Valutier Larano
July 2015

Also by David Denby

Snark

American Sucker

Great Books

Do the Movies Have a Future?

David Denby

Simon & Schuster

New York London Toronto Sydney New Delhi

Simon & Schuster
1230 Avenue of the Americas
New York, NY 10020

First Simon & Schuster hardcover edition October 2012

SIMON & SCHUSTER and colophon are registered trademarks
of Simon & Schuster, Inc.

For information about special discounts for bulk purchases,
please contact Simon & Schuster Special Sales at
1-866-506-1949 or business@simonandschuster.com.

The Simon & Schuster Speakers Bureau can bring authors
to your live event. For more information or to book an event,
contact the Simon & Schuster Speakers Bureau at
1-866-248-3049 or visit our website at www.simonspeakers.com.

Designed by Nancy Singer

Manufactured in the United States of America

10   9   8   7   6   5   4   3   2

Library of Congress Cataloging-in-Publication Data

Denby, David, date.
    Do the movies have a future? / by David Denby. —1st Simon & Schuster hardcover ed.
        p.   cm.
    Includes index.
1. Motion pictures—United States—History—21st century. 2. Motion pictures—United
States—History—20th century. 3. Motion pictue industry—Technological innovations.
4. Film criticism—United Sstates. I. Title.
PN1993.5.U6D46 2012
791.430973—dc23   2011052982
ISBN 978-1-4165-9947-0
ISBN 978-1-4391-1009-6 (ebook)

To Roger Angell, Richard Brody,

Virginia Cannon, Bruce Diones,

Henry Finder, Ann Goldstein, Adam Gopnik,

Anthony Lane, David Remnick, and Daniel Zalewski,

Who know that all of this still matters

Contents

Do the
Movies Have
a Future?

PREFACE

Except for the review of *Pulp Fiction,* all of these essays and reviews were written in the years 1999 to 2011. I have revised some of them, and, in two cases (the articles on James Agee and Pauline Kael), combined two pieces into one. When I revised, I didn't change any of the opinions, or alter the happy or angry mood in which the pieces were first written, or fiddle with the phrasing. I restored a few things that were cut for space, while dropping some passages about, say, business conditions in Hollywood that are no longer of much interest or relevance. I've also cut some matters covered in other pieces. I've noted at the end of each piece when and where it appeared. When I've revised, I've noted that as well.

INTRODUCTION /
THE WAY WE LIVE NOW

ONE: THE BIG PICTURE

I want to make it clear what world a mainstream movie critic lives in. I want to make appalling statements, rend the air with terrible cries (i.e., deal with the actualities of the situation), indulge end-of-the-movies fears, celebrate good and great pictures, and herald Lazarus-like signs of hope, rebirth, and regeneration. I hope that no part of this book will be taken as an expression of regret over my job. I know that I am very lucky to be a movie critic at all, and still luckier, at a time in which many print critics have been canned, to hold a job on a national magazine.

I make this presumption of your interest because most moviegoers live in the same world as I do. When I speak of moviegoers, I mean people who get out of the house and into a theater as often as they can; or people with kids, who back up rare trips to the movies with lots of recent DVDs and films ordered on demand. I don't mean the cinephiles, the solitary and obsessed, who have given up on movie houses and on movies as our national theater (as Pauline Kael called it) and plant themselves at home in front of flat screens and computers, where they look at old films or small new films from the four corners of the globe, blogging and exchanging disks with their friends. I'll try to suggest the strengths and weaknesses of a renewed cinephilia later on. But, for the most part, I'm not thinking of

1

such movie lovers, extraordinary as some of them are; I'm thinking of the great national audience for movies—what's left of it. For those people, the answer to the rhetorical question posed by the book's title is a resounding, trumpet-like, "Well, maybe. Sort of. *Perhaps*. If certain things happen."

The flood of six hundred or so movies opening in the States every year includes films from every country; it includes documentaries, first features spilling out of festivals, experiments, oddities, zero-budget movies made in someone's apartment. Even in the middle of the digit-dazed summer season, small movies never stop opening—at least in New York. There is always something fascinating to write about, and I hope this book gives at least a hint of the variety of filmmaking activity over the last dozen years or so. Yet most of the pieces I've selected are devoted to mainstream commercial and mainstream independent American filmmaking, which is what most people mean by "the movies"—that is, the movies as they are able to experience them in most cities, suburbs, and college towns. New York, after all, is a special case—a city which hosts a continuous world cinema festival, with groups of films from France, Germany, Romania, Korea, or Spain playing somewhere or other in sponsored events in every season; revivals at such institutions as the Museum of the Moving Image, the Film Society of Lincoln Center, the Museum of Modern Art, Film Forum, and many other places. When I speak of "the movies" in the title of this book, I mean what can be generally seen. It's the health of *that* cinema which obsesses me.

Many people have suggested that TV, not movies, has become the prime place for ambition, for entertainment, for art. Cable television has certainly opened a space for somber realism, like *The Wire*, and satirical realism, like *The Sopranos* and *Mad Men*. But there are risks that an artist can't take on television. I have been ravished by things possible only in movies—by Paul Thomas Anderson's *There Will Be Blood*, Julian Schnabel's *The Diving Bell and the Butterfly*, Terrence Malick's intolerable, magnificent *The Tree of Life*, which refurbished the tattered language of film. Such films as *Sideways*, *The Squid and the Whale*, and *Capote* have a fineness, a nuanced subtlety that would come off awkwardly on television. Would that there were more of them!

Nostalgia is history filtered through sentiment. Defiance, not nostalgia, is what's necessary for critical survival. I'm made crazy by the way the business structure of movies is now constricting the art of movies. I don't understand why more people are not made crazy by the same thing. Perhaps their best hopes have been defeated; perhaps, if they are journalists, they don't want to argue themselves out of a job (neither do I); perhaps they are too frightened of sounding like cranks to point out what is obvious and have merely, with a suppressed sigh, accommodated themselves to the strange thing American movies have become. A successful marketplace has a vast bullying force to enforce acquiescence, even among journalists.

A critic's world, then, and your world, too. A single example of life as it's lived now: On May 6 of 2010, the science fiction comedy-spectacle, *Iron Man 2,* starring Robert Downey, Jr., began its run in the United States at 4,380 theaters. That's the number of *theaters.* Multiplexes often put new movies on two or three screens within the complex, so the actual number of screens was much higher—over 6,000, most likely. The gross receipts for the opening weekend (Friday to Sunday) were $128 million. These were not, however, the movie's first revenues. As a way of discouraging piracy and cheap street sale of the movie overseas, the movie's distributor, Paramount Pictures, had opened *Iron Man 2* a week earlier in many countries around the world. By May 9, at the end of the weekend in which the picture opened in America, cumulative worldwide theatrical gross was $324 million. By the end of its run, the cumulative total had advanced to $622 million.

But that was just the beginning. For many big movies, the opening weekend and the worldwide theatrical gross serve as a branding operation for what follows—sale of the movie to broadcast and cable TV, and licensing to retail outlets for DVD rentals and purchase. *Iron Man 2* is of course part of a well-developed franchise (the first *Iron Man* came out in 2008). The hero, Tony Stark, a billionaire industrialist-playboy, first appeared in a Marvel comic book in 1963 and still appears in new Marvel comics. Rattling around stores and malls all over the world, there are also *Iron Man* video games, soundtrack albums, toys, bobblehead dolls, construction sets, dishware, pillows, pajamas, helmets, T-shirts, and lounge pants. There is a hamburger available at Burger King named after Mickey

Rourke, a supporting player in the movie. Such companies as Audi, LG, Mobile, 7-Eleven, Dr Pepper, Oracle, Royal Purple motor oil, and Symantec's Norton software signed on as "promotional partners," issuing products with the *Iron Man* logo imprinted somewhere on the product or in its advertising. In effect, all of American commerce is selling the franchise. The marketing operation for the second installment was set up perhaps ten months before the movie was released, or even earlier, at the time of the first *Iron Man*. The movie's success did not depend on word of mouth; it depended on a calculated strategy put into place way before the movie came out.

I know many of you are aware of this in general, if not in detail. But I'm afraid there's more. I chose *Iron Man* so as not to make a loaded case, since the *Iron Man* movies have a lighter touch than many comparable blockbusters—for instance, the clangorous *Transformer* franchise, based on plastic toys, in which dark, whirling digital masses slam into each other, or thresh their way through buildings, cities, and people, and the moviegoer, sitting in the theater, feels as if his head were repeatedly being smashed against a wall. The *Iron Man* movies have been shaped around the temperament of their self-deprecating star, Robert Downey, Jr., an actor who manages to convey, in the midst of a $200 million super-production, a private sense of amusement. By slightly distancing himself from the material, this charming rake offers the grown-up audience complicity, which saves it from self-contempt. The *Iron Man* movies engage in a daringly flirtatious give-and-take with their own inconsequence: The disproportion between the size of the productions, with their huge sets and digital battles, and the puniness of any meaning that can possibly be extracted from them, is, for the audience, part of the frivolous pleasure of the two films.

Iron Man 2 is soaked in what can only be called conglomerate irony, a mad discrepancy between size and meaning. So are many other such films—for instance, Christopher Nolan's 2010 *Inception,* which generates an extraordinarily complicated structure devoted to little but its own workings. Despite its dream layers, the movie is not really about dreams—the action you see on screen feels nothing like dreams. A businessman hires experts to invade the dreaming mind of another businessman in order to plant emotions which would cause the second man to change corporate plans. Or something like that; the plot is a little vague. Anyway, why should we care? What's at stake? You could say, I suppose, that the movie is about different levels of representation; you could refine that observation and say that the differences between fiction and reality, between subjective and objective no longer exist—that what Nolan has created is somehow analogous to our life in a postmodernist society in which the image and the real, the simulacrum and the original have assumed, for many people, equal weight (the literary and media theorist Fredric Jameson has made such a case for the movie). You can say all of that, but you still haven't established why such an academic-spectacular exercise is worth looking at as a work of narrative art, or why any of it matters emotionally. The picture is an over-articulate nullity—a huge, fancy clock that displays wheels and gears but somehow fails to tell the time. Yet *Inception* is nothing more than the logical product of a recent trend in which big movies have been progressively drained of meaning. Two thirds of the box office for these films now comes from overseas, and the studios appear to have concluded that if a film were actually *about* something, it might risk offending some part of the worldwide audience. Aimed at Bangkok and Bangalore as much as at Bangor, our big movies have been defoliated of character, wit, psychology, local color.

Please understand that I do not hate all over-scaled digital work. "God works too slowly," said Ian McKellen in *X-Men*, playing Magneto, who can produce mutations on the spot. So can digital filmmakers, who play God at will. Digital moviemaking is the art of transformation, and, in the hands of a few imaginative people, has produced sequences of great loveliness and shivery terror—the literally mercurial reconstituted beings in *Terminator 2*, the flying, floating, high-chic battles in *The Matrix*. I loved the luscious beauty of *Avatar*, but *Avatar* is off the scale in visual allure, and so is Alfonso Cuarón's *Harry Potter and the Prisoner of Azkaban*, the best of the Potter series until the final moments of *Harry Potter and the Deathly Hallows Part 2*. The apes in *Rise of the Planet of the Apes*, produced by motion-capture techniques and digitization, are not made-up creatures but enhanced animals—the quintessence of apeness, free-charging around San Francisco, which is one hell of a thing to see. These are all exceptions, however, and I will remind you that many of us have logged deadly hours watching superheroes bashing people off walls, cars leapfrogging one another in tunnels, giant toys and mock-dragons smashing through Chicago, and charming teens whooshing around castles. The oversized weightlessness gets to one after a while.

Moviegoers who first saw this stuff at ten may still love it. For those of us, however, who first experienced the startling beauties of the early CGI movies as adults, and were ravished by them, the omnipresent spectacle—it quickly moved into television shows and commercials—may often seem fatiguing, even brain-deadening. You can never get away from the stuff. The liberation of the fantastic has led, in less than twenty years, to the routinization of the fantastic, a set of convulsive tropes—crashes, flights, explosions, transformations—that now feel like busy blank patches on the screen. At this point, the fantastic is chasing human temperament and destiny—what we used to call drama—from the movies. *The merely human has been transcended.* And if the illusion of physical reality is unstable, the emotional framework of movies has changed, too, and for the worse. In time—a very short time—the fantastic, not the illusion of reality, may become the default mode of cinema.

At the same time as the fantastic has been conventionalized, the old stubborn integrity of space in the best Hollywood films—appraised in theory by the great French critic André Bazin and others and lovingly evoked as art by Manny Farber—has been largely destroyed in the commercial cinema. Space has been extended, bent, or contracted by digital painting, or chopped into fragments held together by cutting so rapid that one sees little of what's going on, the action merely grazing the eyes like a rapid brushing of feathers. What we see in bad digital action movies has the anti-Newtonian physics of a cartoon, but with real figures. Rushed, jammed, broken, and overloaded, action now produces temporary sensation rather than emotion and engagement. Afterward, these sequences fade into blurs, the different blurs themselves melding into one another—a vague memory of having been briefly excited rather than the enduring contentment of scenes playing again and again in one's head. In the piece in this collection called "Conglomerate Aesthetics," I try to detail the amazing breakdown of film language in big movies and the way it devastates emotional response.

There were, of course, B movies in the 1950s devoted to comic book and other pop-cult material, but the combination of digital technology and full-court-press marketing have propelled this material into the center. Such skillful but hollow-spirited pictures increasingly dominate the commercial life of the cinema worldwide, sucking up resources that might be devoted to producing smaller, more interesting movies. Again and again, writers, directors, and producers spend years in Hollywood developing fascinating projects, knocking themselves out against a wall of indifference or time-wasting semi-acquiescence, only to have the projects shelved in the end. If, by studio calculation, an ambitious movie has little chance of grossing at least $100 million in domestic box office, the studio has little interest in making it. With some exceptions, like Sony's *The Social Network,* which I adored, the zero-degree-of-meaning films are really all that the studios are excited about.

Yes, they make other things with greater or lesser degrees of enthusiasm—thrillers and horror movies; chick flicks and teen romances; comedies with Jennifer Aniston, Katherine Heigl, and Cameron Diaz; burlesque-hangover debauches; animated pictures for families. All these movies have a (mostly) assured audience. The studios will also distribute an interesting movie if their financing partners pay for most of it. And, at the end of the year, they distribute small good movies, like *The Fighter* or *The King's Speech,* which are made entirely by someone else. Again and again, these *serioso* films are honored at Oscar time. But for the most part, the studios, except as distributors, don't want to get involved in them. Why not? Because they are "execution dependent"—that is, in order to succeed, they have to be *good.* It has come to this: A movie studio can't risk making good movies. Doing so isn't a *business.* The business model depends on the assured audience and the blockbuster. It has for years and will continue to do so for years more. In 2010, *Transformers: Dark of the Moon,* the third film in the series, a thundering farrago of verbal and visual gibberish, grossed $1 billion worldwide in a month. Nothing is going to stop such success from laying waste to the movies as an art form. The big revenues from such pictures rarely get siphoned into more adventurous projects; they get poured into the next sequel or a new franchise. Pretending otherwise is sheer denial.

On April 30, 2010, a week before *Iron Man 2* made its American debut, an independent film called *Please Give,* written and directed by Nicole Holofcener and starring Catherine Keener, Rebecca Hall, and Oliver Platt, opened in five theaters in the United States. The theatrical gross for the first weekend was $118,000. Holofcener's movie is a modest, formally conservative but sharply perceptive comedy devoted to a group of neighbors in Manhattan—a "relationship" film, arrayed around such matters as the ambiguous moral quality of benevolence and the vexing but inescapable necessity of family loyalty. Holofcener, like a good short story writer, has a precise and gentle touch; moments from the picture have lingered in the affections of people who saw it. I'm not saying that *Please Give* is a great movie. But look at how hard it has to struggle to make even the slightest impression in the marketplace. *Please Give* cost $3 million, and its worldwide theatrical gross is $4.3 million. Once the ancillary markets are added in, the movie, on a small scale, will also be a financial success. But, so far, no more than about 500,000 people have seen it in theaters. Around 83 million have seen *Iron Man 2* in theaters. Maybe 175 million have seen *Transformers 3*.

Nostalgia is lame, so let us confine ourselves to simple fact. The great directors of the past—Griffith, Chaplin, Murnau, Gance, Renoir, Ford, Hawks, Hitchcock, Welles, Rossellini, De Sica, Mizoguchi, Kurosawa, Bergman, and, recently, the young Coppola, Scorsese, and Altman, and many others—did not imagine that they were making films for a tiny audience; they did not imagine they were making "art" movies, even though they worked with a high degree of conscious artistry (the truculent John Ford would have glared at you with his unpatched eye if you had even used the word "art" in his presence). They thought that they were making films for everyone, or at least everyone with spirit, which is a lot of people. But, over the past twenty-five years, if you step back and look at the movie scene, you see the mass culture juggernauts, triumphs of heavy-duty digital craft, tempered by self-mockery and filling up every available corner of public space; and the tiny, morally inquiring "relationship" movies, making their modest way to a limited audience. The ironic cinema, and the earnest cinema; the mall cinema, and the art house cinema.

I can hear the retorts. If such inexpensive movies as *Please Give* (or *Winter's Bone,* an even better movie, which came out in the same season in 2010) get made, and they find an appreciative audience, however small; if Judd Apatow and Steven Soderbergh and David O. Russell and Kathryn Bigelow and Noah Baumbach and David Fincher and Wes Anderson are doing interesting things within the system; if the edges of the industry are soulfully alive even as the center is often an algorithm for making money, then why get steamed over *Iron Man* or the *Transformer* franchise? The reason is this: Not everything an artist wants to say can be said with $3 million. Artists who want to work with, say, $30 million (still a moderate amount of money by Hollywood standards) can't get their movies made. At this writing, Paul Thomas Anderson (*There Will Be Blood*), one of the most talented men in Hollywood, has finally, after five years of pleading, received the money (from a young millionaire, inheriting cash) to make his film about Scientology. After making *Capote,* Bennett Miller was idle for six years before making *Moneyball.* Six unproductive years in the life of a great young filmmaker! Alexander Payne waited seven years (after *Sideways*) before making *The Descendants.* Alfonso Cuarón hasn't made a movie since the brilliant *Children of Men,* in 2006. At this writing, Guillermo del Toro, the gifted man who made *Pan's Labyrinth,* is also having trouble getting money for his projects. By studio standards, there isn't a big enough audience for their movies; they can work if they want to, but only on very small budgets. You can't mourn an unmade project, but you can feel its absence through the long stretches of an inane season.

And why isn't there a big enough audience for art? Consider that in recent years the major studios have literally gamed the system. American children—boys, at least—play video games, read comic books and graphic novels. Latching on to those tastes, Disney has licensed the right, for $4 billion, to make Marvel's superhero comic book characters into movies. Paramount has its own deal with Marvel for the Captain America character and others. Time Warner now owns DC Comics, and Warner Bros. will make an endless stream of movies based on DC Comics characters (the *Superman, Batman,* and *Green Lantern* pictures are just the beginning). For years, all the studios have tried to adapt video games into movies, often with disastrous results. So Warner Bros. went the logical next step: It bought a video game company, which is developing new games *that the studio will later make into films.* "Give me the children until they are seven, and anyone may have them afterwards," Francis Xavier, one of the early Jesuits, is supposed to have said. The conglomerates grab boys when they are seven, eight, or nine, command a corner of their hearts, and hold them with franchise sequels and product tie-ins for fifteen to twenty years. Producer Jerry Bruckheimer is threatening to make a fifth *Pirates of the Caribbean* movie, but by the *third* go-round the films had become a bilgy, incoherent mess without any narrative strategy or point. The beat goes on: This is not a passing fashion or a temporary market phenomenon; it's not some paranoid fantasy of my own. It's everyday corporate practice. The *Twilight* series of teen vampire movies, which deliciously sell sex without sex—romantic danger without fornication—are catching girls in the same way at a slightly older age. The more inspiring *Hunger Game* series fires up young women—the teen heroine is a huntress. We'll see, in later films of the series, if she also becomes a full human being, a real heroine.

In brief, the studios are not merely servicing the tastes of the young audience; they are continuously creating the audience that they want to sell to. Which raises an inevitable question: Will these constantly created new audiences, arising from infancy with all their faculties intact but their expectations already defined—these potential *moviegoers*—will they ever develop a taste for narrative, for character, for suspense, for acting, for irony, for wit, for drama? Isn't it possible that they will be so hooked on sensation that anything without extreme action and fantasy will just seem lifeless and dead to them? I ask; I don't know the answer.

These observations annoy many people, including some of the smartest people I know, particularly men in their late forties and younger, who have grown up with pop culture dominated by the conglomerates and don't know anything else. They don't disagree, exactly, but they find all of this tiresome and beside the point. They accept the movies as a kind of environment, a constant stream. There are just *movies*, you see, movies always and forever, and, of course, many of them will be uninspiring, and always have been. They have little interest in hearing what the current business structure is doing to the art form or how the all-or-nothing promotional efforts are distorting the reception of movies. Critics, chalking the score on the blackboard, think of large-scale American moviemaking as a system in which a few talented people, in order to make something good, struggle against discouragement or seduction. For my young, media-hip friends, this view is pure melodrama; they see the movies not as a moral and aesthetic battleground but as a media game which can be played either shrewdly or stupidly. There is no serious difference for them between making a piece of clanging, overwrought, mock-nihilistic digital roughhouse for $200 million and a searingly personal independent film for $2 million. They're not looking for art, and they don't want to be associated with commercial failure; it irritates them in some way; it makes them feel like losers. If I say that the huge budgets and profits are mucking up movie aesthetics, changing the audience, burning away other movies, they look at me with a slight smile and say something like this: "There's a market for this stuff. People are going. Their needs are being satisfied. If they didn't like these movies, they wouldn't go. Anyway, some of the story values that you love are simply showing up in new forms. And there are plenty of other movies."

But who knows if needs are being satisfied? The audience goes because the movies are *there*, not because it necessarily loves them. Needs? The need for drama, character, complexity, and so on, has to be cultivated, fed, and expanded. Or it has to be created, as Steve Jobs would say, by something new. My friends' attitudes are defined so completely by the current movie market they don't want to hear that movies, for the first eighty years of their existence, were essentially made for adults. Sure, there were always films for families and children, but, for the most part, ten-year-olds and teens were dragged by their parents to what the parents wanted to see, and this was true well after television reduced the size of the adult audience. More fact, rather than nostalgia: The kids saw, and half understood, a satire like *Dr. Strangelove,* an earnest social drama like *To Kill a Mockingbird,* a cheesy disaster movie like *Airport,* and that process of half understanding, half not, may have been part of growing up; it also laid the soil for their own enjoyment of grown-up movies years later. They were not expected to remain in a state of goofy euphoria until they were thirty-five. My friends think that our current situation is normal. They believe that critics are naive blowhards, but it is they who are naive.

They are right, of course, when they say that there are many other kinds of movies. And yet, despite the variety of openings, the financial and marketing strategies of the film business—at least in America—are inexorably pushing movies to extremes of large and small. The American outfits that in recent years have done the most creative work in the space in between—the studio "specialty divisions," including Paramount Vantage, Fox Searchlight, Warner Independent Pictures, and Universal's Focus Features, which were responsible for *Before Sunset, Sideways, Brokeback Mountain, There Will Be Blood, No Country for Old Men,* and many other good movies—have been either closed or weakened by their parent companies. (Sony Classics, which makes few movies but buys completed work for distribution, alone remains untouched.) Such movies made now that are equivalent to *Brokeback Mountain* are financed by eccentric millionaires with aesthetic ambition, and, as I said, by their children; also by smaller production companies (Relativity Media, The Weinstein Company, et al.); by hedge funds and money from Germany, France, Italy, Abu Dhabi. (Abu Dhabi! Louis B. Mayer stirs uneasily in his sleep.) There is no regular system, no *structure* that makes good movies possible. Even if a small movie makes a fortune, as *Black Swan* and *The King's Speech* did in 2011, the movie is considered an anomaly. Each such success is a special case—indeed, a miracle, with financing often secured, after years of pitching and hustling, at the very last minute. It has no successors. Without the bullying force of a few men with taste— most notably, Harvey Weinstein and Scott Rudin—the Academy Awards nominations might be barren.

Most of these movies are directed at older audiences, which, after being abandoned like downsized workers to wander aimlessly the rest of the year, get rounded up and shunted into a dolorous ten-week fall season (the Holocaust, troubled marriages, raging families, self-annihilating artists). The intentional shift in movie production away from adults is a

sad betrayal and a minor catastrophe. Among other things, it has killed
a lot of the culture of the movies. By culture, I do not mean film festivals,
film magazines, and cinephile Internet sites and bloggers, all of which are
flourishing. I mean that blessedly saturated mental state of moviegoing,
both solitary and social, half dreamy, half critical, maybe amused, but
also sometimes awed, that fuels a living art form. Moviegoing is both
a private and a sociable affair—a strangers-at-barbecues, cocktail-party
affair, the common coin of everyday discourse. In the autumn-leaves
awards season, there's plenty of good things to see, and, for adult audiences, the habit flickers to life again. If you've seen one of five interesting
movies currently playing, then you need to see the other four so you can
join the water-cooler or dinner-party conversation. If there's only one, as
there is most of the year, you may skip it without feeling you are missing much. Instead, you retreat into television, where producer-writers
like David Chase, Aaron Sorkin, David Simon, and David Milch now
enjoy the same freedom and status as the Coppola-Scorsese generation
of movie directors forty years ago. Hats off to them. They know what
they are doing. David Simon, creator of *The Wire* and *Treme*, grabbed
me at a festival in 2010 and said "As long as I don't have to sell tickets,
I'll be fine." In other words: "My business model—a subscription service
on cable aimed at adults—works well to make serious stuff. The one you
write about mostly doesn't."

TWO: DOES FILM CRITICISM
MATTER ANYMORE?

Much anguished and contemptuous copy has been turned out in the last
few years on "the death of film criticism." Though hardly a situation that
troubles America's sleep, the crisis is genuine—if, by criticism, you mean
writing in newspapers and magazines. In recent years, as movie advertising has moved to the Internet, and many publications have suffered general revenue losses, more than sixty film critics have been fired by daily
and weekly newspapers, magazines, and movie trade journals. Some very
good soldiers have fallen. Yet, at the same time that print critics have begun disappearing, or have withdrawn to the Web outlets of their publica-

tions, seemingly anyone who has an opinion has taken to the Internet. There is a new horizontal Babel of critical discourse, which leaves the traditional critics a little nonplussed. In the midst of a conglomerate marketing apparatus so powerful and at the same time so constricting, a media environment so voluminous and chaotic, a critic still holding a print position begins to wonder if he is fully alive—or if he's just hanging on, a show horse chained to a wheel. At this point, what on earth can be the function of print criticism?

Movie critics, of course, are hardly alone among arts journalists in facing trouble. Art, dance, music, and book critics disappeared from many magazines and newspapers first. In a tough time for everybody, the employment troubles of film reviewers would be no more than a parochial professional issue—and certainly no worse than anyone else's employment troubles—if movies themselves were not in some danger. The crisis in criticism has been produced not only by the shifting economics of journalism and the changes in movie financing and marketing, but by the drastic shifts in film language I mentioned earlier, which are beginning to maim the movies as an art form. As a collateral effect, they kick criticism into a corner.

A simple confession: We critics are mostly story and character people. We like conflict, atmosphere, wit, style, violence that means something emotionally, form that means something dramatically, visual eloquence that means something philosophically; we don't, as a rule, flip over special effects and sheer movement. A critic now faces a situation in which many of the most prominent American movies are based on material whose strengths are precisely that they are neither morally accountable nor formally articulate. Comic books, graphic novels, and even video games can be startlingly beautiful. But the exhilaration of a comic book is produced by eliminating the preparations and consequences found in carefully worked-out stories. One thing happens after another, space collapses, gravity and the ground disappear, clashing forces jump at each other. The more the movie is true to a source like that—and some try very hard to be true to it—the more the critic with her training in moral or formal coherence or simply hundreds of old movies is going to find herself attacking a landslide with a tennis racquet.

She has to face, for instance, something as arbitrarily plotted as the formidable Batman movie, Christopher Nolan's *Dark Knight* (2008), in which the story elements slam into each other without transition, preparation, release—enraging as a strategy for a movie with flesh-and-blood characters whose fate we may care about. Individual sequences in *The Dark Knight* have a shocking power, but if you look at the movie closely, or even casually, the narrative dissolves. The sequencing doesn't make any sense in time or in space: The anarchic Joker (the late Heath Ledger) is everywhere at once. The climactic moment when the virtuous district attorney, Harvey Dent (Aaron Eckhart), is corrupted by the Joker is simply passed over. The movie depends on such cheap devices as ticking bombs, characters in disguise substituting for one another, people seemingly dead springing back to life. *The Dark Knight,* of course, is not an avant-garde experiment like the savage Buñuel-Dalí collaborations of eighty years ago (*Un Chien Andalou* and *L'Âge d'Or*)—movies in which perversely abrupt juxtaposition was a good part of what the films were about. No, *The Dark Knight* has all the elements of commercial melodrama—good and bad guys, victims, the pretense (in mock form) of a civic consciousness. Yet it moves ahead by jolts and kinky thrills. It's a true comic book movie, abrupt and ruthless, and its remorseless panache depends on the pleasures of cruelty. So how do you review it without holding it to standards that are irrelevant to its entire aesthetic? You can say that it's chic and senseless; that it's corporate art-trash, a terrorizing movie for an age of terror (the novelist Jonathan Lethem did say something like that). But all those terms come out of a critical discourse that has little to do with comic books. What made the movie cool for a lot of people was precisely that *it didn't make any sense;* for them, the arbitrariness as well as the cruelty was a turn-on. Movies like this one—and responses like those—leave critics at sea, trying to find a landmark that's stable enough to steer by. And there are many more comic book movies that aren't nearly as skillful, that are just dull and stupid—both *The Green Hornet* and *The Green Lantern.*

Someone will surely point out that there were earlier changes in the language of movies that also threw critics for a loop. The eclipse of the silent film by sound brought forth a chorus of mourning for the death of cinema (see Rudolf Arnheim's book, *Film as Art,* first published in 1932, for the eloquent version of this nonsense). The use of color irritated many critics who loved the elegance, suggestiveness, and moody eloquence of black-and-white. A few critics, in the early 1950s, including Kael, insisted that the new, expanded wide screen (VistaVision, CinemaScope, and the like) would destroy the art of composition. In the 1960s, the lightweight handheld camera initially produced jangled, jiggling, out-of-focus images which gave many people headaches.

After a while, it became obvious that the critics were wrong and that, on the contrary, the alleged disaster had beaten a path to a new expressiveness. Sound brought the gurgling, crooning music of voices, the murmurs of the city, Fred Astaire tapping, Judy Garland singing. Color brought the strange beauty of Liv Ullmann's translucence, Paul Newman's blue eyes, the malevolent or caressing power of industrial and natural landscapes. The wide screen allowed shots of men conquering vast spaces in *Lawrence of Arabia* and in Clint Eastwood's Westerns. The handheld camera allowed documentary filmmakers like Frederick Wiseman to move in close to people in hospitals, welfare centers, police stations, schools, stores, and performing arts groups. It would be lovely to report that the same thing has happened with digital. When the commercial excitements of fantasy calm a little, perhaps something like that *will* happen (some people believe it happened in Scorsese's *Shutter Island*; I thought it was a cheat). But, apart from the stunners mentioned earlier, and the animated masterpieces from Pixar, most of digital fantasy has been opportunistic, dazzling in an immediate way that was meaningless and dissatisfying. And there's something else setting off digital from earlier revolutions: None of the earlier developments dehumanized the cinema. If anything, they increased the human presence in movies.

The movies are now in an odd place, a turmoil of transition as alarming as the shift from silence to sound or the early '50s period, when television became a mass medium and Hollywood panicked. The movies have been engulfed by digital technology and the Internet. This book, in part, is a product of that turmoil, an attempt to hold on and let go at the same time. So far, with some magnificent exceptions, digital, I believe, has done movies more harm than good, though the sky is the limit in digital spectacle (thank you, James Cameron), and nothing but talent is the limit at the low end of budget-making, where a movie can be made in a studio apartment for $15,000. The Internet is a means of distribution just now beginning to be exploited and also a home for criticism in endless floods (more on that in a second).

When the dominating spectacle movies now are bad or just pointless, a critic has three options. He can punch away at what bored him. Rage, as Kael used to say, isn't demeaning. But how do you get enraged at something silly? Or at stuff that wasn't supposed to make much sense to begin with? There's a job-holding issue, too: A critic who hits the heavy bag too many times risks tiring his readers and himself. Option two: He can create a fresh aesthetic of spectacle, giving up on unity and accountability as beside the point, praising the craftsmanship of individual sequences—coruscating, thunderous clashes; sudden, riotous exfoliations of color; bizarre alterations of the natural world. *Transformers* forever! The world entirely in motion! Galvanization as the new stasis! If a movie is little more than a series of excitements, however, it doesn't offer much for sustained analysis. (Task for a young critic: Create an intellectually convincing theory of digital spectacle.) Option three: He can have fun with the mess or meaningless complication that so many big movies have become, allowing the movie, as he re-creates it, to fall into the ridiculous. At *The New Yorker,* my extraordinary colleague Anthony Lane has turned the big-movie pan into an art form. Lane's literary skill transcends the obvious danger: Writing with irony about big-money pictures which are themselves conceived ironically puts the critic in danger of joining his tone to what he's writing about. He can become a knowing media jester, hip to the meaninglessness of what he's covering, amused by his situation, eventually so amused that he ironizes himself out of existence. A lot of "smart" criticism and movie journalism now has this nervously joshing, self-mocking, I-can't-believe-I'm-writing-about-this-stuff-but-hey-it's-happening desperation. Nothing is more destructive of critical writing than the fear of being thirty seconds behind the zeitgeist.

What is the most valuable thing that critcs do? We point audiences toward exciting new work, new directors, new performers, new themes; we make connections among a wide variety of films, coax out an impulse, a tendency from the ground plan or the unconscious of a movie and make it part of history, politics, or a director's biography. Evocation, interpreta-tion, evaluation, resistance to the industry, defense of the artists, an ac-counting with history and an opening to the future—the tasks remain the same as ever. Surely critics are eager to serve; there's likely as much (if not more) critical talent around as there was fifty years ago.

Movie criticism in print is hurting, but it's not dying. (When I say "print critics," I include writers like Stephanie Zecharek [*Movieline*], An-drew O'Hehir [*Salon*], and Dana Stevens [*Slate*], who write for online pub-lications but operate like newspaper and magazine critics. They have the space and the means to fill it.) The remaining print critics (if they haven't been thrown behind a pay wall) can be read on their publications' websites or on sites like Metacritic and Rotten Tomatoes, which aggregate links to these reviews—a lot easier and cheaper way for a reader of criticism to sample opinion than waiting for a batch of magazines to show up in the mail. At the same time, a number of critics also blog, extending their reviews and giving readers a chance to argue with them—an exhilarat-ing rumpus if the exchanges don't degenerate into the snark, abuse, and madcap agendas so often plaguing conversation threads in the Internet. In truth, those critics who have survived in print have more readers than ever before. Yet at this point, with hundreds of voices clamoring on all sides, print critics can no longer claim any special authority. The best they can do—the only thing they can do—is to demonstrate their ability as writ-ers again and again. If they can't write well, and don't perform some sort of serious cultural function, they risk falling among such bottom-feeders as the itchy-fingered tweeters who send out their views in the middle of screenings—in some cases, kids eager to gain access to parties by turning out sycophantic ballyhoo for pop movies; or ignorant young sports hoping for a moment's renown by posting jauntily thuggish attacks ("It sucks").

The vox populi bloggers, fortunately, command only one part of the endless terrain. In late 1995, Susan Sontag mourned the death of cine-philia—"the conviction that cinema was an art unlike any other: quint-essentially modern; distinctively accessible; poetic and mysterious and erotic and moral—all at the same time." But that conviction has been reborn on the Internet in ardent exchanges among the knowledgeable—both critics and movie lovers who find a voice. The exchanges are charged by the excitement of an immediate response. If something happens at a film festival in Austin or Hong Kong, the tribes send drumbeats back and forth long before the movie opens. Cinephiles, obsessional by definition, may be more isolated socially than poetry lovers, birders, or sexual adventurers, but the Internet connects all passions. Those with a hunger for, say, Antonioni or Dreyer or Bresson or the South Korean director Bong Joon-ho or the American horror and science fiction writer-director Dan O'Bannon can talk, illustrating their blogs with frames or sequences from the movies, and keep those directors, as well as their own interests, alive. Cinephiles copy and swap DVDs of a few good films that have failed to get aboveground distribution—conducting a samizdat operation, for instance, on behalf of banned Chinese movies, a singularly honorable activity.

At its best, the new Internet cinephilia generates an unstoppable, exfoliating mass of knowledge and opinion, a thickening density of inquiries, claims, reference points, agreements, outraged and dulcet tweets, rebuttals, summations, dismissals. Critic-scholars like Jonathan Rosenbaum, Girish Shambu, Ignatiy Vishnevetsky, Jim Emerson, and Richard Brody hold forth on new and old movies, film aesthetics, film history (my friend and colleague Brody is particularly encyclopedic and brilliant—it's as if the Internet Movie Database had been written by Schopenhauer). I learn from these writers and am grateful for them. The New York–based writer Farran Smith Nehme ("The Self-Styled Siren"), one of the few genuine wits on the Web, celebrates old-Hollywood lore, the particulars of studio style, glamour, and costuming. Some of the writing on the blogs is first-rate, some of it is soreheaded and self-serving, and some of it is knowledgeable but dull, with the genteel, deferential tone of logrolling at a low-level academic conference. Yet sooner or later great critics will arise from the Internet forests and mazes. Pay is minimal, editing usually nonexistent, but it's a sensationally *available* place for young critics to find a voice. As the Internet critic Paul Brunick has pointed out, Kael and Andrew Sarris, if they were starting out now, would be blogging.

Internet cinephilia keeps film appreciation boiling in a way that university film courses and scattered revival houses can't. Yet it's fair to ask: What is all this activity doing for the living art form—for movies in their current state? What is the *use* of this kudzu growth of criticism? Many of the Internet cinephiles, when they review new movies at all, review only the few things that interest them. In general, they put everything on the same level—a film by Carl Dreyer from the 1920s, a new documentary from Iran, a new American independent film, a horror "classic" from the 1950s. They have withdrawn from mainstream movies, from worrying over the economic organization of a business which forces artists out to the margins—given up fighting the inexorable division into mass and class, given up on film as a public art. If they see a good new movie from China or South Korea, and only ten or twenty thousand other Americans also see it, they don't (as I do) regard the near-invisibility of the movie as a sad failure of both critics and audience alike; they have appreciated the movie, and the experience is complete. But endless appreciation isn't enough. Filmmakers need a sizable audience to survive. The cinephiles are an innocently arrogant group. The mainstream critics fail, too, attracting a far smaller audience than we would like for such challenging films as Michael Haneke's *The White Ribbon,* Debra Granik's *Winter's Bone,* and Abbas Kiarostami's *Certified Copy,* but at least we're pushing the rock up the hill.

Certainly, the thought of a film culture without widely read print critics standing between the marketing machine and the public is more than a little frightening. For years, the studios have been trying to kill the power of critics in any way they can (except when they need us at awards season). They advance screenings for critics likely to give them favorable reviews, retard or drop them for others who are likely to be "tough." They use such devices as the junket and the embargo as marketing tools—ways of manipulating a disempowered press. A junket brings critics to New York or Los Angeles in advance to see the movie and to bask for ten minutes in the radiance of Angelina Jolie; the critics (at least some of them) then repay the favor with advance quotes that garland the ads before the movie opens. The more serious critics get drowned in the sea of hackish praise. An embargo, by contrast, prohibits reviews until a certain date, at which point the reviews will hit the public with shock-and-awe maximum impact as part of a coordinated ad campaign. To an astonishing degree, the studios, and the noncritical movie press (industry reporters, mainly), talk of embargoes as if they were a solemn promise between journalists and, say, the Pentagon—an agreement to withhold news because lives in a secret operation might be at stake. But this is hooey. Nothing is at stake but marketing. That the movie press has acquiesced in observing embargoes is a function of how weak it has become, how dependent on the studios and producers as sources.

Having enfeebled the mainstream press in any way they can, the studios would be thrilled if a hundred Internet niches were the only place in which criticism flourished.

Advocacy, even prophecy—that's what good critics, in inspired moments, have provided, rousing the public to the aesthetic, moral, and ideological value of a new group of filmmakers: say, the Italian Neorealists in the 1940s; the New Wave (in which case, Godard, Truffaut, Chabrol, and Rohmer, preparing the ground as critics, *became* the insurgency); the American film school generation of the 1970s (Scorsese, Coppola, Spielberg, et al.). Is there an insurgency at hand? The conditions for it exist. Digital equipment has lowered the cost of filmmaking to almost nothing—a few thousand dollars. In the last six or seven years, full-length movies, starring unpaid or barely paid actors, or just a group of friends gathered together for the occasion, have worked in freedom in the streets or in someone's apartment. These movies chronicle touchy personal relations, career anxieties, the all-around uncertainties of people in their twenties (often of the filmmaking group itself). They have semi-improvised scenes of agonizing diffidence and embarrassment, but sometimes there's a stumbling breakthrough, and the movie touches depths that Hollywood shies away from. One longs, so far in vain, for the American equivalent to the vivacious intellectual and lyrical power of the New Wave, but it may come.

What's sure to come in the very near future is a flood of inexpensive digital movies, both fiction and documentary, made available through the Internet or through on-demand cable channels. The regular movie press, overwhelmed, won't be able to sort them out, much less review them, and some very good things could easily disappear. The Internet critics, with their limitless space, are better equipped to do the job. The digital revolution that is stripping criticism of its print platforms could rev criticism up again. Will not a new kind of Internet film magazine—intellectually accomplished, combative, yet popular in style—emerge sooner or later? I'm not rooting for anyone to lose his independence, but it's inevitable that, within a few years, consolidation will be forced on the many separate voices by the need to earn a living. Groups of critics, some bloggers, some refugees from the print world, could join together, submit to professional editing, take on a corrupt industry, defend artists, carry on debates in a way possible only on the Internet. If they did all of that, they could establish a decent-sized audience, and independent film distributors would advertise in the magazine. (Several have told me that they would be happy to advertise in such an online publication.) When the low-budget filmmaking revolution comes, such magazines will be the first to herald it. Without them, and the regular press, too, the revolution might never happen. Meanwhile, the regular press will carry on with its work, claiming such victories as it can, forever waiting for the next *Tree of Life* to get excited about.

THREE: THIS BOOK

The pieces in this book were all written for specific occasions, but, when I put them together, I realized the fragments formed something like a composite portrait: A critic—me—watches and waits like a harried wife on a widow's walk as cherished elements of an art form capsize and others struggle to reach port. What has been lost in movies? What are we missing? What still thrives—and what has been gained? The book could be seen as an obsession with the present in the light of film history—and also as an attempt to assemble the primary elements of a workable film culture. In the first section, I describe the aesthetic and emotional fallout from the conquering business structures in the conglomerate period—the alterations in film language, in the ways we look at movies, in the ways we get enthralled or repelled by them. Does the shift to spectacle as a dominant style in big movies cut us off from the narrative pleasures of the past? Are there more intense pleasures in the work of independents? They have escaped the conglomerate system, carving a bit of open aesthetic space for themselves—either through violent thrusts of imagination or a steely yet cheerful grip on some of the harder realities of American life. I've included reviews of some of the best. Movies over the last dozen years are unimaginable without them.

Loving movie stars, hopelessly, beyond reason, was always the most enjoyable part of going to movies. It was central to film culture, never more so than in the widespread adoration of Joan Crawford, who now seems so dislikable and troubled a figure that we may wonder at our ancestors while longing for the immersion in a star's life and works that they reveled in. In the piece that follows, on movie stars today, I pass out of the old, grateful trance into, I suppose, disenchantment, and I look hard at the economic and institutional structure of stardom in our time, when our betters have now become, disappointingly and gratingly, our familiars. Still, a movie culture without star adoration is another thing impossible to imagine.

A steady audience holds genre films in place, yet something more than commerce allows a genre to flourish. Almost by definition, a genre is a record of communal obsession. Genre lovers are connoisseurs; comparison is the substance of their talk. Why? Because genre films often mean more to us than individual films; their repetitions and variations tell us what we need and want, what we desire and fear. The directors I've included are more a case of personal obsession—disposition triumphing over industrial convention. In the past, temperament and style operated, as it were, in the shadows; the auteur critics can at least claim to have made visible what was buried in the system. I'm no auteurist, but I recognize temperament when I see it, and the directors I've written about have it to spare. At this point, we assume an artist in film will want to express himself openly, even flagrantly (it's hard, at the moment, to think of a director as talented as William Wyler avoiding "signature" flourishes); some of the contemporary directors I've included, like Quentin Tarantino and the Coen brothers, know that we are looking at them for identity marks, and they play with our expectations, teasing, reversing, pulling the rug from beneath "film appreciation." The two great critics I've celebrated—James Agee and Pauline Kael—defined movie love in their eras; I hoped to re-create the exhilaration of work that has meant a lot to me and to other readers, and to place the two of them in the movie history that they both embodied and exultantly transcended. Their writing has made movies more exciting; it has made life more exciting. I don't think it's mere vanity to insist that, as I suggested earlier, a healthy movie scene can't exist without critics. Those two set the standard. Among other things, they leaped like hungry animals at anything that represented a fresh moment in the cinema, and I've taken a cue and pointed to some possible new directions for movies at the end of the collection.

PART ONE / TRENDS

INTRODUCTION

Movies have always been a big-money game. Those of us who lament the present conglomerate system know that perfectly well. But what if the structure of the movie business, as it operates now, actively discourages quality? The piece called "Conglomerate Aesthetics," written in 2001, and never printed, registers my amazement over what was happening to the way stories were shot and edited in the commercial cinema. The piece may occasionally have the sound of a professor rapping the lectern, but I don't apologize for it. I was stunned by the awfulness of the movies I was seeing in the summer of 2001, and I thought a return to basics was necessary in a time of disintegration. In *"Pirates on the iPod,"* I sample screens in many sizes, and I tilt against the new conglomerate ethos of "platform agnosticism"—the notion that a movie can be seen anywhere, on any device, no matter how small. What do the different screens do to movies? What do they do to us emotionally? What are we gaining and losing by having images constantly around as, not as narrative, but as *company*? Spectacle movies come and go, but Mel Gibson's Jesus movie deserves special notice as the most appalling example of hypocrisy in recent years—a sadomasochistic revel passing itself off as a devotional film. Anyone who loves color and movement has to be seduced by *Avatar,* but the constant reliance on airborne fantasy gets me down, and I attempted, in the "Endless Summer" piece, to name the ways in which digital fantasy was eviscerating narrative. Each of the independent movies reviewed here has an idiosyncratic tone—meditative or compassionate or fearful or enraged—which makes reviewing them so extraordinary a pleasure.

CONGLOMERATE AESTHETICS / NOTES ON THE DISINTEGRATION OF FILM LANGUAGE

It's hard to imagine a moviegoer who wouldn't get drunk or at least buzzed from a single tumultuous scene in *Apocalypse Now*. You know the scene: Robert Duvall, as Colonel Kilgore, war lover and surfing nut, destroys a village in the Mekong Delta while searching for a perfect wave. Francis Ford Coppola's crowning moment in his 1978 epic is driven by the kind of savage excitement—the sheer physical exuberance of power and violence—that propels the greatest, most ungovernable and barbaric scenes in Griffith, Eisenstein, and Kurosawa. And yet the meanings of this episode (and others in the movie) are complex and discordant, tearing up our responses. Duvall, half naked, strutting around like a Peking duck gone mad, performs random acts of gallantry even as he calls in the napalm. In some way, this murderous lunatic is a hero and a courageous man. The mixed exhilaration and contempt of the moment carries in its wake an American shame beyond words, and, for anyone who lived through the 1960s and 1970s, this scene and others in *Apocalypse* bring back the period in all its torment and foolishness. In all its movie glory, too. Whatever its failures—and they are enormous—*Apocalypse Now* comes out of a movie world so different from our own that sitting through it again in its expanded form (*Apocalypse Now Redux*) is almost a masochistic experience. We could be pale civilians at a campfire listening to tales of brazen ancestors, wondering at a time when studios, directors, and audiences expected much more out of movies than anyone does now. A single scene, even a single shot—the language of the best movies then was strong enough to haunt your dreams. It's language I want to talk about—nuts and bolts, shots and cuts, story strategies and audience responses. There are always a few, and sometimes more than a few, good movies every year (many of them low- or medium-budget films). Yet the late Pauline Kael, in her last published interview, in May 2001, said that "it was clear twenty years ago that the movie companies were destroying movies," and Kael left an unmistakable impression that they had completed the job. What did she mean by "destroying movies"?

Kael was speaking of mainstream Hollywood films, which she believed in and fought for (and often against) throughout her career. She called them "our national theater"—a forum that meant something wrenching or definitive or endlessly invigorating or funny to us; movies that took over conversations, took over lives. That relationship to movies has obviously changed over the last fifteen years. Some of us still go to mainstream movies obsessively, but few of us beyond the age of fourteen or fifteen live our lives in constant reference to movies, the way millions of people did thirty years ago. Movies, as everyone has said, are now only one part of a de-centered media world. How many nights have I spent on the Internet, reading a little here, watching a clip of something there, writing emails to friends, sitting down with a book for an hour, then checking in again at the computer before bed? Many nights. Our habits have changed; the nature of big commercial movies has changed, too. If you listen to the comments in the back of the theater or in the lobby after the show, you can hear layers of irony and derision thicker than the Coke syrup at the concession stand. The audience is distancing itself not just from the movies but from the way movies are packaged and sold to them. There is a kind of new mass cynicism in which the weekly promotional convulsion over a Friday opening often means exactly nothing, since it gives way immediately to the next week's convulsion, and the movies themselves are often so bad, and so quickly consumed, that even the most ballyhooed picture may drop 60 percent at the box office by the second weekend. My guess is that the constant rhythm of din and disillusion leaves a good part of the audience feeling not angry or cheated but just indifferent—without serious hope. Going to a big commercial American movie now is like reaching into the fridge for a watery beer. If you're thirsty, you have to drink something.

A friend calls and says, "Why are you grading these things as attempted works of art when they're really industrial products?" Okay, I get the point, but many of us like big movies—or at least we used to—and we're not about to give up on them. Why should we? It's not as if it were impossible to make serious money with a good big picture. The careers of Robert Zemeckis, Amy Heckerling, and James Cameron suggest that it's highly possible, as does the success of such artistically ambitious directors as Steven Spielberg, Martin Scorsese, Ang Lee, and Steven Soderbergh. Commercial hits like *Saving Private Ryan, American Beauty, The Sixth Sense, Erin Brockovich,* and *Traffic* were extremely well made; *The Matrix* was intricate and daring, and so were parts of the first *X-Men.* There are always some good big movies, but the tragedy of this period is that it's not only possible but increasingly easy to attract audiences by making movies badly. It turns out that the 60 percent drop-off, steep as it is, doesn't kill the movie's chances of profitability. The marketing for that weekend brands the movie, and then, down the road, the ancillary markets kick in—sales to cable TV, DVD sales and rentals, and the rest. Since only certain kinds of movies can be sold this way—teen comedies, action pictures, sci-fi and comic book concepts, animated movies for families, and sequels to all these things—then such movies will get made again and again (and not just for the summer season), and will force other kinds of movies off the table.

We've been watching this syndrome develop and "destroy" movies for two decades, and last summer it reached the tipping point. In culturally frightened periods, lucid speech falls into demagoguery or jargon, music into sentimental slop or formula. Much the same sort of thing is happening to movies. I'm not speaking merely of infantile themes or subjects—the famous "dumbing down" of the last decade. If movies mean less to people than they once did, it's because of something more central than changing leisure habits and simple-minded scripts. The language big movies are made in—the elements of shooting, editing, storytelling, and characterization—is disintegrating very rapidly and in ways that prevent the audience from feeling much of anything about what it sees. The creepiest part of this is that the distancing of the audience from its own natural responses is intentional, and the audience seems to like it that way. Or not know what it's missing.

/ / /

You can see what I mean in all sorts of big pictures, in both *Pearl Harbor* and *Moulin Rouge,* in both *The Mummy Returns* and *Swordfish,* in both *Gladiator* and *Planet of the Apes* (not to be confused with the splendid *Rise of the Planet of the Apes,* from 2011). All these movies are afflicted with incoherent or trivial narratives, uninteresting or stupid characters, rapid or fragmented editing schemes. What we are seeing in such movies is not just individual artistic failures and crass commercial strategies but a new, awful idea of how to put a picture together. Sixty years ago, the look of a given studio's films reflected the ambitions and fantasies of the men who ran them as well as the film genres they cultivated and the writers, directors, and craftsmen they hired. But now the studios are just one part—and not always a very profitable part—of enormous conglomerates, and the head of the motion picture division is mainly responsible for a revenue stream that will please board members and shareholders. Looking around him, he sees divisions of his conglomerate that have a greater profit ratio than his own—video games, for instance. Imitating these commercially successful forms won't hurt him among the people he needs to please. Under pressure like that, style quickly fades away. Apart from some of the animated work, it's hard now to tell the films of one studio from another. All the studios are ruled by what you could only call conglomerate aesthetics.

The phrase falls uneasily on the ear. Let me say right away that I don't mean to pile into the tumbrils every large movie recently made by conglomerates. I am talking about a widespread portent, even an onrushing engine, but not a universal practice. I realize as well that "conglomerate aesthetics" has a cranky, accusatory, sub-Marxist ring to it, the sound of an assistant professor warming the prejudices of an academic conference. Naïveté is a poor excuse for false moralism, both for me and for the professor. We both should know that Hollywood movies have always been made for profit, that money is the lifeblood of large-scale picture making. Yet the desire to be profitable doesn't, in itself, dictate one style or another. The dreadfulness of current big movies can't be waved away on the grounds that the studios have to make them that way. They don't have to make them that way; they just think they do. They *chose* this style.

The old 1968 *Planet of the Apes*, directed by Franklin J. Schaffner, had stunning action scenes, but it was also a pungent, wounding look at cruelty and intolerance and a great spoof of evolutionary theory; Charlton Heston's Macho Agonistes, humiliated by an unexpected reversal of the species hierarchy (the apes were superior), gives a performance of thwarted potency that has only increased as a joke over the years. The new *Planet* is mostly a sexless dark chase with Mark Wahlberg as a blank-faced little hero. The apes jump around so much that, as a fourteen-year-old of my acquaintance put it, you have to possess the flitting movements of a hummingbird to follow the action. The physical scale of the material has increased, but the spirit and intelligence, and the audience involvement in it, have been brutally diminished. And this movie's rush of meaningless action was all too reminiscent of many, many other moviegoing experiences of recent years. The action scenes in the Oscar-winning *Gladiator*, for instance, were mostly a blur of whirling movement shot right up close—a limb hacked off and flying, a spurt of blood, a flash of chariot wheels. Who could actually see anything? The old ideal of action as something staged cleanly and realistically in open space has been destroyed by sheer fakery and digital "magic"—a constant chopping of movement into tiny pieces which are then assembled by computer editing into exploding little packages.

The shape of conglomerate aesthetics can be seen as well in the narrative gibberish of too many creatures, too many villains in the overstuffed, put-on adventure movie, *The Mummy Returns*; it can be seen in the frantic pastiche construction of the musical *Moulin Rouge*, with its characters openly borrowed from other movies, its songs composed of many other songs—music that alludes to the history of pop rather than risking the painful beauty of a ravishing new melody. The conglomerate aesthetic seizes on the recycled and the clichéd; it disdains originality and shies away from anything too individual, too clearly defined—even a strong personality. (Angelina Jolie wasn't required to be a person in *Lara Croft Tomb Raider*—she got by on pure attitude. Ewan McGregor in *The Phantom Menace* didn't even have attitude.) The last genuine protagonist in a big movie was Russell Crowe's Jeffrey Wigand in Michael Mann's *The Insider*, two years ago, and that movie failed commercially. None of this can be waved away with a few knowing remarks about "postmodernism." In Hollywood, where they know little of academic theory, the lesson has been learned: No complex protagonist. As the visual schemes grow more complicated, the human material becomes undernourished, wan, apologetic, absent—or so stylized that you can only enjoy it ironically (Angelina Jolie as a svelte, voguing super-killer).

Constant and incoherent movement; rushed editing strategies; feeble characterization; pastiche and hapless collage—these are the elements of conglomerate aesthetics, and there's something more going on than bad filmmaking in such a collection of attention-getting swindles. A strange and unpleasant element has crept into the filmmakers' relation to the subjects of these movies and the audience they are made for. Again and again in recent years, I have had the sense that filmmakers are purposely trying to distance the audience from the material—to prevent them from feeling anything at all but sensory excitement, to thwart any kind of significance in the movie. They seem eager to achieve a cinema of pure weightlessness, a zero degree of meaning. At their wittiest and most ironic (*Independence Day* or *Men in Black*), such zero-degree movies offer a plot that is no more than a shared joke between the moviemakers and the audience—a pretext for allusions to old pictures, a series of jazzily inverted clichés. The large-scale frivolousness of those two movies was entertaining enough, but you may have come out of them, as I did, a little rattled, as if you had been walking across an open manhole on wax paper. It turns out, of course, that blowing up the White House in *Independence Day* was not such a cool joke after all. Yes, after 9/11 that remark hits below the belt, and what of it? Doesn't the movie deserve it? You don't have to believe, as movie historian Neal Gabler does, that the terrorists were actually replicating movie images to find something creepy in a movie that joins so much violence to so little emotion. The studios and filmmakers may have gone a little too far in emptying out meaning. What we have now is not just a raft of routine bad pictures but the first massively successful nihilistic cinema.

That's quite a mouthful. But consider, as an example of what's gone wrong, a single scene from last summer's most prominent artistic fiasco. Forget Ben Affleck's refusal to sleep with Kate Beckinsale the night before going off to battle; forget the rest of the frightfully noble love story. Look at the action sequences in Michael Bay's *Pearl Harbor*, the scenes which many critics actually praised (Todd McCarthy of *Variety* was a notable exception). Here's the moment: The Japanese have arrived, dropped their load, and gone back to their carriers. Admiral Kimmel (Colm Feore), the commander of the Pacific Fleet, then rides through the harbor in an open boat, surveying the disaster. We've seen Kimmel earlier: He's not a major character, but he's a definite presence. Before December 7, he had intimations that an attack might be coming but not enough information to form a coherent picture. He did not act; now he feels the deepest chagrin. Dressed in Navy whites, and surrounded by junior officers also dressed in white, he passes slowly through ships torn apart and still burning, ships whose crews, in some cases, remain trapped below the waterline. Now, the admiral's boat trip could have yielded a passage of bitterly eloquent movie poetry. Imagine what John Ford or David Lean—or Coppola in his prime—would have done with it! We have just seen bodies blackened by fire, the men's skin burned off. Intentionally or not, the spotless dress whites worn by the officers become an excruciating symbol of the Navy's complacency before the attack. The whole meaning of this movie could have been captured in that one shot if it had been built into a sustained sequence.

Yet this shot, to our amazement, lasts no more than a few seconds. After cutting away, Michael Bay and his editors return to the scene, but this time from a different angle, and that shot doesn't last either. Bay and his team of editors abandon their own creation, just as, earlier in the movie, they jump away from an extraordinary shot of nurses being strafed as they run across an open plaza in front of the base hospital. People who know how these movies are made have said to me that they *couldn't* have held those shots any longer, because audiences would have noticed that they were digital fakes. But that point (if it's true) should tell you that something is seriously wrong. If you can't sustain shots at the dramatic crux of your movie, why make violent spectacle at all? It turns out that fake-looking digital filmmaking can *disable* spectacle. When bombs drop on an airfield, the action is so rapid and patterned that even a child—no, especially a child—can tell that the effects are done digitally. The digitally realized airplanes, flitting around the sky—too close to one another, too

close to the buildings they fly through—look glib and unconvincing. All
that abrupt, unconvincing movement and the unsettling cuts curtail the
emotions of horror, awe, and pity. And what good is a war epic without
horror, awe, and pity? What did Bay imagine he was doing? By going for
mere surface excitement and speed, he wipes out the national tragedy that
caused him to make the movie in the first place. If he wanted the look of a
video game, why not design the game? It would have been more profitable.

Twenty-three years ago, the battle scenes in *Apocalypse Now* moved
swiftly, too, but not too swiftly. Coppola loads a great deal into the shots;
he dazzles us with his generosity. As the helicopters hover and circle, havoc
breaks loose in the burning village, the soldiers herd groups of Vietnamese this way and that, and the hero, Captain Willard (Martin Sheen), and
his men wander forlornly among Kilgore's soldiers as they try to figure out
what in the world is going on. The moment is crowded, it is complex, it
is crazy; and yet it is utterly lucid, too, and at Loew's Imax theater in New
York, sitting before an enormous screen, I lost the edges of the frame and
got pulled right into the maelstrom, as close to an out-of-the-body experience as this nonmystic has ever had. No matter how much movement
there is, everything in the Kilgore scenes matters, in part because the helicopters have the weight of real objects, in part because the scene is cut so
much slower than the action in *Pearl Harbor*. There's much more here at
stake than the comparison of a good movie to a bad one; the language that
each one uses—and the moviemakers' and audience expectations—have
altered in a way that is devastating.

One of the tendencies of conglomerate aesthetics is to replace action and
drama as much as possible with mere movement. Big movies are now full
of needle-nosed flying pteranodons and cars on fire floating through the
air (at a recent year-end critics meeting, one reviewer suggested an award
for the "best shot of a couple holding hands as they run away from an exploding building"). But the movies are no longer about much of anything
else. The characters get shoved off the sets by special effects that multiply
thrills in repeated exfoliating climaxes or by legions of creatures obviously
put on the screen in order to be zapped or by digital masses barging into
each other like loose cargo. Conglomerate aesthetics requires a dozen

trash epiphanies (explosions, transformations, rebirths) rather than the arc of a single pure visual climax; mass slaughter rather than a single death. The job of luring the big audience to the Friday opening—the linchpin of the commercial system—has destroyed action on the screen by making it carry the entire burden of the movie's pleasure. You leave the theater vibrating, but, a day later, you don't feel a thing; there's no after-image, no deeper imprint, just the memory of having been excited. The audience has been conditioned to find the absence of emotion pleasurable.

The accumulation of big terrible movies this past summer shocked me into seeing the sheer oddity of conglomerate style, and I hate the thought that this oddity might be accepted as the way things have to be. To understand what is so strange about big movies now, you have to remember a little of what movies once were and what audiences once wanted from them—how stories were told in different periods, how movies were put together. Please excuse the basic-aesthetics lecture; I have a point in mind. We are now trapped by an exasperating irony: Employing all the devastating means at their command, movies have in some ways gone back to their crudest beginnings and are determined, perhaps, to stay there forever, or at least as long as the box office and ancillary market mother lode holds out.

PRIMITIVE

A long time ago, at a university far away, I taught film, and I did what many teachers have done before and since—I tried to develop film aesthetics for the students as a historical progression toward narrative. After all, many of the first movies in the 1890s were not stories at all but just views of things—a train coming into a station, a wave breaking toward the camera. These visual astonishments caused the audience (or so the legend says) to stare open-mouthed or duck under the seats for cover. I wanted my students to be astonished, too—to enjoy the development of film technique as a triumph of artistic and technical consciousness. I worked in straight chronological order, moving from those early "views" through Edwin S. Porter's 1903 experiments in linear sequencing in films like *The Life of an American Fireman* and *The Great Train Robbery* and then on through D. W. Griffith's consolidation a few years later of an actual syntax—long and medium shots, close-ups, flashbacks, parallel editing, and the like. But I now think there was something merely convenient in teaching that way. The implication of the lesson plan was that the medium had by degrees come to a realization of itself, discovering in those early years (say 1895 to 1915) its own true nature embedded within its technology—the leafy oak of narrative lodged within the acorn of celluloid. It's a teleological view, and it's probably false. In truth, there is nothing inherent in the process of exposing strips of film to light sixteen or eighteen times a second (later twenty-four times) that demanded the telling of a story.

At the beginning, after the views of trains and oceans, movies offered burlesque skits or excerpts from theatrical events, but still no stories. A completed movie was often just a single, fixed, long-lasting shot. It's likely, as David Bordwell, Janet Staiger, and Kristin Thompson explain in the superb 1985 volume *The Classical Hollywood Cinema*, that movies gradually took their shape as narrative from outside influences—from novels and short stories and from plays, and also from the sheer economic pressure to create work of greater power to attract customers, not from something inherent in the medium itself.

If creating fictions is not encoded in the DNA of film, then what is happening now has a kind of grisly logic to it. As the narrative and dramatic powers of movies fall into abeyance, and many big movies turn into sheer spectacle, with only a notional pass at plot or characterization, we are returning with much greater power to capers and larks that were originally performed in innocence. The kind of primitive chase, for instance, that in 1905 depended on some sort of accident or mischief rather than on character or plot has been succeeded by such scenes as the orgiastic car rumble in *Swordfish* that just springs out of nowhere. A half dozen or more cars get torn up or explode, John Travolta happily blows away fellow drivers (who are they?) with a machine gun, and none of it has any connection to anything else. The 1905 scene has a harum-scarum looseness and wit; the chases and destructive action scenes in movies now are brought off with a kind of grim, faceless glee, an exultation in power and mass. We can do it; therefore we *will* do it, and our ability to do it is the meaning of it, and if you're not impressed, it's still going to roll over you.

Neoprimitivism is one of the great strategies of modern art—Bartók refashioning folk materials in his powerfully angular music; Chuck Berry drawing on "hillbilly" rhythms for his own supercharged songs, and then the Rolling Stones enriching Chuck Berry's licks. Neoprimitivism cleared away the mush of Viennese or Edwardian sentiment, the perfume and pallor of Paris salon art, the Philadelphia softness of early 1960s rock. In movies, a great deal of mush has also been cleared away (the tyranny of niceness that ruined so many family movies in the 1940s, the physical, verbal, and sexual coyness of the 1950s). But the continuous motion of conglomerate product has removed much else as well, such as the mysteries of personality, sophisticated dialogue, any kind of elegant or smart life. The movie companies are now engaged in the systematic de-culturation of movies and the casting away of all manner of dramatic cunning laboriously built up over decades.

CLASSICAL

Sparked, perhaps, by the absence of sound, filmmakers developed the visual possibilities of film very quickly, and by the end of World War I, the vocabulary of editing and the overall strategy of Hollywood moviemaking was set. Celluloid may not have carried storytelling in its genes, but, as Bordwell and his collaborators put it, "Telling a story is the basic formal concern, which makes the film studio resemble the monastery's *scriptorium*, the site of the transcription and transmission of countless narratives." Storytelling may not be the essence of cinema (there is no essence of cinema), but the movies do it well, or used to, and in the scriptorium an unspoken vow was repeated daily: Audiences need to get emotionally involved in a story in order to enjoy themselves. The idea is so obvious that it seems absurd to spell it out. Yet in recent years that assumption, and everything that follows from it, have begun to weaken and even to disappear. It's shocking to be reminded of some of the things that are now slipping away: the notion that whatever is introduced in a tale has to mean something and that one thing should inevitably lead to another; that events are foreshadowed and then echoed, and that tension rises steadily through a series of minor climaxes to a final, grand climax; that music should be created not just as an enforcer of mood but as the outward sign of an overwhelming emotional logic, as if the characters had swallowed a love potion delivering them to an irresistible destiny; that characterization should be consistent; that a character's destiny was supposed to have some moral and spiritual meaning—the wicked punished, the virtuous rewarded or at least sanctified. It was a fictional world of total accountability.

For decades, these rules of the scriptorium signified "Hollywood"— a system dismissed by the humorless and pleasureless as "bourgeois cinema" but also enjoyed around the world by millions and praised in majestic terms by the greatest of French critics, André Bazin. Looking back to the late 1930s from some dozen years later, and passing judgment on precisely such conventions, Bazin announced that "In seeing again today such films as *Jezebel* by William Wyler, *Stagecoach* by John Ford, or *Le Jour se Lève* by Marcel Carné, one has the feeling that in them an art has found its perfect balance, its ideal form of expression, and reciprocally one admires them for dramatic and moral themes to which the cinema, while it may not have created them, has given a grandeur, an artistic effectiveness, that they would not otherwise have had. In short, here are all the characteristics of the ripeness of a classical art."

The ripeness of a classical art. The words are stirring but, at this point, almost embarrassing. What on earth did Bazin mean? Let's leave out *Le Jour se Lève* as impossible to understand without evoking French literary and philosophical traditions. *Jezebel* (1938), then. In *Jezebel,* everything revolves around a central character of extraordinary perversity—Julie Marsden (Bette Davis), a rich belle in pre–Civil War New Orleans. Julie's situation is paradoxical: She exercises the largest possible freedom within the confines of a social tradition that allows women no other career than that of coquette. Taut and over-defined emotionally—she demands categorical approval or rejection—Julie values the predominance of her own will more than love, more than society, more than anything. In other words, she is, in equal measure, admirable, dislikable, and crazy. She torments her high-minded beau (Henry Fonda) and wears a scarlet dress to a society ball at which unmarried women have traditionally worn white, knowing full well that the act must compromise her fiancé and destroy her own social position. Around this central incident—which at first seems trivial, and then, by degrees, more and more momentous—a portrait of antebellum Southern society as both noble and savagely inadequate unfolds with surprising power. Yet Davis's will-driven Julie dominates the movie. All the other characters lean toward her or shy away from her; they fuss before her arrivals and flutter after her departures. William Wyler is often said to have used an "invisible" technique, which means, in this case, that the camera glides, dollies, cranes, goes wherever it has to go, leading the eye from one shot to the next in an unbroken continuity that illuminates a story that is essentially psychological and social. The style is dedicated to the defining moment—the upturned face, the instant of self-definition, the rapid concentrics of astonishment and scandal spreading through a room as a young woman enters and gazes around herself in defiance. All the physical details are tightly arrayed around the outrageous, mesmerizing central figure.

In *Jezebel*, a rigidly structured society is falling into decay. In Bazin's other choice from 1939, *Stagecoach*, a new society is taking shape—the West as caravan of American democracy. The movie is perhaps the most popular and well-known Western ever made, and yet, seeing it again, one is struck by how fresh it is—how very funny and sharply edged, how bracingly decisive and swift the many little scenes are. An entire fluid American world is moving West: a high-type Virginia lady, a fallen Southern gentleman, an alcoholic doctor, a hypocritical banker, a good-hearted prostitute; all these people plus an ineffably relaxed young male beauty, John Wayne. They all go to Lordsburg, but they also move into their future, in a series of brief vignettes that are pitched at a level of temperament and humor that is like the warmth of a steady embrace. In *Stagecoach*, it is not so much a matter of a dominating individual as of an evolving group. All through the trip, the writer, Dudley Nichols, and the director, John Ford, make it clear what each of these highly wrought people thinks of the others. By degrees, they all come to understand that the alcoholic doctor is something more than an irresponsible lush, that the Southern gambler and murderer is suffused in self-disgust and has some genuine tenderness in him, and so on. Apart from all the fun and excitement it generates, *Stagecoach* is a drama of perception.

It is also—please forgive me—a drama of space. What audiences feel about characters on the screen is probably affected more than most of us realize by the way the space surrounding the people is carved up and re-combined. In John Ford, the geographic sense is very strong—the poetic awareness of sky and landscape and moving horses but also the attention to such things as how people are arrayed at a long table as an indication of social caste (the prostitute at one end, the fine lady at the other). The best use of space is not just an effective disposition of activity on the screen, it's the emotional meaning of activity on the screen. Directors used to take great care with such things: Spatial integrity was another part of the unspoken contract with audiences, a codicil to the narrative doctrine of the scriptorium. It allowed viewers to understand, say, how much danger a man was facing when he stuck his head above a rock in a gunfight, or where two secret lovers at a dinner party were sitting in relation to their jealous enemies. Space could be analyzed and broken into close-ups and reaction shots, and the like, but then it had to be reunified in a way that brought the experience together in a viewer's head; so that, in *Jezebel,* one felt physically what Bette Davis suffered as scandalized couples backed away from her in the ballroom. If the audience didn't feel that, the movie wouldn't have cast its spell.

This seems like plain common sense. Who could possibly argue with it? But spatial integrity is just about gone from big movies. For instance, what Wyler and his editors did—matching body movement from one shot to the next ("continuity editing")—is rarely attempted now. Hardly any-one thinks it important. The most common method of editing in big mov-ies now is to lay one furiously active shot on top of another, and often with only a general relation in space or body movement between the two. The continuous whirl of movement distracts us from noticing the uncertain or slovenly fit between shots. In *Moulin Rouge,* the camera swings wildly over masses of men in the nightclub, Nicole Kidman flings herself around her boudoir like a rag doll. *Moulin Rouge* is meant to be farce, of course. But if the constant buffoonishness of action in all sorts of big movies leaves one both overstimulated and unsatisfied—cheated without knowing why— then part of the reason is that the terrain hasn't been sewn together. You've been deprived of that loving inner possession of the movie that causes you to play it over and over in your head. You can't *see* Nicole Kidman the way you can see Bette Davis kneeling in apology to Henry Fonda, or John Wayne swiveling his big body into the stagecoach, or Al Pacino coming out of the gents' room, hesitating, looking at the two thugs he wants to kill, their looking quizzically back at him, his hesitating an instant more, and then their astonishment as he pulls out his gun and kills them both at point-blank range. That scene worked because you knew where Pacino was in relation to the two men at every second. But the new movies burn up one's senses, and leave behind nothing but a jangled nervous system, a blank memory, and a vacuum where emotion should be.

MODERN

A dominating individual, a dynamically evolving group—the classical cinema was always centered in character one way or another. Hollywood's normative style emerged at the happy crossroads of commerce and art, from 1928 to 1948, when an audience of 70 or 80 million people went to the movies every week without being bullied into it. It was an ideal, but it's hardly the only ideal, and I'm not suggesting we need to return to 1939. Most movies, of course, were nowhere near as good as *Jezebel* and *Stagecoach,* and, at their worst, Hollywood movies in the classical period were draped in the molasses of sentiment and reassurance.

After the war, it was time to pull off the drapes. Bazin and also James Agee loved the Italian Neorealists of the 1940s and 1950s, who produced a plainer image and a harsher moral tone than Hollywood ever did; and, if Bazin had lived past 1958, when Truffaut, Godard, Rivette, and the others were just getting started, he would have loved the flowing, open rhythms and offhand literary flavor of the New Wave. In America, television and other media entered the arena, luring viewers away, and the studios, in their old form, lost their power (in their new form, they have as much power as ever). The old tropes got stretched or broken into new shapes. To name just a few: There's the point-of-view camera and shock cutting of Hitchcock; the Expressionist lighting and radio studio echo chambers of Orson Welles; the dynamic architecture of widescreen composition in David Lean; the breathtaking, deeply moving tracking shots of Max Ophuls, Martin Scorsese, and others; the sustained, lens-scarring monologues and duologues of Ingmar Bergman and his satirical disciple Woody Allen; Stanley Kubrick's cold, discordant tableaux; the savagery, both humane and inhumane, of Akira Kurosawa and Sam Peckinpah; the crowded operatic realism of Coppola; the richly allusive, layered dialogue and sour-mash melancholy of Robert Altman; Steven Spielberg's visually eccentric manipulation of pop archetypes; Quentin Tarantino's discontinuous time scheme in *Pulp Fiction;* and many others. Sometimes directors subtracted conventional elements from the old syntax; sometimes they overloaded the medium, refusing an obvious emotional payoff while reaching a purer, more intense emotion through the exaggeration of a single element in filmmaking—the intensity of an enormously prolonged close-up, say, which might reveal the soul of a performer so powerfully that it exposes the soul of the viewer (to himself) as well.

Audiences were no longer enveloped by movies in the same comforting way; at times, they were affronted or even assaulted, both shocked and flattered by a greater aesthetic daring and moral realism. On the whole, this felt good. To be exposed to ugliness and horror, to be stunned rather than cosseted, overburdened rather than babied never hurt a moviegoer yet, and it made many of us happy not to have everything prepared and cushioned for us. Abruptness in the form of, say, the jump cuts in *Breathless* or the breaks in continuity in *Annie Hall* and dozens of other movies injects little spurts of energy into a scene. In such cases, we were not bothered by discontinuities from shot to shot—not when the sequences worked well within an exciting overall conception whose continuity may have been intellectual and emotional rather than physical. After the war, modernist filmmakers also found it impossible to believe in a coherent moral world, and their narratives no longer meted out punishments and rewards in the old Burbank bookkeeper's manner. Moral realism felt closer to the way we viewed our own lives, in which we and our friends may be reluctant heroes or not heroes at all.

The glory of modernism was that it yoked together candor and spiritual yearning with radical experiments in form. But in making such changes, filmmakers were hardly abandoning the audience. Reassurance may have ended, but emotion did not. The many alterations in the old stable syntax still honored the contract with us. The ignorant, suffering, morally vacant Jake LaMotta in *Raging Bull* was as great a protagonist as Julie Marsden. The morose *Nashville* was as trenchant a group portrait and national snapshot as the hopeful *Stagecoach*. However elliptical or harsh or astringent, emotion in modernist movies was a strong presence, not an absence.

In the period of conglomerate control, however, a very different kind of contract has appeared. Both the reassuring warmth of the classical period and the needling intelligence of modernism (apart from its appearance in a few recent movies like *American Beauty* and *Traffic*) have vanished. The new contract says that in order to enjoy themselves, audiences need to be detached from the emotions of a story. Filmmakers no longer seduce the audience; they treat it as if it were afraid of violation: Don't touch me, don't try to get at me. The Hollywood love story, for instance, gives way to lewd but amazingly anti-erotic sex comedies ruled by anxiety, skittishness, the fear of homosexuality. Jason Biggs, in *American Pie 2,* gets his hand glued to his ding-dong. That's about the situation of the audience for the new movies—stymied. But does the audience want more? It's often hard to tell.

POSTMODERN

Film, a photographic and digital medium, is perhaps more vulnerable than any of the other arts to the postmodernist habits of recycling and quotation. Imitation, pastiche, and collage have become the dominant structural devices, and there's an excruciating paradox in this development: Two of the sprightly media forms derived from movies—commercials and music videos—have themselves begun to dominate movies. It's a case of blowback in the arts.

As everyone knows, we can read an image much more quickly than anyone thought possible thirty years ago, and in recent years, many commercials have been cut faster and faster. The filmmakers know we aren't so much reading the image in those commercials as getting a visual impression, a mood, a desire. A truly hip commercial has no obvious connection to the product being sold, though selling is still its job. What, then, is being sold at a big movie that is cut the same way? The experience of going to the movie itself, the sensation of being rushed, dizzied, overwhelmed by the images. Michael Bay wasn't interested in what happened at Pearl Harbor. He was interested in his whizzing fantasia of the event. *Pearl Harbor* was about itself; so was *Planet of the Apes*. So was *Moulin Rouge*. The larger the movie, the more "content" becomes incidental, even disposable.

In recent years, many of the young movie directors (including, when they were young, Michael Bay and Baz Luhrmann) have come out of commercials and MTV. If a director is just starting out in feature films, he doesn't have to be paid much (perhaps a million dollars), and the studios can throw a script at him with the assumption that the movie, if nothing else, will have a great "look." He's already produced that look in his commercials or videos, which he shoots on film and then finishes digitally—adding or subtracting color, changing the sky, putting in flame or mist, retarding or speeding up movement. In the new Nissan commercial, the blue-tinted streets rumble and crack, trees give up their roots, and the silver SUV, cool as a titanium cucumber, rides over the steaming fissures. Wow! What a filmmaker! Studio executives don't have to say to such a young director, "Cut this feature very fast and put in a lot of thrills" because they hire only the kind of people who will cut it fast and put in thrills. That the young director has never worked with a serious dramatic structure or with actors before may not be considered a liability.

The results are there to see. At the risk of obviousness: Techniques that hold your eye in a commercial or video aren't suited to telling stories or building dramatic tension. In a full-length movie, images conceived that way begin to cancel each other out or just slip off the screen; the characters are just types or blurred spots of movement. The links with fiction and theater and classical film technique have been broken. The center no longer holds; mere anarchy is loosed upon the screen; the movie winds up a mess.

Written in September 2001; published here,
with revisions, for the first time

PIRATES ON THE iPOD /
THE SOUL OF A NEW SCREEN
Searching for movie bliss in the digital world

The device was as elegant as an old cigarette case and not much larger than a child's palm. But where do you put the damn thing? I was holding a video iPod in my hand, poised at the cutting edge of something or other—a new digital age, perhaps; a new platform for movies; a new convenience that would annihilate old paradigms. Last spring and summer, when I visited a number of executives and tech guys in big-studio Hollywood, I kept hearing disdain for the malls and movie complexes. And I heard a new mantra that went like this: "Content on demand—when you want it, where you want it, and how you want it." By the end of summer, movies were beginning to flow home and into portable devices through the Internet. In September, Apple began offering previously released movies from Disney through its iTunes Store. The pickings were slim, but I downloaded *Pirates of the Caribbean* onto my hard drive, and from there dumped it onto an iPod. The screen was only two inches across.

If you are sitting down, your lap is the natural place to rest an iPod; that way, your arms, leaning on your thighs, don't get weary. At that distance, however, my myopic eyes couldn't read the image clearly. So I pulled the screen up to my stomach, where the focus was good. And there it sat, riding up and down every time I took a breath. I was on the *Black Pearl,* all right, standing on her foredeck like a drunken sailor as she plowed through heavy seas. The horizon line kept pitching and heaving, and I couldn't see much of anything else. *Pirates* has lots of wide vistas and noisy tumult—a vast ocean under the dazzling sun and nighttime roughhouse in colonial towns, with deep-cleavaged prostitutes and toothless drunks falling out of bawdy houses. What I saw, mainly, was a looming ship the size of a twig, patches of sparkling blue, and a face or a skull flashing by. The interiors were as dark as bat caves. My ears, fed by headphones, were filled with such details as the creaking of the deck and the chafing of hawsers, but then, there below me, rising and falling, were Johnny Depp and Orlando Bloom dueling each other like two angry mosquitoes in an empty jar.

My arms got tired, so I lay down on a bed, turned on my side, propped my head on an elbow, and held the iPod in my free hand, resting on the mattress. Not bad—for a while. But after about twenty minutes, my neck and wrist developed shooting pains. This was nuts. In a theater, you *submit* to a screen; you want to be mastered by it, overwhelmed by it; you don't want to struggle to get cozy with it. The iPod screen will no doubt get larger, and other handheld devices with bigger screens are now emerging to challenge it, but, at this point, the little machine, which, in its musical role, produces Wagnerian torrents and Gillespian subtleties, now seemed not the neatest appliance ever invented but just plain silly. Of course, no one will ever be forced to look at movies on a pipsqueak display. Most grown-ups will look at downloaded films on a computer screen, or they'll transfer them to a big flat-screen TV. Yet the video iPod and other hand-held devices are being sold as movie exhibition spaces, and they certainly will function that way for kids. According to home entertainment special-ists I spoke to in Hollywood, many kids are "platform agnostic"—that is, they will look at movies on any screen at all, large or small. Most kids don't have bellies, and they can pretzel their limbs into almost any shape they want, so they can get comfortable with a handheld device; they can also take it onto a school bus, down the street, into bed, cuddling it under the covers after lights-out.

The movies currently offered by Apple and other downloading ser-vices are the first trickles of an approaching flood. Soon, new movies will come pouring through the Internet and through cable franchises as well, and people will look at them on screens of all sizes. For those of us who are not agnostics but fervent believers in the theatrical experience, this latest development in movie distribution is a momentous affair. Every kind of screen comes with its own aesthetic, and imposes its own social experience on moviegoers. We've all watched hundreds of movies on old TVs, but to watch *Citizen Kane* on TV for the first time is a half-fulfilled promise; to see it on a big screen is a revelation. Kids who get hooked on watching movies on a portable handheld device will be settling for a lesser experience, even if they don't yet know it—even if they never know it. And their consumer choices could affect the rest of us, just as they have in the music business. We're all in this together. Digital technology opens enormous possibilities for filmmakers and even for exhibitors, but it also offers a radical break with the many ways of watching movies that have given pleasure in the past.

On my belly, the *Caribbean* skeletons danced; their bones looked like pieces of string dipped in Elmer's glue. With a groan, I tried to suppress memories of camels making their stately way across a seventy-foot-wide screen in *Lawrence of Arabia*. On the iPod the camels would traverse my thumb. Is this any way to see a movie? What of the other ways?

They have been gone so long that to think of them at all is to indulge nostalgia for nostalgia, a faintly remembered dream from childhood of cathedral lobbies, ushers with red uniforms and gold braids, interiors done in Egyptian revival—King Tut meets Cecil B. DeMille. The old picture palaces, which graced the downtown streets of Dallas, Kansas City, San Francisco, Chicago, New York, not to mention thriving industrial cities in central Pennsylvania and Ohio, had names like the Alhambra, the Rialto, the Roxy; they had auditoriums evocative of pagoda pavilions or of Persian courts or perhaps of some celestial paradise with flocks of fleecy blond cherubim suspended in blue ether. Some of the interiors were an unaccountable combination of the Paris Opera and a seraglio, with hints of wicked luxuries and lewd liberties in upholstered scarlet boxes off to the side. The gents' rooms were suffused with the odor of mentholated raspberry nesting in dry ice—you peed into fragrance. A few of the ladies' rooms were furnished with cast-off pieces from the mansions of the Vanderbilts and other plutocrats. The picture palaces were uninhibited American kitsch, the product of a barbarian commercial culture amazed by fantasies of European or Oriental magnificence. The absurdity of the theaters was reassuring—an ersatz environment for an art form that was so lovable precisely because it was devoted to the unending appeal of illusion.

The neighborhood theaters that thrived at the same time were easier to deal with. Slipping in and out of them, we avoided the stern white-shoed matrons who patrolled the aisles with flashlights, and who told us twice, three, four times not to put our feet up on the seats in front of us. Sometimes we arrived in the middle of the movie and stayed until we reached the same point in the next show—we just wanted to go to the movies. Even now, moviegoing is informal and spontaneous, and people often go with low expectations. Which doesn't mean we don't hope that something extraordinary will happen. We long to be dominated by the merging of image, language, movement, and music; we long to be bullied into synesthesia—one sensory impression stimulating another. Hoping to get the most out of the experience, we may make a fetish over where to sit. Ideally situated, in the middle of the theater, close enough to lose the edges of the frame and disappear within it, a moviegoer has as many people in front of him as behind, all undergoing oceanic rapture, locked together in responses that spill from one to another. We enter from the crowded streets, and suddenly we are not alone, the sighing and shifting and laughing all around hitting us like the shifting pressures of the weather in an open field. It is a public space that nevertheless encourages private pleasures: The unconscious reaches out to the actors, to the cities and open spaces on-screen. The experience is the opposite of escape; it is more like absolute engagement. Emerging from the theater, our eyes are glazed if the movie is any good, and we walk like zombies, still playing it in our heads. The images and emotions will be there when we wake the next morning, as strong as the taste of a great banquet.

Such is the ideal. But how often does this happen now? Consider the mall or urban complex. The steady rain of contempt I heard from Hollywood executives directed at the theaters has been amplified, a dozen times over, by friends and strangers alike. The complaints start with the concussive din created by ten-year-old boys as they blow away invaders on video games in the mall complex lobby. The refreshment stands were lovingly noted, with their "small" Cokes in which you could drown a rabbit, the candy bars the size of elephant patties; and then came the pre-movie purgatory stretched out to twenty minutes and longer with ads, coming attractions, public service announcements, theater chain logos, enticements for kitty-kat clubs and Ukrainian bakeries . . . *anything* to delay the movie and send you back to the concession stand, where, it turns out, the theaters make 40 percent of their profits. If you go to a thriller, you may sit through coming attractions for five or six more action movies, with bodies bursting out of glass windows and enflamed cars flipping through the air—a long stretch of convulsive imagery from what seems like a single terrible movie that you've seen before. At poorly run complexes, projector bulbs go dim, the prints develop scratches or turn yellow, your feet stick to the floor, people jabber on cell phones, rumbles and blasts, like the sound of trains on an adjoining subway line, bleed through the walls. At some of the multiplexes showing *Pirates of the Caribbean 2* last summer, teens in eye patches and head scarves dueled in the parking lots. Those kids were having a hell of a time. But for anyone over thirty, moviegoing at a multiplex entails a very small rumpus factor.

If we want to see something badly enough, we go, of course, and once everyone settles down, and our own worries turn off, we can still have a great time. But we go amid murmurs of discontent. And the discontent will only get louder as the theater complexes age. Many of them were thrown up rapidly in response to what George Lucas demonstrated with *Star Wars* in 1977—that a movie massively advertised on national television could open in thousands of theaters simultaneously and pull in enormous opening weekend audiences. Those theaters were created for surging young audiences playing their part in the new blockbuster business model. When they get old, the gold leaf doesn't slowly peel off a fluted column, as it did at the Alhambra; they don't fade into folkloric shabbiness, like the neighborhood theaters. They turn into East Germany. They rot, like disused industrial spaces.

I visited my friend Harry Pearson, a music and film nut who reviews high-end audio and video equipment for erudite consumer magazines. Together we looked at movies on what must be close to the ultimate in home theater systems—a setup priced at $200,000. Expensive new technologies filter down, in a few years, to less and less costly equipment, so I thought that a glimpse of the best now available might be a way of anticipating the affordable future. Harry's system used not a flat screen but a digital projector suspended from the ceiling, which fed a traditional movie

screen ten and a half feet across the diagonal. Various electronic compo-
nents decoded or upgraded the digital information or sent the sound to
multiple speakers positioned around the room. The player was one of the
new high-definition DVD sets made by Toshiba, and what it produced on
that screen was certainly something to see.

The experience was like putting on a stronger pair of glasses for the
first time: Everything was brighter, crisper, more sharply defined—*newer*
somehow, as if it had been freshly created, even though one of the movies
was a half century old. With amazement, we watched John Ford's masterpiece *The Searchers,* from 1956, in a new high-definition transfer. (Digital
transfers are made by scanning a film negative or a print; technicians then
digitally enhance the images.) The southwestern sky above Monument
Valley was a brilliant azure; the desert was not a mass of orange-brown
glop but grains of sand and pieces of rock; and, inside the pioneers' cabin,
details normally hidden in shadow, like the drying cornstalks hanging
from the ceiling, were clearly visible. And so it was with a recent film.
When Clint Eastwood's *Million Dollar Baby* opened two years ago, I referred to the Hit Pit—the gym where so much of the action takes place—
as "moldy" and a "sweat-stained relic." But the high-definition transfer of
the film, bringing shapes and textures out of the murk, revealed a gym
that was certainly old and shabby but also Lestoil clean. Suddenly, *Million
Dollar Baby* was a rather different movie—the gym was no longer a place
where everything stank of defeat except the two elderly gents (Eastwood
and Morgan Freeman) running it. It was more like an ordinary workplace.

Harry and I got a little giddy noticing things we had never noticed before. But the look of the image was different from a film image, and strange
in some ways. In film, the illusion of three-dimensionality is produced by
the manipulation of focus and by the subtleties of lighting: We are led into
depth by the tiny gradations of color or, in black-and-white movies, by the
many shades of gray between white and black. A digital transfer gathers
and compacts the colors, and also increases contrast, and so, in the worst
instances of early digital transfers of film—say, from a decade ago—the
actors looked almost like cutouts against a flat background, their flesh
tones waxy and doll-like. Everything was too smooth, even congealed.
The images didn't breathe the way the original film images did—the faces

seemed to have lost their pores. But now, high-definition digital, by re-trieving more information from the negative, produces a more nuanced gradation of color and a more definite molding of the face—one saw planes and hollows. To my eyes, flesh still looked a little synthetic, but certainly it looked better than before, and no doubt will get better still in a few years. ("You want pores, we'll give you pores," a digital technician in Los Angeles said to me.) The image was steady, too, in a way that a film image is not. A film, after all, gets pulled into place in the projector by pins entering and then withdrawing from sprocket holes; the image on-screen can jiggle a bit, and if the projector's pressure plate is not evenly applied to the celluloid, the image blurs at the corners. But on Harry's system, I no-ticed an absolute evenness, steadiness, and hard focus into the far reaches of the screen; I also noted the absence of earlier digital artifacts, like a black edge around shapes or a flaring of solid whites.

All in all, high-definition is a big step forward over standard digital imagery, though I'm not used to it yet, and, in truth, I admire it with-out really loving it. To get a release print of a regular film, the image has to go through at least four generations—from negative to positive, and then back and forth again, and, by the end, the multiple printing produces some minor softening and blending of color. I like the way color blends on film: The image is sensuous, painterly, and atmospheric; more poetic, perhaps, than a digital image; lyrical rather than analytic. I may have seen more of the Hit Pit in the high-definition transfer, but I was happier with my earlier sense of what the place meant. Expressive metaphor had given way to a more prosaic reality. And I think that Clint Eastwood, having directed more than thirty films, may have intended *Baby* to look exactly the way it looks on film.

At home, re-creating the memory of a movie experience that once en-gulfed us, we struggle for more—more emotion, more color, more mean-ing. If we can't get it, we fill it in from memory, the way someone listening to a familiar piece of music on the beach will fill in instrumental color and rhythms wiped out by a roaring surf. For almost a half century, we looked at movies at home on ordinary cathode ray tube TV sets, but the last time I tried it, I felt as if I had the flu, and were wrapped in a shawl, afraid of too much movement, too much involvement. The new flat-panel screens have spoiled us. A few days after my bash at Harry's, I went to a friend's house and sat alone, looking at movies on an excellent forty-inch liquid crystal display fed by a standard DVD player.

Alone, I indulged myself. The classic dialogue comedy from 1940, *The Philadelphia Story,* starring Katharine Hepburn, James Stewart, and Cary Grant, came pretty fully to life. The high-def screen yielded such benefits of MGM's glamour years as the sheen (from backlighting) on Katharine Hepburn's hair and the satiny white look of MGM's imagined Main Line mansion. *The Philadelphia Story* had been a successful Broadway play, and the movie adaptation emphasizes the theatricality—the characters are always putting each other on or telling each other off. Few of the movie's visual qualities were lost, and the fanged upper-class banter is so peculiarly intimate that it plays very well at home. And a black-and-white dialogue comedy from almost forty years later, Woody Allen's *Manhattan,* also lost very little on the big home screen. Much of the movie was shot on the streets of New York at night, or in half-light—at dawn, in one case, as Woody and Diane Keaton, sitting in the little park near the Queensboro Bridge, natter on and on. The high-powered technology retrieved the half-tones from what I remembered of old-TV shadows.

Switching to color and to something that was digital and high-tech to begin with—the first *Spider-Man,* from 2002—I scored again. The director, Sam Raimi, went for a hard-edged look, with solid colors and the surging, swinging movement of the Marvel Comics style, and Raimi's graphics still looked sensational. There was no reality to capture—the movie, at its best, was pure artifice and pop rapture. But a neo-noir movie that exaggerated aspects of reality into something that was the very opposite of pop—Martin Scorsese's urban-expressionist *Taxi Driver,* from 1976—was a dud at home. What I loved in the theater was the encompassing lurid rawness, the hookers and pimps and thugs taking over the neon-red streets. On the home screen, the steam rising from the manholes—Dante's burning underground lake percolating in Manhattan—didn't loom up and envelop me, the bloody violence at the end didn't explode in my face as I remembered. For the first time, the big LCD screen seemed inadequate; I was constantly aware of the outer edge of the frame just when I wanted to abandon myself within it, yielding to the power and sensuality that Scorsese and cinematographer Michael Chapman had achieved. No, it wasn't good enough. It wasn't good at all; it was worse than a diminution, it was betrayal. And this was a forty-inch screen. People were looking at movies on a lot smaller screens than that.

Fifty years ago, the length of a pop single was determined by what would fit on those ubiquitous 45 rpm seven-inch disks. The length and the episodic structure of the Victorian novel—Dickens's novels, especially— were at least partly created by writers and magazine editors working on monthly deadlines. In its early days, television, for a variety of commercial and merely spatial reasons, developed the single-set or two-set sitcom. And, of course, the form of the feature film—the usual length, the visual grammar—evolved in relation to the mechanics of the recording and delivery systems, including studio-owned theaters with their hungry maws yearning to be filled every week. Format always affects form. Whether we see movies on a seventy-foot screen or on a toothbrush, no exhibition method is innocent of aesthetic qualities. Platform agnosticism may flourish among kids, but when it comes to grown-up experience of different movie platforms, neutrality doesn't exist.

"Content where you want it, when you want it." That's what I kept hearing in Los Angeles. And also its corollary, "The portability is its functionality." Okay, then, I looked at *Brokeback Mountain* on a portable DVD player with a seven-inch screen and headphones—the kind of rig people use on airplanes and in jury waiting rooms. Portable and functional. The focus was precise, the color very bright—the sun sparkling on a mountain stream had a diamond brilliance. And, through the headphones, I heard extraordinary details—the *flip-flip-flip* of the rain on the tent when Jake Gyllenhaal and Heath Ledger are up in the mountains, the creaking of the leather saddle as Ledger rides through the woods. All of this companionable real-world texture—dramatic punctuation as well as ambient atmosphere—would, in a theater, be lost, or minimized amid the sighing and stirring of the sainted collective beast.

Yet there was something wrong: Watching on a little screen, I was not *in* the mountains. After all, this is the men's workplace for the summer. In so much of the first half of the movie, as their feelings for each move into anger and affection, and then into something else, the action of the movie is the routine work of herding, cooking, loading, washing up. The grandeur of the terrain is not something the men are necessarily conscious of, but the massiveness of the mountain range, the startling clarity of the air, the violence of the weather—all of that enlarges the experience of emotions they haven't words for and can't control. If you watch the movie on a little screen, you're not living within this great breathing, palpable place, you're merely appreciating it as a series of pretty images. The small screen takes the emotion out of the landscape.

The experience was emotionally unsatisfying in other ways, too. Having highly detailed sound in your head and a reduced image before your eyes is an oddly disjunctive and unsettling experience. It's as if the movie had been pulled back to the editing stage, before the sound and picture were "married" on the release prints. You are reminded of the obvious reason theaters have put the speakers behind the screen all these years—so the words seem to be coming out of the characters' mouths. In *Brokeback,* as a storm breaks, the lightning flashed on-screen, but the thunder roared in my head. Disoriented, I half expected the rain to land on my hand. It turns out that too much aural detail at home can dispel or confuse certain kinds of illusion. In *A Star Is Born,* from 1954, Judy Garland, performing with musician friends in a late-night club after closing time, sings "The Man That Got Away," the devastating torch song written for the movie by Harold Arlen and lyricist Ira Gershwin. Heard through headphones, it's a wrenchingly intimate experience. But before the song is over, there's a bitter surprise. The sound is so revealing, you notice that the syncing of Garland's voice, which was probably recorded afterward and dubbed in, is just slightly off. It's not something you would notice in a theater, where the tidal pull of audience emotion would blur the sharpness of perception. A paradox, then: The technology which brings us close to the experience, can, in the end, dislodge us from it, and, listening to Garland, I felt as if a spider had settled on the perfect pleasure of the moment.

I'm hardly a theatrical fundamentalist: At home, with friends, and with children, too, watching a movie can be the greatest entertainment in the world. But it's silly to pretend that watching movies at home in a group is the same as going to the theater. At home, everyone talks. The kids ask questions, and the adults make jokes or play off one another, showing off their knowledge of movies, especially if it's anything old. An old movie seen in a group becomes an occasion for lowbrow cultural anthropology. We can be amazed by the clothing styles—the men in a mid-1960s movie all in suits and ties and parted hair, the women in modified Jackie O bouffants. The movie becomes a way of skipping through our past, rummaging around in memory, marking the strangeness of recognition. In an old movie, the places at which we have left a little of ourselves—a hotel lobby, a street corner, touristic bits of sidewalk-café Paris or Rome—become a startling reminder of age. But time isn't always tragic—a patch of Central Park, say, brownish and threadbare in that movie from thirty-five years ago, is now, in the actual park, verdantly restored. The home movie party can be a time of happiness—we have gratefully left *that* part of ourselves behind. Talk and memory and renewal are the great benefit of the home theater party as much as murmurous silence is the spiritual glue of the theatrical experience.

But watching a movie at home by yourself, on a small screen, can be a discomforting experience, and not just because technology alters the film. Anything intimate on-screen makes you feel like a voyeur in a way that seeing it in a theater, surrounded by hundreds of other curious people, does not. Let's put it this way: Group voyeurism is shared involvement; individual voyeurism is slightly shameful. I enjoyed *The 40 Year Old Virgin* in the theater, but at home, without laughing people on all sides, I felt my loneliness was only slightly less oppressive than that of the Steve Carell character, who is so flummoxed that he can't go to bed with anyone. In the theater, Carell's hang-ups play off a shared notion of what a normal sex life should be—the rough good sense emanating from the experience of three or four hundred people, straight and gay, sexually active and merely lustful. At home, alone, you almost feel that you *are* Steve Carell; the experience is close to self-abuse.

Looking at *Brokeback* on a seven-inch screen diminishes it. Looking at *Pirates of the Caribbean* on an iPod annihilates it. At what point does diminution of the image end the movie experience altogether and turn it into something else? Mobile phones and personal digital assistants serve people who need to be in touch, or can't bear being out of touch. They feed an essential anxiety but never quite eliminate it—there's always a message that you might be missing, another call that you might be making, and, after a while, convenience can turn into an addictive yearning that only increases the anxiety. Visual material is now moving into the same orbit of need and compulsion; it's becoming a near-therapeutic companion for people who can't bear the loneliness of imagination or just plain looking at the world. Understandable enough: We enter a movie theater, in part, because we don't want to be alone, and, in a marvelous paradox, the people around us both relieve us of loneliness and drive us deeper into our own responses. But a portable device is just *company*. It doesn't liberate anything, and it throws us back into the isolation that we longed to escape from.

A movie opening, for better or worse, remains an event. The theatrical opening aggregates the publicity—the ads, the magazine covers, the newspaper and television interviews, the cable "documentaries" about the making of the picture, the hundreds of reviews, the ceaseless nattering of blogs. If the studios send too many movies home, it will be hard to distinguish them from television. How do they sell them as *movies*? The studio executives may be scheming to get movies sent home through the Internet, but they can be as eloquent as anyone about the spiritual communion of five hundred souls in the dark. I'm convinced that at some level they mean what they say. They all grew up in theaters, they know that something magical happens among strangers—they know the excitement of a full house. And the executives remember what it was like to be twenty-one. "You want to have sex with someone," said the blunt James Schamus, the head of Universal's specialty division, Focus Features. "You say, 'Do you want to watch a movie at my house? Or do you want to go to the movies with me Friday night?' Movies are a pretext for social interaction. So don't think of the future in terms of technology. It's not a question of platforms but of how people want to use social spaces, how given ethnic and age groups want to interact."

The lobby is a broad, high vault that shelters a restaurant, a bar, a book-and-gift shop. Couples hang out at the bar, eat and talk, leaf through the pages of a hot new novel or a movie star biography; sometimes they get together again after the movie or meet with strangers who just came out of the same picture. The bathrooms are spotless, with slatted oak doors on the stalls and classic movie music piped in. At the concession stand, the coffee is strong and hot. All the seats are reserved, and the seats are plush, with plenty of legroom. The steeply raked auditorium is very dark—a "black box" design—and insulated from the sound of the many other theaters in the same multiplex. Is this some sort of upper-bourgeois dream of the great good place? A padded cell for wealthy movie nuts? No, it's an actual multiplex, the ArcLight, on Sunset Boulevard, near Vine, and the idea may be catching on. Sumner Redstone's daughter Shari, the president of the family-owned theater business, National Amusements, has vowed to convert about half the lobbies of the chain's fourteen hundred theaters to social spaces with comfortable lounges, complete with martinis, couches, and newspapers on racks. If theaters go in this Starbucks direction, not only will some of the older audience come back, with a positive effect on filmmaking, but the greatness of the movies as an art form and an experience could be preserved. After you are seated at the ArcLight, an usher standing at the front tells you who wrote and directed the movie and how long it is. He and another usher will stay for a while to be sure that projection and sound are up to snuff. Then he shuts up. There are no advertisements following his speech, and only four coming attractions. The movie begins, and you are lost, utterly lost in it.

The New Yorker, *January 8, 2007; revised 2011*

SPECTACLE

THE PASSION OF THE CHRIST

In *The Passion of the Christ*, Mel Gibson shows little interest in celebrating the electric charge of hope and redemption that Jesus Christ brought into the world. He largely ignores Jesus' heart-stopping eloquence, his startling ethical radicalism and personal radiance—Christ as a "paragon of vitality and poetic assertion," as John Updike described Jesus' character in his essay "The Gospel According to Saint Matthew." Cecil B. DeMille had his version of Jesus' life, Pier Paolo Pasolini and Martin Scorsese had theirs, and Gibson, of course, is free to skip over the incomparable glories of Jesus' temperament and to devote himself, as he does, to Jesus' pain and martyrdom in the last twelve hours of his life. As a viewer, I am equally free to say that the movie Gibson has made from his personal obsessions is a sickening death trip, a grimly unilluminating procession of treachery, beatings, blood, and agony—and to say so without indulging in "anti-Christian sentiment" (Gibson's term for what his critics are spreading). For two hours, with only an occasional pause or gentle flashback, we watch, stupefied, as a handsome, strapping, at times half-naked young man (James Caviezel) is slowly tortured to death. Gibson is so thoroughly fixated on the scourging and crushing of Christ, and so meagerly involved in the spiritual meanings of the final hours, that he falls in danger of altering Jesus' message of love into one of hate. And against whom will the audience direct its hate? As Gibson was completing the film, some historians, theologians, and clergymen accused him of emphasizing the discredited charge that it was the ancient Jews who were primarily responsible for killing Jesus, a claim that has served as the traditional justification for the persecution of the Jews in Europe for nearly two millennia. The critics turn out to have been right. Gibson is guilty of some serious mischief in his handling of these issues. But he may have also committed an aggression against Christian believers. The movie has been hailed as a religious experience by various Catholic and Protestant groups, some of whom, with an ungodly eye to the commercial realities of film distribution, have pre-purchased blocks of tickets or rented theaters to insure *The Passion* a healthy opening weekend's business. But how, I wonder, will people become better Christians if they are filled with the guilt, anguish, or loathing that this movie may create in their souls?

The Passion opens at night in the Garden of Gethsemane—a hushed, misty grotto bathed in a purplish disco light. Softly chanting female voices float on the soundtrack, accompanied by electronic shrieks and thuds. At first, the movie looks like a graveyard horror flick, and then, as Jewish temple guards show up bearing torches, like a faintly tedious art film. The Jews speak in Aramaic, and the Romans speak in Latin; the movie is subtitled in English. Gibson distances the dialogue from us, as if Jesus' famous words were only incidental and the visual spectacle—Gibson's work as a director—were the real point. Then the beatings begin: Jesus is punched and slapped, struck with chains, trussed, and dangled over a wall. In the middle of the night, a hasty trial gets under way before Caiaphas (Mattia Sbragia) and other Jewish priests. Caiaphas, a cynical, devious, petty dictator, interrogates Jesus, and then turns him over to the Roman prefect Pontius Pilate (Hristo Naumov Shopov), who tries again and again to spare Jesus from the crucifixion that the priests demand. From the movie, we get the impression that the priests are either merely envious of Jesus' spiritual power or inherently and inexplicably vicious. And Pilate is not the bloody governor of history (even Tiberius paused at his crimes against the Jews) but a civilized and humane leader tormented by the burdens of power—he holds a soulful discussion with his wife on the nature of truth.

Gibson and his screenwriter, Benedict Fitzgerald, selected and enhanced incidents from the four Gospels and collated them into a single, surpassingly violent narrative—the scourging, for instance, which is mentioned only in a few phrases in Matthew, Mark, and John, is drawn out to the point of excruciation and beyond. History is also treated selectively. The writer Jon Meacham, in a patient and thorough article in *Newsweek,* has detailed the many small ways that Gibson disregarded what histori-ans know of the period, with the effect of assigning greater responsibility to the Jews, and less to the Romans, for Jesus' death. Meacham's central thesis, which is shared by others, is that the priests may have been willing to sacrifice Jesus—whose mass following may have posed a threat to Ro-man governance—in order to deter Pilate from crushing the Jewish com-munity altogether. It's also possible that the temple elite may have wanted to get rid of the leader of a new sect, but only Pilate had the authority to order a crucifixion—a very public event that was designed to be a warning to potential rebels.

Gibson ignores most of the dismaying political context, as well as the likelihood that the Gospel writers, still under Roman rule, had very prac-tical reasons to downplay the Romans' role in the Crucifixion. It's true that when the Roman soldiers, their faces twisted in glee, go to work on Je-sus, they seem even more depraved than the Jews. But, as Gibson knows, history rescued the pagans from eternal blame—eventually, they came to their senses and saw the light. The Emperor Constantine converted in the early fourth century, and Christianized the empire, and the medieval pe-riod saw the rise of the Roman Catholic Church. So the Romans' descen-dants triumphed, while the Jews were cast into darkness and, one might conclude from this movie, deserved what they got. The Passion, in its con-fused way, confirms the old justifications for persecuting the Jews, and one somehow doubts that Gibson will make a sequel in which he reminds the audience that in later centuries the Church itself used torture and ex-ecution to punish not only Jews but heretics, nonbelievers, and dissidents.

I realize that the mere mention of historical research could exacer-bate the awkward breach between medieval and modern minds, between literalist belief and the weighing of empirical evidence. "John was an eye-witness," Gibson has said. "Matthew was there." Well, they may have been there, but for decades it's been a commonplace of biblical scholarship that the Gospels were written forty to seventy years after the death of Jesus, and not by the disciples but by nameless Christians using both written and oral sources. Gibson can brush aside the work of scholars and histori-ans because he has a powerful weapon at hand—the cinema—with which he can create something greater than argument; he can create faith. As a moviemaker, Gibson is not without skill. The sets, which were built in Italy, where the movie was filmed, are far from perfect, but they convey the beauty of Jerusalem's courtyards and archways. Gibson, working with the cinematographer Caleb Deschanel, gives us the ravaged stone face of Calvary, the gray light at the time of the Crucifixion, the leaden pace of the movie's spectacular agonies. Felliniesque tormentors gambol and jeer on the sidelines, and, at times, the whirl of figures around Jesus, both hostile and friendly, seems held in place by a kind of magnetic force. The hounding and suicide of the betrayer Judas is accomplished in a few brusque strokes. Here and there, the movie has a dismal, heavy-souled power.

By contrast with the dispatching of Judas, the lashing and flaying of Jesus goes on forever, prolonged by Gibson's punishing use of slow motion, sometimes with Jesus' face in the foreground, so that we can see him writhe and howl. In the climb up to Calvary, Caviezel, one eye swollen shut, his mouth open in agony, collapses repeatedly in slow motion under the weight of the Cross. Then comes the Crucifixion itself, dramatized with a curious fixation on the technical details—an arm pulled out of its socket, huge nails hammered into hands, with Caviezel jumping after each whack. At that point, I said to myself, "Mel Gibson has lost it," and I was reminded of what other writers have pointed out—that Gibson, as an actor, has been beaten, mashed, and disemboweled in many of his movies. His obsession with pain, disguised by religious feelings, has now reached a frightening apotheosis.

Mel Gibson is an extremely conservative Catholic who rejects the reforms of the Second Vatican Council. He's against complacent, feel-good Christianity, and, judging from his movie, he must despise the grandiose old Hollywood kitsch of *The Robe, The King of Kings, The Greatest Story Ever Told, and Ben-Hur,* with their Hallmark twinkling skies, their big stars treading across sacred California sands, and their lamblike Jesus, whose simple presence overwhelms Charlton Heston. But saying that Gibson is sincere doesn't mean he isn't foolish, or worse.

He can rightly claim that there's a strain of morbidity running through Christian iconography—one thinks of the reliquaries in Roman churches and the bloody and ravaged Christ in Northern Renaissance and German art, culminating in such works as Matthias Grünewald's 1515 *Isen-*

heim *Altarpiece,* with its thorned Christ in full torment on the Cross. But the central tradition of Italian Renaissance painting left Christ relatively unscathed; the artists emphasized not the physical suffering of the man but the sacrificial nature of his death and the astonishing mystery of his transformation into godhood—the Resurrection and the triumph over carnality. Gibson instructed Deschanel to make the movie look like the paintings of Caravaggio, but in Caravaggio's own *Flagellation of Christ* the body of Jesus is only slightly marked. Even Goya, who hardly shrank from dismemberment and pain in his work, created a *Crucifixion* with a nearly unblemished Jesus. Crucifixion, as the Romans used it, was meant to make a spectacle out of degradation and suffering—to humiliate the victim through the apparatus of torture. By embracing the Roman pageant so openly, using all the emotional resources of cinema, Gibson has canceled out the redemptive and transfiguring power of art. And by casting James Caviezel, an actor without charisma here, and then feasting on his physical destruction, he has turned Jesus back into a mere body. The depictions in *The Passion of the Christ,* one of the cruelest movies in the history of the cinema, are akin to the bloody Pop representation of Jesus found in, say, a roadside shrine in Mexico, where the addition of an Aztec sacrificial flourish makes the passion a little more passionate. Such are the traps of literal-mindedness. The great modernist artists, aware of the danger of kitsch and the fascination of sadomasochism, have largely withdrawn into austerity and awed abstraction or into fervent humanism, as in Scorsese's *The Last Temptation of Christ* (1988), which features an existential Jesus sorely tried by the difficulty of the task before him. There are many ways of putting Jesus at risk and making us feel his suffering.

What is most depressing about *The Passion* is the thought that people will take their children to see it. Jesus said, "Suffer the little children to come unto me," not "Let the little children watch me suffer." How will parents deal with the pain, terror, and anger that children will doubtless feel as they watch a man flayed and pierced until dead? The despair of the movie is hard to shrug off, and Gibson's timing couldn't be more unfortunate: Another dose of death-haunted religious fanaticism is the last thing we need.

The New Yorker, *March 1, 2004*

AVATAR

James Cameron's *Avatar* is the most beautiful film I've seen in years. Amid the hoopla over the new power of 3-D as a narrative form, and the excitement about the complicated mix of digital animation and live action that made the movie possible, no one should ignore how lovely *Avatar* looks, how luscious yet freewheeling, bounteous yet strange. As Cameron surges through the picture plane, brushing past tree branches, coursing alongside foaming-mouthed creatures, we may be overcome by an uncanny sense of emerging, becoming, transcending—a sustained mood of elation produced by vaulting into space. Working with a crew of thousands, Cameron has reimagined nature: The movie is set on Pandora, a distant moon with thick forests, alpine chasms, and such fantastic oddities as wooded mountains hanging in the sky. The geographical center of the movie is a giant willow tree where a tribal clan, the Na'vi, worships the connections among all living things—a dubious-sounding mystical concept that the movie manages to make exciting. In *Titanic,* Cameron turned people blue as they died in icy waters, but this time blue is the color of vibrant health: The Na'vi are a translucent pale blue, with powerful, long-waisted bodies, flat noses, and wide-set eyes. In their easy command of nature, they are meant to evoke aboriginal people everywhere. They have spiritual powers and, despite their elementary weapons—bows and arrows—real powers, too. From each one's head emerges a long braid ending in tendrils that are alive with nerves. When the Na'vi plug their braids into similar neural cords that hang from the heads of crested, horselike animals and giant birds, they achieve zahelu, which is not, apparently, as pleasurable as sex, but somewhat more useful—the Na'vi's thoughts govern the animals' behavior. Cameron believes in hooking up: This world is as much a vertical experience as a horizontal one, and the many parts of it cohere and flow together. The movie is a blissful fantasy of a completely organic life.

The Na'vi's turf is also rich with an energy-yielding mineral called Unobtainium (which is as close as Cameron comes to a joke in this movie). Eager to harvest the mineral, corporate predators, joined by heavily armed military contractors, have established a base on Pandora. They've been feeding people's DNA into long, pale blue versions of their bodies—

avatars—and setting them loose among the Na'vi, where they learn their lingo and try to argue them off the land. A high-powered biologist (Sigourney Weaver), who loves the Na'vi, has been to the woods and back many times. She is followed by Jake (Sam Worthington), an ex-Marine. He has withered legs, but, reconditioned as an avatar, he can spring and jump anywhere; he's fearless, and as wild as a monkey. His job, if he can't persuade the Na'vi to leave, is to find out enough about them so that contractors can come in and kill them. The next stage of the fable isn't exactly a surprise: Living among the Na'vi, Jake falls in love with a warrior princess, Neytiri (Zoë Saldana), who looks like a painted Amazon on a Milan runway. She teaches him the native ways, and protects him from the other Na'vi, who discover that he's a spy. It's the old story of Pocahontas and John Smith, mixed, perhaps, with the remnants of Westerns (like *Dances with Wolves*) in which a white man spends some time with the Comanche or the Sioux and then, won over, tries to defend the tribe against the advancing civilization that will annihilate it.

Science is good, but technology is bad. Community is great, but corporations are evil. *Avatar* gives off more than a whiff of 1960s counterculture, by way of environmentalism and current antiwar sentiment. "What have we got to offer them—lite beer and bluejeans?" Jake asks. Well, actually, life among the Na'vi, for all its physical glories, looks a little dull. True, there's no reality TV or fast food, but there's no tennis or Raymond Chandler or Ella Fitzgerald, either. But let's not dwell on the sentimentality of Cameron's notion of aboriginal life—the movie is striking enough to make it irrelevant. Nor is there much point in lingering over the irony that this anti-technology message is delivered by an example of advanced technology that cost nearly $250 million to produce; or that this anti-imperialist spectacle will invade every available theater in the world. Relish, instead, the pterodactyls, or the flying velociraptors, or whatever they are—large beaky beasts, green with yellow reptile patches—and the bright red flying monster with jaws that could snap an oak. Jake, like a Western hero breaking a wild horse, has to tame one of these creatures in order to prove his manhood, and the scene has a barbaric splendor. The movie's story may be a little trite, and the big battle at the end between ugly mechanical force and the gorgeous natural world goes on forever, but what a show Cameron puts on! The continuity of dynamized space that he has achieved with 3-D gloriously supports his trippy belief that all living things are one. Zahelu!

The New Yorker, *January 4, 2010*

ENDLESS SUMMER—DIGITAL ALL THE TIME

In J. J. Abrams's *Super 8*—one of the twenty or so digital spectacles storming the malls this summer, including *X-Men: First Class* and *Green Lantern*—a bunch of kids in a small Ohio town, in 1979, are making a zombie movie. It's their first super-production, and the director, a rotund middle-schooler named Charles (Riley Griffiths), is as driven as Hitchcock in his perfectionism. He gets an excitable shrimpy kid with braces, Cary (Ryan Lee), who plays one of the undead, to take a bullet and fall, while Charles's best friend, Joe (Joel Courtney), applies ghoulish makeup to the film's leading lady, Alice (Elle Fanning), a tomboy beauty. We can't help noticing that the kids are not making a documentary about the steel plant in their town, a fading industrial site where Joe's mother recently died in an accident. Anything but. J. J. Abrams and his mentor, Steven Spielberg (who produced the film), both began making movies as boys, with 8mm cameras, and they appear to be saying that art making as a passion is born not in reality but in fantasy, horror, the supernatural. The crew in *Super 8*, however, doesn't have much in the way of special effects to work with—just blank plastic eyes for the ghouls and some fake blood—so the movie is partly an affectionate joke about innocence. The kids are so obsessed with making their fantastic fiction that they don't see the uncanny things happening around them—dogs and people disappearing, objects zipping like bullets through the air.

Spielberg and Abrams are fond of their moviemaking past, but their nostalgia is double-edged. To shoot the large-scale fantasy scenes in *Super 8*, the filmmakers use millions of pixels, not still images photographed at twenty-four frames per second. A way of making movies—the kids' way, the filmmakers' way when *they* were kids—has passed. Film history is right there in the center of the movie; the possibilities for wild invention,

and the temptation to make junk, too. That shift—from film to digital—
has been momentous, even frightening, in its implications. Computer-
generated imagery began a couple of decades ago, and gathered steam with
George Lucas's all-digital *Star Wars Episode II: Attack of the Clones* (2002),
and now it's finding its way into all kinds of movies and TV shows. Just look
at the coming attractions and the fall TV lineup: We get dream and fantasy
sequences, mind reading and mind control; spinning, fanged, red-purple-
green airborne warriors, male and female; life just before death; life just *after*
death; alternate realities; solid worlds crumbling, upended, or fading into
the surreal subjective. Aerated fantasy and sci-fi transmigrations are everywhere. In all, it's as important a shift as the move from silence to sound or
from black-and-white to color. In a few years, we may even say that fantasy,
not reality, is the default illusional mode in movies. Whether it's an improve-
ment is another matter altogether.

Fantasy and spectacle have always been a big part of moviemaking, going
back to Georges Méliès's *Le Voyage dans la Lune* (1902). If the fantasy movies made now are just grander, wilder, and freer than those of decades ago,
why complain about them? Hasn't digital technology liberated imagination
and created many forms of visual rapture? Remember the dinosaurs hopping
across an open field in the original *Jurassic Park* way back in 1993? That was
breathtaking. I would say, "Yes, digital has liberated imagination—some of the
time." CGI has yielded sequences of great loveliness—the mercurial reconstituted beings in *Terminator 2: Judgment Day* (1991); the flying battles in *The
Matrix* (1999). In Alfonso Cuarón's *Children of Men* (2006), a dystopian
adventure about a world without children, digital technology produced
a darkening of the color palette and ominous chaos looming around the
corners of torn-up cities. In 2009, we were engulfed by the purple-green
floricultural lusciousness of *Avatar*. These are all digital triumphs. But one
reason that CGI has become so widespread is that it makes the fantastic available not just to the artists but to the unimaginative and the graceless as well.
Computer-generated imagery (CGI) allows any body or machine to rise
and fly, flame to fill any conceivable volume, water instantly to harden
into ice; it turns humans into furry, skeletal, or serpentine creatures and
then back again. Any plot difficulty can be resolved by turning a man into
a beast, or a beast into a man, or by having a character vanish altogether, or

by hurling someone across a room and smashing him against a wall without his suffering more than an itty-bitty bruise. What's at stake in any of these astonishments? We're getting excitement without end, but the merely human has been eclipsed.

Another reason that digital has become so prevalent—this will not come exactly as a surprise—is that it feeds the opening weekend box office ambitions of conglomerates eager to exploit comic-book-style filmmaking for teen audiences. (*X-Men* took the top spot in its first weekend—with $55 million— and *Green Lantern* looks primed to do the same.) The studios have committed more than a billion dollars to next summer's batch of spectacles. (The end of *Green Lantern* sets up a sequel.) As long as teens keep turning out on opening weekends, and the franchise movies can be cross-marketed as toys, shirts, books, beer mugs, and music, the business model will hold, pushing other kinds of movies off the table. Who knows how many more interesting projects have been shelved and forgotten? That's one alternate universe that we'll never see—the unmade movies. But do these comic book movies really satisfy anyone except kids and overgrown boys? The exhilaration of a comic book is produced by dropping the preparations and the consequences of carefully worked-out plots. One thing happens after another, gravity and the ground disappear. The same can be done in movies: The frame may feature a vertiginous angle, facing down into city canyons or up to the sky, where bodies and machines slam into one another like loose cargo. Movies based on that kind of imagery may be sensational as design, but they aren't likely to fill us with the empathy, dread, and joy inspired by fictions about people making their way through a world where walls are solid, gravity is unrelenting, and matter is indissoluble. Storytelling thrives on limits, inhibitions, social conventions, a world of anticipations and outcomes, fears and consequences. It needs limits as well as freedoms. Can you have a story that means anything halfway serious without a wall between lovers, without gravity's pull, without the threat of mortality?

I admit to a realist bias, a this-world bias. I'm a plot-and-character man, an action-has-consequences man. Pixar's movies may be computer-generated animation, but, in such masterpieces as *Ratatouille* and *Up,* the world very definitely exists—the world in all its tangled complication, and I love these movies. I don't think my bias is merely temperamental. In movies, representation is obviously more intimately joined to physical reality than, say, books or paintings are. In the past, that intimacy was the starting point for mainstream filmmakers. Leaving aside fantasy films for a second, a director composes his film with real people, moving in a simulacrum of real space, in snippets of real time. Then he edits and makes magic. His subjectivity controls the illusion of the real; he can quicken that illusion or slow it down, jump from one place to another, color the moods emotionally. In *Vertigo*, Hitchcock, in order to intensify James Stewart's nausea when he looks down a bell tower staircase, pulled the camera back on a dolly while bringing the image closer with a zoom (the shot was actually made horizontally, with a mocked-up tower). Hitchcock pushed slightly past physical plausibility—and went further past it in *The Birds*—but he was too witty and malicious to abandon it. He wanted to scare us. It was the intrusion of the inexplicably hostile creatures into a workaday, even banal, reality that made *The Birds* so unsettling.

Spielberg and Abrams probably understand this sort of thing as well as anyone. Their filmmaking passion may have come out of a love of the fantastic, but they know that audiences want to believe that the stories they're watching could actually happen. *Super 8* begins well. Abrams, a co-creator of *Lost* and the director of *Star Trek* (2009), lovingly establishes the small-town world of 1979: the ranch houses, with their boxy rooms; the noisy family dinners; the rattly cars hanging on from the 1960s. Abrams's images have a full-bodied zest reminiscent of early Spielberg; he likes a bursting frame, with the eccentric movement of many people scurrying around. But, as the movie goes on, he falls into digital madness. When Abrams designs a train wreck, the cars don't just fall off the tracks; they buckle and spin, and some of them explode, shooting high into the air and landing with a deafening crunch. It's not a derailment; it's digital Armageddon. And Abrams concocts a giant, spiderlike creature that's too much like other monsters, and he uses the beast with remorseless opportunism—it's vicious in one scene and gentle in the next. The magic fades, and *Super 8* becomes just another digital spectacle.

At least *Super 8* acknowledges the world. Like so many comic book movies, *Green Lantern* and *X-Men: First Class* are set everywhere and nowhere. Movies like these are devoted to the flimsy monumental—combats between good and evil so obvious and repetitive that they are of zero interest morally (they're more like premises for endless warfare). In *Green Lantern,* directed by Martin Campbell, the Guardians use the ethical power of will to protect the universe from the destructive force of fear. They deploy the Lanterns, who wear green plastic suits and have purple faces with pointy ears, or heads like fish; they talk slowly and solemnly, like the hierophants of some forgotten Egyptian religion gathered in an underground crypt. The movie dares you to laugh. The bad force is an undulating, pullulating filthy dark mass, at the center of which a hell-mouth—dagger teeth and lips—spews scalding yellow mist. It takes any form it wants, goes anywhere; it can't be extinguished because it must survive into many installments of a franchise. As a representation of evil, it's meaningless. In Matthew Vaughn's *X-Men: First Class,* a prequel to the three earlier movies in the series, the world is also at risk. The mutants, absurdly, intervene in the Cuban missile crisis, planting false orders in the minds of Soviet commanders, sending artillery shells back at the guns that fire them. By touching on history, Vaughn may have conceived the single silliest scene in all these big digital movies.

Both movies are at their best in self-mocking moments, and for some of us, such moments are a kind of reassurance—we're being acknowledged as an audience whose exasperation needs to be acknowledged now and then. In *Green Lantern,* Ryan Reynolds, who developed a light, self-deprecating comic style when going up against Sandra Bullock in *The Proposal,* is perfectly cast as a weightless hotshot, an earthling appointed to continue the Guardians' struggle against fear. Reynolds looks amused, abashed, and highly dubious as he pledges allegiance to a green lantern, the source of ultimate power. The jokes in *Lantern* are not bad, but when the movie turns to action, it just looks cheesy. Reynolds, in a green suit, raises his fist, and he can make absolutely anything happen that he wants to happen—machines and roadways to emerge out of nowhere. Someone will say, He's a comic book movie hero—what do you expect? But the rest of us will retort: How can anyone be a hero when he doesn't have to struggle? If there are no limits, there's no heroism.

X-Men is fun when the mutants, assembled by their leader (James McAvoy), undergo training exercises in an effort to control their extraordinary powers: Digital technology amplifies their mistakes and their misjudgments into sloppy, destructive sprees. For once, excess makes sense. What I enjoyed most in all three of these movies, however, was the little old-tech zombie film in *Super 8*. The kids manage to complete their picture. Poor Alice becomes a ghoul, but the hero, plunging a syringe into her, brings her back to life. The film ends happily, and its threadbare, sincere trashiness, its tawdry illusionless illusion of the undead, is more touching than the whoosh and slam of the epic fantasies. Digital filmmakers need to get a few things straight: If there are no rules, there's no reason to care how the story turns out. If a hero can do anything, nothing he does much matters. When everything is at stake, nothing is at stake.

The New Yorker, *July 4, 2011; revised 2011*

PART TWO /
INDEPENDENT GLORIES

INTRODUCTION

Way back in the 1950s there were "independent" movies—films financed, or partially financed, outside the studio system, but often made with a studio sensibility tipped into daring by a strong script or by a director like Otto Preminger or Douglas Sirk. What we have meant by "independent" in recent years is something smaller and more intense, a movie aimed at a subsection of the audience—what used to be called (sometimes derisively) the "art house audience." I may lament the disappearance of the notion that movie art is for everyone—a big national audience—but it's impossible to lament any of the movies reviewed below, which assume a level of curiosity and understanding in the viewer, and are made with a subtlety of perception, that would have been un-

71

imaginable in the 1950s. At that point, it would have been hard to inject them into the national distribution system. Now, there's a fragile, weakened, but still existing structure of studio specialty divisions, or indie distributors, which gets them into theaters or makes them available on demand from cable channels. The trouble, as I've said earlier, is that producing a commercially successful independent film doesn't allow directors and writers to begin work on something new. Each time, they have to start all over again, from the beginning—hustling, taking endless meetings, begging for money. Some of the directors of the movies below had to wait five and six years before getting another movie going. For that reason alone, apart from sentiment and gratitude, one treasures each of them for its special qualities.

CAPTURING THE FRIEDMANS

Capturing the Friedmans, an extraordinary new documentary directed by Andrew Jarecki, is both a meditation on perversion and truth and one of the most heartbreaking films ever made about an American family. Baldly stated, the facts at the center of the movie are these: In 1987, in Great Neck, Long Island, Arnold Friedman, a retired schoolteacher in his fifties who taught computer classes for kids in his home basement, and his youngest son, Jesse, then eighteen, were arrested and charged with committing repeated acts of sexual abuse on boys who attended the classes. Despite its sensational subject, the picture has been made with tact, dedication, and respect for the unending mysteries of family life. For the five Friedmans (father, mother, and three sons), their sense of themselves as a family was central to what was at stake for them as individuals during the crisis. "I'm a Friedman, therefore I am" might have been their slogan, for they rise and fall as a loving and then suffering brood.

Jarecki's movie owes its existence, it turns out, to the Friedmans' habit of memorializing themselves in films, tapes, and photographs. The audience searches for clues to the catastrophe in the successive layers of technology: There's 8mm footage of Arnold Friedman as an ebullient little boy, then photographs of him as a young musician, passing himself off in the Catskills as "Arnito Rey," Latin bandleader; and then, later, more films and stills of him as an honored schoolteacher and a happy father—a round-shouldered, middle-aged man with glasses and a bemused expression. A lot of the footage shows Arnold and his three sons (David, Seth, and Jesse) horsing around—clowning in crazy costumes, putting on mock playlets, interviewing one another. The nagging hilarity, reminiscent of the Marx Brothers' delirious shenanigans, was a bond among them as strong as steel. Arnold's wife, Elaine, however, does not appear to be in on the jokes. A reserved, put-upon woman, she resists the constant pranks as well as the cameras whirring away in her house. Her slogan might be "I'm a Friedman, therefore I struggle to exist."

The three boys, then in their late teens and early twenties, were home for the Thanksgiving holiday when the unimaginable happened. The police busted in, searched the basement, and found a stack of child pornography magazines. It seems that the Nassau County authorities had been tipped off by postal inspectors, who had been monitoring Arnold's mail. The police then interviewed the children who attended the computer classes—boys reportedly ranging in age from seven to twelve—and a collective tale of violation emerged. Jarecki gives us enough of the local TV news and tabloid coverage to bring back the scandal in all its dismaying squalor. But his real interest is in the memory of each person—including policemen, defense and prosecuting attorneys, and court officials—as it has been shaped over the years in the telling and the retelling. The movie is a stunning demonstration of the subjectivity of recollection. Not even *Rashomon* itself is more ambiguous or many-sided.

All through the arrests and trials, the oldest son, David, made videotapes, which play a central role in the movie. Of the three boys, David was perhaps the closest to his father—the one who drew most directly on his father's humor and love of imposture. As an adult, he became a successful professional clown, an entertainer at family parties in Manhattan. We see him in 1988, during the trials, taping himself as he sits on his bed in his underwear, pouring out his rage and bewilderment to the camera. "If you're not me, you're not supposed to be watching this," he says. But why make the video if there was not an intention to tell the family story somewhere, someday? David is a showman, an ironic entertainer. He also videotaped family dinners, a Seder, conversations in the kitchen and the car. He recorded the scenes not only to tell the story but also, perhaps, to assert some measure of control as the family fell apart under pressure from the police and the community. And he may have wanted to capture what he considered a betrayal: the refusal of his mother to support her husband (who pleaded guilty on some counts) and then her insistence that Jesse, who claimed innocence, plead guilty, too, so as to avoid the maximum sentence. Interviewed in the present, David, sad-eyed and vengeful, loyal to his father, is still living the torment of the family breakup—living it every time he goes out to entertain children as a clown.

What's astonishing about the videos is that they turn from comedy to tragedy and then back again. Even on the day Jesse is given a sentence of six to eighteen years in prison, the boys are larking together—an act of solidarity which a police officer in the case, years later, takes as a sign that Jesse lacked remorse. (It doesn't occur to him that the joking might have been a defiant protestation of innocence.) Within the family, there are taunts and threats as well as jokes: At dinner, all three boys gang up on Elaine while Arnold sits quietly and begs them in a whisper to desist. The boys, clinging desperately to the illusion of the Friedmans' family health, refuse to believe that their dad is guilty, and he refuses to speak. The entire fantastic mess unfolds before our eyes with the power of some appalling biblical story or one of the bloodier Greek myths—the House of Atreus reincarnated as a middle-class Jewish family in Great Neck.

Jarecki and the film's editor, Richard Hankin, shift back and forth in time, intercutting contemporary interviews with family footage and trial records. In the end, the filmmakers capture the Friedmans but not, alas, the truth, which keeps slipping into the distance like a silvery fish; it quivers and flashes, but we can't quite see it in its entirety. Arnold Friedman, we find out, was certainly a pedophile—there were previous instances of molestation that he admitted to. But what happened in the basement? A man sitting with his face in the dark insists that he was raped years earlier. Another man, photographed in close-up, fully lit, says that nothing happened at all. Back in 1987 and 1988, the police put the case together from the discovery of the pornographic magazines and the testimony of the children. But there wasn't any physical evidence—no semen or blood on the children's clothes, no bruises, no complaints at the time from the kids, some of whom had, before the arrests, enrolled for another round of classes. Were the charges exaggerated? Completely false? The investigative journalist Debbie Nathan talks of hysteria, panic, group pressures. One parent says he was urged by other parents to get his kid to confess. And yet the police, the prosecutors, and the judge, interviewed now, come off as cautious and temperate people. After watching the movie, audiences will debate for hours about who is telling the truth, who is telling a half-truth, and who wants to believe so passionately in something false that it becomes a vivid memory to be defended against every hint of doubt.

Seth Friedman chose not to be interviewed for the film. Jesse served thirteen years and now, ravaged in appearance, is a free man. Arnold, sentenced to ten to thirty years, died in prison; the death itself is part of a generous gesture that becomes one of the many revelations offered late in the film. Yet Arnold remains a cipher, a guilty man hounded by the rival furies of shameful desire and family responsibility. In the end, his wife was one of his principal victims. Now in her seventies, Elaine talks of her bewilderment, of her distance from her husband, of being lied to. Touched, we try to imagine the unbearable solitude of her married life. *Capturing the Friedmans* reaffirms the family as the inescapable cauldron of great drama—as the birthplace and feeding ground of the most powerful emotions, including perverse sexual desire, and as the site of reconciliation and solace, too.

Andrew Jarecki started out as a musician and was the founder of Moviefone, which he sold to America Online in 1999. *Capturing the Friedmans,* made with assistance from HBO and many angels, is his first feature-length film, a work that nevertheless demonstrates the audacity, the evenhandedness, the sense of detail and structural power worthy of such accomplished documentary filmmakers as Marcel Ophuls and Frederick Wiseman. I'm not sure how Jarecki is going to top *Capturing the Friedmans.* To begin your career with a masterpiece is so remarkable a feat that one can only hope Jarecki finds another subject as rich as this family, which was obsessed with itself but needed a filmmaker to begin to see itself at all.

The New Yorker, *June 2, 2003*

SIDEWAYS

Early on in the wonderful new movie *Sideways,* the hero, Miles (Paul Giamatti), does the *Times* crossword puzzle while driving his Saab on the San Diego Freeway. Sharp details are not enough in themselves to make a movie great; still, when Miles props his paper up on the steering wheel, it's clear that the filmmakers—Alexander Payne, the director and screenwriter, and Jim Taylor, his cowriter—know what they are up to. Miles, a wine-loving failed novelist in his early forties, is, we quickly discover, the kind of guy who seizes every opportunity for trivial bravura (he does the crossword in ink). Two years earlier, his wife, who shared his love of wine ("the best palate of any woman I've known," he says), left him flat; at the moment, his 750-page experimental novel ("It sort of devolves into a Robbe-Grillet thing") is forlornly making its way around the New York publishing houses. He has no choice but to kill time. When his old college buddy Jack (Thomas Haden Church), a washed-up TV actor in Los Angeles, announces that he is finally getting married, the two set off for seven days of prenuptial wine tasting and golf in the gold-and-green Santa Ynez Valley.

Miles is clearly a bibliophile, apparently a cinephile, and compulsively an oenophile; he likes to show off what he knows. At every stop, he tells Jack how to feel the "structure" of the grape, how to recognize "externals," "good concentration," and such flavors as asparagus and passion fruit; he instructs him to disdain the commonplace Merlot and to prize the delicate and cranky Pinot. Jack, however, couldn't care less; he would happily drink rotgut, and he'll sleep with any woman who comes along—he's blissfully undiscriminating. A heavily muscled, good-looking lummox, with the kind of thick, brushed-back hair that only TV actors can manage to grow, Jack has a wide smile and a cornball line of patter with women that makes Miles cringe, in part because it works. Payne and Taylor, adapting a novel by Rex Pickett, let us know right away that Miles is furtive, duplicitous, and self-destructive, and that Jack gets laid a lot because it's the one thing he's good at. At first, we wonder what holds these two together. *Sideways,* a comedy poised at the edge of despair, asks the question: How do you stop moving sideways? Or, more metaphorically: Won't a Cheval Blanc '61, left too long on the shelf, lose its savor?

Things happen on trips; that's why the road movie genre, with its radical concentration of means, never seems to tire. An opening to landscape, movement, adventure, and the eternal American desire to drop everything and light out for the territories, the form is both inherently dramatic and supremely flexible. It has served as the basis for crime thrillers (*They Live by Night, Bonnie and Clyde*), for violent explorations of the limits of freedom (*Easy Rider, Thelma & Louise*), for bruising tests of love and friendship (*Two for the Road, Scarecrow*). *Sideways* is one of the last: Each man experiences the glories and the horrors of the other's character and is forced, willy-nilly, to look himself in the face in a motel room mirror.

Payne and Taylor have always made movies about the melancholy middling-to-lower range of achievement and ambition, the near-losers that Americans hate but that so many of us at our most demoralized become. Up until now, the dead-eyed blandness of Omaha, Payne's home town, has dominated his work. He and Taylor have repeatedly satirized the emotional flatness and evasiveness of the place, while treating with tender respect their characters' hesitant, inarticulate yearnings for something more. Together they have created a gallery of memorably mediocre people: the dumb, paint-sniffing, but tenaciously enduring Ruth Stoops (Laura Dern) in *Citizen Ruth;* the vindictive schoolteacher (Matthew Broderick) in *Election;* the soured widower (Jack Nicholson) in *About Schmidt.* There is, I believe, a quiet but persistent spiritual ethos at the heart of their intention. The blinkered, semi-unconscious sinners stumble toward grace—a moment of clarity, of self-realization. Some of them may even get there.

Payne is a patient and orderly director; he wants character revelation and eruptive moments, and he carefully builds his scenes and gets both, but some of the elements in *Sideways* are no more than commonplace. The jazz score, by Rolfe Kent, plunks along uninterestingly, and when it accompanies the Saab zipping through loamy hills, or plays over a prolonged eating scene, the movie feels like an episode of *Great Getaways.* Some of the camera setups are too obvious—the shots of faux-Tudor inns and luscious vineyards come off as conventionally handsome. Payne has finally got himself out of Nebraska—you can feel his limbs warming in the sunshiny beauty of California—but he hasn't come close to developing a visual style that can sweep the audience along. He never breaks free into anything like the startling, brutal lyricism of the French director Bertrand Blier, whose own two-men-on-the-road movies, *Going Places* (1974) and *Get Out Your Handkerchiefs* (1978), were exhilaratingly beautiful, amoral fantasies. Perhaps Payne, given his obsession with emotional inadequacy, can't abandon strict realism. Blier's heroes (Gérard Depardieu and Patrick Dewaere) were thoughtlessly carnal outlaws; Payne's are stunted men who need to grow up, and some of the tone of *Sideways* emerges from the American therapeutic instinct. Still, I fervently want Payne to lift off from the Omaha in his soul.

He's certainly ready. *Sideways* is his largest, most candid work. Miles and Jack have the scathing intimacy of friends who waded through each other's dirty laundry as freshmen, and the bluntness of their talk is raffishly enjoyable. The picture is leisurely in tempo but funny and intense, alternating between furious exchanges and stops to drink more wine. I can't think of another movie that has taken such sensual pleasure in the many forms of tippling (sipping, imbibing, downing, bingeing), and no one before Payne has thought of making amateur wine tasting both a sublime ritual and a slightly ridiculous display: the firm, quick pour; the pause to swirl and sniff; the liquid held in the taster's mouth, followed by rhapsodies of praise or a rapid emission into the spit bucket. For the dissatisfied Miles, wine is both spirit and eros; he discovers in its velvety folds the happiness he gets cheated out of everywhere else. We notice immediately that he's diffuse and vague when he talks about his novel but precise, detailed, and ardent when he takes up his glass. On the road, as Jack presses for action, the men meet two vinously hip women: Maya (Virginia Madsen), a divorced graduate student who works as a waitress; and Stephanie (Sandra Oh), a sexy "pour girl" at one of the larger vineyards. Chattering about wine becomes a springboard into bed. Jack, only a few days before his wedding, begins carrying on with Stephanie; Miles and the blond, husky-voiced Maya, both of them taking their time (Miles is terrified), retreat to a quiet nook, where they earnestly discuss "the life of wine . . . the people who picked the grape." This could easily become embarrassing—parody is just a beat away—but we are held breathless by the way that Paul Giamatti suspends Miles between bitter shame and desire.

Giamatti has no chin to speak of, a round-shouldered physique, an adenoidal snarl, and the nervous grin of a craven dog. He's the national anti-ideal, and he's making a brilliant career out of it. In *American Splendor,* as the cartoonist Harvey Pekar, he dragged his miseries around the deserted lots and slag heaps of Cleveland. Pekar is a genuine oddball but Miles is closer to common dreams and chagrins, and in this role Giamatti gives his bravest, most generously humane performance yet. Women may be repelled, but men will know this man, because, at one time or another, many of us have been this man. Miles demands an unlimited license to mock himself but is outraged if someone else slights him. When he talks about his beloved Pinot grape—it's thin-skinned, difficult to handle, but potentially sublime—he's talking about himself, of course, but we feel that he's posing, that he's extravagantly demanding of life so that he will always fail, and that he would rather fail than pull himself together and make the best of what he's got. His voice rising in pitch, his dark eyes bulging in rage (Miles's novel gets rejected), Giamatti is physically explosive in this movie—at one point, in an act of supreme self-loathing, he pours the spit bucket into his mouth and all over his body. The scene is Shakespearean in its emotional violence. When Giamatti goes over the top, he transcends Everyman shmuckiness and attains acting immortality.

As the week goes on, the adventures of the two men become more and more absurd and dangerous, and by the end of the movie we know what holds them together. Thomas Haden Church, from the NBC series *Wings*, has been all too well cast as a second-rate TV actor; his Jack really is a bit of a dull fellow, but he loves Miles and believes in him, and that belief frees Miles to confront the worst in himself and to find a bottom to his self-pity. At the end of the journey, redemption awaits each man; each, in his own way, will drink the Cheval Blanc before it begins to fade.

The New Yorker, *October 25, 2004*

CAPOTE

On November 15, 1959, while luxuriating in abundant literary and social success in New York, the young Truman Capote was called to an unexpectedly spartan test. On that day, in Holcomb, Kansas, two ex-cons looking for money and thrills murdered four members of the Clutter family on their farm. A few weeks later, Capote, who had been eager to expand the boundaries of journalism, went to investigate the case for *The New Yorker*. Whatever his ambitions, Capote was an odd man for a police blotter job. He was born in 1924 in New Orleans, and grew up in Alabama, Connecticut, and New York, where he went to the Trinity School for a while and worked briefly as an office boy at this magazine. For years, many readers (and, in particular, writers) have wondered how this habitué of Le Pavillon and La Côte Basque, with his high, thin, goose-quill voice and his floating palms, could possibly have gained the trust of the straightforward men and women of rural Kansas. In *Capote,* which stars Philip Seymour Hoffman, the writer, Dan Futterman, and the director, Bennett Miller, satisfy that curiosity. *Capote,* which draws extensively on Gerald Clarke's 1988 biography, is devoted almost entirely to the five years in which Capote lived and wrote *In Cold Blood,* an assignment that became a four-part series, a best-selling book, and a literary classic. Small-scaled and limited, *Capote* is nevertheless the most intelligent, detailed, and absorbing film ever made about a writer's working method and character—in this case, a mixed quiver of strength, guile, malice, and mendacity.

Moviegoers who have followed Philip Seymour Hoffman's supporting work in such films as *The Talented Mr. Ripley* and *Cold Mountain* sensed that he had a lot more to give, and here it is. As the cinematographer, Adam Kimmel, moves in close, Hoffman's Capote looms up like some strange Rushmoric outcropping—heavy-domed skull, golden hair, pink skin, double-peaked upper lip, owlish glasses, and blue eyes that occasionally peer directly at the bruised ego and longings of the person in front of him. Hoffman starts with the physical and works inward to the soul. He's only a few years older than Capote was when he went to Kansas, but his thicker features seem to forecast the coarsening of face and body and the spreading spiritual rot that afflicted the writer in the years after the book came out. As Hoffman plays him, Capote is an actor, too: a wounded personality who remade himself; a public figure capable of facing down scorn. Holding forth at parties with cigarette and glass in hand, he dispenses rancorous gossip in a way that cuts off any possible life beyond his perfect sentences.

Although Capote, working hard, eventually befriended several people in Holcomb, his first foray there would have been a disaster were it not for his childhood pal Nelle Harper Lee (Catherine Keener), who was soon to publish *To Kill a Mockingbird,* and who came along as his assistant. As Capote waltzes around the dour courthouses and landscapes in a sheepskin coat and an enormous Bergdorf's scarf, Lee makes the initial contacts and performs the introductions. Never taking a note, he boasts of near-total recall; he boasts, too, of the book he's going to write before he has written a word of it. He sobers up only when he sets eyes on one of the captured murderers, Perry Smith. (The movie almost dispenses with the other killer, Dick Hickock.) As Perry, Clifton Collins, Jr., is not as sensual and insinuating as Robert Blake, who crooned his way through the role in the frightening 1967 movie version of *In Cold Blood,* but he's darkly handsome, with an abashed, yearning manner. Alone with Perry in his cell, Capote is stunned: This beautiful sociopath is material—a gold mine, in fact—and also a sympathetic human being whose miserable childhood and need for recognition match Capote's own history and ravenous hungers. "It's O.K. It's Truman. It's your friend," Hoffman says in his strangely incisive baby voice. In those early moments of interest and empathy, the masterpiece is born.

Perry warms to Capote's attentions, and the rest of the movie turns into a complicated struggle between the two of them, with a desperate Perry telling Capote enough of his story to try to motivate the writer to help him, and a devious Capote both kid-gloving and bullying Perry until he opens up and describes the night of the murders. Determined to create a new form—the "nonfiction novel"—Capote gets in deep with Perry. As the court appeals go on, staying the executions, their relations become an artistically necessary but morally questionable mixture of affection, fascination, and exploitation. But by 1965, Capote, exhausted from his bouts of research and writing, turns ruthless and antic; Hoffman swings back to party mode as Capote privately and publicly longs for the men to hang so that he can finish his manuscript.

Strictly speaking, this intense little movie is not an independent film: It was a dying major, United Artists, that entrusted a reported $7 million to the former high school friends Dan Futterman, an actor, and Bennett Miller, who had directed only the documentary *The Cruise.* But *Capote* is unimaginable without the independent film movement of the past twenty years or so. Apart from some sweeping shots of an extremely horizontal Kansas (the movie was actually shot in Manitoba), the filmmakers work intimately, with an easy, unstressed understanding of such things as Capote's homosexuality and the fervent solicitude that his friends felt for him—solicitude mixed with jealousy, exasperation, and dismay. No doubt people will pick at inaccuracies in the portrait and say, "That's not Truman," but *Capote* is Truman enough—and an image likely to make any writer grimace in recognition. There are some oddities: Harper Lee's character is a little fuzzy, and the filmmakers turn William Shawn (Bob Balaban), the editor of *The New Yorker*, into an aggressive force who pushes the plot along. For the record, Shawn was not in the habit of demanding the bloody details in stories about murder, or of rushing off to the Midwest to keep his writers company at executions. Finally, the filmmakers' suggestion that Capote never recovered from the death of Perry Smith, or from the success of *In Cold Blood*, strikes me as doubly sentimental. Capote was ultimately done in by alcohol. Yet, however one interprets it, the finale is acrid: The chronicler of death triumphs, and then has nowhere to go but to his own inglorious end.

The New Yorker, *October 10, 2005*

THE SQUID AND THE WHALE

When little kids look up, they see gods hovering over them. Parents are big, they make things appear and disappear, and they know just about everything, which is one reason kids keep secrets and tell lies—they need to claim a little power for themselves. As children get older, however, their parents seem less and less like gods. They may even seem grasping and dangerous—more like monsters. At the center of Noah Baumbach's remarkable *The Squid and the Whale* are two brothers—Walt (Jesse Eisenberg), who is sixteen, and a bright and fluent poseur, and Frank (Owen Kline), a twelve-year-old in a sexual uproar—and both boys, as they look at their parents, are caught between feelings of adoration and disgust. The time is 1986, in Brooklyn's Park Slope, the land of frontage-envy, fine old furniture, and dark-stained, well-stocked bookshelves. In these idyllic streets, the boys' parents, both writers, are breaking up and behaving badly. The dad, Bernard (Jeff Daniels), a college English teacher and an increasingly unsuccessful novelist, has become a sour and selfish liar; the mom, Joan (Laura Linney), can't stop leaving evidence of her love affairs around the house. Desolate over the breakup, and trying to hold on to their love for their parents, the boys fall into nutty imitative behavior. Walt parrots every one of his dad's huffy opinions; Frank reenacts his mom's indiscretions by rubbing his crotch against library shelves and depositing his substance on schoolbooks and lockers. *The Squid and the Whale* is a satirical comedy—ruthless and heartbreaking, but a comedy nonetheless. The movie is also about disintegration and the possibility of rebirth. In other words, it's a small miracle.

We are so used to seeing semi-verbal characters on-screen—taciturn Diesels and blank-eyed Pitts, funny goofs of both sexes—that, at first, the sound of fully articulate people may be a little embarrassing. "*This Side of Paradise* is minor Fitzgerald," Walt announces to a friendly girl at school, and he describes the ending of Kafka's "Metamorphosis" as . . . "Kafkaesque." Since Walt hasn't read either author, the lines are meant satirically, but some of us may wince as well as laugh. Listening to pomp-ous Bernard, who puts down a local tennis pro as a nothing and patron-izes *A Tale of Two Cities* to his son—who then says at dinner that he can't be bothered to read "minor Dickens"—educated moviegoers may feel a shock of recognition. It's a shock that's more like a sting. Is this what we're like at our most fatuous? Ranking every person and book so we won't be associated with anything suspected of being second-rate? The sting, how-ever, gradually lessens without quite becoming a caress; it begins to feel like a way of observing closely.

Noah Baumbach, the thirty-six-year-old director of *Kicking and Screaming* (1995) and two other independent movies, draws on elements of his own life. He grew up in Brooklyn, and both his parents are writ-ers. But the best qualifications in the world wouldn't have helped him if he didn't know what he was doing, and Baumbach gets some very tricky things exactly right: the way educated parents project both their self-love and their career anxieties onto their children; the way the kids respond to parental misconduct like pilot fish shimmying around a wayward shark. Baumbach has an irrepressibly critical eye. The movie is a fictionalized memoir: Walt is the artist as a young man, the filmmaker-writer-to-be, but, in Baumbach's telling, the autobiographical figure is no more pro-tected than anyone else. Walt begins his artistic journey as a phony and a plagiarist; at a school talent show, he tries to pass off a Pink Floyd song as his own. The film's four principals are smart and wily, and yet they always get caught. The memoirist, of course, is the one tripping them up, but, in a project like this, memory must give way to convincing invention. Baumbach persuades us that the characters are so guilt-ridden and bound to one another emotionally that they don't really want to get away with anything.

Working with relatively inexpensive Super 16 film, Baumbach shot *The Squid and the Whale* in twenty-three days, mostly in a borrowed Park Slope house, for about a million and a half dollars. He's startlingly sure-footed. The main ideas are set up clearly and developed carefully—much more so than in *Junebug,* another good family film. Yet there's nothing constricted about the form or the feel of the movie. Family arguments and conferences, and interactions between the boys and their friends, are staged simply and straightforwardly, yet many of these scenes, pointed and touching from the start, take off in surprising directions and come to a climax with a sudden rush of hostility or hurt. The tight editing, which often cuts to a character in need of reassurance or enlightenment, is itself a form of wit. Perhaps it's easier to create an organic form if you're making a film about people who have a lengthy shared history; what they say can naturally be fashioned into a single quilt of endearments, quarrels, jokes, and disappointments. Repeated phrases echo off the narrow walls of the Park Slope house; nothing gets lost—the cashew that Frank shoves up his nose at a dinner scene in the beginning pops out after one of his sessions with Onan and alcohol many scenes later. Louis Malle's scandalous family drama *Murmur of the Heart* (1971), which Baumbach credits as an influence, has a similar coherence, intimacy, and speed, and this is a middle-class American *Murmur*—not as daring or perverse, perhaps, but more tender and enveloping, and better acquainted with failure.

As Joan, Laura Linney is affectingly abashed, though she has one great moment of defiance: Bernard says that he wants to come back—he will reform, he will *cook*—and Linney erupts in uncontrollable laughter. As Jeff Daniels plays him, Bernard is a classic study in wounded narcissism. Daniels has a long, thick beard—not a 1960s-style, free-spirit beard but a nineteenth-century, Old Testament beard—and he speaks in a toneless rumble. When someone assails him, his eyes narrow; the hostile glint that remains suggests that Bernard knows the truth about himself but is unable to grant it more than an instant's recognition. His disappointment makes him hell to be around, and treacherous, too. Walt, nearly drowning himself in the effort to keep his dad afloat, calls his mother a whore out of loyalty to his father's suffering. The plot hinges on Walt's rediscovery of his love for her; Baumbach, in the end, holds out the possibility that Walt, at least, will see his parents as neither gods nor monsters but as screwed-up, very foolish adults. The movie is proof that Walt grew into a man.

The New Yorker, *October 24, 2005*

THE DIVING BELL AND THE BUTTERFLY

Most filmmakers regard subjects like illness and despair as dangerous traps—mawkish sentimentality lying on one side of the high road of art, pleasureless suffering on the other—but the challenge of an impossible subject can bring out the best in a director, and now, after Paul Haggis's mournful and touching *In the Valley of Elah,* there's another dark victory, Julian Schnabel's *The Diving Bell and the Butterfly.* The Schnabel movie is about an unlucky man—Jean-Dominique Bauby, the real-life editor of French *Elle,* who, in 1995, at the age of forty-three, suffered a massive stroke. Lying speechless and outraged in a hospital near Calais, a victim of "locked-in syndrome," Bauby (Mathieu Amalric) was restored to full mental clarity but could move nothing but his left eye. Yet Schnabel's movie, based on the calm and exquisite little book that Bauby wrote in the hospital, is a gloriously unlocked experience, with some of the freest and most creative uses of the camera and some of the most daring, cruel, and heartbreaking emotional explorations that have appeared in recent movies.

At first, we see only what Bauby sees—a blur of faces floating into view in fearsome close-up, like deep-sea monsters. Consciousness arrives: The blurs solidify into clear images of doctors and nurses and the surprisingly beautiful decor of Bauby's cell—a turquoise-colored hospital room, with a curtain flapping in the breeze. Bauby's Cyclopean gaze swings wildly from one place to another, and visitors, embarrassed and grief-stricken, pass in and out of his vision, which operates as a kind of microscope peering into the soul of whoever comes into its view. The doctors offer diagnoses and reassurances; Bauby is caressed, shoved, lifted, held, deposited, and washed with hands both rough and gentle, and, through all this, we hear his thoughts on the soundtrack—baffled and angry at first, then bitter (he faintly enjoys the black comedy of his situation), and, finally, soulful and eloquent. Ronald Harwood, adapting the text, has made Bauby's complex internal life fully expressive, and Schnabel fleshes out brief descriptions of therapists and visitors into major psychological portraits. The movie, which was shot by the great Janusz Kaminski (Spielberg's cinematographer), more than fulfills the promise of the sultry early scenes in Schnabel's previous picture, *Before Night Falls*. Bauby's book is concise and lyrical; the film is expansive and sensual, pungent and funny—a much larger experience. The impossible subject has yielded a feast of moviemaking.

Bauby has been reduced to a thing, an object—the ultimate patient—but the emotional and animal life in him hasn't died, and for that we are profoundly grateful. We needn't merely feel sorry for this man—unlike his caretakers and his guests, we know what's going on in his head. Schnabel neither avoids nor softens the hospital room procedures, yet slowly the movie opens up. The camera shifts away from Bauby's limited gaze and moves to a third-person point of view that takes in everything, including Amalric's face, with its hanging lip and wandering left eye. The sight of that face—as grotesque as an image from a horror movie yet expunged of titillation—is a shock, but we quickly get used to it, and the picture moves steadily ahead on two tracks: We see the stages of Bauby's treatment, including the tortuous but productive way he learns to write; and the tumult and ecstasy of his inner life. When Bauby, liberated from terror, says, "I can imagine anything," Schnabel, in a burst of exhilaration, takes us on a speed journey through Bauby's visions and hopes and fantasies—boyhood skiing and surfing, Marlon Brando made up as Pan and horsing around (an image of something that Bauby wanted to be). Later, as Bauby begins to write his book, memories of driving with his girlfriend, her hair blowing in the wind in an open landscape, come flooding back. In the present, he's visited by his small children, who scamper around the paralyzed body on an empty beach.

Schnabel is openly emotional, and Kaminski at times approaches commercial imagery, but there's always something astringent or off center in the moods and compositions which pulls the movie back into art. A memory of Bauby shaving his ninety-two-year-old dad (Max von Sydow, more powerful than ever as a powerless old man) reverses the caregiving polarities, but bathos is averted by the matched vanity of loving father and loving son. After each flight, whether to the past or to a moment outside the hospital, we're sent back to Bauby, his neck askew, eye ravenously taking in the world, as he rests on a long, hauntingly beautiful terrace near the sea, as empty and poignant a place as one of Antonioni's desolate streets. Stillness and frenzy oscillate in almost musical rhythm. Feverishly, Bauby imagines the history of the hospital, with the Empress Eugénie visiting tubercular children and the young Nijinsky, temporarily rehearsing there, leaping through the air. The associations are wild and free, yet nothing feels arbitrary or garish (one thinks of the visionary episodes in silent film rather than of Fellini). We need this extravagant beauty; we deserve it. The diving bell of the title refers to a recurring shot of Bauby trapped inside ancient deep-sea equipment, helplessly sinking in water. The butterfly is his mind and, of course, the cinema itself, which can go anywhere it wants.

A literary man working for a commercial magazine, Bauby, we gather, is not a very nice guy. Or, rather, in the scenes from the past, he comes off as full of life, a lover, a power in the fashion and magazine worlds but not particularly courageous or loyal. Mathieu Amalric has a round face and slightly bulging eyes, and an easy way of swinging his body through a room; he's avid, restless—not handsome, exactly, but an actor with a sexual presence. Sometime before his illness, Bauby left the beautiful, soft-voiced Céline (Emmanuelle Seigner), the mother of his children, in favor of a big-boned, exotic, and demanding girlfriend, Inès (Agathe de La Fontaine). In the hospital, he longs for Inès, but it's Céline, a wife in all but name, who comes to visit and stays. This mild-tempered woman, we realize with a pang, is paralyzed in her own way—she's hopelessly in love with her man even though he finds her a little dull. Both the doctors and the therapists know that Bauby's recovery depends on keeping his libido alive, and Schnabel brazenly dramatizes the treatment as an exchange in which eros and caring become inextricable. The physical therapist (Olatz López Garmendia, Schnabel's wife) teaches Bauby to swallow by twirling her tongue, and the speech therapist (Marie-Josée Croze), a more earnest sort, flirts with her patient morally. She runs through the alphabet in the order of letters most frequently used in French, and Bauby blinks when he wants to choose a letter. After a while, the therapist anticipates his words from the initial letter, and she becomes enraged when his first sentence announces his desire to die. Her demand for a retraction is itself a complete drama of rejection, hurt feelings, and renewed adoration.

Bauby seems to attract the love of religious women who pray for a miracle to save him, but, a freethinker, and anticlerical in a long French tradition, he will have none of it. A beefy attendant cradling his slack, naked body in the hospital's pool suggests Mary holding the crucified Jesus, but Bauby will rise again only in art: The miracle this movie celebrates is his ability to compose his book. Still, *The Diving Bell* surges toward redemption—a man fully realizing his humanity only when mobility and sexuality have been taken away. Imperially free and generous as Schnabel's work is, the imagery—medical, erotic, religious—hangs together with enormous power. The birth of Bauby's soul feels like nothing less than the rebirth of the cinema.

The New Yorker, *December 3, 2007*

THERE WILL BE BLOOD

Early in *There Will Be Blood*, an enthralling and powerfully eccentric American epic, Daniel Plainview climbs down a ladder at his small silver mine. A rung breaks, and Daniel (Daniel Day-Lewis) falls to the base of the shaft and smashes his leg. He's filthy, miserable, gasping for breath and life. The year is 1898. Two and a half hours later (and more than thirty years later in the time span of the film), he's on the floor again, this time sitting on a polished bowling lane in the basement of an enormous mansion that he has built on the Pacific Coast. Having abandoned silver mining for oil, Daniel has become one of the wealthiest tycoons in Southern California. Yet he's still filthy, with dirty hands and a face that glistens from too much oil raining down on him—it looks as if oil were seeping from his pores. The experience chronicled between these two moments is as astounding in its emotional force and as haunting and mysterious as anything seen in American movies in recent years. I'm not quite sure how it happened, but after making *Magnolia* (1999) and *Punch-Drunk Love* (2002)—skillful but whimsical movies, with many whims that went no-where—the young writer-director Paul Thomas Anderson has now done work that bears comparison to the greatest achievements of Griffith and Ford. The movie is a loose adaptation of Upton Sinclair's 1927 novel *Oil!*, but Anderson has taken Sinclair's bluff, genial oilman and turned him into a demonic character who bears more than a passing resemblance to Melville's Ahab. Stumping around on that bad leg, which was never prop-erly set, Daniel Plainview—obsessed, brilliant, both warmhearted and vi-cious—has Ahab's egotism and command. As for Daniel Day-Lewis, his performance makes one think of Laurence Olivier at his most physically and spiritually audacious.

At the start, Daniel Plainview and a small group of workers, wild-catting for oil, give themselves entirely to their perilous labor. There isn't a word of dialogue. Again and again, Anderson creates raptly muscular passages—men lifting, hauling, pounding, dragging, working silently in the muck and viscous slime. Yet this film is hardly the kind of glory-of-industry documentary that bored us in school. *There Will Be Blood* is about the driving force of capitalism as it both creates and destroys the future, and the film's tone is at once elated and sickened. A dissonant, ominous electronic wail, written by the Radiohead guitarist and composer Jonny Greenwood, warns us of trouble ahead. Once the derricks are up, Green-wood imitates the rhythmic thud of the drill bits and pumps with bustling passages of plucked strings and pounding sticks. *Blood* has the pulse of the future in its rhythms. Like the most elegiac Western, this movie is about the vanishing American frontier. The thrown-together buildings look scraggly and unkempt, the homesteaders are modest, stubborn, and reticent, but, in their undreamed-of future, Walmart is on the way. An-derson, working with the cinematographer Robert Elswit, has become a master of the long tracking shot across still, empty landscapes. The movie, which cost a relatively cheap $25 million to make, has gravity and weight without pomp; it's austerely magnificent, and, when violence comes—an exploding oil well, a fight—it's staged cleanly, in open space, and not as a tumult of digital effects or a tempest in an editing room.

One of the workers holds and kisses a baby, then dies in an accident, and Daniel raises the child, whom he calls HW (Dillon Freasier), as his son and partner. The movie skips to 1911, when Daniel and HW are traveling around California in a tin lizzie, buying up land leases, at bargain rates, from ranchers and farmers who are sitting on underground oceans of gold. Daniel takes advantage of their ignorance to pay them less than they deserve, and, as he addresses a group of them, Day-Lewis's performance comes into focus. He lowers his chin slightly, and his dark eyes dance with merriment as he speaks in coarse yet rounded tones, the syllables precisely articulated but with a lengthening of the vowels and final consonants that gives the talk a singing, almost caressing quality. It is the voice of dominating commercial logic—an American force of nature. Day-Lewis, at fifty, is lean and fit, and his scythelike body cuts into the air as he works or stalks, head thrust out, across a field. Much of the time, he projects a wonderful gaiety, but his Daniel never strays from business. He ignores questions, reveals nothing, and masters every encounter with either charm or a threat. He has no wife, no friends, and no interests except for oil, his son, and booze. He drinks heavily, which exacerbates his natural distrust and competitiveness. Even when he's swimming in the Pacific, he looks dangerous. In his later years, however, Daniel disintegrates, and the iconic associations shift from Ahab to Charles Foster Kane.

Upton Sinclair was a longtime socialist, yet he understood that nothing in American life was more exhilarating than entrepreneurial energy and ruthlessness. The movie retains the novel's exuberance, but turns much darker in tone. HW becomes a victim of the oil rush, and Anderson drops Sinclair's moral hero, a communist who organizes the oil workers. Sinclair was a reformer who wanted to ameliorate the harsh effects of capitalism, but Anderson apparently reasoned that social radicalism did not—and could not—stop men like Daniel Plainview. Sinclair, the garrulous, fact-bound literalist, has been superseded by a film poet with a pessimistic, even apocalyptic, streak.

But Anderson does retain Sinclair's portrait of an unctuous young man who thinks he has the word of God within him: Eli Sunday (Paul Dano), who creates, in the oil fields, the revivalist Church of the Third Revelation. Dano, who was the silent, philosophy-reading boy in *Little Miss Sunshine*, has a tiny mouth and dead eyes. He looks like a mushroom on a long stem, and he talks with a humble piety that gives way, in church, to a strangled cry of ecstatic fervor. He's repulsive yet electrifying. Anderson has set up a kind of allegory of American development in which two overwhelming forces—entrepreneurial capitalism and evangelism—both operate on the border of fraudulence; together, they will build Southern California, though the two men representing them are so belligerent that they fall into combat. The movie becomes an increasingly violent (and comical) struggle in which each man humiliates the other, leading to the murderous final scene, which gushes as far over the top as one of Daniel's wells. The scene is a mistake, but I think I know why it happened. Anderson started out as an independent filmmaker, with *Hard Eight* (1996) and *Boogie Nights* (1997). In *Blood,* he has taken on central American themes and established a style of prodigious grandeur. Yet some part of him must have rebelled against canonization. The last scene is a blast of defiance— or perhaps of despair. But, like almost everything else in the movie, it's astonishing.

The New Yorker, December 17, 2007

THE HURT LOCKER

The Iraq War has been dramatized on film many times, and those films have been ignored just as many times by theater audiences. But Kathryn Bigelow's *The Hurt Locker* is the most skillful and emotionally involving picture yet made about the conflict. The film, from a script by Mark Boal, has a new subject: the heroism of the men who defuse improvised explosive devices, sloppily made but lethal bombs planted under a bag or a pile of garbage or just beneath the dirt of a Baghdad street. Bigelow stages one prolonged and sinister shoot-out in the desert, but the movie couldn't be called a combat film, nor is it political, except by implication—a mutual distrust between American occupiers and Iraqi citizens is there in every scene. The specialized nature of the subject is part of what makes it so powerful, and perhaps American audiences worn out by the mixed emotions of frustration and repugnance inspired by the war can enjoy this film without ambivalence or guilt. *The Hurt Locker* narrows the war to the existential confrontation of man and deadly threat.

Over and over, Staff Sergeant William James (Jeremy Renner), following a tip, walks to a bomb site in a heavy protective suit and tries to figure out how to pull apart clumsily tangled wires and flimsy triggering devices. We've seen James's predecessor die on the job: A man watching him from a nearby store detonated the bomb with a cell phone. As James goes in, slowly, under a hot sun, treading like a spaceman through trash-filled streets, people gather in doorways or look out windows. Which of them is hostile, which friendly, which merely curious? The two other members of James's team, the frightened young Eldridge (Brian Geraghty) and the wary, experienced Sanborn (Anthony Mackie), cover James, screaming at anyone who moves. The two men feel entirely vulnerable; they both admire and detest James, who pulls them into situations they would rather leave to someone else.

In the past, Kathryn Bigelow, now fifty-seven, has outdone the macho movie boys at their own game. In her *Blue Steel* (1989), as Jamie Lee Curtis, playing a cop, geared up for a day's work, Bigelow focused on her revolver, her leather holster, and her shoes, in gleaming close-up. The sequence hovered somewhere between fetish and parody. Bigelow went into the ocean with Patrick Swayze and Keanu Reeves in the surfer-crime movie *Point Break* (1991), and brought off scenes of languorously slo-mo destruction in the cultish sci-fi crime movie *Strange Days* (1995). By the mid-1990s, I had her figured as a violence junkie with a strong tendency to stylize everything into stunning images that didn't always mean much. As a filmmaker, Bigelow is still obsessed with violence, but she's become a master at staging it. In *The Hurt Locker*, there are no wasted shots or merely beautiful images. As Eldridge and Sanborn jerk their guns this way and that at a bomb scene, Bigelow, working with the great cinematographer Barry Ackroyd, jerks the camera around, too. She wants us to *be* there, to feel the danger, the mystery.

This kind of immediacy is commonplace in action filmmaking, but, unlike so many directors today, who jam together crashes, explosions, and people sailing through the air in nonsensical montages of fantasy movement, Bigelow keeps the space tight and coherent. No matter how many times she cuts away, you know exactly where James is in relation to a bomb—whether he's in the kill zone or far enough away to be safe. (You can't break up the integrity of space when space is the subject of your movie.) And Bigelow prolongs the moment, stretching out our anxiety almost to the point at which it becomes pain. *The Hurt Locker* is quite a feat: In this period of antic fragmentation, Bigelow has restored the wholeness of time and space as essentials for action. Occasionally, a plaintive reader writes me a note after I've panned some violent fantasy movie and says something like "Some of us *like* explosions. Ease up." Well, I like *these* explosions, because I believe in them. Realism has its thrills, too.

The insistence on plainness, the absence of stylization, carries over to the performances as well. Jeremy Renner has played the serial killer Jeffrey Dahmer and many minor roles in action movies. He has a round face, with a beautiful smile that he mostly keeps hidden, and a strong but unglamorous body. Bigelow's idea in casting him, I think, was to make her star a competent but physically ordinary American serviceman whose greatest gifts are within. William James, it turns out, is implacably heroic. He never steps away from danger. You might say that he's drawn to it and needs it, but he never makes a fuss about what he's doing. His charisma consists of having no obvious charisma except phenomenal concentration and guts. And since he knows, handling bombs, when to be cautious and when not to be, he can be hair-raisingly casual, tossing aside a disabled device as if it were an empty juice carton. At one point, he shucks his headset, too, and Sanborn, who needs to stay in touch with what James is doing, is so enraged that he slugs him. In the 1950s, Aldo Ray played men like William James—war lovers, completely at home on the battlefield but hapless in the normal relations of life. (When James and his partners relax and get drunk, the only way they can show their affection is to punch one another in the stomach.) But Ray's military men were unreachable, stone-cold killers, while James has strong emotions, which he keeps pent up.

Bigelow and Mark Boal (the journalist who developed the real-life material that served as the basis of Paul Haggis's *In the Valley of Elah*) don't always let us know exactly what's going on. As the soldiers swing into action, the filmmakers want a sense of strangeness and disorientation, a craziness that's on the verge of taking over the moment. As James is walking toward a bomb, an Iraqi drives into the scene in a taxi and won't obey commands to go back. What is he up to? Another man, strapped with explosives, changes his mind about suicide and tearfully begs James to rescue him. Is he a lure? The anguish of uncertainty is part of the men's daily life, and James himself, so sure in his odd profession, gets into a serious mix-up over a friendly Iraqi boy who he thinks has been murdered by insurgents. Suddenly, he loses his bearings and charges around Baghdad like a madman. *The Hurt Locker* is a small classic of tension, bravery, and fear, which will be studied twenty years from now when people want to understand something of what happened to American soldiers in Iraq. If there are moviegoers who are exhausted by the current fashion for relentless fantasy violence, this is the convincingly blunt and forceful movie for them.

The New Yorker, *June 29, 2009*

WINTER'S BONE

In the extraordinary independent film *Winter's Bone,* the large Dolly clan lives off the grid. The movie is set in the Missouri Ozarks, in back country—way back, where the front yards are filled with dead cars and cracked toilets, and the children ride wooden horses and hunt squirrels. There are no telephones, much less cell phones or computers, and not a TV in sight. Poverty is not necessarily the issue: The Dollys, we can see, don't particularly *want* to join the consumer society; they live among cast-off things because they're used to them. Their indifference to the outside world turns hostile when they're visited by "the law." Ree Dolly (Jennifer Lawrence), the brilliant, determined seventeen-year-old who is the heroine of the movie, is a law unto herself. She takes care of her withdrawn mother and her kid brother and sister, and she treks across a colorless winter landscape, visiting relatives as she looks for her father, Jessup, who cooks methamphetamine for a living. Jessup was arrested and then released when he put up his house and land as bond. If he doesn't appear in court, Ree and the rest of her immediate family will lose everything. The script—which the director, Debra Granik, and her collaborator, Anne Rosellini, adapted from the 2006 novel by Daniel Woodrell—doesn't spell things out, but, as Ree travels around, we slowly get the point: All the Dollys, in one way or another, are involved in the meth trade. They guard secrets that they don't wish Ree to know about or even ask about. Without making an actual appearance, meth is a character in the film, creating paranoia and corruption everywhere. *Winter's Bone* is something new in movies: a "country-noir" thriller.

Daniel Woodrell writes with insistent rhythm and an evocative and poetic regional flavor. It's a good style, but a literary one, and the film-makers, while drawing heavily on Woodrell's plot and dialogue, don't try to imitate it. The movie, which was plainly and beautifully shot by Michael McDonough, is matter-of-fact, with a strong feeling for the dailiness of life. Yet the Ozarks are a world so little known to most of us that the physical details seem a revelation, a fulfillment of realism's promise to show us what we have never seen or noticed before. And the plainness never goes slack, so the thick physical texture is entirely dramatic. Debra Granik, who earlier made *Down to the Bone,* with Vera Farmiga, creates an aura of violence through suggestion, half-finished sentences, or a threatening or sorrowful look; she envelops us in mysteries that can never quite be solved, because the Dollys don't want them solved. Truculent and reserved, eloquent only in brief outbursts garnished with a twist of perverse wit, the Dollys operate with a double-edged sense of kinship—they will protect you up to a point but, at the same time, your life belongs to them. Ree never knows what she's going to face: A relative will be helpful one moment and intimidating the next.

There have been a lot of earnest, methodical movies coming out of the Sundance Film Festival lately, but *Winter's Bone,* which premiered there and took the Best Picture prize, is what we've been waiting for: a work of art that grabs hold and won't let go. It was shot with digital equipment, for a mere $2 million, buoyed by tax incentives from the state of Missouri. The cast members seem rooted, marked by tough times, and utterly authentic. Some of them are local people, but the main roles are taken by professional actors, including Jennifer Lawrence, who has flowing blond hair, lidless blue eyes, and a full mouth. Her Ree is the head of a household, a womanly girl with no time for her own pleasure, and Lawrence establishes the character's authority right away, with a level stare and an unhurried voice that suggest heavy lifting from an early age. The movie would be unimaginable with anyone less charismatic playing Ree. In a series of soul-shaking confrontations, Lawrence is matched by the veteran character actress Dale Dickey, who plays the wife of the clan's crime boss with an uncanny bitter intensity, and by John Hawkes, as Ree's uncle, who at first seems antagonistic and wasted—no one has ever dragged on a cigarette with greater need—but becomes something else: Ree's protector, and a moral man unafraid of death. In all, the acting and the milieu are so closely joined that when the final shot goes to black, and the spell is broken, the audience gasps.

An album of snapshots from an earlier time suggests that the Dollys have fallen from a stable, prosperous, middle-class life. We don't know why they've fallen, though the drug trade and the military seem to be the only career paths that they consider following. *Winter's Bone* isn't a liberal sociological study of poverty; nor does it rely on genre conventions. We feel so apprehensive for Ree because we have no idea which way the story will go: Mafia behavior is predictable; the Dollys are unfathomable. We look to the older Dolly women for clues. They work at protecting their mangy, surly men, but they know how to get around them, too, and, when they have to, they do the dirty business of cleaning up crimes. Ree is the only hope amid this sordid life. She's not just the most interesting teenager around, she's more believable as a heroic character than any of the men we've seen peacocking through movies recently. In its lived-in, completely nonideological way, *Winter's Bone* is one of the great feminist works in film.

The New Yorker, *July 5, 2010*

PART THREE / STARS

INTRODUCTION

We had a relationship, once, a relationship in our heads with proudly beautiful and fascinating people, talking and arguing with them, imagining how we would act as they did in a given situation, as lovers, as defenders of the weak, as honorable men walking down dark alleys, as women running a ranch or nailing Gary Cooper after a hard campaign. Millions of women, many of them very smart, lived and breathed with Joan Crawford. Why? For a man, Crawford's appeal—in which her strenuous unhappiness was an obvious part—is a puzzle that has to be solved, or at least understood. Star worship can't be understood unless Crawford is understood. Whatever Crawford's absurdities, however, and whatever demands her fans made on her, she did not suffer the indignity of the coarse, intimate, hazing *possession* which we now subject stars to. To put it crudely: It was once a commonplace that moviegoers did not want to see more of a star's body than the star chose to reveal. Nakedness was for porno stars; their distance from us—their impersonality—was part of what made them erotic objects, and nothing more than that. But now, whatever the star's inclination, his picture, and her picture, starkers, is sure to be found on the Internet somewhere, which leaves us with a peculiar problem. Which will win out—respect or curiosity? That we have this choice at all is a mark of how invasive the media have become and how far the stars have fallen—and perhaps how far we have fallen, too. Respect for acting has never been greater than it is now, and movie culture can't live without star worship, so we're left with this: It would be nice if the barriers that once existed between us and Humphrey Bogart, or even between us and Jack Nicholson or Warren Beatty, would go up again. We can't look at Angelina Jolie shopping, or naked on a beach, without trespassing on ourselves as much as on her, but that's the world we live in. We could stop looking, but how likely is that?

ENDURING JOAN CRAWFORD

Must we hate Joan Crawford? The question seems a little odd. Must we think about Joan Crawford at all? That's perhaps a little more like it. It's true that she always had, and still has, a group of fans who caress every glamour photo, every gown, sable, and lover in her dauntingly complicated life. But some of her fans get lost in their appreciation of her, their need of her; they are *with* her; they don't always *see* her. For the rest of us, Crawford the always posing, eternally hardworking star, with her affairs and marriages and triumphs and miseries and comebacks, inspires as much exasperation as wonder. Her ferocious will to succeed seems like a version of the life force itself; a grim version of the life force. Among the great female stars of the studio and immediate post-studio period—Greta Garbo, Bette Davis, Katharine Hepburn, Barbara Stanwyck, Ingrid Bergman, Marilyn Monroe, Elizabeth Taylor—she is the least likely, at this point, to inspire deep affection. Few men go weak in the knees dreaming about her, as they do when dreaming of sultry Lana, generous Rita; nor is she the kind of woman men could imagine bantering with as a lover, as they might with Hepburn or Stanwyck. She's the date who raises your blood pressure, not your libido. She was always a bigger hit with women, but, at this point, women eager to emulate her drive and success may shudder a bit. The ravenous smile, the scything broad shoulders, the burdensome distress, the important walk and complicated hair—she's too insistent, too laborious and heavily armed, and also too vulnerable. She lacked lyricism and ease, except, perhaps, when flirting on-screen with Clark Gable, her off-screen lover and friend, with whom she made eight movies. She almost always tried too hard—it was Crawford who uttered the grammatically ambitious sentence, "Whom is fooling whom?"—and she demanded that you capitulate to her vision of herself. Many people dismiss her as crazy.

Yet if Joan Crawford is not very likable, she would, in a just world, be widely honored for a series of fiercely effective performances and for her emblematic quality as a twentieth-century woman. She was no feminist, but, willy-nilly, she got caught up in the dilemmas of world-conquerors who are also highly sexual women who need men. Constantly refashioning her appearance through one era after another, Crawford was also the prototype of the modern celebrity (Madonna is the obvious heir) who remains indestructible by placing herself at the vanguard of current erotic taste and thereby becoming attractive and slightly threatening at the same time—a combination that no one can ignore. In her more than eighty movies, she played flappers, working girls, adulteresses, matrons, crazies, and, most notably, the anguished heroines of melodrama—women embracing the reality principle whose iron tenets are that life is hard, satisfaction elusive, happiness never without cost. Whatever her characters did, their acts had consequence. Life was serious then. Cigarettes were portentously lit, martini glasses were flung against the wall, cars driven off the road. People rose and fell socially, committed murders, went crazy—Joan Crawford did all of those things. If there was something grindingly literal-minded and overinsistent about her, who could say that she ever ducked anything difficult? Who has half her courage now? (Kate Winslet, definitely, and Charlize Theron, maybe, but she doesn't work very often.)

Any call for justice to Joan Crawford, however, runs into a nasty dead end: The image of Crawford as a mad woman is so juicily entertaining that few people want to give it up. In 1978, the year after Crawford died, her estranged and disinherited adopted daughter Christina, a failed actress, threw together, with a great deal of editorial suggestion from the publisher William Morrow, a venomous portrait of her mother, *Mommie Dearest*, which alleged both physical abuse and bizarre tests and punishments (Christina's uneaten steak accusingly placed before her for days). The book became an enormous best-seller. But who knows how truthful Christina was? Certainly the style is not inflated: Parts of the book are surprisingly well written. But her younger twin sisters, also adopted, said that their mother was strict but loving and that Christina was lying. In any case, in 1981, the director Frank Perry made the sensationally vindictive movie of the same title in which Faye Dunaway, her career as a star fading, grabbed at a chance for glory, or at least notoriety, by launching herself into a spangled caricature of Crawford—hysterically tensed neck and back, painted eyebrows like Gothic arches, crowbar voice. "No wire hangers!" has remained a dorm-room joke even among youths who have no idea what it refers to. The collective memory of Crawford quickly hardened into the remorselessness of camp—the image of a dictatorial harpy, evil sister to Maleficent, the wicked fairy godmother in Disney's *Sleeping Beauty*. Christina Crawford certainly knew what she had done. When she brought out a twentieth anniversary version of the book, in 1998, she promoted it around the country with a variety of female impersonators doing an imitation of her mother.

In truth, I'm not sure that Joan Crawford can be entirely rescued from camp. She wasn't crazy, but she was certainly strange, and her exemplary qualities as a hard-fighting American woman can't quite be freed from her personal fixations and obsessions. In a new biography, *Possessed: The Life of Joan Crawford* (William Morrow), Donald Spoto, who did good early work on Hitchcock thirty years ago and has since become a rolling mill of star bios (Grace Kelly, James Dean, and Ingrid Bergman among many others), tries to cleanse her portrait, separating rumors from fact, alleged hysteria from garden-variety unhappiness. Spoto chronicles her alcoholism and her occasional fits of rotten behavior around rival stars like Norma Shearer, but he insists that she was a loyal friend and unfailingly generous to the crews that she worked with. He sees her strenuous, often difficult life as noble. But Spoto, writing with the most benevolent intentions, can't bear to say that her tragedy—for it was a kind of tragedy—was also a malevolent black comedy of American success from beginning to end.

Joan Crawford came out of nowhere, or as close to nowhere as is consistent with actually having a birthplace and a past. She was born Lucille LeSueur, in San Antonio, Texas, in 1906. Her father, Thomas LeSueur, may never have married her mother, Anna Bell Johnson. Either way, he took off when his daughter was born. Crawford had an older brother, and the family moved to Lawton, Oklahoma, where Anna married a man named Henry Cassin, who ran a theater that booked traveling shows, including dance acts. He was good to Lucille, and let her hang around backstage and watch the performers. He gave her the nickname Billie, and, for a while, she was known as Billie Cassin. But after a few years, Henry was accused of embezzlement; he moved the family to Kansas City, and, eventually, he ran off, too, leaving Anna with no choice but to move her kids into a room behind a laundry, where she took in wash to get by. Anna's next husband, Henry Hough, fondled Lucille, who was then thirteen, and her mother sent her to a local boarding school, the Rockingham Academy, to get her away from him.

This was the second boarding school that Lucille went to. In both cases, there wasn't enough money for tuition, so she spent more time scrubbing dishes and floors than going to class. At Rockingham, the head mistress whacked her with a cane and the kids razzed her, so she left, returning home, and worked with her mother washing clothes. Crawford never had much education past the fifth grade; in her early Hollywood days she got through scripts by looking up words she didn't know and sounding them out.

Many other girls might have gotten stuck in the room behind the laundry for the rest of their lives. Lucille escaped by dancing. In the clubs built along the old Santa Fe Trail, just south of downtown Kansas City, the postwar dance crazes—the Charleston, the black bottom, the shimmy— had taken over. She danced half the night at such places as the Jack O' Lantern and, starting when she was sixteen, entered competitions and began working as a backup behind nightclub singers. She moved from one Midwestern city to another, until she was spotted by two seasoned judges of talent: the New York theater producer J. J. Shubert (of the Alley), who saw her in Detroit and brought her to Broadway as a chorine; and Maurice Rapf, one of Louis B. Mayer's producers at MGM, who caught her in a New York show in 1924, when she was eighteen, and sent her to Hollywood with a $75-a-week contract. Leaving out the obvious explanation (Crawford was never shy about getting ahead), what caused the two men to pull her out of a line of dancers? She was only five feet three; she had freckles, a mop of reddish hair, and broad, square shoulders; she was a little heavy (140 pounds) for her size. But the men must have seen—they couldn't have missed—an insatiable hunger. If you look at pictures of her at any age, the whites of her eyes show not just above her irises but below them. Her body may be stretched out and relaxed, but her eyes are so wide open that she seems to be devouring the future.

Hollywood gave her a name of her own at last. In silent movies, she appeared as Lucille Le Sueur, but Mayer ordered MGM's publicists to run a contest in which a new name was chosen for her. She hated it, but, much as Archie Leach spent an entire life being "Cary Grant," she spent her remaining fifty years enacting "Joan Crawford," which, as she fashioned it, meant a day-and-night, fan-courting, picture-signing, dress-up-to-go-grocery-shopping devotion to stardom as destiny and institution. She did not venture forth from her house without clothes, makeup, attendants. In her only known *mot,* Crawford said, "If you want the girl next door, go next door." At first, MGM put her in small roles, and sent her all over town to cavort for photographers. The shots of her leaping into the air at the studio or horsing around on a beach have a fantastic vitality, a sheer pleasure in moving and being watched, as do her early performances in movies like *Our Dancing Daughters* (1928), *Dance, Fools, Dance* (1931), and *Dancing Lady* (1933), in which she's pleasure-loving and wild yet candid and friendly, a likable straight-shooter who gets the guy.

Still, despite her quick success (she became a star in her mid-twenties), Spoto suggests that something was tearing away at her—her past, her sense of her own ignorance, and, with it, persistent feelings of degradation, even worthlessness. By the early 1930s, she was sick of dancing roles, although she continued to play them. She told one interviewer, "I like the drab. I like to play human beings in the gutter." In Clarence Brown's *Possessed* (1931), she is convincingly morose as a small-town Pennsylvania girl in a print dress walking out of a box factory at the end of her shift. What promise does life have for her? *There,* in that town? She wants more. As she spurns a mediocre and possessive suitor, her disgust has an anguished edge. But she doesn't stay in the box factory long. She moves up fast, to New York, where she falls in with a rising young lawyer (Gable), and soon she's a kept woman on Park Avenue, with city views, a French maid, a regally cultivated accent, terrific slinky gowns, and a none too convincing way with French and German love songs at the piano.

In the movies, Crawford would touch base with her origins only to reenact, again and again, her escape. During the Depression, she made a number of these shack-to-penthouse journeys, but she did her best-known acting in this period in the famous *Grand Hotel* (1932), as a Berlin stenographer who's not going anywhere and is willing, however wistfully, to sleep with a repulsive industrialist (Wallace Beery) in order to get some new clothes and a week's vacation in Manchester (not even London). The performance has a bittersweet quality, a spirit of resignation relieved by bursts of hope. Her popping eyes don't seem excessive when she's playing someone who grabs at pleasure—say, when she flirts with John Barrymore's charming aristocrat, and uses her thick, mobile shoulders both as a shield and a fence to look over, eagerly, hungrily. I prefer this melancholy but eager stenographer to her more famous work years later for George Cukor in the all-female *The Women* (1939), in which she's harsh and grating as a perfume counter saleswoman preying on rich married men. Candor was her strength and her weakness, too. In *The Women*, she seemed determined to show the audience what a bitch a woman faced with few choices can become, and she took the nastiness further than she needed to. In Crawford, self-contempt and courage were inseparable—each spurred the other—and the combination made her an agonized performer, overearnest, overexplicit, discomforting, but enthralling for those who trusted her to act out and overcome their own dilemmas. She entered into a relationship with her public that depended on will and fantasy and woman-alone courage. No female star has that kind of relationship with the public now. To love her must have been exhausting and inspiring at the same time.

Almost from the beginning, she earned plenty of money, but a longing for class and elevation—a redemptive break with the past—never left her. In 1929, she married Douglas Fairbanks, Jr., when she was twenty-three, and he all of nineteen. Fairbanks, who was acting in small roles, was the son of a great silent star and the stepson of Mary Pickford. He was handsome and socially accomplished, and women chased him wherever he went. As a child, he had spent time in Europe, and he held forth on poetry and culture to Crawford during a two-year affair before they married. Spoto makes it clear that Fairbanks was largely faking his knowledge of the arts, but at the time Crawford believed him. She had bought an eight-thousand-square-foot house in Brentwood, and the couple lived there, yet she was intimidated by evenings at Pickfair, the Beverly Hills residence of Fairbanks's parents. If the gods had granted her even a trace of irony she might have been less impressed. Pickfair, with its reproduction French furniture, wasn't Balmoral; it wasn't the Breakers; it wasn't even Fifth Avenue. Fairbanks Sr. and Pickford were of middle-class background, he from Denver, she from Toronto. They were early-generation movie colony celebrities, with the first private swimming pool in Los Angeles. Crawford, desperate to make herself worthy, studied French and took opera-singing lessons while trying to instill some of her ambition into the languid Fairbanks. It was a dreadful basis for a marriage: He slept with the attractive women who asked him, and she slept with Clark Gable, an affair that continued, on and off, for decades.

Gable was Crawford's true mate. When he was young, he had knocked around, too, and had made two marriages to older women who taught him bearing, elocution, couth. He and Crawford shared an understanding of how the world worked. "We were both peasants," she later said. However, in 1935, a year after the relationship with Fairbanks was dissolved, she didn't wait for Gable to be free but instead married Franchot Tone, who was from a socially prominent family in the East; Tone had performed onstage in New York with Katharine Cornell and had been a member of the avant-garde Group Theater. In Brentwood, the same domestic comedy played itself out again. A high-minded alcoholic, Tone enraptured her with readings of Shakespeare, Ibsen, and Shaw. At their dinner parties, a harp or a string trio noodled in the background. It was the period of Hollywood's cultural aspiration, dutiful and gummy—ridiculous, no doubt, but touching, and perhaps too easy to mock now, when ambitious taste among actors has shifted to the safer habit of collecting avant-garde paintings and displaying them on museum-smooth white walls.

The only time Crawford felt good enough, Spoto says, was when she joined with her audience. She escaped into the rituals of stardom that the fans expected of her and that she gloried in. George Hurrell, then MGM's staff photographer and chief artificer of glamour, saw that she had a good set of bones—magnificent forehead, strong chin, serious nose—and, in more than fifty sessions with her over the years, he played lights on her face, extended her eyelashes, and tilted her neck so far back that she

seemed to be gazing at some ineffable visitation from the heavens. Hurrell tried to spiritualize her in the same way that other photographers had
spiritualized Garbo, and Crawford, as the 1930s wore on, tended to stiffen
on-screen, as if she were trying to live up to the images of her in magazines. The public had loved her for her fire as a reckless American girl,
and, as she got older, she wanted to be a dramatic actress in touch with
the nasty realities of life. At the same time, she also wanted to be a clotheshorse, whose jewels and gowns were a rebuke to the people who had mis-
treated her in the past. At her most confused, she became lofty and grand,
and MGM—the greatest studio, but, as John Updike once remarked, "the
stupidest"— encouraged her most pretentious side, making her play society women or period heroines in layered curls. By the late 1930s, a trade
paper dubbed her "box-office poison."

Eventually, in the early 1940s, she shifted to the studio where she
should have worked from the beginning—Warner Bros., which made realistic urban dramas, noirs, gangster movies, and the turbulent melodramas that Bette Davis reigned over in eccentric supremacy. Crawford's first
serious vehicle at Warners begins with gunshots at a Santa Monica beach
house. A shimmering dark ocean lies in the background; Crawford, in a
mink coat and hat, drives away in a big car, and launches herself into the
furious black whirl of *Mildred Pierce* (1945), based on James M. Cain's
1941 novel. Mildred is a middle-class housewife who makes a fortune
as a chain restaurant owner—she puts her back into everything, working harder than a stevedore. Yet she's nearly destroyed by her invincibly
rapacious and snobbish daughter (Ann Blyth) and a snarling upper-class
bounder (Zachary Scott, of the baleful voice and pencil-line mustache).
Directed by Michael Curtiz, *Mildred Pierce* softened some of the Depression-era squalor that Cain wrote about, but it's still exciting for its almost
prurient attention to class, sex, and money, its speed and decisiveness,
its general atmosphere of ruthless social circumstance. (In the spring of
2011, Kate Winslet will appear in a more leisurely and faithful adaptation of the book in an HBO miniseries, directed by Todd Haynes.) Crawford took off her fake eyelashes and, except for two face-slapping scenes
with Ann Blyth (much celebrated in the annals of camp), toned down her
tremulous emotionalism. The performance, which won her an Oscar, is

actually remarkable for its plainness, its sense of a woman's life as a bone-wearying job with fringe benefits but no central satisfactions—except, in this case, the neurotic satisfaction of constantly sacrificing oneself for an unworthy daughter.

The plain style was something that Cukor had taught her in one of her last MGM vehicles, *A Woman's Face* (1941), in which she's a disfigured beauty, an accident victim—until Melvyn Douglas's surgeon changes her back into Joan Crawford. She kept her voice angry and flat in that movie, but the plot was nonsense. In *Mildred Pierce,* Crawford was in her proper range at last, able to tell the truth, as she saw it, of American life, which was that women had to work harder than men to get anywhere, only to risk getting shafted in the end. In the same vein, she's remarkably straightforward again, and utterly convincing, in Otto Preminger's superb *Daisy Kenyon* (1947), this time as a New York commercial artist with an open-eyed stare and a hardened voice, a worldly professional who initially accepts as her due the adoration of two intelligent male peacocks (played by a blustery Dana Andrews and a sly Henry Fonda). When Daisy is nearly driven mad by their manipulative antics, Crawford blows up, jumps into her car, races madly, and drives off the road, but Preminger held her within the tight confines of the plot, and the flagrant flare-up works, too.

She was forty, and her face, a mask with severely etched dark eyebrows and a mouth turning down at the corners, fascinated directors with its control and its suppressed emotion plainly quivering below the surface. Spoto thinks that *Mildred Pierce* was raised to "a higher level of disturbing complexity by Joan's complete mastery of her craft," and he speaks of "rich and subtle expression" and "vocal nuance." That's a bit much: Nuance was never her gift, though she certainly had improved since *Rain* (1932), in which, as the prostitute Sadie Thompson who finds God (momentarily), she goes from hip-swaying sluttishness to zombie-like religious exaltation and back again without any modulation. By the time of *Mildred Pierce,* she was able to offer if not subtlety at least a two-level "psychological" performance. There isn't much give, much play in it—nothing that allows you to feel any intimacy with her. Bette Davis's obvious intelligence and brilliant flamboyance and Barbara Stanwyck's mixture of sympathy and acid wit are more like invitations to pleasure. With Crawford, you are forced to admire her strictly on her own terms, and there was an element in the response to *Mildred Pierce* (and there still is) that falls below criticism but remains unavoidable, a degree of ambivalence bordering on malice, as if the audience were saying to her, "You tried that hard, and you still couldn't find happiness." Yet no one could say that Crawford wasn't solid and serious in the role—a dramatic actress at last.

In *Mildred Pierce,* Ann Blyth's wildly indulged daughter constantly throws it in her mother's face that her origins are shabby, her restaurants common. Suddenly, Crawford found herself confronted with a character voicing her own self-distaste. What's curious—and what makes Joan Crawford someone to puzzle over and even, within reason, to grieve over—is that playing Mildred and other troubled roles over the next ten years or so never released her from her own genuine miseries. Catharsis was not one of her gifts, either.

During her marriage to Franchot Tone, she had several miscarriages, and, in 1939, the year the marriage ended, she began adopting babies on the black market—single women could not legally adopt in California. The first child, Christina, was six when *Mildred Pierce* came out. As all the world knows from *Mommie Dearest,* Crawford gave Christina "everything"— fancy clothes, a stuffed menagerie, lawn parties with monkeys and organ grinders—and demanded adoration in return. She spoiled Christina in the years after making *Mildred Pierce* as much as before, and there were other cases where she embodied a character so completely she couldn't separate herself from it. Again and again in the 1940s and 1950s, when Hollywood's interest in mental and emotional aberration was at its height, she played distraught women throwing themselves at worthless men. She brought an almost punitive honesty to these pathetic parts. In *Possessed* (1947; not to be confused with the 1931 movie), she played a nurse obsessed with a callous construction engineer (Van Heflin) to the point of insanity and murder—he sits at the piano playing Schumann while she goes nuts. At the very same time, in Hollywood, she was clinging to the handsome but abusive rogue lawyer Greg Bautzer. She took on the title role in *Harriet Craig* (1950), which is about a woman so obsessed with order and cleanliness that she drives her family out of her house; in her own home, Crawford cleaned and recleaned as compulsively as Lady Macbeth washing her hands. Some stains, apparently, can never be removed. The cliché that actors are essentially people with no fixed identity—ciphers who must play a role in order to become someone—obviously didn't apply to her. Her psychological patterns were so strong that they both created her roles and destroyed her life.

As well as the falling-in-love-with-a-worthless-man movies, there was the other side of the coin, *Humoresque* (1946), in which she feels worthless herself and is overawed by the man she falls in love with. Her Fifth Avenue socialite, Helen Wright, alcoholic and myopic, takes up with, and nearly ruins, John Garfield's Lower East Side genius, a cocky violin player with a jutting jaw that nearly crushes his instrument. She suffers and drinks, in soft focus, to the sounds of Beethoven and Tchaikovsky, and finally commits suicide by walking into the ocean during a mangled version of the "Liebestod" from *Tristan und Isolde*. *Humoresque* is the ripest of Hollywood kitsch, but, in the midst of the overwrought production, with its temperamental clashes and many moist close-ups of Crawford (Jean Negulesco was the director), something desperately honest, even confessional comes through, a sense that there is no escaping one's character. "You don't need me," she says to Garfield. "I'm too wearing on people's nerves." She was, indeed—arrogant, needy, and self-deprecating all at once. It's perhaps her most touching performance. Near the end of the movie, you can feel her relinquishing her will, her desires, her ability to control anything. When you watch the final scenes, as Wagner swirls around her, laughter may overcome tears, but at least the stifled sobs are real. No one ever gave a more convincing performance as a woman who has everything—Fifth Avenue, beach house, sables, servants, acquiescent husband, limo—and can't find a trace of happiness in any of it.

Of course, in her own career, she didn't willingly give up a thing. She held on. But, as she neared fifty, she became almost grotesque, answering her own needs and the wiles of directors eager to exploit her. In Nicholas Ray's odd, beautiful, impassioned Western, *Johnny Guitar* (1954), she's Vienna, a tough businesswoman in a gunbelt who runs a saloon and constantly faces down groups of armed men. Vienna is both an icon of self-reliance and a woman uncontrollably in love with a handsome young gunslinger (Sterling Hayden). The performance, lodged somewhere between nobility and absurdity, is so peculiarly willed that the young François Truffaut, then a critic, was stunned. "She is beyond consideration of beauty," he wrote. "She has become unreal, a fantasy of herself. Whiteness has invaded her eyes, muscles have taken over her face, a will of iron behind a face of steel. She is a phenomenon. She is becoming more manly as she grows older. Her clipped, tense acting, pushed almost to paroxysm by Ray, is itself a strange and fascinating spectacle."

In 1951, after three marriages to handsome, cultivated, weak-willed actors (Phillip Terry was the last), Crawford wed a different kind of man—the rotund but self-assured business executive Alfred Nu Steele, the president of Pepsi-Cola. She moved to New York, set up an enormous apartment on Fifth Avenue, and then, grandly dressed, and accompanied by a pasha's collection of luggage, traveled around the world with Steele, promoting the soft drink. She was genuinely happy. At last, she had linked up with a man her equal in drive and ability; she had attained the kind of class and respectability she had always wanted. But, in 1959, at the age of fifty-seven, after less than four years of marriage, Steele had a heart attack in the lavish new apartment and died, leaving her with debts incurred from the expensive redo. She continued traveling for Pepsi, and kept working. Her fans never left her, but after *Johnny Guitar* the spectacle that so mesmerized Truffaut lost its fascination. As a top fiction editor in *The Best of Everything*, bullying and then advising young Hope Lange, she's a gallant, unhappy older woman, and almost painful to watch. She passed into tawdry roles, as if she were still in the grip of self-loathing, including a horror film with Bette Davis, *What Ever Happened to Baby Jane?* (1962), in which she plays a washed-up movie star confined to a wheelchair while Davis, playing her sister, a washed-up child actress, torments her. As much as his subject, Spoto refuses to let go, either, seeing a severe and disciplined art in some of the late performances. *Baby Jane* offered a fitting role for a masochist, perhaps, but the only way to enjoy it is to become a sadist. She retired, in 1972, at the age of sixty-six, and retreated, alone, to a smaller apartment in New York. She died in 1977.

Her epitaph is a gloating monstrosity. The lighting in *Mommie Dear-*

PART THREE / STARS   113

est is overbright, the sets astonishingly ugly. (Crawford may have lacked taste, but I doubt that her decorators were inept; anyway, a noir heroine needs some shadows.) As far over the top as you remember Faye Dunaway, she's that much further over it on second viewing. Squatting on her haunches and roaring, her face in cold cream, she's a samurai in Kabuki drag, beating Christina with the famous hangers and then with a can of Old Dutch cleanser. As she rides her voice higher and higher, she goes after innocent rosebushes in the garden with castrating shears and savagely axes a tree. Of course, it's all intended to be absurd—grotesque farce. But farce about what? The movie chronicles one power struggle after another between mother and child, and the joke gets buried in sordid emotional and physical violence. *Mommie Dearest* was an act of posthumous assassination. The movie discharged the assorted resentments that not only Christina but a part of the country had built up in its long assent to Crawford's presumptions and demands, and to her stardom itself. For Faye Dunaway, however, it was more like a murder-suicide pact than a simple crime. She has appeared in many movies and TV shows since, but *Mommie Dearest* finished her career as a star. It's as if Crawford's convoluted aggressive and self-destructive force had carried Dunaway down with it. When the movie is over, you can only whisper, like some pious mourner longing for relief, "Peace, Joan, peace."

The New Yorker, *January 3, 2011; revised 2011*

FALLEN IDOLS / MOVIE STARS TODAY

Clark Gable, the most famous male movie star of the 1930s, drank heavily, hit the road and slept with prostitutes when he felt like it, had false teeth and bad breath, fathered an illegitimate child with Loretta Young, carried on an affair with Joan Crawford when they were both married, and, on at least two occasions, wrapped his car around a tree. He settled down somewhat when he fell in love with Carole Lombard, whom he married in 1939, and he apparently did not, as rumor has long insisted, run over a female pedestrian in 1945 when drunk. Over the years, however, he got into plenty of trouble, and almost all of it was either kept out of the press or appeared in the papers in garbled and anodyne form. In their syndicated newspaper columns, the industry gorgons Louella O. Parsons and Hedda Hopper wrote benevolently of stars except on those occasions when a star crossed one of them or the studios wanted an insubordinate actor punished in public. There were famous Hollywood romances, of course, like Greta Garbo's with John Gilbert, and scandals like the Fatty Arbuckle case in 1921, and also an underground of terrific gossip, but, in general, newspapers and fan magazines published gently whimsical prose about romance and home life in the movie colony. The stars, it seems, were *good*. They were helpful, kind, grateful for their enormous luck. Paired up and dressed in evening clothes, they went to clubs like Ciro's or Mocambo, acting out studio-created liaisons, while their private lives, sometimes thrillingly dirty, sometimes sedate and ordinary, mostly remained out of sight.

Gable had a long-term contract with MGM, and if you were on MGM's payroll and got in trouble, you did not call your lawyer. You called Howard Strickling (or his colleague Eddie Mannix), the talented head of publicity and all-around fixer at the studio. Strickling's duties included bribing the police, planting nonsense in the papers, arranging abortions for MGM's actresses, and shipping off to Europe directors who threw too many orgiastic parties. In 1932, when Jean Harlow's husband, the MGM staff producer and bigamist Paul Bern, was found shot dead in their Benedict Canyon house, Strickling arrived at the scene with Louis B. Mayer and Irving Thalberg, and worked hard, and successfully, to keep Harlow out of court. In those pre-Code days, MGM thought it fine to treat Harlow on-screen as a kind of snarling dirty girl, but it was another thing to have her tinged with crime. (Bern may have been shot by his first wife, but the death was ruled a suicide.) The invaluable Strickling performed his role so successfully that he went to his grave in 1982 with all his secrets intact, an outrageous affront to star biographers and the merely curious.

But consider our daily bread in the new century. Think of Angie and Jen (as if you had the slightest choice not to)—Angie and Jen seesawing on the fulcrum of Brad, who, over the years, has appeared with one or the other, clubbing, attending awards ceremonies, shopping, vacationing, usually with Brad grinning slightly or looking a little lost. In one combination or another, they date, marry, quarrel, break up, "forgive," all of it in public; they deliver, adopt, and lug babies around, sometimes in dusty climes; they gain too much weight, lose too much weight, and so on, forever and ever, until one or another will be hounded into the grave by the excess attention of celebrity mags, TV entertainment shows, and websites. Some of what you hear about them may even be true, but all of it will be written or spoken in an abusively familiar style—chummy, coarse, knowing—that sounds like three girls roughing up the popular kids from a corner table in the cafeteria. The tone of the celebrity media is always junior high: "She's my best friend. I hate her."

US Weekly, one of half a dozen identical magazines, includes, as a regular feature, a shop-and-schlep page called "Stars—They're Just Like US" in which celebrities are caught on the streets hauling the baby in a Snugli or picking up the dry-cleaning. Not just Paris Hilton and Nicole Richie but promising young actors are photographed taking out the garbage. "They Buy Flowers!" "They Pick Up Dry-Cleaning!" Some of the other "stars" are mock celebrities, whose only work is to stone themselves silly and fall apart in public. The feature is lame, but the implied attitude behind it is essential snark: Every part of a star's existence, including the surgical scars and the cellular deposits, belongs to *us*. The digital camera and the Web have turned the entire world into paparazzi, and the public is given unfettered access to the actors' comings and goings and to their flesh. They can't so much as jump naked into the ocean on a secluded beach without someone out in a boat taking their picture. In the past, a star like Rita Hayworth or Marilyn Monroe wore gravity-defying gowns— a negligee negligently hung, and so easy to remove—which offered the *promise* of nakedness; that gown was the difference between a sex goddess and a porno actor. But the actuality of nakedness forces us to choose between prurience and priggishness. You can avoid a lot of this, I suppose, but only if you never watch television, turn on a computer, pass a newsstand, or talk to a teenager.

For the record, I don't think that moviegoers seventy years ago particularly needed "the truth" about Gable. In her recent biography *Circling My Mother,* Mary Gordon records that Anne Gagliano Gordon, born in 1906, a hardworking woman who supported her family, "sat triumphant as a bride" when she heard that Gary Cooper had converted to Catholicism. Anne Gordon made the behavior of the stars a feature of her own moral life. Other fans, however, loved the stars without envy or pride or excessive analysis. Stardom, as John Lahr has said, was proof that the free enterprise system worked—some shnook from nowhere got to the top, and wasn't that great? For those fans, much of the fantasy about stars was probably a self-amused daydream. Why disturb it? If innocent people were not seriously hurt by Gable's roistering and Strickling's deceptions, the phony press images seem harmless enough. Likewise, the crude media usage of a flaunting, voguing actress like Angelina Jolie is hardly the stuff of tragedy. It's more like a joke gone sour from endless repetition. Still, the two extremes of protection and exposure suggest how much the magical aura around movie actors has vanished. In some ways, they have grown too familiar to us.

The shift from knowing nothing to knowing everything about a star's private life puts us in an awkward position, since it's part of our relation to stars to dream of their on-screen characters and their life as in some way unitary. F. Scott Fitzgerald met William Powell at a party in the 1930s and found him merely facetious rather than witty, but, even if true, we don't

PART THREE / STARS   117

want to hear it. We want to think of Powell, with his dark mustache, his Brylcreemed hair parted in the middle, his ironic but not self-regarding manner, as the quintessence of suavity that he was in *The Thin Man* and *My Man Godfrey*. This imagined unity is one element that sets off a star from an actor. No one thought Gable was a great actor, but, unshaven (in his early roles), belligerent, snarling, or seductive, he was a remarkably imposing presence on-screen, and so was Crawford, however absurd her vaunting egotism and coiffed suffering looks to us now. Are there really many stars now like *that*—charismatic, indelibly idiosyncratic people who transcend celebrity and mean something emotionally powerful to the audience? Are there even many stars in the industry's sense of reliable big earners? Hollywood used to breed stars "like minks," as Pauline Kael once said, but we may be breeding a different kind of animal now. And in this new situation, we may be losing some of the ridiculous pleasure—the longing and selfless adoration—that was once at the heart of moviegoing.

Let us not speak of the silent period. The stars are too far from us, too strange, too young, too exotic in their jewels, chinchilla, and velvet, their slinky cars as long as boats, their barbaric aura of leopard-skin splendor. They played tramps (Charlie Chaplin), vamps (Theda Bara), sheiks (Rudolph Valentino), noble lovers (John Gilbert), waifs (Lillian Gish), flappers (Clara Bow), pirates (Douglas Fairbanks), and other extravagant roles, and silence lent them the mystery and cruelty of remote beauty. As working gods—the metaphor for them at the time—they married one another or minor royalty and, in Beverly Hills or Bel Air, built enormous houses in innocently promiscuous Greco-Roman-Tuscan-Spanish style. Gathering together around the marbled swimming pools, or on yachts or polo fields, they enjoyed a kind of sanctified public leisure, relaxing and playing for everyone. It was unthinkable that these people should have children. They burned bright and then were extinguished—in the public imagination, they could not reproduce. In Billy Wilder's *Sunset Boulevard*, which was made in 1950, the sable past of the silent stars was already an object of amazement.

In the sound period, movies became more realistic, more "psychological" and down to earth, and such renewable resources as Gable, Gary

Cooper, Spencer Tracy, John Wayne, Humphrey Bogart, Joan Crawford, Bette Davis, Katharine Hepburn, Ava Gardner, and Rita Hayworth are still complex figures for us. Relished, debated, mocked, or adored, they haven't yet become objects of distant awe or condescending nostalgia; they're still alive. Their careers have been chewed over in endless biographies, so Jeanine Basinger, the film historian and longtime head of Wesleyan's film studies program, decided to do something fresh. In an enormous new book of star lore, *The Star Machine* (Knopf), Basinger keeps the extraordinary people named above just out of sight. Eager to concentrate on the routine workings of the movie industry, when the results may have been merely serviceable, rather than immortal, she takes on what might be called second-level minks—the earnest Tyrone Power and the equally handsome but dashing and playful Errol Flynn, the suave continental lover Charles Boyer, the All-American tap-dancing dynamo Eleanor Powell, the beautiful and tender Loretta Young, and the troubled Lana Turner, whose sullen sensuality and anything-for-love vulnerability have moved John Updike to grateful appreciation in the pages of this magazine. Basinger investigates as well the careers of minor stars like Deanna Durbin and Wallace Beery. Large and small, they were part of a balanced ecology in the great terra firma of the studio. Basinger plots their genesis and rise; she glories in their staying power as proof of the system's strength, even if much of what they appeared in now seems mediocre.

Basinger is half in love with what might be called the Studio System as Rational Paradise. In the twenty years or so from the introduction of sound in 1928 to the late 1940s, just about everyone was on contract to these giant, tentacular organizations. There were variations, of course, and special cases and even a few rebels, but most producers, directors, writers, actors, set designers, cinematographers, composers, sound recordists, and many others were loyal employees reporting to work on a regular, even daily, basis. Films were generally shot quickly on studio sets and the back lots. It was, as everyone has said, a factory process. What couldn't have been known then is that the factories wasted incomparably less money than Hollywood does now. The method turned out forty or so pictures a year at MGM or Paramount or Warners, which, in a stunning instance of vertical monopoly, also owned distribution wings and theater chains.

The Studio System as Rational Paradise is a paradigm most prominently associated with the film historian Thomas Schatz, whose excellent 1988 book, *The Genius of the System,* suggests that studio style, craft, and temperament—Paramount's penchant for sophisticated comedy, Warners' for harsh urban drama and antifascist melodrama, MGM's for lavish period films and literary adaptations—determined the achievement of Hollywood much more than the creativity of individual directors. *The Genius of the System* is an anti-auteurist book. Warners produced the fluent and complex noir miracle *The Big Sleep;* the director, Howard Hawks, added his touches to the extraordinary resources on hand at the studio. He merely directed it.

Basinger nestles with almost delicious comfort into the intimate procedures of star manufacture. The story is familiar yet still startling as an example of the industrialization of the ineffable. Initially, the actors came from everywhere and nowhere—from theater in all its varieties (vaudeville and circus as well as Broadway and nightclubs), from hard-calloused jobs and bumming around, from soda fountain counters, from the recommendations of talent scouts, who attended plays and local beauty contests. If you had some sort of promise, or just looked good and played ball with the scout, you would be invited to Los Angeles, photographed, screen-tested, and then, in many cases, worked on—teeth straightened, nose redone, freckles bleached, eyebrows plucked and redrawn. A mask of perfection was grafted onto natural good looks. You were given lessons in diction, acting, riding, dancing, fencing, and manners. At MGM, if you were a woman, you had to do "the Metro walk"—a peculiar exercise that, as Basinger reconstructs it, required sucking in the stomach, squaring the shoulders, and stepping off with the right foot. Crawford's labored but imperious progress across a room offers the definitive version of it.

Having placed the refashioned young ideal in the Culver City or Burbank version of Louis XV's Deer Park, the studio exercised its rights. The actors were given walk-ons and small roles, and then supporting roles, until the audience "discovered" them. Most of the contracts were for seven years at a fixed rate of pay. The ones who became stars were expected to work forty weeks and to make three or four pictures every year; they could also be "loaned out" to other studios in return for favors or payments that didn't necessarily benefit them. If they refused a role, the time lost was added to the end of the contract period. Even Gable, the king, felt sore over his arrangement with MGM.

Who made it through the mill? Kael and others have asserted that the studios' notion of a beautiful woman—the symmetrical features and a small nose—represented the bland dreams of the Jewish-immigrant studio moguls who wanted to assimilate, and who therefore put what they took to be American physical ideals—WASP stereotypes—on the screen. Norma Shearer, Irving Thalberg's wife, was certainly such a genteel and Gentile ideal. But I think this interpretation is a little glib. There's simply too much variety on the surface: Joan Crawford was tense and ambitious, with arched, worried eyebrows; Margaret Sullavan had a low, musical voice and eyes that conveyed hurt. Hepburn, of course, was high-strung, elocutionary, and both defiant and supple at the same time; her nostril flared when she was enraged. Gary Cooper was tall and very lean, a rural ideal of slow-talking sincerity. Flynn's soft mustache, courtly manners, and rallying mischief suggested a romantic figure out of an illustrated children's book. James Cagney, short, with lustrous blond hair, danced, weaved, and bantam-cocked his way through the maze of the big city.

What they all shared were large eyes with glistening whites. The video "Women in Film," on YouTube, morphs the faces of female stars, from the silent period to the present, in a continuous progression, and the video makes it clear that eyes may be freakishly pinned open (Crawford) or flirtatiously half closed (Marilyn Monroe), but they must be liquid and voluminous. Apart from eyes, the beauty characteristic that unites women as disparate as Lana Turner, Rita Hayworth, and Jennifer Jones is a full, gently crescented lower lip—a lip insolently slung—and a perfect bow for an upper lip. The women were often filmed with raised chin, looking up at men, so the neck had to be a clean line, the shoulders pliant and yielding. Women's hair in the glamour period was curtain and foliage, the luxurious motif of sexual abandon; men's hair, whether gleaming and parted like Cary Grant's or an indeterminate, sensuous swirl, like Burt Lancaster's, was a force field. A male star also needed something contradictory or unresolved in his face, for without that, he could never have been more than a model. Thick but not bushy eyebrows and a full, molded chin, preferably cleft, often matched up with a touch of "feminine" softness about the mouth (Gary Cooper) or a sardonic fold in the eyelids (Bogart). Lighting, costume, and makeup sealed the mask of idealization. In a passionate clinch, the actor's tie remained perfectly knotted. On the beach or in the sweaty Congo, the actress's hair and lipstick remained sprayed and painted. As the French sociologist Edgar Morin put it, Hollywood insisted on the ideal in the midst of the real—a vibrant notion of character stamped onto a splendid physical emblem that hardly ever varied.

Stars hold your attention just by being what they are. In their very existence on-camera, they express a vivid or extreme human possibility, a projection of personal power onto the world. Jessica Lange, by any measure, is a better actress than Lana Turner, yet Turner's Cora, in the 1946 version of James M. Cain's novel *The Postman Always Rings Twice,* is a more arresting figure than Jessica Lange's Cora in the 1981 version. Turner is so single-minded about sex and power that John Garfield, her costar, can hardly breathe in her presence. An earlier version of a star overtaken by celebrity, Turner had an unfortunate tendency to marry men she hardly knew (seven of them) and to consort with gangsters. Her problems couldn't be kept out of the press, but, as Basinger says, her bad girl image fed into her movie roles. She was shrewd enough as an actress to draw on the sordid messes she had gone through in her life. She may have reached the outer limits of her talent early in her career, but her fascination on-screen remained.

Young film actors often say now they don't want to be "typecast"—that is, limited—the way many of the old stars were, but there's a lot to be said for typecasting. Among other things, it makes an easy, involuntary communion with a star possible for the audience. Not every actor hit that unmistakably readable temperament right away. The studios could be awfully slow to realize what they had. Notoriously, Cary Grant didn't become Cary Grant, and Bogart Bogart, until they had each made more than twenty movies. It took Frank Capra's demotic genius to remold the standoffish Jean Arthur into the skeptical but ardent professional woman—a smart cookie with a gurgling voice—whom audiences fell in love with. At some point, however, an actor's looks and temperament would merge with a role that brought out, perhaps, an underlay of humor or menace, and the public would take notice, get excited, and the actor would become a star. The actor then solidified his position when he learned to impose a unifying temperament on his many characters; he became the characters, they became him, and any given performance offered a palimpsest of his past performances. Everything he had done since he assumed his "type" trailed him like a ghost. It's that larger-than-the-role mythic element that distinguishes a star (Gary Cooper, Clint Eastwood) from someone who may be a much greater actor (Fredric March, Robert De Niro). Courageous as he is, De Niro has never pulled us toward himself; he remains his own man, not ours.

According to Basinger, both Tyrone Power and Errol Flynn felt trapped by the types they played. They believed they had talent that they weren't free to develop. Power fought Twentieth Century-Fox to get the role of an ambitious con man in *Nightmare Alley* (1947), and then gave a strong performance in it, so he may have been right. It's a hopeless practice, however, to judge actors by a single performance or by what they wanted to do; Power was generally eager and dull or greasily charming. The trouble with Basinger's strategy of concentrating on lesser stars is that such people are often of lesser interest; and when she exults in the sheer stability of a system which allowed, say, Loretta Young to stay around forever, the book doesn't have much point. To keep us interested in Loretta Young, she needed to make a strong critical case for her films, and she can't, or won't, do that. And maybe it's not possible to do so. The system is a genius when it produces *The Big Sleep,* but it's no more than a system when it produces *The Farmer's Daughter.* Loretta Young won an Oscar in it, yet the movie still strains patience.

By today's standards, the old stars weren't paid very much—$3,000 or $4,000 a week, at the most $7,000, and they almost never got a share of the movie's profits. But these wage slaves were well looked after. The studio functioned for them as business manager, lawyer, publicist, doctor; as exercise room, sexual playpen, and probably a lot else. There's little reason to think that the stars picked up many checks or paid for a lot of their clothes. The smart ones invested in land or art and became rich. Still, the system of paternalist domination was enraging to many. In 1938, Hepburn bought out her contract at RKO rather than appear in a movie called *Mother Carey's Chickens,* and later worked with MGM. Barbara Stanwyck, at various stages in her career, had nonexclusive contracts with three different studios and alternated among them. Cagney walked out on Warners in 1936, formed a company with his brother, failed with the pictures he made independently, and came back to the studio. Bette Davis, often at odds with Jack Warner, also attempted to escape in 1936. She got reeled in after a court case, but she began working with director William Wyler, got much better roles, and became a great actress as well as a star in such pictures as *The Letter* and *The Little Foxes.* However unhappy, the stars who put up with the indignities and stayed in harness accomplished a lot and gave moviegoers enormous pleasure, and who's to say that our pleasure doesn't matter as much as their independence?

The system persisted until 1944, when the seemingly mild Olivia de Havilland refused a role and balked at the notion that the time lost would be added to the end of her contract. Her agent, Lew Wasserman, then discovered an obscure California statute which held that a contract lasting longer than seven years amounted to slavery. When a California court ruled for de Havilland, the contract system began to crumble. In 1948, the courts forced the studios to divest themselves of their theaters. A couple of years later, James Stewart (again with the help of Wasserman) was negotiating profit participation on the Western *Winchester '73,* and actors like Burt Lancaster and Kirk Douglas were beginning to form their own production companies. The modern era had begun. Servitude was over. Independence was at hand.

If the studio system, at its best, was a rational paradise ruled by philistine but occasionally benevolent tyrants, the current system, at its worst, is a semi-chaotic free market in which actors must find their way through a maze of extraordinary opportunities for honor and greed and all the variations in between. A few stars have multi-picture "relationships" with studios, but most of them "float," as Basinger puts it in her Epilogue. They choose their own roles, working as often or as little as they like; their agents negotiate the fees, which may include profit participation as well as salary, and the competition to be top dog is fierce. Most of them have no particular allegiance to any particular studio. Some form their own companies and develop their own properties. They are equally free to create interesting movies and to give in to their worst follies; they may keep screenwriters and other people waiting for years, only to cancel a project in the end. They exercise far greater control of their work, but each movie, begun from scratch, with technicians and members of the cast hired separately, takes much longer to launch and complete; and the enormous rise in production costs (an average of $60 million for a major studio film) has been created, in part, by the staggering increases in what stars are able to demand and receive. A few years ago, twenty million bucks got you Harrison Ford, but you had to pay extra for his cook, his chauffeur, his trainer, and his private plane, fueled and ready to take him home for the weekend. Reese Witherspoon—*Reese Witherspoon!*—recently negotiated a deal to be paid $29 million to act in and produce a movie. But for all her monetary power, is Reese Witherspoon a genuine star or just an ambitious young actress temporarily capable of acing a competitive market?

In the new high-stakes accounting, is a star merely an actor who can get the best money? However crass, the price tags would simplify one's definitions a great deal. But just how much a highly paid star actually contributes to the success of a movie is not so easy to determine. From the industry point of view, Will Smith is the sole actor in Hollywood guaranteed to "open" a movie—that is, to attract at least a $40 million domestic box office gross in the opening weekend of any movie he appears in. Smith earns his $20 million fee. A charmer who can do action (*Independence Day*), comedy-fantasy (*Men in Black*), romance (*Hitch*), and parenthood (*The Pursuit of Happyness*), Smith is a star by any definition. But Chris Tucker, who got $30 million to appear in the rattletrap pop franchise movie *Rush Hour 3*, is not a star; no one will give Tucker that kind of money if he's not rushing. The blockbuster system is at the center of the studios' hold on profitability, yet many of those films, it turns out, don't require stars. Among the thirty-five top-earning films of all time, measured by worldwide theatrical gross receipts (unadjusted for inflation), all but two (*Forrest Gump* and *The Da Vinci Code*) can be classified as spectacle, fantasy, or animation. In these movies, stars may be reduced to burbling voices; they may get shoved aside by scaly creatures, by digital convulsions, or magical columns of light. There weren't any stars in *E.T.* and only minor ones in the *Jurassic Park* cycle. The *Harry Potter* cycle was staffed by the British theater tradition in all its glory, not by Hollywood. Harrison Ford wasn't a star when he appeared in *Star Wars* in 1977, nor was Tobey Maguire at the time of the first *Spider-Man,* in 2002. As everyone knows, the "concept" for a big movie, or the special effects, may be the true star.

But a franchise can certainly propel an actor into stardom—Johnny Depp, say, after his flirtatious, kohl-eyed, twin-bearded turn in the first *Pirates of the Caribbean* movie; or Matt Damon, who has given his nearly wordless role as Jason Bourne an increasing soulfulness, and whose movies, a recent *Forbes* study revealed, earn $29 from all revenue streams (TV and DVD sales as well as theatrical) for every dollar invested in them; or the chin-pointing looker and (also) serious fellow George Clooney, who has his smarty-pants *Ocean's* franchise; or Leonardo DiCaprio, who has no franchise but caused teenage girls to see *Titanic* again and again. DiCaprio was the kind of sexually unthreatening cat-faced boy (TV heartthrob Zac Efron is the latest) that girls love to dream about. Beefed up for Scorsese's *Gangs of New York,* he looked and sounded ludicrous, but he got back on his feet as an art-deco-poster Howard Hughes in Scorsese's *The Aviator* and other movies. These four, along with Tom Hanks and Tom Cruise, have triumphed in the marketplace without the support of a studio contract. Not every one of their movies is a hit, but they've demonstrated earning power, so they now have the freedom to do something unimaginable in 1935—appear in small, intense, off-center films in which they can play sex addicts or losers or anything else that stretches their talents and possibly wins them awards. They can play that part for a fraction of their normal salary at the studio's specialty division or in an independent film. They are stars who can even fail a few times (in commercial terms) without losing their standing. They hold the whip hand. "It's a nice life," a top studio executive said to me ruefully, sounding licked.

Tom Cruise got to this point the old way: He had tiny and supporting roles, and he hit his type in movies like *Top Gun, The Firm, A Few Good Men,* and *Jerry Maguire,* in which he played the same role over and over—a callow young man who has the stuff, the drive, but lacks character. In the course of the movie, he would grow up; he would acquire ethics. Cruise was never an interesting actor, but he parlayed pure energy and a triumphant sense of his own emerging powers, re-created in each movie, into stardom. But for such handsome and ambitious young actors as Colin Farrell, Josh Hartnett, Ewan McGregor, Jude Law, and Orlando Bloom, the way may now be blocked. Seventy years ago, these actors would have been tested in a variety of small roles or in B movies—tested to see whether they could act and whether the audience perked up when they came on-screen. They would have been allowed to grow slowly. Now, with no studio to protect them, they are thrown into big roles in expensive movies, and they're forced to overdraw on themselves before their temperament has found the right shape. They don't know the camera yet, and the camera doesn't always find much in their faces. Blank-eyed beauty in men creates little but audience contempt. If these actors fail, they are quickly dropped, and the media which scattered petals at their feet immediately stomp all over them. Unprotected, they can't find guide rails or progressive steps to success.

Yet people who love the system today say that the market operates ruthlessly but efficiently to create the stars it needs. Well, maybe so, but only if you leave out the development of stars who could make certain kinds of great movies. For instance, market-driven comedies for young male audiences have created a raft of talented buffoons who can play slap-happy guys (Vince Vaughn, Adam Sandler, Will Ferrell, Ben Stiller, Owen Wilson, Luke Wilson, Jim Carrey, Matthew McConaughey, and the Judd Apatow gang), but, apart from Will Smith, DiCaprio, Brad Pitt, Damon, and perhaps Clive Owen or Jake Gyllenhaal, it's hard to think of an actor under forty one could reliably cast in a straight dramatic movie or as a romantic leading man. Ben Affleck and Jude Law are better at projecting weakness than strength. Edward Norton, who has authority and an extraordinary voice, may not want the job of star. (Terrence Howard wants it and with luck will get it—he certainly has the talent.) The paucity of young male dramatic stars means that the large number of brilliant actresses who have emerged in the last few years from mid- or small-budget movies—Cate Blanchett, Charlize Theron, Laura Linney, Hilary Swank, Maria Bello, Naomi Watts—don't necessarily have anyone to team up with. Winslet is hooking up again with her *Titanic* partner DiCaprio in the upcoming adaptation of Richard Yates's novel *Revolutionary Road*.

But it's hard to imagine many possible pairings of male and female actors at the same level of renown. Adam Sandler clearly did not go well with Téa Leoni—a comedienne with the elegance and the daring of Carole Lombard—in the disastrous *Spanglish*. Charlize Theron and Will Ferrell? Naomi Watts and Ben Stiller? You can see the problem. Only minor actresses like Drew Barrymore or Kate Hudson can match up with the male buffoons.

The emphasis on spectacle and comedy has created a disconnect between male and female stars that now makes the return of grown-up dramatic filmmaking, at the big-budget level, virtually impossible to imagine. (The male leads in those small or mid-size movies—Paul Giamatti, Philip Seymour Hoffman, Mark Ruffalo—are not stars but superb character actors.) A star like Gable or Robert Mitchum—a sexual man on-screen—couldn't exist now. There wouldn't be any roles for him. The relentless womanizer appears now only in farce, as a fool to be brought down. And the romantic teams that exalted both members of the team—Gable and Crawford, James Stewart and Margaret Sullavan, Charles Boyer and Claudette Colbert, Fred Astaire and Ginger Rogers, Spencer Tracy and Katharine Hepburn—are also impossible to imagine. Tilting movie production toward families and young audiences has ruled out all kinds of star combinations that once gave enormous pleasure.

Actresses are stepping into fresh territory; they have to, because the old territory has been burned away, and star-making stories are hard to find. Consider that Bette Davis, in her years at Warners, did some of the following: betrayed her lover and died (*Of Human Bondage*); got a brain tumor, went blind, and died (*Dark Victory*); wore a red rather than a virginal white dress in antebellum New Orleans, was humiliated, begged her husband's forgiveness, and then *he* died (*Jezebel*); renounced her lover and took care of his daughter (*Now, Voyager*); brought up another woman's baby (*The Great Lie*). Suffering, renunciation, punishment, and the shuffling of babies played a big part in Davis's career. I intend no mockery: Those were all juicy roles (and *Jezebel*, at least, is a great film), and Davis brought to them her flashing eyes and scalding voice, her mastery of movement and emotional detail, her willingness to be dislikable; she was a truly great and daring movie actress. But roles of that kind have been ruled out by feminism as reactionary, or as embarrassing kitsch, and few actresses will now go near them. They no longer make us cry. The thick, dreamy sensuality of Lana Turner or Rita Hayworth or Kim Novak may be offered now, on a smaller scale, by the diminutive but fleshy Scarlett Johansson, but when Johansson pouts and flirts her way through a picture, she seems like a willing anachronism—a male movie director's delectable toy.

A woman can be selfless now but not self-sacrificing; she can be injured but not helpless. If she's hurt by a man, she takes revenge. Jodie Foster, Ashley Judd, Uma Thurman, Angelina Jolie, and Charlize Theron have played role after role in which they've been pushed too far and have pulled out the knives. Female violence is some sort of step forward in the pop-culture image of women, I guess, but, for an actress, denying so many parts of her temperament in order to be tough all the time may not be much of a gain. The old softness is taboo, but the new hardness may be a trap—a form of exploitation that merely feeds the public's hunger for violent movies. (The male public, that is. It was men, not women, who were excited by Uma Thurman slicing up thirty stooges in *Kill Bill*.) Charlize Theron seems to be selecting roles in which she can play enraged women who give no quarter, which is fine (she's good at it), but it would be crazy for this beautiful woman entirely to reject the lyricism that is the privilege of beauty.

The actresses want independence so they can play strong women, but neither they nor the male stars—initiating their own projects—have better taste in scripts or a shrewder idea about their own talents than did the Hollywood staff producers who made choices for the stars sixty years ago. The studio heads may have been vulgarians and sentimentalists, but some of the men working under them were brilliant at putting movies together. Hal B. Wallis, for instance, who had a long career at Warners, was involved in half the most entertaining movies the studio turned out in the 1930s and 1940s. And someone like Wallis, backed up by the studio, could move quickly. When an actor initiates a project, however, he's responsible for it in a way that no star was in 1946, and he may fuss over it endlessly, going through many writers, many directors, losing the other actors who had initially committed to the film along the way. There are extraordinary actor-initiated triumphs, of course, like Clooney's *Good Night, and Good Luck,* and there will be others in the future, but there's a possible negative side effect to this. The actors and actresses may pass up juicy parts while they're exercising their freedom to dither. Bette Davis complained like hell about the roles Warners imposed on her, but no one could say that, in the end, she didn't give a large number of classic performances. With the exception of Meryl Streep (who doesn't have her own company), American star actresses with all the freedom in the world are not putting together careers as productive as Davis's.

Julia Roberts, just now turning forty, is perhaps the last old-fashioned female star whom audiences wanted to see simply for herself—for her big easy carriage, her beautiful oversized features, her enormous smile which gives way to a racketing laugh. She makes audiences feel good; they want to follow her through a continuous series of episodes in which, so to speak, Julia lends herself now to the part of a prostitute who gets a suave businessman to fall in love with her (*Pretty Woman*), now to a law student who teams up with Denzel Washington to stop terrible people from doing terrible things (*The Pelican Brief*), now to a tough broad taking on a wicked gas-and-electric company (*Erin Brockovich*). In all these roles, Julia moves from point to point in the public narrative of her life. She's imposing without being regal, and the audience could both identify with her trials and aspire to be like her. Nicole Kidman is a comparable talent, but Kidman's career suggests the perverse contradictions of freedom. With a truly valiant generosity, she has worked, at a fraction of her big-movie price, with a variety of young directors, but her choice of material hasn't matched her courage, and she has appeared in too many stinkers like *Fur*. She hasn't quite created, for the audience, a narrative of her life in public. Her mold is indistinct; she needs a myth-making role to reclaim stardom.

The success of *The Devil Wears Prada* should have indicated to Hollywood at least one way of creating roles that both young and older actresses can *play*. Out in the world, women work hard. They have fights with their bosses, they have love affairs on the job, they commit or prevent crimes in corporate boardrooms, they get morally compromised or fired or promoted. Why not unleash Roberts and Kidman, or Cate Blanchett, with her pale-fire intensity, or Charlize Theron, Kate Winslet, or Rachel

McAdams into the morally complicated corporate, financial, and political worlds, where they can misbehave or have a ball and, in the process, claw their way to new or fresh stardom?

Of course movie stars still exist. What is the ungovernable Russell Crowe if not a star? He's like King Kong breaking his chains. But there are fewer stars than in the past, and in many ways they've come down in the world. They are paid more but valued less. Their private lives are not gushed over but chewed to death. Manners, dress, and language have lost what was left of formality—expensive casual is the aspiration for stars and everyone else. Sharon Stone was the last star to carry herself in public like Crawford, but she couldn't find roles equal to her pretensions. Even before the celebrity machine made stars *the same as us,* many of them were learning to cultivate modesty. Henry Fonda and James Stewart were reserved, even dignified, in public. But stars like Tom Hanks—princes of the democratic realm—are downright friendly; they don't want to lord it over us lest we knock them off their low-rise pedestal. In some ways, movie stars now have a lesser hold on the public's imagination than the actors creating a sustained characterization in a TV series. After watching *The West Wing* for a few weeks, I would fall into conversation in my head with Bradley Whitford, the actor who plays Josh Lyman, the White House deputy chief of staff. Whitford, who has a high forehead with lots of blond-auburn hair, seems either preoccupied or hyper-aggressive. His Josh is smart, impulsive, ill-tempered, sometimes successful in getting his way, sometimes not, and I found myself arguing with Whitford, roughing him up for his mistakes, urging him to push harder on some policies. I even imagined myself in his job. Who has that kind of relation with a movie star?

They are not dead gods; not yet. We just don't need them as desperately as we once did. They may be shop-soiled goods, but we're not ready to say goodbye to them. Stars figured not only in the moral life of Anne Gordon, they figured in the erotic life of an urban poet like Frank O'Hara, who, sitting in a theater, insisted that "the blood in my pants mounts to the stars/ as I ponder the silver square." At the movies, loneliness in the anonymous crowd liberated fantasy and a sense of possession. Manuel Puig's 1976 novel *The Kiss of the Spider Woman* was made into a movie in 1985 in which the hero, Molina (William Hurt), a gay hairdresser in an Argentine prison, brings solace to his cell mate, a stern Marxist revolutionary (Raul Julia), by telling him the story of a 1940s-kitsch Hollywood film, which we then see: Sonia Braga plays a French chanteuse who falls in love with a Nazi. In that same year, 1985, Woody Allen made *The Purple Rose of Cairo*, in which Mia Farrow, a dreamy unemployed waitress and lonely wife in Depression-era New Jersey, goes to the same movie over and over until, finally, one of the characters (Jeff Daniels) steps down from the frame and enters her life; he turns out to be real sweet. Each fable, a response to feelings of entrapment, is about a relation to a movie star so intense that the boundaries between the screen and the moviegoer collapse. Growing up as Puig did in the Argentine sticks (where Hayworth wasn't just a beautiful woman but a ray of hope), or waiting out the American Depression, was tough; the movies kept people alive. By 1985, a more prosperous time, we were already engaging in nostalgia for nostalgia: Star worship became a memorializing rather than a fresh passion.

American culture is now frantically demanding. Our attention is split among many kinds of media, and we may not want to invest too much dream time in movie stars. After all, the star system operates in many areas of American life: In a teenager's inner sanctum, the wall is more likely to be postered with musicians and athletes than with movie stars. The rappers, basketball players, and even the ice-skaters are closer to profane liberty, closer to the full freedom of the body in violence or beauty, than the actors.

The actors who are stars by any definition—Smith, Depp, Damon, and DiCaprio; Meryl Streep; George Clooney and Denzel Washington; Russell Crowe and Julia Roberts—have become rarities. The older performers in that group have the size and strength, the sheer imposingness of the old stars, but the system, structured as it is now, isn't going to produce many more of them. (Daniel Day-Lewis, arguably the greatest actor of his generation, can only occasionally bring himself to act in movies.) But perhaps we don't need more than a few at the moment. If you include such actors as Morgan Freeman, Sean Penn, and Tommy Lee Jones; Nicole Kidman, Julianne Moore, Laura Linney, and Hilary Swank;

Téa Leoni, Cate Blanchett, and Kate Winslet; Don Cheadle, Clive Owen, and Daniel Craig; Paul Giamatti and Philip Seymour Hoffman, you have as varied a collection of talent as any assembled in Hollywood's history. American acting has probably never been much better than it is now, so it would be virtuous, and even shrewd, perhaps, to say goodbye to star adoration and simply glory in talent. Some of the smart young actors seem to be avoiding stardom, and their hesitation suggests that the celebrity racket has made their lives hell and that worship has become unclean. For us, however, virtue is its own reward in life, not in a movie theater. We are lost. Star worship transcends movie technique and directorial prowess; it transcends art; it's the wicked or foolish indulgence that once made moviegoing a universal habit, and so, despite every discouragement, there's little to do but wait like suitors with hat in hand for movie economics and American culture to yield a fresh round of stars so we can become fools all over again.

The New Yorker, *October 22, 2007; revised 2011*

PART FOUR / **GENRES**

INTRODUCTION

Nothing might seem more innocuous than high school movies and chick flicks, yet, in their frazzled, fumbling, often candied way, they get at both happy dreams and nightmares—school as battle-field, as collective trauma (well, at least for the people who make these movies); a single woman's life as work, friendship, shopping, and also as one potential humiliation after another. I wanted to write these pieces because no one else seemed to be taking either of the two genres very seriously. Westerns, gangster movies, film noir, horror, science fiction fantasy—these were all subjects for learned commentary, for appreciation, for endless talk, for cults. Dozens of books have been written about each of these genres. But kids and young women in the big city aren't worth much more than a quick summary and a joke, and then a rapid move on to something allegedly more serious. Romantic comedy, of course, has been much written about, and often mourned over, but Judd Apatow's *Knocked Up* was something new—the first real break in patterns that have lasted centuries. The following pieces are my attempt to locate the resonant myth buried in convention, the emotional appeal of artifice, the movie love lost in routine response.

HIGH SCHOOL MOVIES

The most hated young woman in America is a blonde—well, sometimes a redhead or a brunette, but usually a blonde. She has big hair flipped into a swirl of gold at one side of her face or arrayed in a sultry mane, like the magnificent pile of a 1940s movie star. She's tall and slender, with a waist as supple as a willow, but she's dressed in awful, spangled taste: Her outfits could have been put together by warring catalogues. And she has a mouth on her, a low, slatternly tongue that devastates other kids with such insults as "You're vapor, you're Spam!" and "Do I look like Mother Teresa? If I did, I probably wouldn't mind talking to the geek squad." She has two or three friends exactly like her, and together they dominate their realm—the American high school as it appears in recent teen movies. They are like wicked princesses, who enjoy the misery of their subjects. Her coronation, of course, is the senior prom, when she expects to be voted "most popular" by her class. But, though she may be popular, she is certainly not liked, so her power is something of a mystery. She is beautiful and rich, yet in the end she is preeminent because . . . she is preeminent, a position she works to maintain with Joan Crawford–like tenacity. Everyone is afraid of her; that's why she's popular.

She has a male counterpart. He's usually a football player, muscular but dumb, with a face like a beer mug and only two ways of speaking—in a conspiratorial whisper, to a friend, or in a drill sergeant's sudden bellow. If her weapon is the snub, his is the lame but infuriating prank—the can of Sprite emptied into a knapsack, or something sticky, creamy, or adhesive deposited in a locker. Sprawling and dull in class, he comes alive in the halls and in the cafeteria. He hurls people against lockers; he spits, pours, and sprays; he has a projectile relationship with food. As the crown prince, he claims the best-looking girl for himself, though in a perverse display of power he may invite an outsider or an awkward girl—a "dog"—to the prom, setting her up for some special humiliation. When we first see him, he is riding high, and virtually the entire school colludes in his tyranny. No authority figure—no teacher or administrator—dares correct him.

Thus the villains of the recent high school movies. Not every American teen movie has these two characters, and not every social queen or jock shares all the attributes I've mentioned. (Occasionally, a handsome, dark-haired athlete can be converted to sweetness and light.) But as genre figures these two types are hugely familiar; that is, they are a common memory, a collective trauma, or at least a social and erotic fantasy. Such movies of the past year as *Disturbing Behavior, She's All That, 10 Things I Hate About You,* and *Never Been Kissed* depend on them as stock figures. And they may have been figures in the minds of the Littleton shooters, Eric Harris and Dylan Klebold, who imagined they were living in a school like the one in so many of these movies—a poisonous system of status, snobbery, and exclusion.

Do genre films reflect reality? Or are they merely a set of conventions that refer to other films? Obviously, they wouldn't survive if they didn't provide emotional satisfaction to the people who make them and to the audiences who watch them. A half century ago, we didn't need to see ten Westerns a year in order to learn that the West got settled. We needed to see it settled ten times a year in order to provide ourselves with the emotional gratifications of righteous violence. By drawing his gun only when he was provoked, and in the service of the good, the classic Western hero transformed the gross tangibles of the expansionist drive (land, cattle, gold) into a principle of moral order. The gangster, by contrast, is a figure of chaos, a modern, urban person, and in the critic Robert Warshow's formulation he functions as a discordant element in an American society devoted to a compulsively "positive" outlook. When the gangster dies, he cleanses viewers of their own negative feelings.

High school movies are also full of unease and odd, mixed-up emotions. They may be flimsy in conception; they may be shot in lollipop colors, garlanded with mediocre pop scores, and cast with goofy young actors trying to make an impression. Yet this most commercial and frivolous of genres harbors a grievance against the world. It's a very specific grievance, quite different from the restless anger of such 1950s adolescent-rebellion movies as *The Wild One,* in which someone asks Marlon Brando's biker "What are you rebelling against?" and the biker replies, "What have you got?" The 1950s teen outlaw was against anything that adults considered sacred. But no movie teenager now revolts against adult authority, for the simple reason that adults have no authority. Teachers are rarely more than a minimal, exasperated presence, administrators get turned into a joke, arid parents are either absent or distantly benevolent. It's a teen world, bounded by school, mall, and car, with occasional moments set in the fast food outlets where the kids work, or in the kids' upstairs bedrooms, with their pinups and rack stereo systems. The enemy is not authority; the enemy is other teens and the social system that they impose on one another.

The bad feeling in these movies may strike grown-ups as peculiar. After all, from a distance American kids appear to be having it easy these days. The teen audience is facing a healthy job market; at home, their parents are stuffing the den with computers and the garage with a bulky SUV.* But most teens aren't thinking about the future job market. Lost in the eternal swoon of late adolescence, they're thinking about their identity, their friends, and their clothes. Adolescence is the present-tense moment in American life. Identity and status are fluid: Abrupt, devastating reversals are always possible. (In a teen movie, a guy who swallows a bucket of cafeteria coleslaw can make himself a hero in an instant.) In these movies, accordingly, the senior prom is the equivalent of the shoot-out at the O.K. Corral; it's the moment when one's worth as a human being is settled at last. In the rather pedestrian new comedy *Never Been Kissed,* Drew Barrymore, as a twenty-five-year-old newspaper reporter, goes back to high school pretending to be a student, and immediately falls into her old, humiliating pattern of trying to impress the good-looking rich kids. Helplessly, she pushes for approval, and even gets herself chosen prom queen before finally coming to her senses. She finds it nearly impossible to let go.

Genre films dramatize not what happens but how things feel—the emotional coloring of memory. They fix subjectivity into fable. At actual schools,

---

* This was written in 1999. No one would say the same today.

there is no unitary system of status; there are many groups to be a part of, many places to excel (or fail to excel), many avenues of escape and self-definition. And often the movies, too, revel in the arcana of high school cliques. In last summer's *Disturbing Behavior,* a veteran student lays out the cafeteria ethnography for a newcomer: Motorheads, Blue Ribbons, Skaters, Micro-Geeks ("drug of choice: Stephen Hawking's *A Brief History of Time* and a cup of jasmine tea on Saturday night"). Subjectively, though, the social system in *Disturbing Behavior* (a high school version of *The Stepford Wives*) and in the other movies still feels coercive and claustrophobic: Humiliation is the most vivid emotion of youth, so in memory it becomes the norm.

The movies try to turn the tables. The kids who cannot be the beautiful ones, or make out with them, or avoid being insulted by them—these are the heroes of the teen movies, the third in the trio of character types. The female outsider is usually an intellectual or an artist. (She scribbles in a diary, she draws or paints.) Physically awkward, she walks like a seal crossing a beach, and is prone to drop her books and dither in terror when she stands before a handsome boy. Her clothes, which ignore mall fashion, scandalize the social queens. Like them, she has a tongue, but she's tart and grammatical, tending toward feminist pungency and precise diction. She may mask her sense of vulnerability with sarcasm or with Plathian rue (she's stuck in the bell jar), but even when she lashes out she can't hide her craving for acceptance.

The male outsider, her friend, is usually a mass of stuttering or giggling sexual gloom: He wears shapeless clothes; he has an undeveloped body, either stringy or shrimpy; he's sometimes a Jew (in these movies, still the generic outsider). He's also brilliant, but in a morose, preoccupied way that suggests masturbatory absorption in some arcane system of knowledge. In a few special cases, the outsider is not a loser but a disengaged hipster, either saintly or satanic. (Christian Slater has played this role a couple of times.) This outsider wears black and keeps his hair long, and he knows how to please women. He sees through everything, so he's ironic by temperament and genuinely indifferent to the opinion of others—a natural aristocrat, who transcends the school's contemptible status system. There are whimsical variations on the outsider figure, too. In the recent *Rushmore,* an obnoxious teen hero, Max Fischer (Jason Schwartzman), runs the entire school: He can't pass his courses but he's a dynamo at extracurricular activities, with a knack for staging extraordinary events. He's a con man, a fund-raiser, an entrepreneur—in other words, a contemporary artist.

In fact, the entire genre, which combines self-pity and ultimate vindication, might be called "Portrait of the Filmmaker as a Young Nerd." Who can doubt where Hollywood's twitchy, nearsighted writers and directors ranked—or feared they ranked—on the high school totem pole? They are still angry, though occasionally the target of their resentment goes beyond the jocks and cheerleaders of their youth. Consider this anomaly: The young actors and models on the covers of half the magazines published in this country, the shirtless men with chests like burnished shields, the girls smiling, glowing, tweezed, full-lipped, full-breasted (but not too full), and with skin so honeyed that it seems lacquered—these are the physical ideals embodied by the villains of the teen movies. The social queens and jocks, using their looks to dominate others, represent an American barbarism of beauty. Isn't it possible that the detestation of them in teen movies is a veiled strike at the entire abs-hair advertising culture, with its unobtainable glories of perfection? A critic of consumerism might even see a spark of revolt in these movies. But only a spark. My guess is that these films arise from remembered hurts which then get recast in symbolic form. For instance, a surprising number of the outsider heroes have no mother. Mom has died or run off with another man; her child, only half loved, is ill equipped for the emotional pressures of school. The motherless child, of course, is a shrewd commercial ploy that makes a direct appeal to the members of the audience, many of whom may feel like outsiders, too, and unloved, or not loved enough, or victims of some prejudice or exclusion. But the motherless child also has powers, and will someday be a success—an artist; a screenwriter. It's the wound and the bow all over again, in cargo pants.

As the female nerd attracts the attention of the handsomest boy in the senior class, the teen movie turns into a myth of social reversal—a Cinderella fantasy. Initially, his interest in her may be part of a stunt or a trick: He is leading her on, perhaps at the urging of his queenly girlfriend. But his gaze lights her up, and we see how attractive she really is. Will she fulfill the eternal American fantasy that you can vault up the class system by removing your specs? She wants her prince, and by degrees she wins him over, not just with her looks but with her superior nature, her essential goodness. In the male version of the Cinderella trip, a few years go by, and a pale little nerd (we see him at a reunion) has become rich. All that poking around with chemicals paid off. Max Fischer, of *Rushmore*, can't miss being richer than Warhol.

So the teen movie is wildly ambivalent. It may attack the consumerist ethos that produces winners and losers, but in the end it confirms what it is attacking. The girls need the seal of approval conferred by the converted jocks; the nerds need money and a girl. Perhaps it's no surprise that the outsiders can be validated only by the people who ostracized them. But let's not be too schematic: The outsider who joins the system also modifies it, opens it up to the creative power of social mobility, makes it bend and laugh, and perhaps this turn of events is not so different from the way things work in the real world, where merit and achievement stand a good chance of trumping appearance. The irony of the Littleton shootings is that Klebold and Harris, who were both proficient computer heads, seemed to have forgotten how the plot turns out. If they had held on for a few years they might have been working at a hip software company, or have started their own business, while the jocks who oppressed them would probably have wound up selling insurance or used cars. That's the one unquestionable social truth the teen movies reflect: Geeks rule.

There is, of course, a menacing subgenre, in which the desire for revenge turns bloody. Thirty-one years ago, Lindsay Anderson's semi-surreal *If. . . .* was set in an oppressive, class-ridden English boarding school where a group of rebellious students drive the school population out into a courtyard and open fire on them with machine guns. In Brian De Palma's 1976 masterpiece *Carrie*, the pale, repressed heroine, played by Sissy Spacek, is courted at last by a handsome boy but gets violated—doused with pig's blood—just as she is named prom queen. Stunned but far from powerless, Carrie uses her telekinetic powers to set the room afire and burn down the school. *Carrie* is the primal school movie, so wildly lurid and funny that it exploded the clichés of the genre before the genre was quite set: The heroine may be a wrathful avenger, but the movie, based on a Stephen King book, was clearly a grinning-gargoyle fantasy. So, at first, was *Heathers,* in which Christian Slater's satanic outsider turns out to be a true devil. He and his girlfriend (played by a very young Winona Ryder) begin gleefully knocking off the rich, nasty girls and the jocks, in ways so patently absurd that their revenge seems a mere wicked dream. I think it's unlikely that these movies had a direct effect on the actions of the Littleton shooters, but the two boys would surely have recognized the emotional world of *Heathers* and *Disturbing Behavior* as their own. It's a place where feelings of victimization join fantasy, and you experience the social elites as so powerful that you must either become them or kill them.

But enough. It's possible to make teen movies that go beyond these fixed polarities—insider and outsider, blond-bitch queen and hunch-shouldered nerd. In Amy Heckerling's 1995 comedy *Clueless,* the big blonde played by Alicia Silverstone is a Rodeo Drive clotheshorse who is nonetheless possessed of extraordinary virtue. Freely dispensing advice and help, she's almost ironically good—a designing goddess with a cell phone. The movie offers a sunshiny satire of Beverly Hills affluence, which it sees as both absurdly swollen and generous in spirit. The most original of the teen comedies, *Clueless* casts away self-pity. So does *Romy and Michele's High School Reunion* (1997), in which two gabby, lovable friends, played by Mira Sorvino and Lisa Kudrow, review the banalities of their high school experience so knowingly that they might be criticizing the teen movie genre itself. And easily the best American film of the year so far is Alexander Payne's *Election,* a high school movie that inhabits a different aesthetic and moral world altogether from the rest of these pictures. *Election* shreds everyone's fantasies and illusions in a vision of high school that is bleak but supremely just. The movie's villain, an overachieving girl (Reese Witherspoon) who runs for class president, turns out to be its covert heroine, or, at least, its most poignant character. A cross between Pat and Dick Nixon, she's a lower-middle-class striver who works like crazy and never wins anyone's love. Even when she's on top, she feels excluded. Her loneliness is produced not by malicious cliques but by her own implacable will, a condition of the spirit that may be as comical and tragic as it is mysterious. *Election* escapes all the clichés; it graduates into art.

CHICK FLICKS

It's rare that one can find a definitive moment in movies, but there's no doubt about this one: The American cinema hit bottom, absolute bottom, in February 2009, in a single astonishing shot. In *Bride Wars,* Kate Hudson and Anne Hathaway play two lifelong New York friends whose weddings, through an error, get scheduled for the same day at the Plaza Hotel. Neither wants to change her "venue," so each tries, for months, to destroy the other's wedding party. Hathaway sends Hudson succulent boxes of candy so she'll gain too much weight to fit into her $10,000 Vera Wang dress. Hudson secretly pours a dark color into Hathaway's tanning mix, which turns her skin orange. The two women become bratty, petty, snitty, underhanded, vicious. On the fateful day at the Plaza, Hathaway tackles Hudson, and they wrestle on the floor. That's when the shot arrives: Billowing masses of wedding-dress tulle fill most of the screen; the two women, at the bottom of the frame, might be enraged sea creatures sending up a gorgeous cloud of nacreous froth. The moment is so enchanting visually (Frederick Elmes, shot it) and so ugly emotionally that it came to represent, for me, what has happened in chick flicks at their worst in recent years—a joining of great technique to cruddy, hostile, low feeling.

You have to fight off disbelief that you're seeing stuff like this on the screen. *Bride Wars,* it turns out, was not the only chick flick fiasco in the winter of 2009. In *Confessions of a Shopaholic,* women at a sale, trying to get their hands on a pair of red Gucci boots, knock each other around and wind up, again, wrestling on the floor. The heroine, one Rebecca Bloomwood, played by Isla Fisher, fakes her way into a good job while hiding her addiction to shoes, dresses, and scarves, which she caresses, in department store boutiques, as if they were part of a lover's body. All of this, of course, is meant to be satirical: Rebecca, who has built up $16,000 in credit card debt, lives amid a rubble of goods at home; she's a neurotic mess. She needs to be saved, and, eventually, she will be, by Hugh Dancy's debonair magazine editor. But through most of the movie, Rebecca fakes her way through things and hides from a snarling debt collector, a guy presented as a vicious pest. One wonders: A debt collector—is there any work more awful? After a while, you begin to feel sorry for him. He's just doing a job. Rebecca is the jerk in the movie.

Made by Hollywood pros, men and women together, these movies might have been created by barroom meatheads jeering at women as greedy little beasts—dishonest, consumption-mad, hysterical, empty-headed little fools. In *He's Just Not That Into You,* another release from the winter of 2009, the heroine, played by Ginnifer Goodwin, is an anxious single who latches convulsively on to men after a single dinner date and then suffers the humiliation of not hearing from them. The movie is set among a network of Baltimore friends who stay in touch by cell phone (receiving a call, not sex, is the real turn-on for these people), and the theme of the picture, captured in the rug-pulling title, is that women, mis-reading the signs, can't accept that a guy who won't call simply doesn't give a damn. Quite a subject for a movie. It's a sitcom anecdote at best: *Sex and the City,* in its jaunty TV version (which I'm including in the chick flicks genre), would have treated the telephone issue with a few quick jokes. Samantha would then have slept with some guy after calling *him,* and a comment by Carrie would have wrapped up the entire affair in under twenty-five minutes. *Into You,* however, was an interminable 129 minutes and was fleshed out with an A-list cast, including Ben Affleck and Jennifer Aniston, who, in all fairness, seem like Lionel and Diana Trilling, or perhaps Edmund Wilson and Mary McCarthy, compared to the others. The rest of the characters aren't into *anything.* The inanity of the talk is frightening.

It may seem pointless to get into a huff about these pictures, since no one expected much out of them in the first place. But why doesn't anyone expect much out of them? What in the world has happened to funny movies about women? Twenty years ago, Garry Marshall, kicking off the current cycle of chick flicks, directed *Pretty Woman* with such confidence and verve that one thought at the time that the genre might bloom into a major form of entertainment. *Bridget Jones's Diary,* from 2001, was bright and chipper, and, in 2006, David Frankel's *The Devil Wears Prada* had an irresistible drive and a shrewd grasp of comic detail. Nora Ephron's recent *Julie & Julia* is a real charmer and stirring, too, in its gentle way. But those good pictures shine like Waterford crystal in a pile of plastic party plates. In general, the chick flick genre, as Nancy Franklin in *The New Yorker,* and Manohla Dargis in *The New York Times,* have said, is drizzled in condescension—toward the material itself on the part of filmmakers, and toward the audience, too. The very phrase "chick flicks," like its big sister, "chick lit" (many of the recent movies are based on popular books), has the cozily patronizing sound of marketing specialists trading anecdotes at a hotel bar. Horror movies are widely enjoyed as a dirty pleasure, but they're also analyzed and compared with scholarly zeal; sci-fi spectacles and deafening video game derivatives get treated in some quarters as religious texts. Any film director who mucks around with a comic book will have a hundred thousand geeks slamming him on the Internet. But chick flicks are largely conceived, and assessed, as a market phenomenon that ebbs and flows and is otherwise of zero interest.

Part of the problem obviously is that men have very little curiosity about them. The audience for chick flicks is estimated at 70 percent female. Not to put too fine a point on it, the genre usually inspires in men something like the "animal repugnance" that Mark Twain said he felt toward Jane Austen's novels. The repugnance, of course, is produced by immersion in a movie world in which men may be treated as mere appendages, like shoes, or like a power screwdriver that doesn't always work properly.

A male critic entering the field of chick flicks wonders if he won't get tripped up by the La Perla camisoles lying on the floor. Doesn't the genre's obsession with clothes make it a mere extension of the designer-fashion and wedding industries? Well, yes, in part, but leaving it at that is much too easy. Gangster and detective movies probably sold fedoras, every thriller sells cars and guns, but no one suggests we shouldn't write seriously about such movies. Shoulder arms, men! A movie genre—any movie genre—is not just a recurring group of stories, characters, and decors; it's also a set of conventions that say something (perhaps more than does a freshly created, individual work of art) about the way we live—about what we want, what we enjoy, and what we fear. Genre films turn desire and fear into fable. If the movies didn't satisfy those emotional needs, the same picture (with variants) wouldn't get made over and over. Part of the answer to why so little is expected of chick flicks may lie in the pleasure the movies give exactly as they are—the anxieties they engage and propitiate, the hungers they satisfy. And the way to make them better may lie in open recognition of the enormous social change that made the current cycle possible in the first place.

A chick flick is built around a heroine, usually young, who is stumbling through a crisis of some sort. The crisis is worked out as comedy: It may be momentous in the heroine's life, but, in the grand scheme of things, it rates somewhere below plague and floods. The heroine will not undergo grief or lose a home. She will, however, undergo trials and humiliations— or at least excruciating moments of embarrassment. And she will triumph in the end, triumph by making a choice—one man or another, one friend or another, one way of life or another. However much she gets knocked around, however rattled she may seem at times, she possesses what academics, economists, and lawyers call "agency." She chooses, she acts; she is not simply acted upon. Chick flicks are always about a young woman learning who she is, what she wants, and what she needs.

Men are around, but they're never quite at the center of the story, and that distance is what sets off a chick flick from a romantic comedy. In *Notting Hill*, Julia Roberts (essentially playing herself) is charmed by Hugh Grant's mild London bookseller, and the two of them become equals. So are Katherine Heigl and Seth Rogen in *Knocked Up*—she has beauty, he has a crude sort of smarts, an annoying distribution of qualities, I admit, but at least it works as a balance. Both movies are romantic comedies. In *The Proposal*, cranky Sandra Bullock may be the office superior of the much younger Ryan Reynolds, but sexual attraction levels them. Another romantic comedy. But if the romantic story is dominated by the woman's point of view, by a woman's emotions and desires, it's a chick flick. *Bridget Jones's Diary* is narrated by Renée Zellweger's anxious Bridget as she passes back and forth between a witty bounder (Hugh Grant) and an honorable stiff (Colin Firth). In *Legally Blonde*, various men struggle to grab on to Reese Witherspoon's trailing scarves as she flies through Harvard Law. Both are chick flicks. The girl rules.

The most obvious thing to say about this heroine is that with very rare exceptions she's single. She may be looking for a guy, obsessed with a guy; she may have a married lover, or a persistent ex-boyfriend, or a husband who has left (as in *Waiting to Exhale* and *The First Wives Club*, with its angry older heroines). But she doesn't have a good man who's directly and unequivocally devoted to her. Whatever her troubles, however, she lives without the sexual constraints and economic woes that pinned down earlier generations of women in movies. There is no poverty in chick flicks. (No one would call Debra Granik's back-country, dirt-poor *Bone* duo—*Down to the Bone* with Vera Farmiga and *Winter's Bone* with Jennifer Lawrence—chick flicks. Those two movies are serious dramas starring women.) The heroine of a chick flick will not be punished for having sex with a man, or many men. She will not suffer the injuries of class. And, with very few exceptions (two of the women deep into the six-year run of *Sex and the City*), she doesn't have children, the cause of so much anguish and sacrifice for stern, wounded Bette Davis and neurotic, anxious Joan Crawford, whose characters gave up their children, or gave up their lovers for children, or lived their entire lives to support their children, and so on. Childless, the heroine is also, in most cases, parentless—if they exist at all, parents are rarely important in these movies.

The heroine is actually a kind of orphan, though, unlike the orphan heroes of folk tales or Victorian fiction, she lives within a fortress of friends. In the second-rate, obvious, but often funny comedy *The House Bunny,* Anna Faris plays an actual orphan who becomes a Playboy Bunny. A centerfold beckons, but she's suddenly kicked out of Hef's Mansion, and she becomes mentor to a group of overweight, pierced, left-anarchist nerds at a sorority house at a Los Angeles university. "The eyes are the nipples of the face," she tells them, teaching the girls to be hot. The orphan is no longer alone. To turn a Bunny into a person it takes a sorority. . Friendship, as much as romance, is at the center of chick flicks. Women have discovered each other—which may be part of the reason men are so turned off by these movies.

Chick flicks are set in the handsomest parts of London, New York, Chicago, and Los Angeles, where the streets are clean, the parks free of trash, the storefronts gleaming, the food shops bursting with pomegranates, brie, and asparagus. It's an idealized city of pleasure—a sumptuary and gustatory city. The urban environment, purged of rawness and power, has been transformed (even outdoors) into a crowded, big boutique. As in a department store, the interior lighting is uniformly bright. (Noirish shadows do not add their morose moods to chick flicks.) You have to see the goods, even when crammed into the bursting closet of an apartment. Mistress of the city, the heroine usually works in the glamour occupations—journalism, fashion, art, publishing, public relations, law—and, much of the time, she lives in a kind of party world of openings, gallery events, clubs, bars, and, of course, endless brunch.

Independent, single, but not alone, the heroine works, she has money, or at least buying power. There are few bohemian women in chick flicks, and no artists or ascetics; the atmosphere is generally corporate, the mobility upward, the heroine a bold integer of consumer confidence. In all, this heroine is a descendant of Helen Gurley Brown's invention of the early 1960s, the avid, man-hunting *Cosmo* girl. But she's better educated than the *Cosmo* girl and makes more money; she also eats better, dresses better, and has better sex. At least she's not obsessed with eighty-three ways of pleasing men in bed. She expects that a man will please *her,* and, if he does not, she will tell her friends—an implied threat. The controlling "male gaze," a familiar bugaboo in feminist film theory about classic Hollywood movies, has now been reversed; chick flicks are about the female gaze, and, gathered in groups and comparing notes, the women singe the fat of male conceit. Men may be longed after, but they may also be publicly judged as promiscuous, sweet-talking sex hustlers, sticks with no souls, slavering jerks; they can be forgetful, unreliable, condescending, dishonest; they have a stunning inability to hear what women are saying. "Most of them are deaf," as Whitney Houston says in *Waiting to Exhale.*

Since the *Cosmo* girl appeared, the sexual power game has shifted, if not quite in the heroine's favor, at least in her direction. For one thing, the shame of being single has vanished—a social change which, it turns out, makes some people uneasy. *Sex and the City* was created by openly gay men (Darren Star and Michael Patrick King, adapting Candace Bushnell's material), and, when the show got under way, in 1998, straight men who hated the show sometimes said that the four heroines seemed less like women than like male homosexuals. They objectified men, they slept around; Samantha even cruised. But this "insight" now seems a canard; it depends on fixed notions of sexual behavior—that all gay men want multiple partners, that women are always monogamous. It underestimates the variety of women's sexual experience in the last thirty years or so. It sounds more like an expression of panic than criticism. As *Sex and the City* went on, troubles, both real and absurd, piled up for the four heroines, but the early episodes radiated an extraordinary pleasure in freedom. No one had ever seen single women quite so happy on-screen before. In its nattering, shoe-worshipping way, the series was a revolution. No wonder it irritated some men so much.

Chick flicks have an odd, neglectful, surly relation to what made all this possible. The feminists of the late 1960s and early 1970s beat down the doors of law and corporate offices, universities, and hospitals, and women began pouring in and making good money. You will hear almost nothing of this political victory in the movies. Feminism in its theoretical, anatomical, professional, and hectoring form is anathema in Hollywood. What we get instead is the woman warrior—kick-ass feminism in the ferocity of the heroines played by Charlize Theron, in Uma Thurman's laying waste to roomfuls of men in Tarantino's inane *Kill Bill* movies, in Angelina Jolie voguing and nut kicking her way past male patsies in picture after picture. Feminism functions in chick flicks as a necessary but passé and slightly embarrassing mentor; the movies have buried what now is considered a bore.

In bad chick flicks, women may work, but work is often dramatized with no more than a nod. Much of the time, work is represented as talking on a cell phone (this may be true, of course, in male-centered films as well). One liberation, however, that chick flicks explicitly celebrate is the unashamed survival of a girl in the soul of a corporate woman. That's the source of the comedy in *Legally Blonde*. Reese Witherspoon's Elle Woods, who appears to live inside a gift box—everything in her life is pink, fluffy, super-nice—drives right through the stern male keepers of the law, both professors and students, by drawing on such explicitly female qualities as intuition, empathy, and common sense. Elle is very happy as a girly woman. *Legally Blonde* turns the tables on feminism, using it and then trumping it: A woman can be a lawyer and a flouncing girl at the same time. The same writing team—Karen McCullah Lutz and Kirsten Smith—also wrote *The House Bunny*, in which Anna Faris is a dumb bunny (literally) and an inspirational leader at the same time. Feminism is the inspiration, the blond super-female girl-woman the product. Lutz and Smith eat their chocolate sampler and have it, too.

The women in *Sex and the City* and Elle Woods in *Legally Blonde* are exceptions in their contentment. The heroine of a chick flick is often dissatisfied—with her guy, with not having a guy, with herself, with her clothes, with her career, with something. A woman who just wanted to stay the same forever, like the group of bonged-out male buffoons in *Knocked Up*, or the beached young men in the movies derived from Nick Hornby novels (*High Fidelity, About a Boy, Fever Pitch*)—such a woman could never become the heroine of a chick flick. Even in her most hapless moments, the heroine is trying to arrive somewhere. She's a Cinderella who will never eat ashes—she wants to remake herself. At the least, she throws herself into a struggle to look good—a terrific activity of plucking, waxing, mud treating, treadmilling, downward-facing-dogging, often shown in a rapid montage, like the scenes of Rocky pounding a side of beef and running up the steps of the Philadelphia Museum of Art. There are daily exertions (a quick tug of hose and boots in the morning, seen in fragmented close-ups), and there is also the Makeover, in which a frump gets turned, by application of money, into a princess—farcically, in the case of the snarling, ketchup-fingered Sandra Bullock, who falls into the soft hands of disdainful Michael Caine in *Miss Congeniality;* classically, in *Pretty Woman* (1990), one of the ur-texts of the genre.

In *Pretty Woman,* the tale of a prostitute's sudden rise to respectability, Julia Roberts gets undressed and slips into a huge bubble bath, first by herself, then with Richard Gere. But getting *dressed*—that's her real triumph. Severe-minded viewers, who dismiss the importance of clothes in these movies with a few tough sociological aperçus about consumption and the modern single woman, should at least notice that, in *Pretty Woman,* clothes mark the stages of social and even moral elevation. There may be a touch of condescension in the way Gere's sugar daddy plays Pygmalion, dressing Roberts up so he can show her off, but I think you would have to be a prig not to enjoy her leaving a snobby shop, on Rodeo Drive, with a Cerruti bagged and held in triumph. Julia Roberts, with her loose, shambling, cowhand's walk—her touch of commonness and swagger—became a superstar by putting on a red gown and a diamond-and-ruby necklace and turning into a stunner. She combined shyness, wonder, nerves, and frank enjoyment of luxury. That enormous smile, and the cackle that burst out of her, marked the elation of an actress who knew, in her early twenties, that both men and women enjoyed looking at her because it made them feel good.

Pretty Woman may be the ultimate Cinderella fantasy—a candied, money-driven fable of deliverance from drab service through the intervention of a moneyed prince. But it's so likable and funny that it became a kind of universal dream of self-realization. Clothes make the woman; or rather, clothes allow her true nature to come out. She's not a whore at heart, she's an intelligent, lost girl who finds a man capable of appreciating her. Sex is the down payment; money and clothes seal the deal; soul is the shape of the happiness that results.

The Devil Wears Prada (2005), a chick flick masterpiece, seems at first to be going the same way. Anne Hathaway's fledgling journalist, Andy, starts her job at *Runway,* a thick fashion monthly where perpendicular girls in Galliano and heels race through the corridors like cranes en pointe. At first, Andy is a condescending frump. In a brilliantly written scene, the editor-in-chief, Miranda Priestly (Meryl Streep), explains to her with cold contempt that the cerulean color of her lumpy sweater was the result of a chain of decisions that began with Oscar de la Renta designing cerulean gowns, Yves St. Laurent creating cerulean military jackets, the color filtering down through department stores, and so on, until Andy found the "blue" sweater in a clearance bin. Miranda lays out the entire structure of the fashion business as a series of interconnected activities involving thousands of people and millions of dollars—Adam Smith couldn't have traced the linkages any better. Having been stripped to a pathetic clueless consumer, Andy, distraught, and unable to please her vicious boss, dresses herself—she gets the magazine's number two editor, Nigel (Stanley Tucci), to reach into the magazine's vast wardrobe room. She emerges with a Chanel jacket, a Kristina Ti skirt, shoes by Jimmy Choo and Manolo Blahnik, and she keeps on dressing for the rest of the movie, as if the closet door were always open, passing from Donna Karan to Valentino to Roberto Cavalli.

So far, the movie is another Cinderella-shopping fantasy, with Miranda as the wicked stepmother and helpful Nigel as the fairy godmother. Two warring princes (puppyish, dark Adrian Grenier and blond, swinish Simon Baker) compete for Andy in bed. Again, the stages of social elevation are driven by clothes. Everyone now looks at Andy in a different way. "You're very fetching. Go fetch," Miranda says to her when they hit Paris together—Paris, in this fable, serving as the interior of the castle, the seat of ultimate chic and power. Having pleased her boss, Andy is on her way to success in the fashion magazine business. But *The Devil Wears Prada* has an economic and social logic that goes way beyond the simple upward drive of *Pretty Woman*. In this particular Cinderella story, you can never rest. You have to keep reinventing yourself—that is, if you want to climb, like Miranda, from princess to queen. One of the movie's many virtues is its remarkable bluntness about fashion as a business; we realize that Andy's continuous makeover is nothing less than a metaphor of capitalism's relentless drive. If she wants to get to the top, she not only has to live out of Nigel's magic closet and wear different stunning clothes in every scene but she has to lose everything—her friends, her family, and her honor. She has to stab her rival in the back. In order to succeed in business, she must fail as a person.

Prada is almost magically entertaining—detailed and satirically accurate about the working world in a particularly competitive place. The movie captures in its breezy way the ceremonies of power and subservience—the pecking order in the office, the manners and jokes, the convenient lies and honeyed flatteries, the sudden betrayals. It's the only chick flick that consistently, almost obsessively examines the way a young heroine has to confront power. The center of *Prada* is not Andy's relations with her two suitors (they are both, in different ways, decorative) but with two women—her rival, Emily (Emily Blunt), and her boss, Miranda. Indeed, Andy's connection with Miranda is stronger than anything sexual. It's the apprentice-master relationship in all its unstable and endlessly complicated and bruising permutations. On the apprentice's side: awe, fear, eagerness to please, chagrin, emulation, and, perhaps, love and disapproval mixed together. On the master's side: dominance, contempt, applied lessons, applied tests, all of which gives way to a teacherly affection. Director David Frankel worked very closely with Meryl Streep to get the consecutive stages of Miranda's attitude toward Andy exactly right. By the end, Miranda tells Andy that what she sees in her—her instincts, her intelligence—reminds her of her younger self. That remark is what causes Andy, in a fit of revulsion, to bolt.

The Devil Wears Prada is a morality tale in which the princess realizes she doesn't want to live in the castle after all, that it takes too much out of her. In Paris, Andy leaves Miranda flat, and, back in New York, she gets a job at a crusading newspaper. Now, some of us may think of her renunciation as false ("Don't be ridiculous. Everybody wants this. Everybody wants to be us," Miranda says with some truth in the back of a Mercedes limo). Well, "false" may be too strong a word. The movie's conclusion is off because it presents the heroine's career options as a simple choice between honor and power. It's the same choice that *Wall Street* offered Charlie Sheen's fledgling financier almost twenty years ago—either hold on to your soul or become Gordon Gekko. Someday I'd like to see a film suggesting that you can be the boss without giving up your intellectual ideals, and that the proposed alternative—rejecting power altogether—may have its corruptions, too. Still, even if the morality tale ends too neatly, *The Devil Wears Prada* first accepts and then rejects social elevation through dress. Andy has her clothes fantasy and gives it up. In the end, the movie is about a soul's journey. It conceives of a woman's career in the same moral terms as a man's career—not ending simply and happily in marriage but in a professional choice.

Even in *Sex and the City,* where the continuous makeover was part of the appeal that made the show irresistible to women, apparel did not, in the end, rule everything. Sarah Jessica Parker, with her long narrow face and many anxieties, has a shrewdly self-teasing quality that delivers the material into irony. Parker's clothes themselves are often a bizarre mix of princess and gypsy, high and low, designer label and off-the-rack (for instance, a Louis Vuitton top and ordinary jeans). And her Carrie Bradshaw blunders as often as she triumphs. Her pink tutu and tulle skirt get ritually splashed by a bus in the show's famous opening logo; and when Carrie, wearing a black satin bra and jeweled underpants, climbs on a high-fashion runway, as an exemplar of "New York style," she flops onto the floor. Parker, the executive producer of the show, and also the show's male creators, knew that the women in the audience wanted something more than tantalizing makeovers and flamboyant dress. What they wanted was the emotional satisfaction of sustained friendship, surviving every rivalry and calamity. The clothes madness that followed in the show's wake—the shopaholic disasters like *Bride Wars*—turned a controllable comic obsession into an outright perversion.

Moving toward self-creation, the heroine of a chick flick usually stumbles. Chick flicks are built around the constant threat of exposure of weakness or incapacity, and there's no immediate escape, no place to hide. Never mind the shopaholic movies, or something like *27 Dresses,* in which the lovely Katherine Heigl is unaccountably a lifetime bridesmaid. Those movies are bathed in masochism from the beginning. Consider instead that Renée Zellweger's Bridget Jones, doing publicity at a British publishing house, tries to fake her way through a call, in front of her boss, to the long-dead F. R. Leavis; that she asks Salman Rushdie (in the flesh) the way to the toilet. Kate Hudson, allegedly an ace lawyer in *Bride Wars,* falls apart in front of a group of powerful men when she has to make a presentation. Even in *The Devil Wears Prada,* on her first day at *Runway,* Andy doesn't know who Miranda is and then admits to the editor that she has never read the magazine; and Miranda herself has to be seen naked (that is, without her makeup) as a woman defeated by the ordinary miseries of marital failure. These, I admit, are all necessary plot points, but the mere fact that plot after plot is based around them (I could name many more) can't be a coincidence. When men make idiots of themselves in a male-slob comedy, drinking, stumbling, pissing, vomiting, they're forgiven as hopeless, lovable boys; their ultimate worth is not on the line. But the young heroines are trapped; they cringe and stammer; they feel like no-accounts—the female equivalent of impotent. Eventually, they will overcome, but at first they must fail. Moments of excruciating embarrassment are as organic to chick flicks as dating and clothes.

Men cause the heroines the deepest humiliations, and the movies both register familiar complaints and take revenge. The older heroines— Barbara Hershey in *Beaches,* the women in *The First Wives Club*—have been left by husbands for slender tootsies. In *Waiting to Exhale,* Whitney Houston's character realizes, while making breakfast for her soft-spoken married lover (Dennis Haysbert), that he is stringing her along and has no intention of leaving his wife. Betrayed, the women in movie after movie gather together to compare notes. They *see* the men. Mykelti Williamson or Edward Burns or Simon Baker or Chris Noth may be physically ir- resistible, but shouldn't they be resisted? Sexual attraction can go only so far. They have to be told off. Telling men off—chewing them out, dumping their clothes out of a closet, whamming them across the kisser, walking out and slamming the door—is the moment the women take control of their lives. In chick flicks, revenge is self-creation.

The men who make the grade for the long haul are very different. They are gentle. They are candid. They are British. Hugh Grant (in his noncad roles), Hugh Dancy, James McAvoy, Colin Firth, Jude Law—the Brit charm- ers, unthreatening but convincingly male, care for conversation and wit as well as for sex. In romantic comedies as well as in chick flicks, Hollywood has been throwing women against the wall of Matthew McConaughey's stupidity to see what sticks (the answer: Kate Hudson). The Brits provide a relief from American blockheads like McConaughey and Dermot Mul- roney, just as, in the late 1930s, civilized Leslie Howard, Ronald Colman, Robert Donat, and David Niven provided a release from the sexually over- whelming Clark Gable and taciturn Gary Cooper. The British—at least the ones who aren't preening narcissists—can listen, and what they have to say is worth hearing. In chick flicks, women care about words.

The heroine gets her guy in most of these movies, but why are there so many humiliations along the way? A man can't know these things; at this point, I'm just guessing. My guess is that those scenes reappear be- cause the audience wants and needs them. Consider that the women who see these films, as well as the women who make them, may be part of the first female generation consistently to take on high-pressure jobs. Their mothers were teachers, secretaries, nurses, saleswomen, garment workers, or homemakers, while a good part of the new generation are college students, doctors, lawyers, TV producers and movie craft people, journalists, hospital administrators, and corporate and financial executives. That's a big leap, and the surge of upward mobility and power can produce the bends. I've spoken to women friends in their thirties—all of them carrying a heavy load of work while raising children—who love chick flicks. They enjoy the formula plots, the shopping sprees and dating quandaries. "They're like Top-40 radio, easy and fun," they say. They also enjoy them because they're a blessed reminder of what life was like when they had fewer cares and more time. One could say that their enjoyment of chick flicks is a function of their success. The movies remind them not only of freedom but of vulnerable moments experienced a decade before in early days on the job. No matter how successful these women have become, the memory of those blunders survives, and the movies allow them to revisit those fears and see them vanquished again and again. The genre is built around humiliations survived and then overcome.

Good chick flicks can be constructed on the solid foundation of classic folk tales—not just Cinderella, but Snow White and Little Red Riding Hood, all of them archetypal stories that can be varied in infinite ways. Chick flicks are also good when they update the Austen marriage plot (literally in *Clueless,* a delightful 90210 version of *Emma;* and by inheritance in *Bridget Jones's Diary*). In that fable, a young woman is attracted to a witty, glamorous, even devastating man, and then slowly, by degrees, extricates herself from enthrallment and chooses another man who may seem stolid at first but who shows himself, after trials, to be made of finer stuff. Her choice is an act of creating herself as much as giving herself to another. That pattern is close to romantic comedy, of course, but it will remain a chick flick if it's told from a woman's point of view.

Chick flicks also work well, as I've suggested, when they embrace work, in all its miseries and glories—embrace it centrally, not just as a cell phone occupation and a way of launching credit card debt. This may sound like an excessively high-minded prescription for a comedy genre, but the trials of work drive a movie along. What makes *The Devil Wears Prada* so fascinating is the intricacies of how a novice might get shaped by the demands of a high-pressure office. In *Julie & Julia,* the strongest part of the movie dramatizes Julia Child's self-creation sixty years ago in France in a void of indifference and outright hostility. These heroines are smart women, gentle fighters, and they pep up the genre, giving the audience something it can admire without self-mocking irony. The movie version of *Sex and the City* was an aesthetic disaster (commercially, it did fine) in part because it lost the short, anecdotal form of the show, in which the sound of a woman working—Carrie writing a column—unified the adventures and jokes into a brief, tight narrative.

As a genre, chick flicks are generally too scared of tough girls, too shy of heroism. No one, for instance, has yet done a comic movie (not a solemn biopic, a *comic* movie) about a future great athlete or CEO or a young—don't scream—Nancy Pelosi or Hillary Clinton. Yes, such a film would be much harder to do as comedy, though not impossible: Brilliant girls blunder on the job and fall for bad men, too. Filmmakers would have to find the intellectual pride within the neophyte, the genius within the early flutter—or possibly the comedy of a noble spirit who gets teased out of vanity without giving up her ambition. Katharine Hepburn played parts like that for years. How about someone like a young Maureen Dowd or Molly Ivins—a fallible young woman with an instinctive grasp of the absurd? Dramatizing ambition and work is the key to making chick flicks better and even more commercial. These movies should always be funny—comedy liberates their affectionate attitude toward women—but they could do worse than acknowledge and repay, without rhetoric or grinding earnestness, feminism's incomparable gift.

Written in 2009; published here for the first time

ROMANTIC COMEDY GETS KNOCKED UP / THE SLACKER-STRIVER COMEDY

His beard is haphazard and unintentional, neither full nor designer-stubbled, and he dresses in sweats, or in shorts and a T-shirt, or with his shirt hanging out like the tongue of a Labrador retriever. He's generally about thirty, and he spends a lot of time with friends who are like him, only more so—sweet-natured young men of foul mouth, odd hair, and wanker-mag reading habits. When he's with them, punched beer cans and bongs of various sizes lie around like spent shells; alone, and walrus-heavy on his couch, he watches football, basketball, or baseball on television, or spends time memorializing his youth—archiving old movies, games, and jokes. Sports are central to his life, though mainly as a fan, a state of being that he embraces as passion and grace—the Red Sox as grail. Like his ancestors in the 1960s, he's anti-corporate, but he's not bohemian (his culture is pop). He's more like a sullen back-of-the-classroom guy, who breaks into brilliant tirades only when he feels like it. He may run a used record store, or conduct sightseeing tours with a nonstop line of patter, or feed animals who then high-five him with their flippers, or teach in a school where he can be friends with all the kids, or design an Internet site that no one needs. Essentially, he plays all the time, even at work, which is usually just a more organized form of play. Whatever he does, he hardly breaks a sweat, and sometimes he does nothing at all.

He may not have a girlfriend, but he certainly likes girls—he's even, in some cases, a hetero blade, scoring with tourists or love-hungry single mothers. But if he does have a girlfriend she works hard. Usually, she's the same age as he is but seems older, as if the disparity between boys and girls in ninth grade had been recapitulated fifteen years later. She dresses

157

in Donna Karan or Ralph Lauren or the like; she's a corporate executive, or a lawyer, or works in TV, public relations, or an art gallery. She's good-tempered, honest, great-looking, and serious. She wants to "get to the next stage of life"—settle down, marry, maybe have children. Apart from getting on with it, however, she doesn't have an idea in her head, and she's not the one who makes the jokes.

When she breaks up with him, he talks his situation over with his hopeless pals, who give him bits of misogynist advice. Suddenly, it's the end of youth for him. It's a crisis for her, too, and they can get back together only if both undertake some drastic alteration: He must act responsibly (get a job, take care of a kid), and she has to do something crazy (run across a baseball field during a game, tell a joke). He has to shape up, and she has to loosen up.

There they are, the young man and young woman of the dominant romantic comedy trend of the past several years—the slovenly hipster and the female straight arrow. The movies form a genre of sorts: the slacker-striver romance. Stephen Frears's *High Fidelity* (2000), which transferred Nick Hornby's novel from London to Chicago, may not have been the first, but it set the tone and established the self-dramatizing underachiever as hero. Hornby's guy-centered material also inspired *About a Boy* and *Fever Pitch*. Others in this group include *Old School; Big Daddy; 50 First Dates; Shallow Hal; School of Rock; Failure to Launch; You, Me and Dupree; Wedding Crashers; The Break-Up;* and this summer's hit, *Knocked Up*. In these movies, the men are played by Vince Vaughn, Owen Wilson, Adam Sandler, John Cusack, Jimmy Fallon, Matthew McConaughey, Jack Black, Hugh Grant, and Seth Rogen; the women by Drew Barrymore, Jennifer Aniston, Kate Hudson, Sarah Jessica Parker, and Katherine Heigl. For almost a decade, Hollywood has pulled jokes and romance out of the struggle between male infantilism and female ambition.

Knocked Up, written and directed by Judd Apatow, is the culminating version of this story, and it feels like one of the key movies of the era—a raw, discordant equivalent of *The Graduate* forty years ago. I've seen it with audiences in their twenties and thirties, and the excitement in the theaters is palpable—the audience is with the movie all the way, and, afterward, many of the young men (though not always the young women) say that it's not only funny but true. They feel that way, I think, because the picture is unruly and surprising; it's filled with the messes and rages of life in 2007. The woman, Alison (Katherine Heigl), an ambitious TV interviewer in Los Angeles, gets pregnant after a sozzled one-night stand with Ben (Seth Rogen), a nowhere guy she meets at a disco. Cells divide, sickness arrives in the morning—the movie's time scheme is plotted against a series of pulsing sonograms. These two, to put it mildly, find themselves in an awkward situation. They don't much like each other; they don't seem to match up. Heigl has golden skin, blond hair, a great laugh. She's so attractive a person that, at the beginning of the movie, you wince every time Rogen touches her. Chubby, with curling hair and an orotund voice, he has the round face and sottish grin of a Jewish Bacchus, though grape appeals to him less than weed. At first, he makes one crass remark after another; he seems like a professional comic who will do anything to get a laugh. It's not at all clear that these two should stay together.

Authentic as Ben and Alison seem to younger audiences, they seem very strange to anyone with a long memory of romantic comedy. Buster Keaton certainly played idle young swells in some of his silent movies, but, first humiliated and then challenged, he would exert himself to heroic effort to win the girl. In the end, he proved himself a lover. In the 1930s, the young, lean James Stewart projected a vulnerability that was immensely appealing. So did Jack Lemmon, in his frenetic way, in the 1950s. In succeeding decades, Elliott Gould, George Segal, Alan Alda, and other actors played soulful types. Yet all these men *wanted* something. It's hard to think of earlier heroes who were absolutely free of the desire to make an impression on the world and still got the girl. And the women in the old romantic comedies were daffy or tough or high-spirited or even spiritual in some way, but they were never blank. What's going on in this new genre? *Knocked Up*, a raucously funny and explicit movie, has some dark corners, some fear and anxiety festering under the jokes. Apatow takes the slacker-striver romance to a place no one thought it would go. He also makes it clear, if we hadn't noticed before, how drastically the new group of movies breaks with the classic patterns of romantic comedy. Those ancient tropes fulfill certain expectations and, at their best, provide incomparable pleasure. But *Knocked Up* is heading off into a brave and uncertain new direction.

/ / /

Generically, all romantic comedies are examples of what the Greeks called New Comedy. In comparison with the Old Comedy of Aristophanes, which was a satirical comment on public events and famous men, the New Comedy of Menander and, later, the Roman entertainers Terence and Plautus, was lower in tone, sexual in preoccupation, and worldly in its resolution. Northrop Frye, in *The Anatomy of Criticism,* a critical classic published a half century ago, laid out the ground plan as follows:

> What normally happens is that a young man wants a young woman, that this desire is resisted by some opposition, usually paternal, and that near the end of the play some twist of the plot enables the hero to have his will. . . . At the beginning of the play, the obstructing characters are in charge of the play's society. . . . At the end of the play the device in the plot that brings the hero and heroine together causes a new society to crystallize around the hero.

This new society is solemnized by a wedding, and, in some cases, a social promotion: Wedding gowns and robes are donned, property changes hands, and one partner or the other rises in the world. Romantic comedy is both revolutionary and conservative at the same time: The scrambling Roman boy, his legs sticking out beneath his toga as he enlists the help of wily slaves in some ridiculous intrigue, carries the future within his eagerness to bed the girl. He may break up some old pattern, but then social norms are reasserted in the promise of children arriving after the tumult ends. Romantic comedy is driven by desire and tamed by ritual—not just a wedding, but, often, a feast. In one Roman comedy, the actors threw food at the audience at the end. Let the future begin.

Shakespeare knew the Roman farces by Plautus and Terence, and he varied the pattern. His comedies were rarely a simple chase, and the best American romantic comedies have drawn on the forms that he devised— not so much, perhaps, in the coarse-grained *Taming of the Shrew* but in *Much Ado About Nothing,* with its pair of battling lovers, Beatrice and Benedick. Why is the contact between those two so barbed? Because they are meant for each other, and are too proud and frightened to admit it. We can see the attraction, even if they can't. They have a closely meshed rhythm of speech, a quickness to rise and retort, that no one else shares. Benedick, announcing the end of the warfare, puts the issue squarely: "Shall quips and sentences and these paper bullets of the brain awe a man from the career of his humor? No, the world must be peopled."

Romantic comedy is entertainment in the service of the biological imperative. The world must be peopled. Even if the lovers are past child-rearing age or, as in recent years, don't want children, the biological imperative survives, as any evolutionary psychologist will tell you, in the flourishes of courtship behavior. Romantic comedy civilizes desire, transforms lust into play and ritual—the celebration of union in marriage. The lovers are fated by temperament and physical attraction to join together, or stay together, and the audience longs for that ending with an urgency that is as much moral as sentimental. As far as they are concerned, neither war, nor fire, nor plague can stop the couple from getting together—the sexual union is as inevitable as the two halves of a bridge falling into place. But the audience, for its pleasure, doesn't want the bridge to close too quickly. Romance becomes romantic *comedy* only when there is delay. The lovers misunderstand each other; they get pixie dust thrown in their faces. Befuddled, the woman thinks she's in love with a gas station attendant, who turns out to be a millionaire; an unsuitable suitor becomes a proper suitor; and so on. It's always the right guy in the end. Romantic drama may revel in suffering, even in anguish and death, but romantic comedy merely nods at the destructive energies of passion. The confused lovers torment each other and, for a while, us. Then they stop.

The best directors of romantic comedy in the 1930s and 1940s— Frank Capra, Gregory La Cava, Leo McCarey, Howard Hawks, Mitchell Leisen, and Preston Sturges—knew that the story would be not only funnier but much more romantic if the fight was waged between equals. It was the solution appropriate to a democratic society. The couple may not enjoy parity of social standing or money (the social promotion at the end still occurs in many films), but they are equals in spirit, will, and body. Each matches the other's moves and wants to outdo the other—a competition that is actually a form of admiration. And, in the end, no matter how much they batter each other, no one else seems quite real to them. Who else can they talk to? As everyone agrees, this kind of romantic comedy—and particularly the variant called "screwball comedy"—lifted off in February 1934 with Frank Capra's incredibly charming *It Happened One Night,* in which a hard-drinking reporter out of a job (Clark Gable) and an heiress who has jumped off her father's yacht (Claudette Colbert) meet on the road somewhere between Florida and New York. Tough and self-sufficient, Gable contemptuously looks after the spoiled rich girl. He's rude and overbearing, and she's miffed, but it helps their acquaintance a little that they are both supremely attractive—Gable quick-moving but large and, in his famous undressing scene, meaty, and Colbert tiny, with a slightly pointed chin, round eyes, and round breasts beneath the fitted striped jacket she buys on the road. When she develops pride, they become equals.

The cinema added something invaluable to the romantic comedy: the camera's ability to place lovers in an enchanted, expanding envelope of setting and atmosphere. It moves with them at will, enlarging their command of streets, fields, sitting rooms, and nightclubs; rapid cutting then doubles the speed of their quarrels. Out on the road, in the middle of the Depression, Gable and Colbert join the poor, the hungry, the shysters and the hustlers; they spend a night among haystacks, get fleeced, practice their hitchhiking skills. In screwball comedy, the characters have to dive below their social roles for their true selves to come out: They get drunk and wind up in the slammer; they turn a couch in an upstairs room of a mansion into a trampoline; they run around the woods at a country estate—the American plutocrats' version of Shakespeare's magical forest in *A Midsummer Night's Dream,* where young people, first confused and then enlightened, discover whom they should marry.

In many of the screwball classics, including *Twentieth Century, My Man Godfrey, The Awful Truth, Easy Living, Midnight, Bringing Up Baby, Holiday, The Philadelphia Story, The Lady Eve*—all made between 1934 and 1941—the characters dress for dinner and make cocktails, and servants mutter demurely at the fringes. The wealth and high style—the enormous New York apartments, the country mansions with white porticoes, the white-on-white clubs in which swells with monocles and women with diamond tiaras listen to a warbling singer—establish the facade of manners, though the social rules are far less stringent than in, say, England, where dressing for dinner is a kind of armor against commonness and mess (i.e., the jungle). In the American films, except for the Astaire-Rogers dance musicals, in which evening clothes are integral to the lyric transformation of life into movement, the lovers are no more than playing at formality (only shirts already stuffed really love tuxedos). Yet wealth is necessary: It allows the open exercise of will and choice, the unfettered search for happiness. The screwball comedies are less about possessions than about a certain style of freedom in love, a way of vaulting above the dullness and petty-mindedness of the sticks. (In these films, no matter how much money you have, you are out of the question if you hail from Oklahoma or Albany—you are Ralph Bellamy.) Wealth allows the characters to make fools of themselves without consequence, and it allowed the poor and middle-class audiences to enjoy the foolishness without envy. When the characters misbehave, they join the common life, they become human in a way that everyone understands.

Many of the heroines were heiresses, who, in those days, were prized for their burbling eccentricities—Carole Lombard's howl, Irene Dunne's giggle, Katharine Hepburn's Bryn Mawr drawl. Pampered and dizzy, they were nevertheless smart enough, when choosing a man, to favor spontaneity over security, spirit over solidity. The men were in finance, or, in some cases, trying to get out of it, for, in the 1930s movies, Wall Street was a curse—Wall Street was where young men's souls went to die. Yet the men were worldly; they knew how to get things done, how to hand a woman into a taxi at night. There were a few unsophisticated heroes, too, gently cartooned intellectuals: Cary Grant, in *Bringing Up Baby,* a paleontologist who wants to complete the skeleton of a brontosaurus; Gary Cooper, in *Ball of Fire,* a lexicographer who lives in dim celibacy in a New York town house with a bunch of older word hunters; and Henry Fonda, in *The Lady Eve,* who goes "up the Amazon" and tells a wondering Barbara Stanwyck that "snakes are my life." Learned boobies preoccupied with some intricate corner of knowledge, these men may have been a distant anticipation of the recent crop of slackers; they're not lazy like the slackers, but they're beached; they have to be pulled out of the lab into marriage.

The man is the love object here—passive, dreamy, and gentle, a kind of Sleeping Beauty in spectacles—and the woman is the relentless pursuer. Katharine Hepburn in *Baby* nearly drives Cary Grant crazy with her intrusions into his work, her way of scattering his life about like pieces of lawn furniture. She's attracted by his good looks but also by what's unaroused in him, and she will do anything to awaken him. Equality in these comedies takes a new shape. The man is serious about his work (and no one says he shouldn't be), but he's confused about women, and his confusion has neutered him. He thinks he wants a conventional marriage with a compliant wife, but what he really wants is to be overwhelmed by the female life force. In the screwball comedies, the woman doesn't ask her man to "grow up." She wants to pull him into some sort of ridiculous adventure. *She* has to grow up, and he has to get loose—the opposite of the current pattern.

The screwball comedies were not devoted to sex, exactly—you could hardly describe any of the characters as sensualists. The Production Code limited openness on such matters, and the filmmakers turned sex into a courtship game that was so deliriously convoluted precisely because couples could go to bed only when they were married. The screwball movies, at their peak, defined certain ideal qualities of insouciance, a fineness of romantic temper in which men and women could be aggressive but not coarse, angry but not rancorous, silly but not shamed, melancholy but not ravaged. It was the temper of American happiness.

Sometimes the couple in a romantic comedy are already married, or were formerly married, but husband and wife go at each other anyway, because they enjoy wrangling too much to stop. In a case like that, romance becomes less a dazed encounter in an enchanted garden than a duel with slingshots at close quarters—exciting but a little risky. The most volatile of these comedies was *His Girl Friday,* Howard Hawks's 1940 version of the 1928 Ben Hecht and Charles MacArthur play *The Front Page.* In the original, the star reporter Hildy Johnson is a man. In Hawks's version, Hildy (Rosalind Russell) is a woman who has fled the barbarous city desk and plans to marry a timid businessman (Ralph Bellamy). Her former husband and editor, Walter Burns (Cary Grant), will do anything to get her back to the paper. He doesn't seem drawn to her as a woman, yet he woos her in his way, with scams, lies, and one important truth—that she's the only person good enough to cover the hottest story in town. She knows him as an indifferent and absent husband, yet she's attracted, once again, by the outrageous way this man fans his tail. And, despite her misgivings, she's caught, too, by the great time they have together toiling in the yellow journalism that they both love. Vince Vaughn, in some of his recent roles, has displayed a dazzling motormouth velocity, but he has never worked with an actress who can keep up with him. Rosalind Russell keeps up with Grant. These two seize each other's words and throw them back so quickly that their dialogue seems almost syncopated. Balance between the sexes here becomes a kind of matched virtuosity more intense than sex. Every now and then they stop to stare at other people in disbelief: Why are they so slow? Their cynical city room patter is more intense than sex, and endless newspaper stories are the only imaginable offspring they could produce.

As the globe-trotting journalist Tess Hardy in George Stevens's *Woman of the Year* (1942), Katharine Hepburn presses ahead, too, while Spencer Tracy, as a star sports columnist, is deliberate, even adamantine, and that difference in tempo was part of their strength as a working couple in their movies together (nine in all). At the time of *Woman of the Year,* their off-screen relationship, which lasted until Tracy's death, in 1967, had just begun, and their first look at each other on camera—in an editor's office and the hallway outside—is frankly appraising. Stocky and curly-haired, Tracy was a product of a time when the male movie body wasn't yet required to be tapered and sinewy (James Cagney and Alan Ladd were stubby, too), and he acted with his large head, his thick trunk, and his wide-opening eyes, which take in Hepburn with more wonder than desire. Then thirty-five, Hepburn may never have been more beautiful in movies than at that moment. She had the broad-shouldered look and the crowning glory of lustrous hair that was characteristic of female stars in the 1940s, but the bones were more pronounced, the features more sharply defined than, say, Rita Hayworth's or Ingrid Bergman's, and the combination of luxuriance and angularity made her right for romantic comedy. In *Woman of the Year,* she gets out too far, is punished (too severely for our taste), then yields, a stunning intellectual woman whose singularity made her blind to her own vanities. The comedy plays off Tracy's staring disbelief.

By the time of the classic *Adam's Rib* (1949), five pictures later, they were an established on-screen married couple, and the movie nestles into small details of their domestic routine—passing out of sleep in the morning to a state of muzzy wakefulness, dressing, going to work, and, later, drinking a cocktail when they get home from the office. How can you have romantic comedy in a setting of such domestic complacency? But *Adam's Rib*, which was written by a married couple, Garson Kanin and Ruth Gordon, and directed by George Cukor, takes these two through fierce combat—so fierce that it can be ended only with a new and very desperate courtship. They become opposing lawyers in a murder case. He prosecutes, and she defends, a woman (Judy Holliday) who put a couple of slugs in her husband when she caught him in the arms of his mistress. As the two lawyers compete in court, and Tracy gets upstaged by Hepburn, the traditional sparring at the center of romantic comedy intensifies, turns a little ugly, and then comes to an abrupt stop with a loud slap—Tracy smacking Hepburn's bottom in a proprietary way during a late-night rubdown session. The slap is nothing, yet it's everything. The husband has violated the prime rule of mating behavior by asserting a right over his wife physically. The drive for equality in movies can lead to bruising competitions, and in *Adam's Rib* the partnership of equals nearly dissolves. Suddenly anguished, the movie uneasily rights itself as husband and wife make concessions and find their way back to marriage again.

The drive for equality can lead to potentially bruising competitions in which romance becomes nerve-wracking. Tracy and Hepburn, working again with Gordon-Kanin material and George Cukor, found a point of resolution and comfort a few years later in the charming *Pat and Mike*, but, in general, the 1950s and 1960s were marked by a pullback from their kind of special relationship, or almost any kind of easy balance between men and women. The ideal of romantic couple as equals got overwhelmed by sexual obsession—that is, male obsession, the craziness about women. In the past, manners had provided a cover for desire, but sex became uneasily lurid (without being explicit) in the 1950s, both crass and self-parodying at the same time. The old mad dichotomy between virgin and whore was revived. Marilyn Monroe, whispering and cooing, spilling out everywhere, was revered and mocked, and no one, except Tony Curtis in his Cary Grant guise in Billy Wilder's *Some Like It Hot,* knew how to talk to her or (in movies) make love to her. Cheery, tough Debbie Reynolds and Doris Day, a band singer when she was a teenager—a woman who had been around—were turned into professional virgins. Billy Wilder, who had written wonderful romantic comedies as a young émigré in Hollywood in the 1930s, soured as he aged, and poured his new brand of cynical sexual wisdom into films like *The Apartment,* in which the young couple (Jack Lemmon and Shirley MacLaine) are no more than exhausted survivors of manipulation by powerful older men.

Without intending to, the women's movement of the late 1960s and early 1970s probably made the task of putting man and woman together in the movies even more self-conscious and fraught, and, for a while there, in such Robert Redford–Paul Newman flirtations as *Butch Cassidy and the Sundance Kid* and *The Sting* and in many other buddy films, women got pushed out altogether or reduced to sidekicks. It took Woody Allen's love of both New York and Diane Keaton to revive the form in *Annie Hall,* a movie that opened thirty years ago this past April. In defiance of the city's crime rates and bond defaults, and the general urban dyspepsia of the period, Woody Allen created an aura of magic in his beloved East Side streets, in movie theaters and bookshops, in an embrace at dusk in a little park near the Queensboro Bridge. He presented himself as the embodied spirit of the place, a man who had left Brooklyn behind (when Brooklyn needed to be left behind) and had become a professional Manhattanite, sharp and critical, but also didactic, overexplicit, cranky, and frightened of everything—of spiders and lobsters off the leash and crawling about on the floor, alleged anti-Semites everywhere, and also, in the menacing distance, California sunshine and good times. Working with Diane Keaton again (it was their fourth movie together), Allen created a new way of balancing equals. Short and narrow-jawed, with black-framed specs that give him the aspect of a quizzical Eastern European police inspector, Woody dictates what she should read and when they should make love. At first, we're meant to think that his intellect and wit make him sexy for her. A beautiful Galatea, apologetic and even unformed in her floppy hats, loose-tailed shirts, and bland opinions—all sighs and stammers—she initially agrees to be tutored, but, as she gains strength in her own opinions, he overplays his hand and loses her. Intellect and beauty each have their prerogatives, but when she realizes who she is, she can no longer bear his bossy ways. The balance, in other words, is unstable and doesn't last, and the comedy is bittersweet. If Tracy and Hepburn were like a rock and a current mysteriously joined together, these two neurotics were like agitated hummingbirds briefly meeting in midair.

Working with the cinematographer Gordon Willis, Woody Allen created the atmosphere of a marriage plot in the leafy East Side streets—his version of Shakespeare's magical forest. But *Annie Hall* shifts away from marriage. No woman can put up with the quintessential New Yorker. And the specific New York elements that Allen added to romantic comedy—the cult of psychoanalysis and the endless opinions about writers, musicians, and artists—also threaten the stability of the couple. Psychoanalysis yields "relationships" and "living together," not marriage, as the central ritual, and living together, especially in the time of the Pill and the easy real estate market of the 1970s, is always provisional. Opinions about art—the way the soul defines itself in time—are provisional, too. In *Annie Hall*, Keaton outgrows Allen's curriculum for her and moves on, and in *Manhattan*, perhaps the best American comedy about selfishness ever made, she returns to the married man she was having an affair with. Allen loses her both times; the biological imperative goes nowhere. *Annie Hall* and *Manhattan* now seem like fragile and melancholy love lyrics; they took romantic comedy to a level of rueful sophistication never seen before or since.

The louts in the slacker-striver comedies should probably lose the girl, too, but most of them don't. Yet what, exactly, are the men getting, and why should the women want them? That is not a question romantic comedy has posed before.

The slacker has certain charms. He doesn't want to compete in business, he refuses to cultivate macho attitudes, and, for some women, he may be attractive. He's still a boy—he's gentler than other men. Having a child with such a guy, however, is another matter, and plenty of women have complained about the way *Knocked Up* handles the issue of pregnancy. Alison has a good job, some growing public fame, and she hardly knows the unappealing father—there's even some muttering about "bad genes." Why have a baby with him? Well, a filmmaker's pragmatic answer would have to be that if there's an abortion, or if Alison has the child on her own, there's no movie—or, at least, nothing like this movie. And this movie, just as it is, has considerable interest and complication as fiction.

What's striking about *Knocked Up* is the way the romance is placed within the relations between the sexes. The picture is a drastic revision of classic romantic comedy patterns. Ben doesn't chase Alison, and she doesn't chase him. The movie is not about the civilizing of desire, and it offers a marriage plot that couldn't be more wary of marriage. *Knocked Up*, like Apatow's earlier *40 Year Old Virgin*, is devoted to the dissolution of a male pack, the ending of the juvenile male bond. Ben and his friends sit around in their San Fernando Valley tract house whamming each other on the head with rubber bats and watching naked actresses in movies. The way Ben lives with his friends is tremendous fun; it's also as close to paralysis as you can get and continue breathing. Apatow, of course, has it both ways. He squeezes the pink-eyed doofuses for every laugh he can get out of them, but at the same time he suggests that the very thing he's celebrating is sick, crazy, and dysfunctional. The situation has to end. Boys have to grow up or life ceases.

Ben and Alison's one-night stand forces the issue. Willy-nilly, the world gets peopled. Yet the slowly developing love between Ben and the pregnant Alison comes off as halfhearted and unconvincing—it's the weakest element in the movie. There are some terrifically noisy arguments, a scene of Rogen's making love to the enormous Heigl ("I'm not making love to you like a dog. It's doggy *style*. It's a style."), but we never really see the moment in which they warm up and begin to like each other. That part of the movie is unpersuasive, I would guess, because it's not terribly important to Apatow. What's important is the male bond—the way it flourishes, in all its unhealthiness, and then its wrenching end. Alison lives with her sister, Debbie (Leslie Mann), and brother-in-law, Pete (Paul Rudd), and Ben begins to hang out with Alison at the house of the married couple, who are classically mismatched in temperament. Pete is restless, disappointed, and remorselessly funny, and Ben links up with him.

Whooping with joy, they go off to Las Vegas, but they don't gamble or get laid. Instead, they hang out and eat "shrooms." They merely want to be together: It's as if Romeo and Mercutio had left the women and all that mess in Verona behind and gone off to practice their swordsmanship. When Ben and Pete get high, crash, and then return, chastened, to the women, the male bond is severed at last, the baby can be born, and life continues. In generic terms, *Knocked Up* puts the cart before the horse—the accidental baby, rather than desire, pulls the young man into civilization.

As fascinating and as funny as *Knocked Up* is, it represents what can only be called the disenchantment of romantic comedy, the end point of a progression from Fifth Avenue to the Valley, from tuxedos to tube socks, from a popped champagne cork to a baby crowning. There's nothing in it that is comparable to the style of the classics—no magic in its settings, no reverberant sense of place, no shared or competitive work for the couple to do. Ben does come through in the end, yet, if his promise and Alison's beauty make them equal as a pair, one still wants more out of Alison than the filmmakers are willing to provide. She has a fine fit of hormonal rage, but, like the other heroines in the slacker-striver romances, she isn't given an idea or a snappy remark or even a sharp perception. All the movies in this genre have been written and directed by men, and it's as if the filmmakers were saying, "Yes, young men are children now, and women bring home the bacon, but men bring home the soul."

The perilous new direction of the slacker-striver genre reduces the role of women to vehicles. Their only real function is to make the men grow up. That's why they're all so earnest and bland—so nice, so good. Leslie Mann (who's married to Apatow) has some great bitchy lines as the angry Debbie, but she's not a lover; she represents disillusion. As Anthony Lane pointed out in *The New Yorker*, Apatow's subject is not so much sex as age, and age in his movies is a malediction. If you're young, you have to grow up. If you grow up, you turn into Debbie—you fear that the years are overtaking you fast. Either way, you're in trouble.

Apatow has a genius for candor that goes way beyond dirty talk—that's why *Knocked Up* is a cultural event. But I wonder if Apatow, like his fumy youths, shouldn't move on. It seems strange to complain of repetition when a director does something particularly well, and Apatow does the infantilism of the male bond better than anyone, but I'd be quite happy if I never saw another bong-gurgling slacker or male pack again. The society that produced the Katharine Hepburn and Carole Lombard movies has vanished; manners, in the sense of elegance, have disappeared. But manners as spiritual style are more important than ever, and Apatow has demonstrated that he knows this as well as anyone. So how can he not know that the key to making a great romantic comedy is to create heroines equal in wit to men? They don't have to dress for dinner, but they should challenge the men intellectually and spiritually, rather than simply offering their bodies as a way of dragging the clods out of their adolescent stupor. "Paper bullets of the brain," as Benedick called the taunting exchanges with Beatrice, slay the audience every time if they are aimed at the right place.

The New Yorker, *July 23, 2007; revised 2011*

PART FIVE / DIRECTORS

INTRODUCTION

In thinking about directors, I'm always attracted by a play of contraries. Otto Preminger, a mid-century liberal who believed in free speech and debate and balanced views, was an absolute dictator on the set, a terror to younger and more vulnerable actors. Victor Fleming directed the two most famous movies of the late 1930s, *Gone With the Wind* and *The Wizard of Oz*, yet, until Michael Sragow revived him in his 2009 biography, Fleming had been largely forgotten. Pedro Almodóvar is a flagrant sensationalist with a sweet, generous temperament. Clint Eastwood became an American icon by playing men who killed with pleasure, yet, as he got older, he came to revise, even reverse his attitudes toward violence and virtually everything else. The Coen brothers are jokesters with a dark, even savage view of life. Quentin Tarantino has turned pop movies into a quasi-academic canon;

his outrageousness barely masks piety. David Fincher is a visual formalist who embraces chaos. I don't mean to suggest that the contraries are what make them talented, but it certainly makes them fun to write about.

OTTO PREMINGER / THE BALANCE OF TERROR

Otto Preminger's *Anatomy of a Murder,* from 1959, is still the best court-room drama ever made in this country, and, in its occasional forays out of the court, among the finest evocations of place—an Upper Peninsula Michigan resort area in the off-season, leafless, underpopulated, alcoholic, and forlorn. James Stewart, in one of his wonderful melancholy "late" per-formances, plays a former county prosecutor named Biegler, a lifelong bachelor who now spends his time with a nonpracticing lawyer (Arthur O'Connell) and an unpaid secretary (Eve Arden), who sticks around for the wisecracks. The movie is leisurely, detailed, realistic, intensely com-panionable; you get a sense of how people exist at the margins of a profes-sion without losing their dignity. It's my favorite Preminger movie, edging out the celebrated *Laura* (1944), a suave murder mystery set in a studio-built Manhattan. *Laura* is sly and haunting—a Park Avenue ghost movie that anticipates the dark-shadowed noir style that blossomed in Prem-inger's work later in the 1940s. The light in *Anatomy,* on the other hand, is not shadowy but gray and even: In that world, good and evil are not easily identifiable. And the music, in contrast to David Raksin's lush popular romanticism for *Laura,* is pure mockery—a tickling jazz score by Duke Ellington that suggests something unruly going on beneath the surface.

As it turns out, *Anatomy of a Murder* is stunningly ambiguous. Rous-ing himself from his lethargy, Biegler defends an Army lieutenant (Ben Gazzara) who has killed a local man—a hotel owner and saloonkeeper—after the guy has mauled and raped the lieutenant's wife (Lee Remick). Or at least that's what the wife says; the medical evidence is inconclusive, and the bruises she has on her body may have come from her husband knock-ing her around. As played by the young Lee Remick, the wife is almost haplessly flirtatious. She flirts even with the disconcerted Biegler, who disapproves of her but also feels a certain chagrin: She's young, she's sexual, and, looking at her, he feels that he missed the party. What's going on with this surly Army lieutenant and his enticing but anxious wife? Are they playing their lawyer for a sucker? We wait for the trial to make things clear.

Anatomy of a Murder is Preminger at his finest—intelligent, intricate, utterly unillusioned, and evenhanded. Preminger was fair-minded about many things, and particularly so in the late 1950s and early 1960s, when, in a rather odd career move, he came to specialize in enormous fictions about the interior workings of major public institutions. He re-created the legal proceedings in *Anatomy* with something like love; he afforded the same meticulous attention to the British quandary in Palestine and the Jewish nationalist cause in *Exodus* (1960), the deliberations of the United States Senate in *Advise and Consent* (1962), the power plays within the Curia in *The Cardinal* (1963), and the demotions and promotions of Navy officers in *In Harm's Way* (1965). In all, Preminger is a strange case. At his peak, for more than twenty years he created sophisticated entertainments in many different styles for an audience that was composed largely of grown-ups. But was he a great director or just an inquisitive and urbane fellow who respected the audience's intelligence?

Preminger rarely spoke like a man driven to bring formal or expressive pleasure to moviegoers or even to himself. He spoke of daring subjects, of *projects*. By the early 1950s, he was working independently, producing as well as directing his own pictures—two functions that he saw as continuous. Before shooting, he shaped the script with his writers, and, on the set, he practiced a ruthless economy, finishing his pictures on time and on budget. He then delivered much of the publicity himself. Preminger was a master of high-minded ballyhoo—the taboo-breaking story, the battle with obtuse censors, the overflowing press banquet, the chartered plane to Cannes for a screening (those were the days). Tall, bald, fearless, and charming in a slightly menacing way, he spoke a German-accented English that was a delight to hear and to make fun of. By the late 1950s, he was a director second only to Hitchcock as a Hollywood public figure. At the same time, rumors circulated about his spectacular rudeness and his bullying treatment of actors, especially less experienced actors. This highly intelligent man was capable of grabbing a young performer by the shoulders and screaming "Relax! Relax!" into his face. "Sort of a Jewish Nazi," Joan Crawford called him, and she was a fan.

The first notable claim for Preminger as an artist was advanced in 1954 by Jacques Rivette, then a critic and later one of the New Wave directors. Yet Rivette's article, appearing in *Cahiers du Cinéma* during the seedbed years of auteur theory, is a strange affair. Such directors as Howard Hawks, Alfred Hitchcock, and Fritz Lang, Rivette says, "first believe in their themes and then build the strength of their art upon this conviction. Preminger believes first in mise en scène, the creation of a precise complex of sets and characters, a network of relationships, an architecture of connections, an animated complex that seems suspended in space." In other words, he had no overriding thematic obsessions or visual poetry or dramatic motifs—the usual hallmarks of a director given the auteur honorific. It was the physical realization of the movie in space that mattered to him—the manipulation of characters as the camera met, joined, and accompanied actors down streets, along walls, up and down staircases, through passageways. These particular qualities, and Rivette's limited way of praising Preminger, might have deterred exegesis. On the contrary, they spurred it. Preminger the craftsman of genius was a puzzle that needed to be solved, and he was taken up in the 1960s by English and American auteur critics. Film magazines devoted special issues to him. Stylistic consistencies were discovered, and claims were made; *Advise and Consent*, a shrewd, scrupulous, but very prosy movie, was hailed as a masterpiece. All of this led to Preminger's being attacked, even contemptuously dismissed, by anti-auteurists like Pauline Kael and Dwight Macdonald. "Otto Preminger is a great showman who has never bothered to learn anything about making a movie," Macdonald wrote in 1964.

Preminger the man without aesthetic passions had become a cause of passion in others, an irony that he no doubt enjoyed. But, twenty-one years after his death, the irony seems a little stale, and the question of his importance remains irritatingly difficult to settle. In a forthcoming critical biography, *The World and Its Double: The Life and Work of Otto Preminger*, Chris Fujiwara picks up where the 1960s auteurists left off, finding patterns of narrative strategy, physical detail, and characterization. But, in the course of much formal analysis, Fujiwara seems to be straining to stack up similarities, and, reading him, one is reminded of the old complaint against auteurism—that the mere finding of patterns doesn't guarantee that the movies are any good. In another new book, *Otto Preminger: The Man Who Would Be King*, Foster Hirsch, a professor of film at Brooklyn College, takes a more commonsense approach. Hirsch, who has a warmer sense of a movie's human and dramatic meanings (and failings) than Fujiwara, sorts out the good films from the bad and is eager to present a fully developed portrait of a man often reviled as a brute. Yet while Hirsch wants to praise Preminger as an artist, what impresses him most is the vaunting authority of Preminger as a personality. The book inadvertently raises a curious question: Can technical skill and craft, combined with worldliness and urbanity, and presented in a distinct style, rise to the level of art?

Otto Preminger always passed himself off as Viennese, but he was born (in 1905) in Wiznitz, Poland, an obscure corner of the Austro-Hungarian Empire. The Premingers were *Ostjuden*—East European Jews—and therefore suffered from the status chagrins of provincials as well as from the usual Austrian anti-Semitism. A formidable appearance and manner became central to the family's sense of itself; in an early portrait, Otto's father, Markus, a distinguished lawyer, appears with waxed mustaches pointing upward like raised swords. The family moved to Vienna when Preminger was ten, and Markus Preminger quickly became the chief state prosecutor. A privileged and much indulged youth, Otto read the drama classics and attended the theater. At the age of seventeen, he presented himself as an apprentice actor to Max Reinhardt, the founder of the Salzburg Festival and the most celebrated theatrical producer and director in Vienna. Preminger never amounted to much as an actor (early baldness ended any thought of a career as a leading man); he was always more the impresario-in-the-making. He left Reinhardt after only a year, acted and directed elsewhere, and, while attending university, helped start two new theater companies. By the age of twenty-five, he was a seasoned theatrical professional who had also (to appease his father) earned a law degree from the University of Vienna. A few years later, he inherited Reinhardt's position as manager of the prestigious Theater in der Josefstadt. There Preminger let other directors do the classics while he staged the farces—which seems odd, since his movies, though often witty in a sardonic way, never demonstrate much feeling for physical comedy.

Having received offers from both Broadway and Hollywood, Preminger left Vienna in October 1935, a time when a Jew could still depart from, rather than escape, the city. Hirsch records that Preminger sailed on the *Normandie,* hobnobbed with swells and aristos, and then checked into the St. Regis in New York. Though still in his twenties, Preminger radiated success and authority, and many Americans were eager to be impressed; in those years, appreciation of a cultivated European somehow raised their own status. Others may have merely been vanquished by Preminger's implacable desire to receive the best treatment, even when he couldn't pay the bill. On his first day in New York, he was taken to lunch at "21" and was conducted by the co-owner, Jack Kriendler, on a personal tour of the restaurant, which, along with the St. Regis, remained his favorite haunt in New York for years afterward. Throughout his life, he was a connoisseur of hotels, restaurants, mistresses, artworks, furnishings—the luxurious paraphernalia of the big time.

Yet his artistic success in the early years was mixed. After directing a single play in New York, he wound up working at Twentieth Century-Fox for Darryl Zanuck, a vibrantly self-assured and often shrewd lowbrow from Nebraska. Zanuck put him to work as an apprentice, then gave him some B movies to direct. By 1937, Preminger, having proved himself capable, was assigned to direct a big-budget adaptation of Robert Louis Stevenson's *Kidnapped.* Zanuck thought the early rushes looked stiff. He and Preminger began to argue in Zanuck's office; Preminger, neck veins bulging, blew up, and Zanuck quickly froze him out at Fox. This appears to have been the first notable instance of what became famous as the Preminger tantrum—an empurpled complexion followed by a seeming loss of control and shrieking insults.

Preminger returned to the more comforting milieu of New York theater and café society, where he remained for five years, directing plays, until, in 1942, Zanuck left Fox to oversee production of training films for the Army Signal Corps. Preminger jumped back to the studio and was working with three writers on an adaptation of Vera Caspary's suspense novel *Laura* when, in 1943, Zanuck abruptly returned, took the reins again, and immediately assigned *Laura* to the distinguished film and theater director Rouben Mamoulian; Preminger was allowed only to produce. After three weeks of shooting, however, Mamoulian's work displeased everyone—the style was melodramatic, the actors were florid, and Zanuck, taking it out on Preminger, wired him that "you should have stayed in New York or Vienna, where you belong." Despite this sally, Zanuck listened to Preminger when he argued for a cooler, drier style, and, in the end, Zanuck dropped Mamoulian and gave complete control of the movie to Preminger, who began all over again with the actors and technicians and created *Laura* as we know it.

From his years in New York, Preminger had developed an acid sense of the city's upper classes. "Mamoulian is a nice man, isn't he?" he said to Vincent Price, who plays a svelte, predatory gigolo. "I'm not, and most of my friends are these kind of people"—by which he meant not only Price's character but Judith Anderson's vampiric socialite and Clifton Webb's primly snotty columnist, a middlebrow with a boutonniere who manufactures maudlin sentiment for the masses. *Laura* has been subjected to endless formal analysis, but the movie's fascination has always relied on the outrageous bitchiness of the dialogue and the almost comical coldness of its approach to murder. Laura (Gene Tierney), the beauty who is the object of everyone's obsession, has apparently been killed, but then turns out not to be dead—the girl found in Laura's apartment was a model whose face was destroyed by a shotgun blast. No one, including Laura, mourns the actual victim. As the truth is revealed, all the characters calibrate their next move in the game of power, money, and sex. Even the hero—Dana Andrews's police detective, a tough guy in an effete milieu—comes off as both neurotic and calculating. Preminger's candor about what he brought to the material, and the coolness that allowed him to see what people are really up to, is what keeps *Laura* alive and biting after all these years.

Laura was nominated for five Oscars, and Preminger won Zanuck's respect. As a Fox contract director, he had to take assignments that didn't much interest him, but, when you look at his work from the 1940s and the early 1950s, you find, amid many other films, a series of noir dramas that are among the best movies of the period. So many pictures now are bloated with unnecessary spectacle and backstory that the economy and decisiveness of the noirs—violent, saturnine, dark-city crime narratives driven by strongly motivated characters—seems more miraculous than ever. Like many noir heroes, Preminger's are tormented, sleepless men pursuing women, money, and respect. The underrated Dana Andrews, anguish festering under a self-assured surface, worked for Preminger in four other movies, notably *Fallen Angel* (1945), in which he played a failed public relations man and con artist who becomes obsessed with a sullen beauty (Linda Darnell) working in a Pacific Coast coffee shop; and *Where the Sidewalk Ends* (1950), in which he's a troubled New York police detective with a propensity for violence. Yet if the characters are violent and half crazy, Preminger holds back from obsession. The virtuoso moving camera—always miraculously easy and fluent—doesn't take the point of view of one character or another. Nor does Preminger rely on frequent close-ups, which often define characters in isolation as morally pure or damned—the common technique of melodrama. As Andrew Sarris and many other critics have pointed out, he prefers the two-shot, with the actors facing each other, or positioned side by side or one behind the other, an arrangement that forces us to balance conflicting arguments or emotions. Almost everyone in Preminger's noir movies has jumbled motives, or mixed qualities of good and evil, and his refusal to sort out and judge makes these films, for all their period rhetoric of shadow and lust, feel modern and open-ended. Preminger was a dramatist, not a melodramatist, and, as his later career suggested, a dramatist of a particularly dialectical sort; he was an autocrat who believed that differing points of view needed to be honored, or at least listened to.

An overbearing nature, flourished like a sword, was standard equipment among the German and Austrian directors who had come to Hollywood in the teens and 1920s. Before Preminger, there was Josef von Sternberg, wearing boots and carrying a riding crop on the set; Erich von Stroheim, reportedly demanding monogrammed underwear for the Imperial Army extras in *The Wedding March*; F. W. Murnau, after his initial success here, loudly proclaiming his sufferings as an artist in philistine America, and so on. In Central Europe, manners could be authoritarian in ways unknown in America, but, still, some of the carrying-on was sheer imposture. Von Sternberg and von Stroheim were born middle-class Austrian Jews, so the "von" and some of the hauteur were concocted for the occasion—in a new country, these men wanted to be impressive. Was Preminger also acting a part? On several occasions, both onstage and in the movies, he played a Nazi, most famously in Billy Wilder's *Stalag 17,* from 1953, in which he was the bullying camp commandant. As a director, he seems to have been eager for people to think of him as nasty: Fear of his brutal candor kept actors and technicians in line, discouraging most of them from arguing with him or trying out ideas of their own.

The targets of his outbursts were, for the most part, highly selective; his rage at Zanuck was an anomaly. He did not blow up at Frank Sinatra, Laurence Olivier, John Wayne, Deborah Kerr, or the other big stars who appeared in his movies. He reserved his wrath, instead, for the largely untested Tom Tryon, the leading man in *The Cardinal,* or for Jean Seberg, the seventeen-year-old high school graduate he plucked out of small-town Iowa and made into a leading lady in *Saint Joan* (1957) and *Bonjour Tristesse* (1958). Tryon, Seberg, and many others were reduced to tears by his hectoring and became so rattled they couldn't remember their lines; that night, he would take them out to the best restaurant in town, only to humiliate them again the next morning. With one exception, he was always the one dealing out pleasure and pain. On the set of another terrific noir movie, *Angel Face* (1952), he demanded so many takes of a scene that required Robert Mitchum to slap Jean Simmons across the face that Mitchum finally turned around and slapped Preminger.

Did his way with actors work? As both Hirsch and Fujiwara insist, the old pros who knew their lines got along with him easily and performed well (and, for the record, the red-faced Simmons is quite good). Even Joan Crawford, often so stiff and humorless, gave a spontaneous and likable performance as a professional woman unable to choose between lovers (Andrews, again, and Henry Fonda) in *Daisy Kenyon* (1947), Preminger's sole, and very engaging, venture into the modern-woman's-picture genre. But Preminger lacked the patience to coax a good performance out of unformed actors—or actors formed by Method training, which required them to connect the emotions of a scene to past personal experience. He cared only for what an actor could do on the spot. Still, paradoxically his inability to teach could lead to sterling results. To my ears, Jean Seberg's performances for him are excruciating, yet her callow, just-off-the-farm quality was exactly what Godard wanted for the conscienceless American girl in *Breathless* (1960). Inadvertently, Preminger delivered her intact to a modernist master.

Preminger's annoyance with Jean Simmons may have been exacerbated by the way *Angel Face* was made—as a favor to Zanuck, who, in turn, wanted to do a favor for his pal Howard Hughes, who had Simmons under contract. This sort of seignorial trading of talent—the last remnant of a fading studio system, with its exclusive contracts—infuriated Preminger, and in 1954, anticipating a trend toward independence by a number of years, he bought out his own contract with Fox. A free man, he arranged for the financing and distribution of most of his films himself, and he dealt with controversial subjects that challenged the traditional Hollywood squeamishness. We have long taken for granted the liberties he fought for all through the 1950s, so the issues may now seem musty, even absurd: for instance, the right to make lighthearted jokes about virginity and seduction, in the harmless comedy *The Moon Is Blue* (1953); the right to portray heroin addiction with a decent amount of candor, in *The Man with the Golden Arm* (1955), a film now remarkable mainly for Frank Sinatra's touching performance as an addict. But such issues were not absurd at the time. The two films were refused a seal of approval by the industry-backed Production Code, but Preminger, forging ahead, opened them without the seal, hastening both the death of the Code and the liberation of movie content.

Preminger's independent productions in the 1950s and early 1960s often featured jazz scores, along with chic title design by Saul Bass, who animated solid blocks of color—the titles were aggressively informal and cool, almost hip. Preminger had become a kind of high-bourgeois modernist, relinquishing a Bel Air mansion for an austere, white-walled East Side town house furnished with Eames chairs, curved marble tables, and art by Picasso, Chagall, and Dufy. Liberal in his social attitudes, he enjoyed shocking a country that was both easy to shock and quick to recover from shock, rewarding a creator who stayed just ahead of the curve. He hired the blacklisted screenwriters Ring Lardner, Jr., Albert Maltz, and Dalton Trumbo; he made two musicals with all-black casts, *Carmen Jones* (1954), an adaptation of Bizet's opera set in the contemporary Deep South and featuring a stunning Dorothy Dandridge, who was Preminger's girlfriend at the time, and *Porgy and Bess* (1959), a noble but surprisingly stiff-jointed version of the Gershwin opera. He had become an enlightened citizen, a flamboyant show business equivalent of, say, Eleanor Roosevelt or Joseph N. Welch, the anti-McCarthy lawyer, who, in a shrewd bit of casting by Preminger, played the judge in *Anatomy of a Murder*. No one has been able to separate the opportunist from the man of principle in Preminger, and perhaps there's no need to—the two sides of him combined to set his work apart from the doughy liberal films of the period directed by Stanley Kramer and Martin Ritt.

In a familiar typology, the sociologist Max Weber distinguished among three kinds of leaders—the charismatic, the traditional, and the rational-legal embodiment of authority produced by the modern bureaucratic state. In the United States, there wasn't much tradition to draw on, or, at least, none that mattered to Preminger, but he partook of the two other kinds in paradoxical combination—he became an instance of overwhelming personal charisma operating in a society that prized rationality and legality. What Preminger admired about America was the openness of its culture; he disdained ideologues and took seriously the notion of civil discourse and the exchange of opinion. Here was a man who forbade disagreement on the set and humiliated dozens of people, yet he put tyranny in the service of its opposite: His "institutional" films are all about argument, debate, mutual respect, and compromise. In *Exodus,* a half-naked Paul Newman, emerging like a Jewish Triton from the Mediterranean, excited teenage girls from Scarsdale to Shaker Heights, but a significant part of the film is given over to detailed wrangling between Newman's relatively moderate Haganah and the more radical Irgun. Preminger had refashioned the epic as disputation: Celebrating the birth of Israel, he also gave the British and the Arabs their due. *Advise and Consent* is an enormously articulate structure of warring points of view, in which the most appealing character is the Senate majority leader (played by Walter Pidgeon), who is willing to make all sorts of deals to push the president's nomination for secretary of state through the Senate; the least appealing character is a liberal demagogue who uses blackmail as a tactic. In *The Cardinal*, which chronicles the rise of an American priest named Stephen Fermoyle, Preminger obviously loves the spectacle of vulpine cardinals jostling one another amid the Vatican's frescoes, stairways, and antechambers. Out of piety, Fermoyle betrays several women, but Preminger dramatizes the personal issues with such rigorous dialectical balance that one has trouble telling if the man is supposed to be a victim of Church law or just an insensitive fool.

Preminger was perhaps too refined and modulated in his sophistication to achieve more than occasional greatness as a director. He doesn't compare, for instance, with his fellow émigrés Fritz Lang and Billy Wilder. It's hard to think of a heartbreaking or truly exhilarating moment in his work. Yet, at his best, he raised civil discourse to the level of subtle entertainment: One can get caught up in the intricately choreographed give-and-take of *Advise and Consent* without caring whether the nominee gets confirmed or not. And, in at least one case, he was enough of an artist to know that discourse could not be enough. In *Anatomy of a Murder*, the conclusion of the trial settles nothing—the verdict is announced, but we still don't know if the wife was violated. The moral chaos of the Army lieutenant and his wife overwhelms the hyperrationality of the legal process, and truth recedes into mazelike corridors of doubt. The movie ends with Ellington's pointed ironies—a muted trumpet shrieking and then gasping in mock anguish. And the light remains gray.

The New Yorker, *July 14, 2008*

VICTOR FLEMING / THE DIRECTOR THE AUTEURISTS FORGOT

Howard Hughes, whose acumen outside certain areas of expertise (aeronautics and the acquisition of beautiful actresses) was rarely sound, once said something intelligent about the relative merits of two movie directors. The remark was delivered in early 1939, when George Cukor had been shooting *Gone With the Wind* for about three weeks. An adaptation of Margaret Mitchell's thousand-page blockbuster novel, from 1936, about the Old South, the Civil War, and Reconstruction, the movie was the largest and most expensive production in Hollywood up to that time, with a huge cast, massive sets (the city of Atlanta was burned down and then rebuilt), and hundreds of unshaven and bandaged extras trudging across the landscape. As half of Hollywood maliciously cheered, the production slipped into disaster. The script could be kindly described as a mess, and the star—Clark Gable—was in turmoil. The initial rushes displeased David O. Selznick, the legendary, manic producer who dominated every aspect of the film, and he suddenly fired Cukor, who, he later said, couldn't have handled the more spectacular elements of the movie. In Cukor's place, Selznick hired Victor Fleming, who was then directing the other big picture in town, *The Wizard of Oz*. Fleming was a vigorous and resourceful man, but few people considered him an artist. The change pleased Gable but distressed the two female leads—the young stage and film actress Vivien Leigh, just arrived from England and not yet a star, and Olivia de Havilland, who was then Howard Hughes's girlfriend. Both women depended on Cukor, who was known as a "woman's director," and de Havilland brought her troubles to Hughes, who advised: "Don't worry, everything is going to be all right—with George and Victor, it's the same talent, only Victor's is strained through a coarser sieve."

Hughes was almost correct. Fleming's talent was not "the same" as Cukor's, yet he was definitely the right man for *Gone With the Wind*, and he did inventive and powerful work on *Oz*. But in the seventy years since the release of those films, Fleming, whose talent flowed not smoothly or subtly, but roughly, in surges of energy and feeling, has been largely forgotten. The auteur theory critics who, in the 1960s and 1970s, went wild over Cukor, Hitchcock, Preminger, John Ford, Howard Hawks, Ernst Lubitsch, Josef von Sternberg, Frank Capra, and many other directors of the late silent and early sound periods, ignored Fleming, though he had made a number of entertaining movies in the 1920s and 1930s and his two super-productions of 1939 are very likely the most widely seen movies in American film history—not just good pictures but films that have entered the unconscious of generations of moviegoers. *Gone With the Wind*, with its happy plantation slaves—emblems of Noble Toil—posed against reddening skies, has its enraging and embarrassing moments; the racist kitsch is, regrettably, part of the nation's collective past. What remains remarkably modern in the film is the central combat of wills between Leigh's Scarlett O'Hara and Gable's Rhett Butler, each seeking the upper hand in and out of bed. Margaret Mitchell set up the conflict, but it was Fleming who got the two actors to embody it. As for *The Wizard of Oz*, the movie's version of the magical land of Oz, in its combined freedom and unease, happiness and fear, has become a universally shared vision of the imagination itself. Since Fleming was the element common to both movies, his contribution needs to be lifted out of the shadows.

The seventieth anniversary of these two classics has seen deluxe new (and expensive) versions on DVD, and the appearance of two good books: *Victor Fleming: An American Movie Master* (Pantheon), a full-scale biography that shines up the director's reputation, by Michael Sragow, the film critic of the *Baltimore Sun,* who has written for this magazine; and *Frankly, My Dear: "Gone With the Wind" Revisited* (Yale), by Molly Haskell, whose 1973 study *From Reverence to Rape* remains a standard text on women in movies. Haskell has lived in Manhattan for more than forty years, but she grew up in Richmond, Virginia, and as a girl she became obsessed with Margaret Mitchell's rebellious Southern belle, Scarlett, as personified in the movie by Leigh—a selfish, greedy, flirtatious yet sex-hating green-eyed demon who is every inch and flounce a heroine.

/   /   /

When summoned by Selznick, Fleming hadn't read Mitchell's novel, but he took a look at the screenplay and immediately told the producer, "Your fucking script is no fucking good." Selznick had owned the property since the book's publication, and in 1936 he had hired the East Coast playwright and screenwriter Sidney Howard to do an adaptation. Howard turned in a faithful but overlong version, and Selznick began fiddling. At one time or another, as many as fifteen writers worked on the movie, until finally, in early 1939, as production stalled and hundreds of salaried people sat around idle, Selznick turned to Ben Hecht, the greatest and most cynical of Hollywood screenwriters. Hecht agreed to work on the script as long as he didn't have to read the book. Selznick told him the plot, but he couldn't make any sense of it, so Selznick retrieved Howard's version, and, as Hecht listened, Selznick and Fleming read it aloud, Selznick taking the role of Scarlett, Fleming reading Rhett.

In this manner, the three men worked eighteen or twenty hours a day, sustained by Dexedrine, peanuts, and bananas, a combination that Selznick believed would stimulate the creative process. On the fourth day, according to Hecht, a blood vessel burst in Fleming's eye. On the fifth, Selznick, eating a banana, swooned, and had to be revived by a doctor. Many good Hollywood movies have been saved by last-minute revisions, but this ill-fed, hazardous, all-male acting-and-writing marathon must be the strangest of all interventions. Oddly, it may also provide a key to the movie's success: Selznick, an epic (and often hapless) Hollywood womanizer, nevertheless had, Molly Haskell claims, genuine and delicate insights into women's feelings, and, in some crucial way (strengthened, perhaps, by his reading her part), he identified with Scarlett. Fleming, tall, strong, and startlingly handsome—Selznick ruefully called him "the most attractive man, in my opinion, who ever came to Hollywood"—did not chase women; they chased him. The director was considered by everyone to be a "man's man"—shrewd, funny, but bluff and demanding—and he was close in temperament to the hard-nosed character of Rhett Butler. It's possible that the extraordinary balance between Scarlett and Rhett was sealed at this moment.

Gable had been worried all along about his ability to play Rhett, an emotionally demanding role, and he yearned for Fleming's support. He had worked with him before, in 1932—in the deliciously entertaining sex-in-the-jungle romantic drama *Red Dust,* in which he costarred with Jean Harlow—and he had taken a lot from Fleming's manner of brusque masculine humor. Cukor, however, as people noted at the time, made Gable nervous and angry. Gable was afraid that Cukor might swing the movie toward its actresses, especially Vivien Leigh. In recent years, a more piquant speculation has surfaced: that Gable, in his early days in Hollywood, had been a gigolo and had had a few gay encounters. In this telling, someone in Cukor's circle had been gossiping about Gable's past, and Gable, jealous of his reputation as the hetero "king" of Hollywood, grew alarmed.

Fleming's presence restored the star's self-assurance. After Hecht edited Sidney Howard's script (in the end, Howard got sole credit), the production got under way again, and Gable, once more imitating Fleming's manner (Sragow calls the director "the real Rhett Butler"), wound up doing the best, most expressive acting of his career. The actresses did well, too. De Havilland provided the movie with a moral center, and Leigh, though hardly fond of Fleming, gave one of the most electrifying performances in the history of movies. As Fleming pulled together Selznick's monster production during the day, he supervised the editing of *The Wizard of Oz* at night. He may have been an artist after all.

Victor Fleming's mother was of Pennsylvania Dutch extraction (the longtime Hollywood rumor that Fleming was part Cherokee is nothing more than that); his father was from Missouri. The family went West, and Fleming was born, in 1889, near Pasadena, then a hamlet so primitive that his father, a citrus rancher, helped lay the public water supply system. He died of a heart attack, in a family-managed orange orchard, when Fleming was four. Years later, the director wrote, "There is little room in my life for sentiment and soft words," which is the kind of statement that tough American men in the 1920s and 1930s often made to cover a deeper current of feeling. Dropping out of school in his mid-teens, Fleming became fascinated by speed and by the new machines that produced it, cars and airplanes, as well as by the new machine that captured it, the motion picture camera. In his early twenties, he briefly tried his hand at car racing, but wound up a chauffeur in Santa Barbara, where he fell in with the pioneer movie director Allan Dwan. Taking over as a cameraman on Dwan's films, Fleming found a trade. A photograph of him from this period reveals an almost unnervingly forceful young man with hostile eyes and a wedged pompadour. He looks less like a movie person than like a young officer out of uniform.

By 1915, he was shooting the films that Dwan made with Douglas Fairbanks, and, four years later, Fleming became Fairbanks's director. They made just three movies together—*When the Clouds Roll By* (1919), *The Mollycoddle* (1920), and the mock documentary *Around the World in 80 Minutes* (1931)—but they became lifelong friends. Fairbanks's movies often had a satirical bent: The smiling young man, throwing himself around the set and showing off his skills as a gymnast, outraged the boors and the stuffed shirts. Off the set, the two men carried on in the same way. They jumped over chairs and couches in hotel lobbies, swung through trains by holding on to overhead racks; they leaped from a twelve-foot height (in one version of the story, from a burning hayloft), first Fleming and then Fairbanks, and each broke an ankle.

In the early 1920s, Fleming became close to Howard Hawks, and, in the same spirit of macho competitiveness, they took up aviation, building and flying ramshackle planes that smashed their landing gear on hitting the ground. The risk-taking shenanigans, the strenuous, dangerous fun, were an essential part of the carefree ethos that found its way into countless movies and that formed, for better or worse, a good part of the American masculine ideal in the twentieth century.

Sragow is immensely attentive to Fleming's films, and he traces in detail the fortunes of all the people connected to them, but his book is held together by what can only be called the romance of moviemaking in the studio era—the large, free, hard-drinking life that the men (but rarely the women) enjoyed when movies were still made quickly and relatively cheaply, craft was spoken of with respect, and art was barely mentioned. Some of the episodes in Fleming's life play like scenes from the movies of the time—for instance, his killing a charging rhinoceros in East Africa an instant before it slammed into one of his friends. Or his showing up with a case of Scotch after the alcoholic Spencer Tracy had gone on a bender and had failed to report to the set of Fleming's 1937 film *Captains Courageous.* According to Tracy, Fleming told him to drink up the entire case—he was through with worrying about him. Abashed, Tracy sobered up and got back to work. Fleming, in effect, administered the reviving smack that figured in so many movies of the period (including his own)—the slap across the kisser that brought people to their senses.

As Sragow points out, Fleming had learned something essential from his capering association with Douglas Fairbanks—how to position a performer within the frame and time his performance in such a way that the camera brought out his temperament and his strength. This would seem an essential skill for any filmmaker, yet a surprising number of directors, obsessed with visual expressiveness, are inattentive to it. Fleming didn't give detailed instructions to his actors; rather, he talked about the character, and located and enlarged a set of defining traits—a strain of feeling or humor—in whomever he was working with. Then the actors, working intimately for the camera, performed what in effect were idealized versions of themselves, creating a persona that connected with a widespread public fantasy. Fleming, along with such directors as Ford and William Wyler, had the star-making skill that Hollywood has now lost.

It was Fleming, directing the canonical Western *The Virginian* (1929), who shifted Gary Cooper's minimalist stoicism into a subtly but steadily revealing undercurrent of emotion. In *Captains Courageous,* he helped Tracy focus his threatening manner into a single strong shaft of feeling with the slightly off-center rhythm that became Tracy's signature. Gable, Cooper, and Tracy all produced variations on the ideal of a courageous, good-humored American male, and they all borrowed, to some degree, from Fleming. What they found in him was ease and authority. What women found in him, apart from good looks, fun, and romance (he had affairs with many of his actresses, including Clara Bow and Norma Shearer), was a current of self-confidence that they could draw on. "Despite his later reputation as a 'man's director,'" Sragow says, "Fleming launched or cannily revamped a host of female stars from the 1920s on." The hot-wired Bow did her sexiest, best work for him, in *Mantrap* (1926), and he got sensationally funny performances out of Jean Harlow in *Red Dust, Bombshell* (1933), and *Reckless* (1935). The sacred male companionships of seventy years ago did not have the effect of downgrading women—anything but. Fleming, along with his friend Hawks, created women on-screen who were resourceful, strong-willed, and sexual—the kind of women they wanted to hang out with, partners and equals who gave as good as they got. For a while, they, too, were an American ideal.

The auteurist critics look for recurring patterns, the incandescent joining of visual style and idea. You can't find such patterns, or even a consistent visual motif, in Fleming's movies. But you can find a powerful grasp of fable—the emotional progression of a small number of clearly drawn characters through a decisively shaped tale, leading to a series of wrenching encounters and a satisfying climax. In *Captains Courageous,* a brilliant but snotty American rich kid (Freddie Bartholomew) falls off an ocean liner. Tracy's Portuguese fisherman pulls him out of the sea and throws him in with the crew of his trawler, who knock him into shape. As Sragow points out, what the boy becomes is not a decent jolly fellow but the superior young man he was bred to become. The movie is less sentimental than it at first appears, as was Fleming's *Treasure Island* (1934), starring Wallace Beery and Jackie Cooper, which caught the scariness and the strangeness felt by a boy cast among thieves and scoundrels. In these two movies, growing up is a trial—a passage through fear, a test of character.

In retrospect, it seems hard to imagine anyone but Fleming directing *The Wizard of Oz,* the greatest child-centered movie of all. Yet he wasn't the first choice on this film, either. In October 1938, the film began shooting at MGM under Richard Thorpe, a journeyman who had directed a Tarzan picture in 1936. Thorpe's footage was flat, and the producer, Mervyn LeRoy, threw it out. (Bizarrely, Cukor also briefly worked on *Oz.* After Thorpe was fired, Cukor dropped in, changed Judy Garland's makeup and hair style, and fled; the material didn't interest him.) LeRoy then turned to Fleming, who initially said no, as much of the production, including the screenplay and the sets, was already in place. A few years earlier, however, Fleming had gotten married—to Lu Rosson, who had been the wife of a close friend—and he was the father of two little girls, whom he adored. He left few memos or letters, but, from what he wrote about *Oz* for an internal MGM publication, one gets the impression that he changed his mind because he wanted to make an entertainment that both adults and children could see.

The screenwriters Noel Langley, Florence Ryerson, and Edgar Allan Woolf adapted *The Wonderful Wizard of Oz,* L. Frank Baum's classic 1900 novel, and they made two momentous changes. In Baum's book, Oz is a wondrous place, but it's real—Dorothy, still in her house, is carried there by a raging cyclone. In the movie, Dorothy (Judy Garland), conked on the head during the storm, spins into Oz in a dream, and Oz becomes the blossoming of her unconscious, populated by strikingly familiar faces joined to weird bodies: Her intimidating neighbor Miss Gulch (Margaret Hamilton) shows up as the lime-green Wicked Witch of the West, and the farmhands employed by Dorothy's stern Auntie Em become her sweetly despondent companions with missing parts—the Scarecrow (Ray Bolger) and the Tin Man (Jack Haley). Fleming, working with his favorite screenwriter, John Lee Mahin, added a third farmhand, Zeke, who became the Cowardly Lion (Bert Lahr). He also reconceived the Kansas scenes, giving them a sharper edge. He changed what had become (unbelievably) yellow ovals in Thorpe's production back to the immortal yellow bricks, and commissioned the signature song "Follow the Yellow Brick Road" from Yip Harburg and Harold Arlen. Fleming did not direct the Kansas scenes, which were shot in black-and-white (and then released in sepia). They were scheduled for the end of the shoot; by that time, he had gone off to work on *Gone With the Wind,* and they were done by the director King Vidor. But the main body of the movie, from the moment that Dorothy opens the door to Oz and the screen turns to brilliant Technicolor—a stunner in 1939, and still exciting today—belongs to Fleming.

Dorothy's immortality, in the person of Judy Garland, was not easily achieved. Garland, who had been fussed over and bullied by MGM since she had signed with the studio in 1935, was a very self-conscious, uncertain, but blazingly talented sixteen-year-old, playing a girl of about twelve. Her eagerness and tenderness are still touching, as an idealized portrait of a child, but Fleming wanted Dorothy to be tough as well, and the neurotic star gave him fits. In one scene, Garland bops Lahr's Cowardly Lion on the snout, and Lahr's blubbering was so funny that Garland cracked up, and then lost control of herself, laughing hysterically through take after take. She stood behind a synthetic tree, saying to herself, "I will not laugh. I will not laugh," but, when she ruined yet another take, Fleming slapped her across the face and said, "All right, now. Go back to your dressing room." (The slap was something of a Fleming trademark, on-screen and off.) She came out later and got on with the rest of the movie. In the end, her Dorothy, an orphan raised by a Depression-era aunt (her uncle hardly exists), turns out to be surprisingly strong. The way Fleming directs her, Dorothy has a clumpy farm girl's grit—she's a literal-minded kid fiercely clinging to her hopes and desires among witches, blue-faced flying monkeys, and squeaking little people. She undergoes a journey of epic proportions, only to arrive back in Kansas, where she finds that her true self was there all along. It's an ending that Salman Rushdie, in an affectionate short book he wrote about the movie, deplores: Dorothy, he says, no longer needs the inadequate adults in her life; she's ready to go out on her own. Yet we assume—don't we?—that Dorothy has been changed by what she has imagined. In her dreams, she has faced down demons, overcome a loss of faith—she has been tested, just like Fleming's child heroes in *Treasure Island* and *Captains Courageous*.

Apart from the scenes with the hoodoos and the winged monkeys, Fleming's direction is earthbound, and that's the way it should be. The picture's veteran music hall stars—Bolger, Haley, and Lahr—need to work on the ground; indeed, they have an intimate, virtuosic relation to the ground. When Lahr lands on his rump, his legs shoot up like a moving swing suddenly emptied of its child. Bolger does flailing, rubber-legged collapses and recoveries—he teases the ground, engaging it and then taking off from it. And Haley, in his rusting metal case, leans perilously, like a telephone pole in a storm. Academics have told me that *Oz* is a mythic structure, a descendant of the *Odyssey* or the *Aeneid*, but they look at me blankly when I say that the movie is also a summa of 1930s show business. Fleming framed his vaudevillians and musical comedy performers as he had framed Cooper and Tracy—he brought out their individual genius as performers. He might have moved the camera more, or done some point-of-view shooting, but his square, stable, front-and-center view is essentially the right directorial strategy for this performance-dominated fantasy. Many talented people worked on *Oz*, but, as Sragow says, without Fleming's enthusiasm and discipline "the movie would have collapsed into campy chaos." Fleming combined the elements into an emotionally overwhelming fable, which was always his supreme gift.

Judged as an example of storytelling (if not for the story it tells), *Gone With the Wind* can't be much faulted, either. The Civil War begins, crests, and reaches a disastrous conclusion with the destruction of Atlanta, and mournfulness holds sway through the middle of the epic. Yet, if keening over the Old South had been the movie's sole thematic line, *Gone With the Wind*, as Molly Haskell notes, would have been forgotten, along with many mossy plantation novels and films of the period. Barbarous Rhett and ungovernable Scarlett push the gracious-plantation nostalgia out of the way. A Southern-born war profiteer, Rhett doesn't believe in "the cause" of secession, while Scarlett finds the war merely tiresome (the foolish young men run away to get killed, spoiling the parties). For all its fustian, the picture offers an enchanting idiosyncrasy: A saga of a broken nation is told from the point of view of a vain and restless girl. At the beginning, in one of the cinema's indelible images, Leigh's sixteen-year-old Scarlett floats rapidly across the grass and through the trees in a virgin-white layered dress. Pauline Kael once compared Leigh to a Dresden-china shepherdess, an image that captures the delicacy of her features and her body but not their mobility. As the small mouth puckers, the lynx-eyed glance, with head slightly turned, appears to see around corners. The quickness of her responses is almost frightening. Wariness and avidity, coquetry and rage, preening and despair—unrelenting egotism plays on her face like sunlight on a fast-moving stream. Amid the terrible events of the war, her Scarlett, the implacable "me," is obsessed with nothing but her own affairs, and Fleming urged Leigh to give Scarlett's bitchiness full rein.

Introducing his couple, Fleming gave Gable perhaps the most glamorous entrance that any movie actor has ever enjoyed. As Leigh looks down while ascending a grand staircase, Gable, broad across the shoulders and pulled in (actually girdled) at the waist, stands at the bottom and brazenly gazes up at her. She says to a friend, "He looks as if—as if he knows what I look like without my shimmy." Gable's appreciative stare was usually enough to make the women in his movies tumble, but Scarlett resists for a long time, marrying two men, both nonentities, before marrying Rhett, and then she does so mostly for his money. Her resistance to him even after marriage—her choice of power over sex and romantic love—fascinates Haskell. "Inside the tinkling charms of a Southern-belle saga," she writes, "are the rumblings of a feminist manifesto." After the war, Scarlett not only takes over America's most famous fictional turf, the ruined plantation Tara, but scandalizes Atlanta society by becoming a hard-driving lumber entrepreneur—apparently the first female capitalist of the New South. Margaret Mitchell had enjoyed a brief fling as a flapper, and Haskell maintains that she transposed the rebellious spirit of women of the 1920s into the heart and body of a nineteenth-century social butterfly. This compositional strategy not only retrieved Scarlett from the past but projected her into the future, and Leigh, abetted by Fleming, sustained Scarlett as a perverse, good-bad heroine for our times, a shrew who won't be tamed.

For seventy years, ever since teenage girls started reading the novel with a flashlight under the covers, this romantic misalliance has remained a subject of speculation and debate—a pop-culture obsession serving as a template for a nation's romantic dreams and regrets. In the famous "rape" scene, Gable, with an unwilling Leigh in his arms, surges up a crimson stairway to the bedroom, and after that point the movie, as Haskell says, astonishingly lurches from bodice ripper to something like tragic drama. Tracking the stages of the struggle between husband and wife, Haskell discovers a conflict in her own responses: She loves Scarlett's ambition but finds the marital disaster, which is partly produced by it, almost heartbreaking, especially since Rhett isn't the usual villain of feminist critique—a dominating husband who wants to crush his spirited wife. On the contrary, he loves his wife for exactly what she is. Looking at the movie again, one can glean the truth from certain shadings in Leigh's performance: Her rage at Gable contains more than a hint of panic, a suggestion by the actress that, for Scarlett, sexual happiness might lead to an intolerable loss of will. In all, as a portrait of a couple at war, there's nothing quite so intense and sustained in American movies, and Fleming sharpened it to the point of violence. No surprise: On a much smaller scale, and largely as comedy, he had done something similar in the rowdy give-and-take between Gable and Harlow in *Red Dust*, a romance in which each partner is initially too proud to admit to loving the other.

On the *Gone With the Wind* set, Fleming teased and cajoled Leigh; at times, they battled as much as Rhett and Scarlett. Walking off after a bad day, he said, "Miss Leigh, you can stick this script up your royal British ass," a not particularly elegant variant of "Frankly, my dear, I don't give a damn." But their dislike for each other may have kept the movie dramatically alive. In one of the scenes in which Rhett moves in on Scarlett, Fleming instructed her, "Resist but don't resist too much." Yet, as Gable reached for her, she slapped him. This particular blow, one imagines, may have been a retaliatory act aimed as much at Fleming as at Rhett. In any case, Fleming was very pleased with the scene ("That's swell!"), and it stayed in the movie. The ethos of toughness was applied to Gable, too, and with unprecedented results. If Gable began the project afraid that episodes from his past life might make him look effeminate, he nevertheless gave way, under his mentor's insistent prodding, to "feminine" emotions he had never shown before (nor after), including bafflement when a beautiful woman doesn't want him, increasing despair, and even, at times, tearful grief.

All through the shoot, Fleming took vitamin shots to keep up his energy, and downers at the end of the day, and he became so jangled and tired, and so enraged by Selznick's daily memos about virtually every shot, that he retreated, under a doctor's orders, to his beach house in Balboa. For eighteen days, the MGM staff director Sam Wood took over. But Fleming came back and, muttering mildly anti-Semitic remarks to friends, reshot scenes as Selznick requested, and assisted in the editing. He directed, by common estimate, about 60 percent of the film. A few of the scenes that Cukor shot (none with Gable and Leigh alone) survived the final cut, and, after he was dismissed, on days off from shooting, Cukor coached both Leigh and de Havilland at his house, so he may be responsible for some of the nuances in those two performances. Yet it was Fleming who saved the project from dissolution and got the man-woman struggle at the heart of it down right, and he deserves a good part of the credit for the movie's becoming the cultural monument that millions still adore.

/ / /

The best movie Fleming made after his exhausting labors of 1939 was a new version of *Dr. Jekyll and Mr. Hyde* (1941), with Spencer Tracy in the title roles and, as Hyde's victim, a startlingly sexual Ingrid Bergman, who was Fleming's last movie star girlfriend. He died eight years later, of heart failure, in the arms of his wife, Lu, at the age of fifty-nine, and immediately slipped into obscurity. What should history make of him? He didn't direct the entirety of either of his two classics, and he wasn't, by definition, an auteur. But this absence from the list of the blessed suggests a fault in auteur theory and not in Fleming—a prejudice against the generalists, the nonobsessed, the "chameleons," as Steven Spielberg called them, who re-created themselves for each project and made good movies in many different styles. Talent, when poured through "a coarser sieve," can assert itself in rough-and-ready humor, resilience, and all-around hardiness and strength. Cinema's historians should celebrate, as audiences always have, not only the obsessed geniuses but also the adaptable ruffians who made many of the most entertaining movies ever to come out of Hollywood.

The New Yorker *(published as "The Real Rhett Butler"), May 25, 2009*

PEDRO ALMODÓVAR /
IN AND OUT OF LOVE

Let me tell you a story. In a Catholic school in a small town in rural Spain, two boys, Ignacio and Enrique, fell in love. They went to the movies together and touched each other—a consummation of sorts. But the boys were only eleven, and their friendship was broken up by the schoolmaster, a priest named Manolo. Father Manolo, however, wasn't simply enforcing the rules. He had already laid hands on Ignacio, a sweet-faced choirboy, and he wanted him entirely for himself. Pedro Almodóvar's triumphantly accomplished *Bad Education,* which is both a summation of his career thus far and a deepening of his recent style, opens sixteen years later, in 1980. Ignacio (Gael García Bernal), now a young actor, brings a manuscript to Enrique (Fele Martínez), who has become a well-known movie director in Madrid. The manuscript chronicles the boys' friendship and what happened to Ignacio—he became a drag queen and a blackmailer. As Enrique reads the story, we see it enacted. Later, he turns it into a movie, only to be interrupted by the appearance of the priest, who tells his version of events. By now, the priest has turned his collar around—he is Mr. Berenguer, not Father Manolo—but he's still in love. Complex and devious beyond easy recounting, *Bad Education* is about the fallout from the ending of a "pure" love between boys, consecrated in an Almodóvaran temple—a movie theater. Like so many of Almodóvar's films, it's also about memory and the dangerously self-serving act of telling stories. Storytelling, lying, and the eager trying on of selves have always been at the core of Almodóvar's alarmingly literal demand for liberty. La Agrado, one of Almodóvar's gabby, warmhearted transsexuals—from *All About My Mother* (1999)—puts it this way: "You are more and more authentic the more you look like someone you dreamed of being."

In *Bad Education,* Almodóvar draws on elements from his own life, but the movie is not a confession. He has stated, for instance, that he was not abused as a boy. The movie is explicitly homoerotic, but then so was *Law of Desire* (1987), along with scenes in many of his other movies. Almodóvar, now fifty-three and, in recent years, the recipient of the kind of adulation offered to Bergman, Fellini, and Kurosawa four decades ago, revels in flagrantly disreputable material—cross-dressing and transsexuality, carnal dreams and rhapsodies, sex with an aura of violation. He has put theatricality and fantasy back into lust. As far as anyone can see, he has always been happily "out," and he may have little to confess. What's come "out" in *Bad Education* is a confirmation of the formal control he displayed in *Talk to Her,* the somber and beautiful movie he made in 2002. The two films are not a break with the past, but they might be seen as a liberation from a famously liberated style. For the first time since *Law of Desire,* Almodóvar has made movies centrally about men, and both, perhaps not coincidentally, are resolutely serious.

Magnificent, unbridled Medusas, broad-shouldered and long-waisted; tense housewives and avid professionals enraged over the misbehavior of some worthless lover; haggard mothers and bereft daughters, longing for connection even as they are repelled by each other's need—the films of Pedro Almodóvar have celebrated women. And not just women but women in an uproar. They are in love, they are betrayed, they lie, dissemble, commit murder. Their lives are defined by the feverish calamitousness of soap opera, by the conventions of Spanish movie melodrama, and, in particular, by Hollywood "women's pictures" of the 1940s and 1950s, the mere sound of whose starring names—Lana, Ava, Bette, Rita, Joan—conjures up an era of sumptuous glamour and tempestuous emotionalism. Most of Almodóvar's movies are romantic melodramas goosed into near-parody. He loves absurd reversals of fortune. In *Tie Me Up! Tie Me Down!* (1990), for instance, an unhinged young man entraps a former porn star he's crazy about and demands not just sex with her but a family and children, and she winds up falling in love with him. Even when Almodóvar renders homage to a director utterly unlike himself, as he did in the mother-daughter epic *High Heels* (1991)—a mad retelling of Ingmar Bergman's *Autumn Sonata*—he squeezes the original story for its underlay of hysteria and competitiveness. By the end of *High Heels*, a mother and daughter have shared a lover, the daughter has killed him and her stepfather, and a drama of female temperament begins to seem like a comedy of female temperament. Not just Bergman but such directors of glossy Hollywood melodramas as Michael Curtiz, Otto Preminger, King Vidor, and Douglas Sirk probably never imagined that the world of grand female emotion could be reconfigured as farce. How could they? In different ways, as serious artists or as masters of kitsch, they were immersed in creating illusions for an audience that wanted and needed to believe in what it saw. Almodóvar, in contrast, always lets us know that his actresses are performing, that what they offer is not a piece of life but a convulsively entertaining fiction. There's an Oscar Wilde paradox at work in the physical appearance of these women: They seem to have taken off their faces so that we can see their masks. Almodóvar is not interested in discovering something profound in an actress. He's interested in electric immediacy, in presence. What could he do with a guileless, vibrantly natural, "transparent" performer like Liv Ullmann? He likes an actress who appears to be onstage even when she's sitting in a living room. A madcap couturier, he dresses women in reds and oranges, in tippy-tappy high heels and miniskirts, and celebrates their most unconventionally attractive features—Picassoesque hatchet noses, large ruby lips, masses of thick black hair, and sharply outlined eyes.

Leaving out the transvestites, the men in the movies Almodóvar made before *Talk to Her* are mostly handsome stiffs. Straight or gay, they are all caught up in the comic insanity of machismo. The Almodóvaran male was a Lothario, a betrayer who muttered fatalistic Spanish nonsense into a woman's ear; he was a relentless predator who longed to dominate some love object; he was a luscious young virgin, slender, cherubic, bare-rumped. (Antonio Banderas, with dark, liquid eyes and swollen lips, played both the second and third types in his youth.) Until recently, Almodóvar had shown little interest in men as people. Is he a caricaturist, then? An ironist? How could a director working out of what appears to be a gay-cabaret sensibility achieve such renown? Surely there has never been a world-famous director whose work is essentially camp. Or is Almodóvar's work not camp at all? The most readily enjoyable of all art house directors—a natural-born entertainer—Almodóvar also has his mysteries. This teasing melodramatist-modernist may be something unprecedented in movie history.

Almodóvar's life is an urban gay man's version of a hero's tale. He was educated in the small town of Cáceres, during the Franco era, at a school run by Salesian Brothers. He escaped, whenever he could, to watch movies and listen to American and British pop. In the late 1960s, at the age of sixteen, he left school and headed to Madrid, where he got a job at Telefónica, the Spanish national telephone company. He made connections: He finished work at three and, at night, frequented the Madrid underground. In the next decade, as Franco's reign came to an end, Almodóvar worked at the triple nexus of pop, gay, and commercial culture. He wrote music and comedy skits, designed fotonovelas and comics, and performed in curlers and a housedress as half of a parodic punk rock duo called Almodóvar y McNamara. He collaborated with the avant-garde theater troupe Los Goliardos, where he met his future star and muse, Carmen Maura. He shot his first movies in Super 8 film, without a soundtrack, and showed them in bars and at parties, performing all the speaking parts himself. In 1980, he moved into features, and became as much the chronicler of nighttime Madrid as Brassaï had been the chronicler of Paris cafés. In his movies, the countryside hardly exists, and "nature" may be no more than a poisoned mushroom pushed up by a corpse buried in someone's city garden.

Almodóvar has said, "My rebellion is to deny Franco. . . . I refuse even his memory. I start everything I write with the idea, What if Franco had never existed?" This claim is no doubt a way of avoiding an endless quarrel with the past, but it sounds like a myth, and we needn't believe it. The anticlericalism, the erotic fantasias, the love of dressing up and acting out—the efflorescence of liberated expression in Almodóvar's films can no more be understood apart from Franco's clerical-military form of fascism than Joyce's work can be separated from the Irish Catholic Church. To begin with, Almodóvar's way of not taking seriously the sexual transgressions that enrage conservatives is itself a political act. Again and again, he has ridiculed Spanish machismo—most openly in *Matador* (1986), which thrusts a sword of parody deep into the blood-and-cape solemnity of the national stereotype. Diego, a famous bullfighter who retired after he was severely gored, is a kind of mountebank philosopher of death. He masturbates to movie scenes in which women are offed, and he kills a few himself. At last, he meets his female counterpart, a lawyer in swirling capes who seduces young matadors and, just as they are about to reach orgasm, inserts an ornate hairpin into their necks. Not entirely to our surprise, the bullfighter and the lawyer make a pact. In a rush of giddy, gaudy passion, they die in each other's arms, their capes spread out on the floor beneath them. All this spectacular, highly patterned erotic play makes hash of the traditionalist version of Spanish character that Franco's authorities encouraged—the gestural majesty, the tautly defined, iconic emotions of the dance and the bullring. *Matador* is screwball, dirty-minded flamenco—ritual movement turned into lurid spoof. On the evidence of this movie, and others, Almodóvar seems to have nothing but distaste for the Spanish cult of cruelty. There is violence in his movies, but very little sadism; evil functions formally, as a plot device, but not emotionally, as a definer of character. Almodóvar identifies with the victim rather than with the conqueror, and he fills his movies with benevolent gestures and the pathos of lost love, the half-serious, half-ludicrous fatality of past acts replaying themselves in the turmoil of the present. He is Tennessee Williams's most talented heir.

Almodóvar's interest in molten-eyed transvestites and vamping, sequined drag queens may be the product of more than sexual curiosity. Such men open the floodgates of emotion without shame, and, however wistful and mixed up, they represent hope, as do the tall, restless street hustlers who become not transsexuals but omnisexuals—they have beautiful new breasts, which they show off to anyone who's interested, but they still have a male organ. They haven't changed gender—they've added one. Almodóvar's embrace of such men is so affectionate that we think less about perversion than about the manifold carnal possibilities of life—the unwillingness to give up anything. In *Law of Desire*, Carmen Maura plays Tina, an actress who was born a boy. As a child, she ran off with her father and, at his urging, had a sex change operation. Then he left her, and she became a lesbian and mother—she's raising her lover's daughter. Tina could be a joke on all the solemn talk of "gender" in recent years: Her identity is not so much unstable as universal. In Almodóvar's films, identity is not "constructed" by social forces but created by fantasy, will, and humor. Self-generated, his people don't behave according to traditional stereotypes, but they don't behave according to liberationist stereotypes, either. What matters to the director is not whether they are straight or gay (the issue is hardly discussed) but what they want and what they do.

In *High Heels,* there is a tall drag queen named Femme Letal (pronounced "Lay-thal," which sounds a lot more lethal). At the end of her act, a young woman walks backstage to say hello, and, to her astonishment (and ours), Letal, still in lipstick and mascara, jumps her. Gorgeous, hilarious, and highly gymnastic sex follows, and, eventually, a child is born. Fellini made people like Letal into grotesque freaks; Almodóvar unfreaks them. A credit at the end of *All About My Mother* reads, "Dedicated to Bette Davis, Gena Rowlands, Romy Schneider. . . . To all actresses who have played actresses. To all women who act. To all men who act and become women. To all people who want to be mothers. To my mother." In Almodóvar's world, you begin with the nurturing images of Hollywood and you end with Mom. Just like everyone else, the transvestites and omnisexuals get grouchy, hungry, or tired, and some of them long for children. They leave the audience in remarkably good humor, relieved by the appearance of what the Spanish director Miguel Albaladejo called "the daily ordinariness of the extraordinary." That doesn't sound like camp at all.

As a boy, Almodóvar would go to a movie and entertain his family afterward by telling them the story, and making it juicier in the telling. For years, he's been doing the same thing as a filmmaker. It makes sense, I think, to regard his fourteen completed films as retold movies, as stories relished for spectacle and emotion, pleasure and suffering, with all the boring parts left out—the cumbersome narrative supports, the "motivation." Almodóvar jumps to the transactional moments: People meet and size each other up; they connect or rebuff each other on the spot. He rarely shoots gauzy, meandering love scenes. The sex is immediate, overwhelming. His is an anti-Freudian cinema: The connection between repression and violence, so important to his predecessor the surrealist Buñuel, has been broken—in Almodóvar's movies, everyone acts out. And by using multi-sexual characters, he expands his narrative freedom. All sorts of linkages suddenly become possible; plots, hinged by changing desire, turn radically in an instant, establish parallel lines, double back on themselves.

Terse and decisive, the films are not full-scale dramatic fictions but fables, in the tradition of work by racy, fast-moving writers like Boccaccio or the creators of *A Thousand and One Nights*. And, like Cervantes, Almodóvar multiplies narratives, laying stories within stories or piling closely related tales on top of one another. In *All About My Mother,* a nurse named Manuela loses her son in a street accident in Madrid when the boy runs after Huma, an actress he adores who has been playing Blanche DuBois in *A Streetcar Named Desire*. The grief-stricken Manuela goes to Barcelona and scours the pickup scene there for the boy's father, who, it turns out, has gained breasts and become Lola, a transsexual junkie. Manuela can't find him, but she falls in with two people—a nun who is also pregnant by Lola, and the high-flying Huma, who is now playing Blanche in Barcelona. Like the Thelma Ritter character in *All About Eve* (the reference is explicit), Manuela gets a job taking care of the star. At the same time, onstage, she fills in for Huma's female lover—who has run off—in the role of Stella, a role she performed years earlier in an amateur production. Both as Stella and in her relationship with Lola, Manuela is a woman sexually enthralled by an overpowering man. In the end, Lola shows up, only to die of AIDS; the nun dies in childbirth; and Manuela gets a son—the nun's baby, who has the same name, Esteban, and the same father, Lola, as her dead child. Nutty as that story is, it parses. If anything, it intentionally over-parses.

A movie like *All About My Mother* is an example of Almodóvar's insistence on the productive artificiality of storytelling. A story is not a version of life but an interpretation of experience; it's a way of telling, not a way of being, and it reverberates in every direction. Eager to make the audience concentrate on his meaning, this fabulist is extremely disciplined; his imagery may be flamboyant, but he keeps his camera still or gliding gently, and he arranges the visual design around a dominant color or pair of colors (red and black in *Matador,* pale blue in *Talk to Her*). The color unifies the shocks and agitations of the tale, and the music, like Bernard Herrmann's throbbing scores for Hitchcock, exaggerates the characters' turmoils in a wash of overcharged strings. Almodóvar hasn't dropped the traditional narrative logic of temporal sequence, or cause-and-effect action, but the speed and the heated-up emotionalism of his dizzy plots are exhilarating. As you're watching, you consciously enjoy the pretense that life could be like this.

What strengthens the mocking, overdetermined fables and makes them real movies, not just sizzling erotic cartoons, is the intensity of the performances. Almodóvar may experiment with narrative plausibility, but, at the same time—and this is his great secret—he gets his actors to put real feelings into his loopy stories. His characters may be strange, but they express common emotions—sexual obsession, love, the pain of loss, compassion. Their responses to the bizarre circumstances they find themselves in burst through the flimsy walls of plot. As a jilted lover in *Women on the Verge of a Nervous Breakdown* (1988), Carmen Maura skitters on high heels, rushing from one ridiculous confrontation to the next. *Women* is farce, and, physically, Maura gives an expertly stylized performance. But her eyes are alive with outrage. The way Almodóvar turns the plot inside out may be a joke, but the situation of a woman abandoned is not, and Maura holds your emotions even as the pinwheeling movie makes you laugh. In other Almodóvar movies, Marisa Paredes, another favorite, has a haunted, mask-of-tragedy face, like Joan Crawford or Melina Mercouri. Big-boned, a growler, often rattled yet always generous, Paredes is close to exultation or breakdown; her despair is like blackest night. This is acting in the grand manner, but it's not ironic, and it's certainly not camp. Paredes never places quotation marks around her moods. People all over the world have been moved by Almodóvar's transvestites and roiling women. He's afraid of nothing, but he's a generous, playful, warm-spirited director—the last great humanist in cinema.

In *Talk to Her*, the first of Almodóvar's recent male-centered movies, two men, strangers, attend a Pina Bausch ballet. Onstage, women, their eyes closed, bounce off the walls in anguish, while a man rushes to and fro in front of them, hastily moving chairs out of their way. The two spectators are touched, and they later form a bond, in a clinic where each cares for a comatose woman he idolizes. The ballet, with its themes of isolation and dependency, sets up the narrative in a manner that's poetically satis-

fying rather than explicit. Earlier, in his celebrations of female temperament, Almodóvar's dominant colors were oversaturated and bright, and
he loved abrupt shifts of tone, but in *Talk to Her* the colors are soft-hued
and blended, the imagery is smooth and harmonious. Past and present
flow together, too; everything seems touched with melancholy longing
and the power of what's not stated. The movie has the feeling of a chastened reckoning. Could *Talk to Her* be interpreted as an allegory of the
way a gay director imagines his relationship to women—caring for them,
even adoring them, but never quite reaching them? For the moment, Almodóvar has stopped trying to understand women. Male homosexuality
is front and center in *Bad Education,* and the mood is one not of longing
but of bitter acceptance of the deceptions and manipulations that accom-
pany desire. In Ignacio's story, we see him grown up, in drag, confronting
Father Manolo, and claiming to be his own sister. Almodóvar is still playing with alternate selves, though the play has gotten more dangerous, the
lying more selfish.

Gael García Bernal (from *The Motorcycle Diaries*), with his pout and
sudden smile, is the male successor to the lying scarlet women who lived
at the center of old Hollywood and Almodóvar films. At one time or another in *Bad Education,* García Bernal plays the drag queen, a desirable
gay cupcake, and a straight young actor. The trying on of selves has suddenly taken on a darker cast; Ignacio is perhaps the first character in Almodóvar's movies to be judged completely amoral, and the movie asks, Is
love possible between men, or is it possible only between innocent boys?
Love expressed by women is suffering and theater; when it's felt by men, it
may be suffering, too, but it's also a series of manipulations and traps. The
truth of what happened to Ignacio and Enrique in *Bad Education* emerges
in pieces: The three narratives, as they expand and correct one another, become mirrors producing endless off-angle reflections. The playful young
Almodóvar was a carefree dazzler who settled on one charged emotion at
a time. At fifty-three, he still plays, but in a formally complex and sinuous
style that embraces ambiguity and regret. In the next stage of his extraordinary career, Almodóvar may become the most bitterly intelligent director since Billy Wilder.

The New Yorker, *November 22, 2004*

CLINT EASTWOOD /
THE LONGEST JOURNEY

On a beautiful day in Wyoming, in 1880, three men gather on a slight rise behind some rocks, ready to do a bit of killing. Two of them—William Munny (Clint Eastwood) and Ned Logan (Morgan Freeman)—are retired professional assassins, disgusted with their past but broke and therefore willing to shoot a couple of cowhands, unknown to either of them, for cash. The third is the excitable "Schofield Kid" (Jaimz Woolvett), who has read Western dime fiction all his life and is hot to become a legend by plugging someone—pretty much anyone will do. Logan is the best shot, and he raises his Spencer rife, aiming at one of the cowhands, who are rounding up cattle with some friends below. But Logan, after hitting the guy's horse, can't pull the trigger again. He just can't kill anymore. As the Schofield Kid loudly complains ("He ain't killed? What's goin' on?"), Munny takes the rifle and mortally wounds the cowhand, who howls so persistently for water that Munny shouts at his friends, "Will you give him a drink of water, for Christ's sake? We ain't gonna shoot."

The scene, which appears more than halfway through Clint Eastwood's 1992 Western, _Unforgiven_, is excruciatingly long—almost five minutes—and, watching it for the first time, you sensed almost immediately that the episode was momentous. The clumsy realism of it has a cleansing force: At least for that moment, ninety years of efficient movie violence—clean shots and quick death, a resolution central to the Western and police genres—falls away. Old myths dissolve into the messy stupidity of life, which, as rendered by Eastwood, becomes the most challenging kind of art. It's idiotic to kill a stranger for money, and, not only that, it's hard. Particularly hard on the stranger, but hard on you, too. The Schofield Kid, it turns out, gets to shoot the other cowhand a bit later, as the guy is sitting in the crapper. But afterward, the Kid is sickened and scared. Everything about the two killings feels wrong, which is all the more surprising since the creator of this sobering spectacle is an actor-director who became famous playing men who killed without trouble, whose pleasure in eliminating scum had become a kind of surrogate for social disgust. The worm had turned, the snarling cub had become a sober bear, the lean jackal was now the protector of the pack—use whatever metaphor you like. No personal transformation in movie history has been any greater than Clint Eastwood's.

Being underestimated is, for some people, a misfortune. For Eastwood it became a weapon. Certainly, no one meeting him in his twenties, before his movie career began, would have seen much more than a good-looking Californian (frequently in a bathing suit, which made him look even better), a handsome guy with a seductive smile who loved beer, women, cars, and nighttime noodling at the piano. The young Clint was a mover, 1950s-style—early photos show him with a big head of James Dean hair and two girls, sometimes three. Since those pleasurable but unprepossessing days, he has done the following: starred in a hit TV show, *Rawhide,* for six years; appeared in more than fifty movies and directed thirty-one, often acting, directing, producing, and composing the music at the same time; added several menacingly ironic locutions to the language, including "Make my day," quoted by Ronald Reagan in the face of a congressional movement to raise taxes; become a kind of mythic-heroic-redemptive figure, interacting with public desire in a way that no actor has done since John Wayne; served as the Republican mayor of Carmel for two years; won four Oscars, the Irving Thalberg Memorial Award for lifetime achievement, and received many other accolades, including a low-angle buss from Nicolas Sarkozy while becoming commander of the Légion d'honneur in November 2008. It's not a straight line—no one's "development" ever is—and there were times in the late 1990s and early aughts, when he made lazy movies like *Blood Work* and *Space Cowboys,* when he seemed to be coasting, resting, declining. But the greatest glory actually lay ahead. For many of us now toting up his career, a kind of retrospective upping of judgment has been inevitable, his later achievements making us aware of earlier strains that were present but not much noticed at the time. There's a certain comedy in all this. My own conversion, after early contempt, came in Clint's midcareer, with *Tightrope* (1984); some critics shifted later; a few, particularly Richard Schickel, Jay Cocks, Richard Corliss, Richard T. Jameson, and Dave Kehr, have always liked him. (So have audiences.) Wherever a critic falls on this spectrum, the point is that those who were skeptical of him forty—or even fifteen—years ago have long since capitulated, retired, or died. There isn't anyone he hasn't outlasted.

Early on, his outsider heroes operated with an unshakable sense of right. Such men were angry enforcers of order defined not by law but by primal notions of justice and revenge. A biblical avenger in a Western poncho, or a ratty sports jacket, he was inexorable, unyielding, amusingly two-dimensional, not of this world. "Nothing wrong with shooting as long as the right people get shot," Dirty Harry famously said in *Magnum Force* (1973). Like a lot of Harry's soft-snarl pronouncements, the remark is meant to be grimly funny; at the same time, it's not so funny. Removed from normal social existence, these low-tech terminators eliminated "the right people" and drew back into bitter isolation again. Noblesse oblige— or, perhaps, vigilante oblige.

Yet by midcareer, in the late 1970s and early 1980s, even as the later films in the Dirty Harry series were still coming out, Eastwood began showing signs of regret, twinges of doubt and self-reproof, admissions of sadness and failure, along with a broadening out of interest and a stunning increase of aesthetic ambition. His movies shifted from stiff, stark, en-raged fables, decisive to the point of patness, to something more relaxed, ruminative, and questioning. In *Unforgiven,* for instance, he holds scenes a few extra beats so that characters can extend their legs, scratch behind their ears, air out some issue of violence or honor. It's a companionable movie with much attention to weather, discomfort, illness, the despera-tion of women in the Old West. How do whores recover their honor when they've been abused?—craftily and with money. How do Westerners sleep in the rain?—badly. Or build a house?—ditto. The movie breathes; it com-ments on itself as it goes along. Clint Eastwood had somehow combined classicism and postmodernism in a single narrative. *Million Dollar Baby,* before it swings into its dire final section, has this grazing, thoughtful quality, too—for instance, the mordant pleasure that Eastwood's fight trainer and Morgan Freeman's employee (a half-blind former boxer) take in conversation, in first wounding and then consoling each other, by implication something they've been doing for years. The corners of Eastwood's gym were filled out with gesture, character detail, atmosphere—the oddities and irrelevancies and silences (in strict plot terms) that made the movie so affecting as a portrait of defeat and illusion in the saddest of all sports.

It's now obvious that *Unforgiven* was less an end point than a significant way station along an uninterruptible career path. Eastwood's most recent film, *Invictus,* a celebration of Nelson Mandela's shrewd and noble way of uniting South Africa in 1995, is not one of his best movies—it's a little too simple—but it's devoted to a public man who is the very opposite of isolated, a man whose sense of right changes an entire society. The transformation is complete: The actor who became famous in Spaghetti Westerns playing the Man With No Name has now made a movie about one of the greatest names in recent history. (Eastwood, a moderate libertarian Republican, has acknowledged parallels with the presidency of Barack Obama, and expressed annoyance with the "morbid mood" of America and the "teenage twits" in Washington.) In all, Eastwood has had an incredibly productive long run, and, in celebration, Warner Bros. issued a DVD box in 2010 with thirty-four movies that Eastwood starred in or directed for the studio, the largest such DVD collection devoted to a single person ever released. Richard Schickel, whose 1996 biography, despite its advocacy of Eastwood's views of everything in his life and work, is the shrewdest writing about the director's films and character, has added some fresh thoughts in a large illustrated book published in 2010, *Clint: A Retrospective,* which goes through the films one at a time, and chronicles Schickel's long friendship with the director.

Yet there is something of a mystery in this fifty-year ascent. The hero of this fable does not, at some dramatic turning point, look down from Mulholland Drive, condemn the frivolous lights of Hollywood, and seize greatness by the neck. Eastwood would sooner commit seppuku under a Carmel cypress than make some sort of grand statement about his intentions. He doesn't talk about his career in large terms; he doesn't talk about individual movies that way, either. His remarks are often low-key, offhand, undetailed—something on the order of "Well, it seemed like a good story to tell; I hadn't played this kind of character before, and I wanted to do it." He embodies the old Hollywood laconic professionalism: Never claim that you're an artist. Never let anything but your movies do your talking for you. Art talk is punk. A man works.

There *is* no dramatic turning point, no sudden coming to consciousness. What one sees is a calculating, shrewdly opportunistic but often honorable march through many projects, some hack, some genial, some slightly shopworn but still fascinating, some fresh and stunningly adventurous, and also a complex weaving back and forth of acting persona and directorial expression. Eastwood's professional life, conducted in the most wasteful business in the world, would seem to exemplify lessons of industry, persistence, and frugality copied out of a nineteenth-century maxim book. Yet the discipline at work has been matched, off-camera, by a prodigality of pleasures. There have been two wives, many affairs, both on and off the set, numerous children, some of them legitimate. But the movies have so overshadowed the rest of his life that one forgets the details of his marriages and romances and paternities as soon as one reads about them. (Yes, I realize this can't be true for the women and children in his life; I'm speaking as an outsider.) Clint Eastwood plays the media game with perfect discipline: In public, he has always been as boring as possible about his life so as to live it in private as fully and selfishly as he likes. At the end of May 2010, rich, propertied (six houses), garlanded, and exceptionally busy, he entered his ninth decade.

He was born big—Bunyanesque big—at eleven pounds, six ounces, in 1930, and grew up mostly in Piedmont, California, a middle-class enclave surrounded by Oakland on most of its borders. During the Depression, his father found and lost many jobs—at various times, he pumped gas, sold refrigerators, sold bonds. During the war, he worked in a shipping yard, and after it as a sales manager at a corrugated box company. Richard Schickel has suggested that the family's moving around may be one cause of Eastwood's lifelong restlessness and also his habit of appearing in movies out of nowhere and disappearing, at the end, into an equally baffling nowhere. The constant in Eastwood's early life was his mother, Ruth, who collected jazz records and got her son excited about music. As a late teen-ager, hanging around clubs in Oakland and Los Angeles (he and friends would drive down there for a weekend), Eastwood heard such icons of the new West Coast cool style in jazz as Gerry Mulligan and Chet Baker and the bebop geniuses in their early days, including Dizzy Gillespie and Charlie Parker. As Eastwood has said, his notion of cool—slightly aloof, giving only the central satisfaction and withholding everything else—is derived from those musicians. That's the picture of the onstage Charlie Parker that emerged in the pained love letter to the frantically disorga-nized musician, *Bird* (1988), which Eastwood created forty years after first seeing him. As played by Forest Whitaker, Parker, however hapless in the rest of his life, is supremely self-contained and confident when holding his sax. Eastwood had learned the lesson: Don't ingratiate, just do the main thing well.

He seems less to have graduated from high school (the record is un-clear) than to have terminated his attendance, which was sporadic in any case, at the age of nineteen. For a year or so, he worked at odd jobs, in-cluding hard work in a lumber mill, poling logs onto a conveyor belt, and easy work on a beach, as a lifeguard. When he was drafted, in 1950, his proficiency as a swimmer, and therefore his presumed competence as a swimming instructor, kept him out of combat in Korea. Assigned to Ford Ord, near the Monterey Peninsula (which turned out to be the geographi-cal center of the rest of his life), he worked at the base pool during the day and manned the piano at local bars when he was off-duty at night—a relaxed existence that he captured in his first film as a director, *Play Misty for Me* (1971), in which Eastwood was a Carmel disc jockey, indolent, seductive and seducible, a character probably as close to the actual young Clint as we would ever see on-screen.

At the suggestion of friends, he took some acting classes at Los Ange-les City College. Such fashionable disciplines of the time as the Method, which insisted on deep and threatening plunges into one's emotional past, he found distasteful, or perhaps frightening, and he seized instead on what he derived in acting studio night classes from a disciple of the fa-mous teacher Michael Chekhov (the playwright's nephew)—that is, "cen-tering" a performance on a given set of physical traits and gestures that projected the essence of the character to the audience. The prescription was comparable in its focus and narrowness to what he gleaned from the jazz greats a few years earlier.

In 1954, he came to the notice of Universal Studios, which still had a "school" devoted to the training of young actors. He signed on as contract player for $75 a week, which was peanuts even then. His teachers noted a certain tentativeness to his demeanor—he didn't, putting it gently, project much—but also some interesting corners in his temperament, and over the next few years he had some small parts in junk movies. There was the talking-mule picture, *Francis in the Navy,* and something called *Lady Godiva of Coventry,* which sounds like a porn feature shot in a cathedral basement. No one much noticed him until he was hired, in 1958, to be the co-lead (alongside Eric Fleming) of *Rawhide,* one of the many TV Westerns of the period, this one a cattle drive formula show complete with a Frankie Laine theme song punctuated with crackling whiplashes. After a few years, bored and ready to jump, Eastwood received a strange, derivative, wordy script by a man named Sergio Leone. It was titled "The Magnificent Stranger," and it was an obvious remake of Akira Kurosawa's funny-bloody samurai classic of 1961, *Yojimbo.* Leone had been assistant director, or uncredited director, of shlock Italian historical spectacles. He was a kind of ruffian movie intellectual—obsessed with America, and convinced, in particular, that the classic Western had turned what was historically a remorseless struggle for commercial dominance into a moralized battle between good and evil. Leone wanted literally to demoralize the Western. He had eccentric ideas about how to shoot a movie, alternating huge vistas with super-tight close-ups. In effect, he took the deep syntax of the genre (the bare street, the stare-downs and sudden draws, the high body counts), raised it to the surface, and dropped almost everything else. *A Fistful of Dollars,* as "The Magnificent Stranger" was eventually titled— and its more entertaining sequels, *For a Few Dollars More* and *The Good, the Bad and the Ugly*—was knowing parody, and Eastwood, with his minimalist technique, fit perfectly into the style of unyielding absurdism.

The Man With No Name enters on a donkey, wearing a poncho and a flat-brimmed hat, chewing on a cigarillo, and he proceeds to play off two warring gangs in a small town against each other. In *Yojimbo,* Toshiro

Mifune acted with his belly, hips, and shoulders; his violence was an exuberant overflow of spirit. But Eastwood, successfully convincing Leone to reduce the number of his lines, must have realized that silence cast a deadlier spell than rumpus. "Who the hell does he think he is?" I remember thinking at the time. "Isn't he going to *do* anything?" But he knew exactly who he was. He kept his head still, at a slight angle; he narrowed his eyes; he scowled and curled his upper lip. It was an arrogant teenager's idea of acting, but he looked mean, amused, coolly amoral. From the beginning, he possessed a secret: For an actor like him, playing a character was less important than establishing an image of implacable male force. Movie audiences want force, and they want style. Many in the audience took Eastwood's immobility not as a weakness of craft but as an actor's conscious revision of a Western hero—a revision which allowed them to enjoy the movie's violence as style, too, and without feeling a thing. Cults spring up when emotion is dropped out, not added, to genres—the absence of emotions makes the old formulas feel cool. The Spaghetti Westerns never did a thing for me, but they attracted an enormous following. (Leone went on to be a much better director in *Once Upon a Time in America.*)

There were comic possibilities embedded in Eastwood's stone mask, and the director Don Siegel (who became Eastwood's mentor) exploited them in the coarsely conceived *Coogan's Bluff* (1968). This time, Eastwood is a contemporary Western sheriff, an émigré from the sun-bleached desert of Arizona, searching for an escaped felon in a crowded, noisy New York, a city filled with chattering neurotics, hippie scum, and hungry women. Apart from taking advantage of the sexual opportunities, the sheriff just glares and holds his ground. The scenes of Lee J. Cobb's saturnine Manhattan cop roaring "Go home!" at this Western paleolith were funny enough, but there was a prickly side to the comedy. Siegel played off the country's growing distaste for the big city and the counterculture. He threw together embarrassingly touristy views of sex and drugs, and created the tall, stoical, mostly silent Westerner as the real American—the man who can take on bureaucrats and do-gooders as well as hippies and thugs, bang a few silly women, and get the job done. Coogan was amusingly single-minded and selfish, yet duty-bound—a ruthless pragmatist who cut to the heart of the matter; all the rest was bullshit.

The ur-American mold was set, and the ruthlessness, without losing its comic edge, turned dire. In that baleful pop-culture time capsule, *Dirty Harry* (1971), also directed by Siegel (with many touches suggested or added by Eastwood), Inspector Harry Callahan catches up to a freakish serial killer (Andy Robinson) terrorizing San Francisco. Brushing aside the mayor's warnings about excessive violence, Harry tortures the screechy madman when he has him in his grip rather than read him his rights (the Miranda warning had only recently become law). The movie had a tone of desperation, a grim, snarling wit alternating with outright fear: Siegel made San Francisco into a paranoid landscape, seething with danger and anxiety; even the sunlight looked unclean. Seeing it again, one gets pulled back into the emotions of this unappetizing movie. For audiences at the time, the law-and-order atmosphere of the Nixon period and Eastwood's screen temperament went together like ammonium nitrate and fuel oil. *Dirty Harry* says criminals are out of control; payback time is at hand. In a drolly violent prelude, Harry stops a bank robbery at lunchtime, crossing the street and blazing away with his .44 Magnum while chewing on a hot dog. Pointing the gun, which may or may not have a bullet left in its chamber, Harry almost croons to the wounded bank robber who's thinking of reaching for his own weapon. "You've got to ask yourself one question, 'Do I feel lucky?' Well, do ya, punk?" The teasing question became one of Eastwood's signature lines; he repeats it at the end of the film, when he has the serial killer under his gun, and this time the question is lethal.

As taglines, "Make my day" and "Well, do ya, punk" don't compare to "Here's looking at you, kid." But those moments of insolent pop cruelty put Eastwood, at the not so young age of forty-plus, over the top. An actor may work for years without becoming a star, as John Wayne and Humphrey Bogart had done throughout the 1930s. But then suddenly, looks, temperament, and role all come together—for Wayne in *Stagecoach* (1939) and for Bogart in *The Maltese Falcon* (1941)—and the public *sees* the actor, sees what it desires. He becomes not only a star but a myth as Garry Wills defined it in his 1997 book *John Wayne's America*—as something that was true for the people who needed it to be true. What the public needed from Eastwood by the time of *Dirty Harry* was both physical and, in a convoluted way, moral.

It began with his appearance. He was six feet, three inches tall, perhaps an inch taller than Wayne. He had gray-green eyes; a forehead like the rock face of Yosemite's Half Dome; a perfect jawline; a soft voice, so surprising in a big man, a voice that suggested a tough guy needn't shout to have an effect. The whisper and croon were deadly. A fitness nut (and a vegetarian), he was broad-shouldered by nature and muscular from many hours in his workout room, but not overly muscled—not a pop-culture joke like Sylvester Stallone or Arnold Schwarzenegger. A mass of light brown hair piled up on his head in a pompadour and flowed back in waves; he had an animal grace, a big-cat tension as he moved. Wayne was graceful, too, but he had an unusually long torso, and he rolled slightly as he walked. As Wills pointed out, Wayne, swinging his bulk down Western streets, couldn't imagine that anyone would challenge him. But Eastwood, always wary, couldn't imagine a world free of challenge. Wayne's confidence, as Wills says, made him especially popular in a country that had won the Second World War and remained armed for the Cold War. One might add that Eastwood's guardedness, and his Magnum, provided reassurance to a country that was losing in Vietnam and feared chaos in the streets.

Harry Callahan is lonely, hard, distant. He is nevertheless not an example of "fascist medievalism," as Pauline Kael, writing in *The New Yorker* (January 15, 1972), asserted in a negative review of *Dirty Harry* that shadowed Eastwood's reputation for years. By any definition, fascism involves state control and leader worship, but Callahan, in *Dirty Harry* and its four sequels, detests the city leaders and is too disaffected to lead anyone anywhere. Kael wrote as if Harry's nature were completely a response to the times, but, actually, he was the latest in a series of individualistic and anti-bureaucratic figures that Don Siegel had created in the past and would create again—with Eastwood, for instance, in *Escape from Alcatraz* (1979), in which he's a prisoner who not only flees the Rock but upends the warden, a stuffy martinet. And Eastwood would play such types in movies made in political climates very different from the law-and-order atmosphere that spooked Kael at the time of *Dirty Harry*. In *Heartbreak Ridge* (1986), he was an aging Marine sergeant with a guttural voice who breaks the rules and sasses his superior officers as he tries to prepare young men for war; in *In the Line of Fire* (1993), a tormented Secret Service agent taking on Fred

Thompson's White House chief of staff. Eastwood's characters have always been disgusted by regulations and proprieties that hampered their effectiveness. It was the *job* that mattered, the piece of brutal work. Why had everyone forgotten that? Duty calls; it never stops calling. In *Dirty Harry,* the cop's fury at the Miranda and Escobedo protections of suspects' rights was less a political position, as Kael assumed, than the contempt and humiliation ("The law is crazy") felt by a policeman who can't intimidate a murderer boasting of his crimes. Harry Callahan's behavior fell somewhere between American "rugged individualism" and outright pathology; at times, he made us realize how closely the ideal and the perversion of it might be drawn together, how easily individualism could collapse into vigilantism. But vigilantism, a very American phenomenon, is a long ways from fascism. Kael's review was a case of critical sensationalism, as much a product of the overheated atmosphere of 1971 as the movie itself.

"Mass culture is a machine for showing desire," Roland Barthes has written. It's also a machine for expressing resentment, a frustration of desire. Eastwood became so popular, in part, because he allowed people to dream that they could be effective without being nice, tolerant, or good. As critic Michael Wood wrote, in the *London Review of Books,* in 1992, Dirty Harry was a man who allowed the audience to enjoy "imaginary violence as a solution to real problems." Yet, apart from an impatience with what later was called political correctness, this vessel of public wrath possessed very little in the way of explicit politics. In the real America, such a loner, muttering to himself, might have climbed into the hills with a supply of ammunition and Spam. But Harry's rebellion would have been meaningless outside the system. He may have thrown away his badge at the end of *Dirty Harry,* but he put it back on for the sequels. He was an outsider by temperament who nevertheless stayed inside, protecting society, protecting *us.* For that reason, Eastwood became, as everyone said, an icon. Millions were fond of him as a righteous bastard, an avenger; he was our authoritarian bad boy, our low-minded protector, our licensed killer. A lesser man, receiving such adoration, might have just repeated himself forever.

As an actor in training at Universal, Eastwood had roamed all over the lot, asking questions about different aspects of filmmaking, and, during his *Rawhide* years, he made several requests, without success, to direct an episode or at least a sequence. In 1970, he prevailed on Universal to let him direct *Play Misty for Me,* a low-budget feature. In return for not taking a fee, he had the freedom to make the movie as he liked. The studio may have been trying to hook him into years of service in Western, crime, and other action vehicles. But they couldn't. In 1968, before he was a superstar, he had set up his own production company, Malpaso, and from that time on if studios wanted Eastwood, they had to make a deal with his company, which allowed him to exercise control over the script, the director, and major casting. He had created the basis of his freedom before he needed to exercise it.

At first it wasn't clear how he would display himself in his own work. The DJ hero of *Play Misty for Me,* Dave Garver, whispers so intimately into the microphone that an impressionable fan (Jessica Walter) imagines that she has a special bond with him. He sleeps with her a few times, thinking he can easily cut her loose, only to discover that she's a knife-wielding psychopath who won't let go. Eastwood directs at a rather languid tempo—the movie, slow to come to a boil, offers many luscious views of Eastwood's beloved Monterey Peninsula before the knife slashing begins. This casually made picture featured plentiful views of Eastwood's bare chest, which appeared in many movies (until late in his career), including *The Beguiled,* which he had made with Don Siegel in 1971, just before *Dirty Harry.* In *The Beguiled,* which has a nearly pornographic scenario, Eastwood is a wounded Union soldier taken in by the itchy women of a girls school at the end of the Civil War. The two portraits of lusted-after men border on narcissism, though, in a surprising turn (which should have alerted us to where Eastwood was going), the hero in each case is a careless opportunist who refuses responsibility for the havoc he creates. Even outside the *Dirty Harry* series, Eastwood's characters were always tainted in some way; they might be selfish and egotistical (though never cowardly), lonely and saddened (though never passive), bullheadedly macho (though never weak), eagerly mercenary (though never bourgeois—the man does not easily wear a business suit). This candor about intentions separated him from such idealized stars of the past as Gary Cooper and brought the wised-up modern audience closer to him. In movie after movie, he would, by implication, do what any American male would do—take what was there for the taking. But, comically, he was always shocked when anyone behaved worse than he did. His indignant stare became a signature, too. As Robert Mazzocco wrote in *The New York Review of Books,* in 1982, "Few other actors convey so naturally, even at their most brutal moments, so outraged a sense of innocence."

Play Misty for Me ends with Dave Garver knocking his murderous lover through a window and down Big Sur's rocky cliffs. Eastwood, in this first film as director, was clearly telling studios and the public that they could admire him, but they could not possess him. The refusal to be trapped, typed, "suffocated" (his word) became the recurring note of Eastwood's dealings with studios, press, and the film medium itself. Universal may have thought that he would be a workhorse on the lot, but he withdrew, and shifted to Warner Bros., where he made, among many other things, Westerns, but only his own, eccentric kind of Westerns. In *High Plains Drifter* (1973), as in *A Fistful of Dollars,* he's again the nameless loner emerging out of nowhere. In a bare, mangy town at the side of a lake, a town with a guilty secret in its past, he quickly establishes his authority, eliminating all opposition and setting himself up as a kind of metaphysical avenger—a godlike destroyer of hypocrisy in boots who literally makes the furtive townspeople paint their buildings red in an admission of sin. *Drifter* was a whimsical, slightly daft spectacle—one didn't know how seriously to take its religious overtones—made with much physical exaggeration (the Leone influence was clear). "What kind of nutty egomaniac is this?" I remember thinking. But Eastwood did one thing straight: He embraced the noble American pictorial ideal: a man on a horse, traversing great open spaces. He had, it seemed, a horizontal imagination.

The Outlaw Josey Wales (1976), his first great movie as a director, is filled with one ravishing image after another of lonely figures crossing vast landscapes as they search for a resting place. This time, the Eastwood character has a name. Initially a rooted man, Josey Wales is a Southern farmer who loses his family to Union marauders during the Civil War. He takes revenge, and then heads West, passing through the driftwood floating in the wake of war—poltroons of all sorts, bounty hunters, cowardly opportunists. Vicious and amused, he wants only to be alone, but, against his will, he acquires, as he moves, a new, irregular family (a talkative Indian, an elderly woman, a young girl) and takes over an abandoned house in Texas, in effect resettling the West. If Leone emptied the West, making Westerns that were all syntax and dead bodies, Eastwood, working in long paragraphs, repopulated it and put meaning back into the genre. *Josey Wales*, which was written by the writer-director Philip Kaufman and Eastwood's associate Sonia Chernus, has a palpable sense of time passing and a frame of stately picaresque filled with violent encounters and only-in-America eccentrics. The bizarre bunco artists and scroungers, combined with a gathering mood of disgust, evoke Huck's adventures along the river.

"America here," as Michael Wood wrote, "is not a place people die for, it's a vast, beautiful, shifting landscape that people keep dying in, killing each other out of sheer smallness of mind, or for reasons they can't remember." In the end, the movie calls a halt to smallness of mind. The Western hero can no longer ride off to nowhere; he needs some sort of community. Josey Wales makes peace with Indian tribes and a man pursuing him, terminating various wars and the cycles of revenge. These pacific events were the first signs in Eastwood of both a wider social sympathy and an incipient distaste for the conventions of genre plotting. Indifferently reviewed when it came out, *The Outlaw Josey Wales* received a stunning compliment six years later. Orson Welles, who had seen the picture four times, said on *The Merv Griffin Show* that "it belongs with the great Westerns. You know, the great Westerns of Ford and Hawks and people like that." And Welles implied that if anyone but Eastwood had directed it, the movie would have been hailed as a masterpiece.

Welles's evocation of names from the past is a startling reminder of the singularity of Eastwood's path. Ford appeared in a few silent movies and never acted again, Hawks not at all. Clark Gable, Gary Cooper, Spencer Tracy, James Stewart, Cary Grant, Humphrey Bogart, William Holden, Steve McQueen, and Sean Connery never directed a feature. John Wayne directed only twice, and badly; ditto Burt Lancaster. Paul Newman, Jack Nicholson, Warren Beatty, Robert De Niro, and Sean Penn have directed a few movies each, with mixed commercial and artistic success. Robert Redford has directed seven; he has also, through his Sundance Institute and the Sundance Festival, warmed the atmosphere for independent film-makers for decades, but Redford has never expressed himself as a director the way Eastwood has. The comparison with Beatty is more interesting. Both were pretty boys who emerged from television in the 1960s. Both were casual piano players, catnip to women. Both cast actresses they were involved with. Both were enormously ambitious, and engaged seriously, at times, in politics. Beatty has had a fascinating career as a producer and hyper-energetic stimulator of persons and projects, but, along with his genuine achievements, the principal activity of his professional life for considerable stretches has been getting people excited about what he wants to do rather than actually doing it. He does much research, holds endless meetings, fusses over details, keeps people waiting for years, dithers brilliantly. In 2007, at the Golden Globes party, after the recent release of Eastwood's *Flags of Our Fathers* and *Letters from Iwo Jima,* Beatty ruefully acknowledged the difference. "Clint, are we not friendly? We're very friendly. I don't understand. First, you do one great movie right after another movie, then you gotta do two more movies that are just as great as the first two movies, but you gotta do them at the same time no less—and you do the score? How do you think that makes me feel?"

For Eastwood, the point has never been to vibrate in a limbo of unproductive celebrity but to try out new things, enjoy the work and the money, and get on with it. The mystery of his longevity turns out to be no mystery at all. As a filmmaker, he is almost comically free of quirks, neuroses, hesitations, fear. Studio politics and the hysterics built into elephantine productions, which he experienced firsthand when he acted and sang (sort of) in the expensive musical *Paint Your Wagon* (1969), leave him cold. If he likes a story, he buys or commissions a script, moves rapidly into production, shoots the film on a short schedule and, until recently, on a modest budget. If he knows an actor's or actress's work, he doesn't ask for a reading. He casts quickly, dislikes extensive rehearsals and endless takes. If a star becomes balky, he gets tough. (When Kevin Costner left the set of *A Perfect World* and lingered in his trailer, Eastwood threatened to shoot the rest of the movie with a double. Costner pulled himself together and gave the best performance of his career.) If someone else is supposed to direct and then falters or becomes too slow or indecisive for

Eastwood's taste—as Philip Kaufman did on *Josey Wales,* and the writer Richard Tuggle on *Tightrope*—he pushes him aside and takes over. Like Bergman, Godard, and Woody Allen, he works hard and fast, an impatient man who likes calm and order, relying on the same people over and over—most importantly, the production designer Henry Bumstead (from 1992 to 2006), cinematographer Bruce Surtees (1971 to 1985), followed by Jack N. Green (1986 to 2000), and then by Tom Stern, who rose out of Eastwood's lighting and camera crew. In recent years, his editor, Joel Cox, has pulled sequences together as the film was being shot; the post-production period is remarkably brief. Eastwood is not devoid of imperial temperament; he demands loyalty from those around him, and I'm not sure he has always surrounded himself with the best people he could find. But, in Hollywood, an Eastwood set is one of the saner places to be. As a professional code, all this seems obvious enough, but, in recent years, who else in big-time American filmmaking but Eastwood and Allen and, recently, the Coen brothers, has practiced it?

"Maturity" is a high school counselor's word, and responsibility is something we rarely ask of artists and entertainers. But Eastwood, by trying out new forms and moods, both light and dark, and by constantly altering his early self as a star, achieved both as he got older, and without becoming a stiff. If his temperament early on led him to narrowness and minimalism, as he got older and more confident he broadened out, step by step but relentlessly. Late in 2009, critic A. O. Scott asserted in *The New York Times* that revenge is "the defining theme of his career." But this is not quite true. Revenge is certainly a major theme, but Eastwood's interests and ambitions as a director became protean and encompassing, and no critic will ever successfully strap him onto the Procrustean bed of a single theme or pattern. The alterations are more interesting and important than the consistencies.

There he was in *Tightrope* (1984) playing a cop again, a member of the vice squad in New Orleans, which, like San Francisco in *Dirty Harry,* is haunted by a serial killer. The difference is that the city is haunted by his pursuer as well. Eastwood's detective, Wes Block, a widower falling apart, is drawn to whores and kinky sex; he scours the bars and clubs for a man who murders prostitutes, and mostly encounters his own desire. Richard Tuggle wrote the script and got screen credit as director, but Eastwood did most of the work and shot the movie in Don Siegel's tawdry, urban-anxiety mode, slowed by episodes of rapt erotic stillness. Eastwood also gave his most complicated and forceful performance up to that date. He was fifty-four, and any trace of the creamy pinup beauty of his youth was gone. The scowl had become a painful grimace, the voice thick and hoarse. He had become his own monument. A few years earlier, in *Parade* magazine, Norman Mailer had granted him "a presidential face." Some president! Eastwood's candor brought the character to the edge of disintegration. The biggest star in the world was implicating himself in the kind of pathologies that his earlier characters had grimly eliminated. Robert Mitchum (and maybe Bogart) would have had the courage to play a role like this, but Gable, Cooper, or Wayne wouldn't have dared. I remember feeling a palpable sense of relief when Wes Block, pulling himself back from the edge, annihilates the killer in order to annihilate part of himself.

If Wes Block came close to self-immolation, was that something Eastwood himself feared? In an odd turn, as if to ward off bad dreams, he made no fewer than three films in the 1980s about self-destructive artists—and made them tenderly, with respect both for talent and the annihilating energies beneath talent. The least of these was *Honkytonk Man* (1982), in which Eastwood directed himself as an alcoholic and tubercular country singer who drives through the Oklahoma dust during the Depression, and, amid much sour-mash joking and occasional one-night stands, gets a tryout at the Grand Ole Opry, only to expire in a cheap hotel room. *Honkytonk Man* was repetitive but touching, and Eastwood spared us nothing of the singer's disintegration. In 1990, stretching himself mightily in *White Hunter Black Heart,* he took on John Huston, playing John Wilson, a lightly fictionalized version of the director during the making of *The African Queen.* A gifted and courageous man, Wilson nevertheless commits the unpardonable sin of ignoring a movie waiting to be shot in order to indulge an obsession—the desire to bag a giant elephant. The African open air was magnificent, but Eastwood, it turned out, didn't have the largeness of spirit or the vocal resources to play Huston. His disdain was the strongest element in the movie. He let us know, once and for all—as if we had any doubt about it—that reckless flamboyance was an egotistical diversion he couldn't afford. The lesson might have seemed prim if he hadn't also applied it to an artist he loved far more than Huston.

Bird (1988), his biopic devoted to Charlie Parker, was the most daring of the three movies. The picture was either art or it was nothing. Those who decided two decades ago that it was nothing should take another look. I trust Stanley Crouch and the other knowledgeable jazz lovers who wrote at the time that Eastwood and screenwriter Joel Oliansky slighted Charlie Parker's fierce intellectual edge, the range of his curiosity, his struggles as a black artist in a racist society. But a biopic can't do everything, and sometimes one has to respond to what's there, rather than mourn what's not. *Bird* plays very well on second viewing. Eastwood niftily transferred his love of open country to a peculiarly tight urban spot, a studio-built Fifty-second Street, at the late-1940s height of bebop. In one continuous shot, Parker (Forest Whitaker) and his new date, Chan (Diane Venora), cross the street talking, wending their way through traffic. Parker stops to exchange half-voiced, half-intimated witticisms with two musicians as Chan climbs the steps of her mother's brownstone, a teeming jazz hangout. The sequence, a densely populated traveling shot, was worthy of Robert Altman.

In all the indoor scenes, Eastwood wanted the harshly lyrical, high-contrast look of early-1950s black-and-white jazz photography. With that ideal in mind, he and the cinematographer Jack N. Green miscalculated: They used too little light for color film, and some of the movie is dark as a tenement back hallway. Still, to an astonishing degree, the furtive, desperate tone of night people—talented, brilliant, sexually ravenous—comes through the murk. As the movie's timeframe moves backward and forward through Parker's life, and Whitaker and Venora flirt, banter, and fight in off-rhythm exchanges (no one has ever done love scenes so quirky as these), the film attains a feeling of fleetingness and improvisation, a true jazz style—one of the few feature films that have come close to it. As played by Forest Whitaker, Parker is a man of great sweetness, who, when he's not on the stage, can't stop himself from getting into trouble. In the end, addicted and helpless, he betrays people close to him and finally himself. *Bird,* directed with subtleties of emotion—a feeling for the elusive and momentary, the words not spoken, the words spoken and immediately regretted—was created out of love and a baffled sense of loss. It was the most generous and demanding movie that Eastwood had made up to that point.

After the disasters of totalitarianism, humanism as a philosophical stance has seemed beside the point. At the moment, in this fretful country, we live within the derisive ironies of a media matrix; and we are teased by the postmodernist notion that the self is a myth, a mere collection of fragments. But the humanistic attitude insists on the opposite—that we are accountable for ourselves as morally coherent beings, which may mean admitting, at times, that we are incoherent, operating with mixed motives, or even that we're thoroughly screwed up. Such an attitude requires a three-dimensional attitude toward character, background, motives. In the arts, humanism's greatest weakness is a tendency to middlebrow dreariness—it can easily become a refuge for the unimaginative. If anyone could tell improbable stories as perversely well as Hitchcock, why would he bother making rounded, realistic narratives? Humanistic filmmaking is always a bet against the heavy odds of dullness. But that's exactly where Eastwood has placed his chips for the last twenty years or so.

When Eastwood was young, his rakish cruelty was pop-hip. He transformed himself without going all soft and cloying. As he hit fifty, a surly macho temperament may have held sway in many of his characters, but, at the same time, he showed the audience the backwaters of macho—the mistakes, the emotional rigidity, the outright stupidity. In the 2002 edition of *The Biographical Dictionary of Film,* David Thomson wrote warmly of Eastwood but made a demand: "The test that awaits Eastwood is whether he can find himself in neurosis and failure." The sentence was written before Eastwood made *Mystic River* and *Million Dollar Baby,* which, in the event, offered the tonalities that Thomson wanted. Still, there were plentiful signs earlier that Eastwood had revealed something of "neurosis and failure." He did it within popular genres and in very broad terms, in movies that occasionally seemed naive, but still, he did it. For instance, in *Bronco Billy* (1980), his seventh film as a director, he plays the cranky, not very bright head of a bedraggled Wild West show that is still hitting the small towns of Montana and Idaho in 1980. The movie at first seems too simple and casual, even a little dumb. A New York heiress, played by Sondra Locke (whose appeal for Eastwood has always escaped me), falls in with Billy and his troupe, a bunch of misfits of stunningly limited talent. The heiress is snooty, dismissive; Billy is irritated by her but attracted; he saves her from rape, and she melts, finding bliss in his arms. The story, a crude version of *It Happened One Night,* is almost embarrassing, but, two thirds the way through, the movie deepens. Yes, the men have little talent, and none of them is a Westerner. Billy, born in New Jersey, was a shoe salesman until he was thirty; two others are ex-cons, one is an Army deserter. They are all desperate to put on a show, to sustain an illusion of themselves, to stay together as a family in the absence of a family—a theme that recalls the gradually expanding irregular group in *The Outlaw Josey Wales.* It's second-level Eastwood but oddly touching in its earnest desire to make a case for not terribly bright people who do the best they can and make a kind of life for themselves.

Years earlier, Billy had shot and wounded his unfaithful wife; he's a damaged man trying to recover, and so is Gunnery Sergeant Thomas Highway, or Gunny, in *Heartbreak Ridge* (1986). Again, a lot of the movie is flat, stunted, semi-believable. The Marine unit that Gunny whips into shape is composed of slackers and jerks who would never have made it into the Marines in the first place. The movie's climax—the mighty victory at Grenada, where Gunny commands his unit against the awesome Cuban army—leaves one a little ashamed. But Eastwood himself is touching in *Heartbreak Ridge.* Grizzled, growling, enraged, he's a man whose military career and attack reflex leave him incapable of dealing with anything in life but training and combat. This is a familiar trope: The men we hire to protect us do so at the price of nearly annihilating themselves. Wayne has played such roles; James Caan did it in Coppola's *Gardens of Stone;* recently, Woody Harrelson did it superbly in *The Messenger.* But no one has taken the idea as far as Eastwood. In this and many movies he played men who are lost outside the specialty that gives them their identity—not a tragedy exactly, and not pitiable, either, but a rueful acknowledgment of how hard it is to get life right. Defeated, Gunny glowers, looks crestfallen, and then beats someone up. Macho cripples him as much as it enables him.

The embittered sense of something inadequate, something missing or lost—the forlornness—was repeated in *The Bridges of Madison County* (1995), in which Clint's roving photographer hero and lover seems baffled, as if his demand for independence and globe-trotting liberty had caused him to miss some larger point. As Meryl Streep, Eastwood's costar, has said, the two of them transformed a junk-novel weepie into something a little tougher—a movie about regret, a life not quite lived. The note of regret, severely repressed but still unmissable, fueled his best work as an actor—his performance as Frankie Dunn, a complicated grouchy old man, estranged from his daughter, in *Million Dollar Baby*. Frankie is the most intellectual of his characters—a constant reader, a questioner of Christian theology whose guilt never lets up on him. With his short hair and piercing eyes, Eastwood, in that movie, looked like a puzzled cobra.

In his sixties, he became conscious of the implications of his work, and in his best movies he added dimensions to situations he had earlier handled simply. Return to that rocky glen in Wyoming, where Eastwood's William Munny has trouble killing a man. Whatever else it is, *Unforgiven* is an argument about how to represent violence, an argument about movies. Eastwood and screenwriter David Webb Peoples are the artificers here, but there's a rival actually present in the movie, a hack writer who creates Western fictions—just the kind of books the doltish Schofield Kid has grown up reading. The scribbler W. W. Beauchamp (Saul Rubinek) turns up in the nearby town of Big Whiskey, accompanying one of his heroes, the raffishly ornate outlaw known as English Bob (Richard Harris, declaiming the Queen's English in the one truly funny performance of his career). The sheriff of Big Whiskey (Gene Hackman) quickly disarms and beats up the prating Bob; and then, sentence by sentence, he deconstructs the nonsense Beauchamp has written, explaining how shoot-outs actually happen. In effect, the sheriff, known as Little Bill, shreds the way that violence is represented in most Western movies—violence which is normally a lot closer, we have to admit, to Beauchamp's rubbish than to the wrenching mess we've seen in the glen. Peoples's script is endlessly complicated, and Eastwood honors its startling turns. We may enjoy Little Bill's scornful realism, but he's a terrifying man. If he's the true West, the West is a nightmare. Hackman makes him rancorous and sadistic—a man completely without honor who later beats Munny's pal Ned Logan to death. In Little Bill, justice and order have collapsed into pure force.

But where does that leave Eastwood's character, who tells us again and again that his dead wife has made him renounce violence—repeating it to himself as a mantra even as he's committing violence? Eastwood appeared to be returning to what was hinted at in *Tightrope,* the capacity of his own surly movie self for criminality and his increasing regret over any glorification of it. He shapes his performance as a study in rueful abnegation; at times, he looks lost and vulnerable, even sickly. Yet William Munny, however weakened, has to avenge his partner's death. *Unforgiven* ends with Munny gunning down Little Bill and his friends and riding away, a return to the kind of familiar Eastwood myth that the rest of the movie seems to reject. What, one wonders, was the use of all that antiviolence business if it all comes to *this?* Eastwood's murderous past characters and his regretful new temper appear to have collided on a Western street. He had gotten himself into the kind of dilemma that artists encounter when they depart from the safety of convention. Westerns, by their very nature (guns must be expertly drawn; bad guys must be killed), depend on myth if they are to exist at all. By taking the Western into three dimensions, and by pushing the moral issues to extremes, Eastwood had exposed the limits of the genre. *Unforgiven* is both an entertainment and a contradiction, a troubled masterpiece at war with itself.

He may have sensed that he hadn't said all that he wanted to say about renunciation. In the lovely movie that followed, *A Perfect World* (1993), Kevin Costner's escaped convict and murderer, having lost his desire to kill, yet unable to outrun his past, dies without a fight in an open meadow. In these two pictures, the protagonists are locked into the imperatives of character, exercising, as they imagine, free will from moment to moment but governed at the same time by the sullen imprint of past crimes, injuries, mistakes. The word for this kind of dramatic structure is tragedy. That's what Eastwood had become capable of. The two movies had depth, nuance, a burnished and reflective nostalgia for a simplicity no longer possible. All this became definitive in *Mystic River,* from 2003, a movie in which every one of Eastwood's late obsessions—guilt, destruction, self-destruction, vengeance—merge into a completely satisfying work of art.

Genre conventions offer enormous narrative strength—I don't mean to belittle them—and in the structure of the story, you can still see some conventions at work. The screenwriter Brian Helgeland, adapting the novel by Dennis Lehane, worked with the elements of a police procedural: A girl has been murdered, and Sean (Kevin Bacon), a homicide detective in the Massachusetts State Police, sets about solving the crime with his partner (Laurence Fishburne). But within this familiar matrix, Helgeland and Eastwood created a shadowed way of life whose roots go back twenty-five years to a crime: the kidnapping and abuse of a young boy. In the present, the grown-up victim of the crime (Tim Robbins), and the two friends who watched years ago as he was driven away (Sean Penn and Bacon), are held together by a bond of shame and disgust. Working without the aid of science fiction or fantasy, Eastwood established a sense of malaise, a community in which the normal dimensions of pleasure, ease, and trust are missing. The movie is set in a white, Catholic, working-class suburb of Boston, and the physical weight of this fallen world—the wood-frame buildings, the gray light, the sour flatness of the accents, the tough, anxious women clinging to their men—pervades every frame of the movie. The neighborhood might be an ancient Greek city fallen under a curse. What remains of the generic elements—the slow gathering and sifting of evidence by the two cops—brings the past, by degrees, into pointed clarification of the present. In the end, the movie's actions and perceptions transcend genre. We are what the past has made us, and Sean Penn's Jimmy, a neighborhood store owner and thug whose earlier life has been marked by acts of vengeance, loses his daughter and then asks if he's not responsible for her death in some way. Eastwood had never worked with an actor as daring as Penn, and he let him loose to explore the outer reaches of sullenness, self-righteousness, and shame. It's one of Penn's greatest performances.

To work with such glum material without falling into middlebrow dreariness requires intellectual force and a steely grip on narrative. *Mystic River* is wonderfully *told,* and it's filled with memorable moments—not just Penn's anguish at the scene of his daughter's death but scene after scene in which one character feels out another, not quite saying what he surmises, not quite asking what he fears. It's a movie of hints, echoes, past betrayals that live on to do further damage. This film, too, turns into an argument about violence. Like Dirty Harry and Little Bill, Jimmy is yet another guy who imagines that he alone embodies justice. He tries to avenge his daughter's death, only to kill the wrong man. But then, a surprise: His wife (Laura Linney), excited by his daring, and maybe by his cruelty, pulls him into bed. Eastwood had moved past easily understood right and wrong, past the simple satisfactions of pattern. Killing for revenge is as idiotic as killing for hire, yet the act is flagrantly rewarded. From the beginning, going back to his performance in *A Fistful of Dollars,* Eastwood had enjoyed a taste for irony, but this ending was a perverse twist worthy of a sardonic modern artist like Brecht or Fassbinder.

He was seventy-three, he had hit the summit (*Mystic River* was commercially successful, too), and one might have expected little afterward— perhaps a pleasant stroll through the high pastures of esteemed old age. Instead, he took stock and moved on. For years, he had played outsiders (by temperament) who worked within the system, angry men who held up authority on behalf of a white male majority beginning to feel besieged. Now, returning to elements from *Josey Wales,* he began noticing and even celebrating true outsiders, people who had much less power than his own characters. Had he become, of all things, a liberal? Probably not, at least not in any overtly political way. It's a better guess that, as he got older, he saw his own prized values embodied in people he had mostly ignored earlier. Women, after all, had rarely figured for much in his movies. One can remember Verna Bloom's tenderness in supporting roles, and, in the late 1970s and early 1980s, a few sassy performances by Sondra Locke, who was then Eastwood's paramour. In *Tightrope,* Geneviève Bujold projected a taut intelligence; Marsha Mason gave body and flavor to her exasperation with Eastwood's Gunny in *Heartbreak Ridge;* Meryl Streep had a never-met-the-right-man wistfulness in *The Bridges of Madison County.* But many of the women were whory, predatory, or adoring, and none of them, even the strong ones, quite prepared us for Hilary Swank's pugnacious jaw and wide smile in *Million Dollar Baby* (2004). At first, the fight club setting gives off the sour-sweat odor of defeat. As Eastwood and Morgan Freeman rag on each other, the movie seems a joke between elderly

friends (the lines are a duet for buzzsaw and cello). But Eastwood himself turns out to be the butt: The bullheaded Maggie Fitzgerald (Swank)
breaks into this second-rate male province, trains as a fighter, and pulls
the snarling old man out of emotional isolation into something like fa-
therhood and, finally, the full humanity of mourning. Maggie could give
and take a punch. The movie was less an expression of feminist awareness
than a case of awed respect for a woman who was tough and enduring
(the respect was rather woodenly repeated in *Changeling,* from 2008, in
which Angelina Jolie's betrayed mother takes on the entire LAPD).

In the same way, Eastwood began to see, in minority groups, even in
America's former enemies, what he had long admired in tough white men.
Certainly, no one in American movies had ever done anything quite as
open-hearted as Eastwood's 2006 feat of recounting the devastating battle
of Iwo Jima from both points of view. In *Flags of Our Fathers,* Eastwood's
critical account of the War Department's crass media exploitation of the
American soldiers took the shine off the victory. Then, a few months later,
he brought out *Letters from Iwo Jima,* a portrait of the Japanese, particularly the island military commander, General Kuribayashi (Ken Wata-
nabe), as supremely dutiful, and honorable in defeat. The two movies,
shot in color but then drained to near-black-and-white, were not great,
but both were intelligent and stirring, and the dual release placed them in
conversation with each other as profiles of national character, dialectical
partners in an imaginary but potent debate. The Japanese came off better.

Part of Eastwood's late curiosity was directed at new aspects of himself, a superb human animal inexorably getting older. Rather than fight
his years, Eastwood, with the entire world watching, explicitly dramatized aging—the slowing of reflexes, the hardening of perception and will.
Back in 1993, in *In the Line of Fire,* he managed to suggest, in the midst
of a first-rate thriller (directed by Wolfgang Petersen), that men his age
(early sixties) compensate for perceived weakness by over-focusing on the
task at hand, a fresh insight. Frankie Dunn in *Million Dollar Baby* was
inflexible, too, holding himself rigid so as not to be crippled by the many
kinds of guilt overwhelming him. Eastwood never revived Dirty Harry,
who would have been a grimly witty old party, but Walt Kowalski, the
irascible retired autoworker in *Gran Torino* (2008), is a clear variation on

Harry. Living in a house outside Detroit next to a family of Hmong refugees, Kowalski is indecently hostile—"gooks" and "slopes" are among the daily epithets—but, by degrees, he's impressed by the family's insistence on discipline, and he rouses himself to protect them against local gangs. Who can doubt that Eastwood's shift from loathing to compassion was an oblique rejection of the endless American rancor over immigration? The man who once walked away at the end now gravely took responsibility for everything, a development enlarged in *Invictus*. As if teasing his limits as an actor, Eastwood literally growled, but Walt Kowalski is also a true terror. Eastwood's skull stood out beneath his skin; his eyes were like coal fire. He was never a more dominating star.

The New Yorker, *March 8, 2010; revised 2011*

THE COEN BROTHERS /
A KILLING JOKE

The Coen brothers' *No Country for Old Men* casts an ominous and mournful spell from the first shot. Over scenes of a desolate West Texas landscape, an aging sheriff (Tommy Lee Jones) ruminates on the new viciousness of crime. He says that he's not afraid of dying, but, he adds, "I don't want to push my chips forward and go out and meet something I don't understand. A man would have to put his soul at hazard." But what does he mean? That he would be debased by the fight? That a devil might take his soul? Without transition, we see an odd-looking man in a modified Prince Valiant haircut (Javier Bardem) murder first a deputy sheriff, then a stranger whose car he needs. (He strangles the deputy and shoots the stranger with some sort of gun attached to what looks like an oxygen tank.) The movie jumps again, to Llewelyn, an early-morning hunter (Josh Brolin) who's out in the desert tracking antelope. In the distance, he sees five pickup trucks arrayed in a rough circle and some dead bodies lying on the ground. He moves in slowly, rifle held low. His attentiveness is so acute that it sharpens our senses, too.

In the past, Joel and Ethan Coen have tossed the camera around like a toy, running it down shiny bowling lanes or flipping it overhead as a naked babe or two, trampolined into the air, rises and falls through the frame in slow motion. Now they've put away such happy shenanigans. There's no music, only silence; the shooting and editing are devoted solely to what the hunter sees and feels as he inches forward—earth, air, a slight brush of wind, and the mess in front of him, which is obviously the remnants of a drug deal gone bad. Only one man, shot in the belly, remains alive amid the trucks. Nothing is explained to us, and nothing has to be; we accept the arbitrariness of disaster—and of goodness, too. Having lifted off a case full of money from the scene, the hunter—he's actually a welder named Llewelyn—returns home to his trailer and banters affectionately with his young wife (Kelly Macdonald), but then decides, in the middle of the night, to go back to the desert and bring water to the wounded man. He gets chased off by thugs from the drug syndicate—the beginning of a very long chase that will go through many moments of terror.

So powerful are the first twenty minutes or so of *No Country*—so concentrated in their physical and psychological realization of dread—that we are unlikely to ask why Prince Valiant, whose name is Anton Chigurh, kills with a captive-bolt gun (the kind used in killing cattle) rather than a revolver; or if it makes any sense for Llewelyn, a likable roughneck, to return to the scene after he's made off with $2 million in drug money; or how corpses lying in open air could have remained untouched by coyotes or vultures; or whether it's probable that absolutely everyone involved in the drug shoot-out could be killed or wounded (such mutual wipe-outs occur in the movies more than in actual shoot-outs). *No Country* is based on Cormac McCarthy's 2005 novel, and the bleak view of life that has always existed in the Coens' work merges with McCarthy's lethal cool. After these initial scenes, Chigurh poses hostile and unanswerable questions to the baffled owner of a roadside gas station (Gene Jones), and the mind games are prolonged to a state of almost unbearable tension. Watching the movie, you feel a little like that gas station owner—impressed, even intimidated.

That's an odd way to feel at a Coen brothers movie. For almost twenty-five years, the Coens have been rude and funny, inventive and sometimes tiresome—in general, so prankish and unsettled that they often seemed in danger of undermining what was best in their movies. Have they gone straight at last? The sheriff's expressions of philosophical despair are meant to carry serious weight, and surely no one could deliver these sentiments with greater authority than Tommy Lee Jones. His creased face is a map of hard times, his voice, in its curious drops and rises, a record of long experience, many earlier ruminations, much defeat. But our questions about plot details and many other things return, and, in the end, one wants to argue with the picture's aura of sinister fatality. How could the Coen brothers pull off a major statement about violence and death—they who have often made a joke out of both?

/ / /

There are the Taviani brothers, the Dardenne brothers, the Farrellys and the Wachowskis, but the Coens are surely the most relaxed and productive of all the fraternal movie partnerships. Joel was born in 1955, Ethan three years later, and they grew up in a Jewish household in a Minneapolis suburb, the sons of two professors (their dad an economist, their mother an art historian). Joel studied film at NYU, Ethan did philosophy at Princeton. During the college years, they weren't that close, but they hooked up in their twenties, drawn together by memories of 8mm filmmaking as kids, a shared catalogue of movie references, a flourishing sense of the absurd. They launched their career in 1984, with the thriller *Blood Simple*. Joel got sole screen credit as director on this film and also on the next nine they made together, with Ethan listed as producer and both of them as writers. But Ethan was always there on the set, whispering into Joel's ear or talking to the actors, and, in their last two films, ending all pretense of sole control, they have shared the director credit. They also edit the films together under the name of Roderick Jaynes, an invented surly Englishman who disapproves of their work.

The Coens form a conspiracy of two—industrious, secretive, amused, and seemingly indifferent to both criticism and praise. Early in their careers, they gave detailed interviews, but in recent years they have discussed only specific and relatively trivial matters concerning their movies, avoiding comments on larger meanings or anything approaching a general intellectual outlook. At times, they are given to sour pragmatic remarks, such as Ethan's "The awards put a movie on people's radars. Festivals are good, even though the idea of putting movies into competitions—this one is the best this, that one is the best that—is ridiculous." Their attitude is, "The only way to avoid bullshit is to say as little as possible." Avoiding art talk is solidly in the tradition of such American movie directors as Ford or Hawks, who presented themselves solely as entertainers. But the Coens, in their hip mulishness, have gone further into insouciance than any old-time director I can think of. In the opening titles for *Fargo* (1996), they announced that the movie was based on a true story, though it wasn't. *O Brother, Where Art Thou?* (2000) begins with a title stating that the movie is "based upon *The Odyssey* by Homer," which they later claimed they had never read. From the beginning, they've been playing with moviemaking, playing with the audience, the press, the deep-dish interpreters, disappearing as artists behind a facade of mockery and silence.

Consider a stinging moment in their first film, *Blood Simple* (1984). Two adulterous lovers, Ray (John Getz) and Abby (Frances McDormand), frightened and at odds with each other, are standing at a screen door. As they talk, we see something flying end over end toward them. It hits the door with a thwack—but it turns out to be just the morning newspaper. *Blood Simple* is the kind of adultery-and-murder story that James M. Cain would have written in the 1930s and Hollywood would have made a decade later into a seductive work of cinematic nightshade—the kind of picture that, as James Agee put it, lulled the audience into "a state of semi-amnesia through which tough action and reaction drum with something of the nonsensical solace of hard rain on a tin roof." But there's no such solace in *Blood Simple*. For the audience, that thwack was more like a slap across the face; it jolts us into noticing the new thing the brothers were doing. *Blood Simple* was full of such noir flourishes as a slowly turning fan, but the drama was set not at night in the labyrinthine city but in the bright sunshine and heat of underpopulated rural Texas. The characters are not shrewdly calculating sophisticates but moral idiots and screwups. The movie is both a homage to noir and a teasing gloss on it.

For example, the illicit romantic attraction between the lovers, which sets the story in motion, doesn't mean a thing; it's completely without heat. What interests the Coens is how foolishly people behave, and how little they understand of what they're doing. The lovers keep misreading signs, misperceiving what's going on. As trouble closes in on them, they can't make themselves clear to each other. The Coens may be the first major filmmakers since Preston Sturges to exploit the dramatic possibilities of stupidity. In Sturges's movies, however, you don't feel that he is putting people down—not even the rubes and yokels who won't shut up. Sturges was an affectionate satirist of gabby democratic vitality, but the Coens can be sardonic, even misanthropic. In their world, stupidity leads to well-deserved disaster. In *Blood Simple,* the cuckolded husband (Dan Hedaya) hires a vicious private eye (M. Emmet Walsh) to get rid of his wife and her lover, but the private eye double-crosses the husband, killing him instead, and sets up the lovers to take the fall. He laughs to himself, enjoying what a bad guy he is, but then, chasing Abby, he reaches out of a window and into an adjacent one, only to get his hand tent-pegged to the sill by her knife. The Coens spread dark blood on the floor in a spirit of play. Even fans of the movie (including me) came away feeling a little wounded.

If *Blood Simple* suggested that the Coens didn't want to make a thriller so much as tease one into existence, *Miller's Crossing* (1990) sported with the form in heavier and grimmer ways. The movie is set during Prohibition, in a nameless, somber-looking city dominated by Irish and Italian gangs. The openly corrupt atmosphere and much of the slang ("What's the rumpus?") come out of Dashiell Hammett's novels *Red Harvest* and *The Glass Key*, as does the hero (Gabriel Byrne), a morose, alcoholic, and mysterious loner who plays the gangs off against each other. Sullenly handsome, *Miller's Crossing* was shot in blended browns and dark greens; it looks serious, and, with the Gabriel Byrne character front and center, the Coens seem to be saying, or confessing, something about the inability to express feeling. But the situations and the dialogue are so stylized—so manically fretted with crime genre allusions and tropes—that the Coens killed whatever interest we might have taken in their story or in their hero. Created as a somber put-on, the movie perversely invented a new form of failure. It canceled itself out, almost as if the Coens had acted in bad faith toward themselves.

If *Blood Simple* and *Miller's Crossing* were almost offensive in their knowingness—and almost undermining in the way the knowingness yanked meaning out of the movies—the Coens in those early days had another side that was more generously eager to entertain. The comedy that the Coens made between those two thrillers, *Raising Arizona* (1987), has the lilt and shock of a disjointed folk ballad. This tall tale is set in a sun-drenched Arizona whose reddish deserts and magnificent mountains are disfigured by trailer homes and Short Stops—paradise giving way to suburbia. A young married couple—H.I. (Nicolas Cage), a semi-retired convenience store thief, and Ed (Holly Hunter), an ex-cop—decide that, since they cannot have a child of their own, they have the right to snatch one of the quintuplets born to a wealthy couple. This time, the Coens expressed open affection for their lunkheads: H.I. and Ed talk in moralistic platitudes culled from the Bible and self-help manuals. Loving their snatched quint, they desperately want to do what's right—that's the comedy built into their outrageous behavior. Their struggle is accompanied by subdued yodeling and Beethoven's Ninth, played on a banjo.

The Coens' joking is inseparable from topography. In every movie, working first with the cinematographer Barry Sonnenfeld and later with Roger Deakins, they establish a specific landscape, and pull whatever eccentricities they can out of it. In *Arizona*, two prison buddies of H.I.'s show up at the house and steal the baby, but then mistakenly leave him in a car seat along the road. Shrieking with remorse (they, too, have fallen in love with the kid), they drive back for him, and the camera sweeps across the blacktop, as if sliding on an oil slick. The wildest scenes in the movie were shot from the tot's point of view. Seen from below, a burning-eyed bounty hunter on wheels—a creature the Coens discovered in the Southwest named Randall "Tex" Cobb—is a caveman figure out of a child's book of monsters. The genre the Coens were leaning on was 1960s and 1970s biker movies, with its bearded creeps and outlaws of the road, but they were the first to think that a tot's point of view might be cooler than a biker's.

These three movies established the emotional and stylistic range of the Coen turf—the flagrancy, the jack-rabbit creativity, and the self-destructive whirl of unhinged pop scholarship. The filmmakers clearly had no interest in ordinary Hollywood realism. They could not—or would not—tell their stories straight or develop themes; their movies were jangled in style, brilliant and flashing but without sensuality or much interest in women. In order to get the right tone of controlled hyperbole, they depended on certain repeated American character types—not just their foolish heroes and heroines but fat, pompous men sitting behind desks and shouting; hulking, pre-mental brutes who murdered at will. They would draw on a stock company of actors—John Goodman, John Turturro, Jon Polito, Peter Stormare, and Steve Buscemi—who were not stars or lookers but rough-and-ready talents eager to play eccentrics, meatballs, killers, obsessives, and grouches. (There was only one woman in the group, Frances McDormand, who married Joel Coen after working on *Blood Simple*. McDormand could play anything—she shows up in *Raising Arizona* as a suburban bitch in a wig.) The Coens traveled to the boonies, working up the slang and commonplaces of the South or the Midwest into their own joshing patter. They could be nasty, heartless, even cruel, though with soft spots here and there. If they couldn't care less about sex—an absence that makes many of their movies seem adolescently skittish—they would take a tender attitude toward marriage.

They made lurid thrillers and screw-loose comedies, all of them shot with a liberated camera that alternated between swooping runs and trancelike fixations on objects dislodged from their context—a hat flying beautifully through the woods in *Miller's Crossing*, a pair of dead fish lying atop a Zippo lighter in *Blood Simple*. These objects were stuck somewhere between gag and symbol—a symbol without a referent. (Gabriel Byrne's fedora, in *Miller's Crossing*, epitomized the decor of 1930s gangster movies, but not their meaning.) The movies were skewed genre commentary—surreal parody, offered without irony; spoof that was too unstable to settle into satire. As in a David Letterman routine, derisive quotation marks surrounded the higher sentiments.

Barton Fink (1991), for instance, was a bizarrely malicious joke on a New York left-wing playwright (John Turturro)—Clifford Odets as he might have been imagined by Nathanael West. The Coens portrayed the Odets character as an open-mouthed prig and phony who goes to Hollywood in the early 1940s and immediately sinks into artistic paralysis. The playwright's sin in the Coens' eyes was his disgust for the task of writing a studio genre picture. They punished him with their own media-hip fluency: They turned the writer's hotel into a flaming, horror-film fantasia out of *The Shining*. In *O Brother, Where Art Thou?* (2000), three more open-mouthed clods (Turturro, George Clooney, and Tim Blake Nelson) horse around in a Depression-era South soaked in myth and legend. The movie is a stunningly uneven mix of cornpone monkeyshines, lovely pastoral imagery, and condescension. The sarcasm was thick. *O Brother* may have revived the blues and country music of the period, but it scorned such affecting Depression-era classics as *I Am a Fugitive from a Chain Gang* and *The Grapes of Wrath*. The Coens, it seems, are irritated by the earlier naive strains of earnestness or pathos. They expended their talent in an indiscriminate taste for ridicule and crazy-salad genre mixes. You might call them nihilists if their subversions were more systematic; or postmodernists if their fooling weren't so random that it shattered any academic category you could place it in.

/ / /

Before *No Country for Old Men,* the Coens had never made a movie that grossed more than $50 million domestically, but, for good or ill, they've never given up their aberrant panache, maintaining their independence by writing their own material and by keeping budgets low—sometimes very low. (*Fargo* was made for just $7 million.) If some of the movies have been misfires or hodgepodges, there are astonishing passages in many of them, like the Ku Klux Klan musical number in *O Brother.* Except for *The Man Who Wasn't There* (2001), a dud academic exercise in absurdist moods, nothing the Coens did was spiritless, and a little more than a decade ago they stopped banging movie references together and made two harmonious masterpieces in a row, the first a tragic comedy, the second a slacker hymn of praise so gentle and goofy that it has floated off the screen into the fantasy life of the nation.

In *Fargo,* the topographical obsession yields a view of landscape as moral destiny. Despite the title, the movie is set largely in Brainerd, Minnesota, where the snow falls so heavily that the fields and the sky merge into a single blinding mass. Watching the horizon line disappear, one thinks of evil's white body—Melville's white whale and Robert Frost's "dimpled spider, fat and white, on a white heal-all." The movie is about the blurring of ethical distinctions. The protagonist, Jerry Lundegaard (William H. Macy), who manages a car dealership, is deep in debt and needs more cash for a real estate scheme. He hires two thugs to kidnap his wife; his wealthy father-in-law, he assumes, will come up with the ransom, which Jerry will use to pay the kidnappers, while keeping the lion's share himself. As played by Macy, who has a face like Howdy Doody gone to seed, Jerry is the most destructive of the Coens' dopes; the confusion that he unleashes is so violent that the movie comes close to farce. Close, but it never steps over the line. The pace is deliberate, the tone deadpan, the style a flattening out of realism (there are no camera tricks or oddly angled shots). The Coens grew up in Minnesota and believed that something strange was going on there—a regional verbal tic that masked a collective nervous breakdown. Jerry's idiocy is a product not just of personal fecklessness but of a way of life in which rampant greed (among other things) gets covered over by an implacable blandness. Committed to politeness and the best of all possible worlds, Jerry has no inkling of his own wickedness—no words to put it in—and not the slightest fear that his idiotic scheme might fail. He's chipper and reassuring and unconscious, but no more so than the other citizens of Brainerd. Allowing for a change in accents, they could all be versions of Samuel Beckett's Winnie in *Happy Days,* who, buried up to her neck in sand, keeps insisting "This *is* a happy day, this will have been another happy day!"

The Coens' steady hand in this movie gives stupidity an astounding power; sarcasm gives way to a calmly amazed observation of chaos. The quiet directorial style takes in not only Jerry's depraved normality but also the brutishness of the two kidnappers (Buscemi and Peter Stormare), who hail from out of state and don't share the local manners. Buscemi, a sour-tempered lowlife, protests against the silence of Stormare's stone killer so frequently that Stormare knocks him out and feeds him into a wood-chipper, leaving only a foot sticking out of the top. The black comedy encompasses even the good folks. The pregnant sheriff, Marge (McDormand), is more shocked by rudeness than by the bloody homicides that she successfully investigates. She and her stolid husband, Norm (John Carroll Lynch), a wildlife artist who paints wooden decoys, demand little; they cuddle together in bed, awaiting their child, far happier than the grasping people outside in the snow.

Sometimes slowness, literalness are only a mask; it was moving to see the Coens acknowledge that. The surface of the Coens' work is jumpy, even hyperactive, but in *Fargo* they associated goodness with, of all things, a state of rest. That state, and its surprising life-affirming qualities, turns up again in *The Big Lebowski* (1998). The hero, known as the Dude (Jeff Bridges), a waddling Los Angeles mammal in candy-striped shorts, T-shirt, and gray hoodie, gets into all sorts of trouble but wants only to be left alone. *The Big Lebowski* received mediocre reviews and did little initial business, but this odd comedy has built, over the years, an enormous obsessive cult following, madly devoted to every detail of the movie. There are minuscule and profane versions of the film on YouTube, as well as costumes, posters, stickers, and frequent regional stagings of a weekend "Lebowski Fest," at which young men consume many White Russians (the Dude's favorite drink). Heroic sloth has been memorialized into a national holiday, into ritual and reaffirmation. The devotion is entirely deserved. As cult movies go, *The Big Lebowski* is much wittier than

Animal House or *Hairspray,* and free of the dumb-bunny silliness of *The Rocky Horror Picture Show* or the fumy mystical pretensions of *El Topo.*

The jumping-off point for *The Big Lebowski* is the insolent Howard Hawks classic *The Big Sleep* (1946). But this movie doesn't taunt its model; it mutely reveres it, and finds a rhythm of its own. As in *The Big Sleep,* an old man in a wheelchair assigns the hero the job of dealing with whoever is blackmailing a wayward young woman in his family—in the Coens' version, the old man's sluttish trophy wife. As in Hawks's film, the hero is pulled into an incredibly complicated set of circumstances—pornography, avant-garde art, conspiratorial groups, a real Los Angeles miasma. But private eye Philip Marlowe, in Humphrey Bogart's devastating performance, always anticipates the next moment and has a thirst for action, whereas the Dude is a man so slack that he can't sit in a chair without hitching his leg over one arm, exposing his crotch. Marlowe always anticipates the next moment, but the Dude, caught up in an indecipherable Los Angeles intrigue, is so vaguely constituted that he can hardly complete a sentence. The Dude, so to speak, resists being drawn into a story; he wants to spend his time bowling with his irascible friend Walter (John Goodman), a Jewish convert who served in Nam and has become a rhetorically enabled face-down-in-the-mud kind of guy. He thinks the fact that Americans died heroically in Vietnam justifies his getting furious over the smallest incidents in his life. Many of the Coens' idiots are obsessives, but Walter, who has burning eyes and a tight beard outlining a mighty jaw, is so fiercely methodical in his false syllogisms that you begin to understand paranoia as a form of intellectual egotism. *The Big Lebowski* is a tribute to harmlessness, friendship, and team bowling. It offers a persistent "no" to the hard-pressing American "yes." No wonder there's a cult; it's the only movie that makes inertia, and the resistance to work, family, and responsibility, seem like a position of honor. Women don't much care for it; for men, it's the Holy Grail. "The Dude abides," Jeff Bridges says at the end, meaning that mere living is enough. Or almost enough. The picture, in an amazing turn, becomes quite touching. After disastrous misadventures, the Dude and Walter realize they have nothing in life but each other. Their final hug completes one of the great movie tributes to friendship. Like *Raising Arizona,* the movie is a ballad held together by tenderness. The Coens, it turned out, had a heart after all.

/ / /

But it's not tenderness that impresses audiences in *No Country for Old Men*. Stimulated by McCarthy's tough little sentences, which record action and thought but not sentiment, the Coens have hardened their style to a point far beyond what they accomplished in *Fargo*. The movie delivers an unparalleled sense of menace. What we're watching seems to fall somewhere between a bitter modern Western and an absurdist parable. The empty West Texas road, which was right there at the beginning of the Coens' career, in the first shot of *Blood Simple*, returns again, suggesting a void of moral order, a wilderness where limitless freedom can lead to chaos. This movie never lets up. As Llewelyn flees, half of the Southwestern drug trade pursues him and his $2 million. But the money is most seriously chased by the strangely named, strangely armed Anton Chigurh, who's working (vaguely) for the American side of the drug network. The movie is essentially a game of hide-and-seek, set in brownish, stained motel rooms and other shabby American redoubts, but shot with a formal precision and an economy that make one think of masters like Hitchcock and Bresson. The killer and the money thief, as played by Bardem and Brolin, are alike in endurance, resourcefulness, and tolerance of pain. We get to know their torn flesh with admiring intimacy. Has there ever been a better chase?

Tommy Lee Jones's sheriff remains on the sidelines (he never really gets into the action of the movie) and continues to make dejected remarks. Impotent as a lawman, he has become a connoisseur of meaninglessness, irresolution, futility. Civilization, it seems, has come to an end, petering out in the yellow-brown fields of West Texas. But does the story support the sheriff's metaphysical dyspepsia? And have the Coens found, in Anton Chigurh, a correlative for their malign view of life? He's very entertaining as a movie creep, but who is he? *What* is he? He kills a cop, and then eleven other people; he walks around carrying what appears to be a vacuum cleaner, yet no one sees him, no one reports him. He enters and leaves motels and hotels, walks the streets, appears out of nowhere, vanishes into nowhere, but the police don't get their act together and come even close to laying a finger on him. The plot, when you parse it from scene to scene, doesn't hang together as a crime story.

Some people have said that you cannot read the movie literally. Chigurh is Death, they say, a supernatural figure, a vengeful ghost. Well, Death shows up bearing a scythe in Bergman's *Seventh Seal,* but that grim movie is set in the Middle Ages, and it's bathed in an atmosphere of magic, superstition, and religious fear. The fabulous, solemn Grim Reaper fits in *The Seventh Seal.* But *No Country* is set in trailer-park West Texas, a setting banal and spiritless and ever so real, and if Chigurh is supernatural, what do you do with the rest of the movie? Tommy Lee Jones's nonhero certainly lives in a realistic world. No, I'm afraid that Chigurh, despite Bardem's gravid tones and elocutionary precision, is not Death but a stalking psycho killer out of a grade-C horror movie, an implacable force who sports a cheap line of metaphysical patter. You keep wondering when he'll return—he's an intellectual Freddy Krueger. He's a trashy element in the book, too, but Cormac McCarthy gave him a shade more reality: He returns the money to the head of the drug syndicate and discusses an ongoing partnership. He murders people, but he wants to continue working in the trade; he's not quite the ineffable spirit of Evil.

The spooky-chic way the Coens use Bardem has excited audiences with a tingling sense of the uncanny. But, in the end, the movie's despair is unearned—it's far too dependent on an arbitrarily manipulated plot and some very old-fashioned junk mechanics. *No Country for Old Men* is the Coens' most accomplished achievement in craft, with many stunning sequences, but there are absences in it that hollow out the movie's attempt at greatness. If you consider how little the sheriff bestirs himself, his philosophical resignation, though beautifully spoken by Tommy Lee Jones, feels self-pitying, even fake. And the Coens, however faithful to the book, cannot be forgiven for disposing of Llewelyn so casually. After watching this foolhardy but physically gifted and decent guy escape so many traps, we are close to him, and yet he's eliminated, off-camera, by some unknown Mexicans. He doesn't get the dignity of a death scene. The Coens have suppressed their natural jauntiness. They have become orderly, disciplined masters of chaos, but one still has the feeling that, out there on the road from nowhere to nowhere, they are rooting for chaos rather than against it.

The New Yorker, *February 25, 2008; revised 2011*

QUENTIN TARANTINO

PULP FICTION

It's not hard to see why actors have been eager to work with the young writer-director Quentin Tarantino. A bad-boy entertainer, "dark" but playful, Tarantino writes an American gutter rant—golden arias of vituperation interlaced with patches of odd, hilarious formality (the formality functions like an outbreak of classical movement in the middle of a modern dance concert). His latest, *Pulp Fiction,* which won the Palme d'Or at Cannes last spring and just opened the New York Film Festival, is an ecstatically entertaining piece of suave mockery. Tarantino serves up low-life characters and situations from old novels and movies, and he revels in every manner of pulp flagrancy—murder and betrayal, drugs, sex, and episodes of sardonically distanced sadomasochism. But the language pours forth with a richness never heard in conventional pulp, and he plays havoc with our expectations. There are three overlapping stories in *Pulp Fiction,* and the structure is bound with words—anecdotes, debates, rococo profanities, biblical quotations. Amazingly, the complex of overturned expectations gets set right by the end.

Like Altman and Scorsese twenty years ago or Godard a decade before that, Tarantino, thirty-one, has quickly become an international film festival celebrity. At the moment, he's an avatar of American hip, perhaps the only one in the movie business. (Jim Jarmusch's stylized ennui has come to look like artistic and personal enervation.) Tarantino, commercial yet intransigent, is the hero of those who long to be produced, those who have daring ideas but no way of realizing them. Like the earlier movie men, Tarantino is immersed in cinema; he even comes garlanded with a myth comparable to Scorsese's asthmatic, movie-enriched childhood. A sort of

Southern California swamp-mall creature, he rises, unschooled, from a clerk's position at a video store with thousands of films in his head and grand ambitions in his heart. Having seen and digested everything, he understands the logic and secrets of movie genres, the hidden strength of their conventions; therefore, he can play, he can mix cruelty and formal inventiveness (sometimes the formal play is itself cruel), teasing, undermining, subverting, while telling a story at the same time.

Pulp Fiction is about Los Angeles crumbums—gangsters, a boxer ordered to take a dive, molls, a pair of sadists. The movie is not meant to be sincere. In a Scorsese movie like *Mean Streets* or *GoodFellas,* the characters, as much as lovers in an opera by Verdi, suffer and die. But Tarantino's gangsters are not "real." *Pulp Fiction* is play, a commentary on old movies. Tarantino works with trash, and by analyzing, criticizing, and formalizing it, he emerges with something new, just as Godard made a lyrical work of art in *Breathless* out of his memories of casually crappy American B movies. Of course Godard was, and is, a Swiss-Parisian intellectual, and the tonalities of his work are drier, more cerebral. *Pulp Fiction,* by contrast, displays an entertainer's talent for luridness. It's a very funky, American sort of pop masterpiece, improbable, uproarious, with bright colors and danger and blood right on the surface. And yet the movie is not heartless like *Natural Born Killers;* and for all its joking, *Pulp Fiction* is not a put-on. Tarantino gives us the great pulp theme without its attendant clichés. It's a movie about loyalty.

What a jump forward! I can't say I was a fan of Tarantino's 1992 debut film, *Reservoir Dogs.* The movie was like a nihilistic film school exercise— a malignant gloss, perhaps, on Stanley Kubrick's early heist picture, *The Killing.* I enjoyed the virtuoso cursing, the grotesque ironies, but Tarantino depended on blood and sadism so thoroughly that the genre tease lost its wit. (Being bullied by hipness is the same as being bullied by anything else.) Apart from enjoying one baroquely nasty scene between Christopher Walken and Dennis Hopper, I also hated *True Romance,* a movie that Tarantino wrote but Tony Scott directed. A commercial hack like Scott working on Tarantino's material revealed what trash unredeemed by irony might look like. *True Romance* was all processed, violent thrills, with cocaine dust for glamour. *Pulp Fiction* isn't nihilistic, and it certainly isn't stupid. If the theme is loyalty, the basic dramatic unit is the couple—men and women and men and men. Two petty thieves sitting in a diner, played by Tim Roth and Amanda Plummer, skinny and intense, mated like rabbits, rise from their seats and announce a stickup. Lightweights, thrill-seeking amateurs, they pull out their guns—and the episode breaks off. That's the beginning of the movie, and we return to them at the end, though what appears in the interim isn't all flashback. Some of it takes place before that moment, some *after*. The chronology of the three stories is daringly skewed so we can see people in the midst of different yet connected actions. Call it collateral narration. What goes around comes around.

The two principal characters are hit men in black suits, white shirts, and black ties. John Travolta, overweight, puffy, with long hair falling from a knot in strands (at times, in his black suit, he looks like a Hasid), and Samuel L. Jackson, lean, curly-haired, with a mean tongue, work for a local crime boss (Ving Rhames). That morning, on the way to the job (killing yuppie punks who have taken something that belongs to their boss), the two hit men have a long conversation about a man who massaged the feet of the boss's wife and was tossed out the window. Is massaging a woman's feet an offense worthy of death, like adultery? The conversation goes on and on, with perfect seriousness—the two thugs could be disputatious monks in the late Middle Ages. The movie is less about crime than about what happens before and after crime—the shadows and echoes of an act rather than the act itself. Tarantino has pushed to an extreme the pleasures of pulp, which are, of course, the pleasures of sensation and cheapness, and moods of shallow, voluptuous despair. Pulp fiction, especially in its aesthetically and intellectually respectable noir forms (the books of Dashiell Hammett and Raymond Chandler, the movies of John Huston, Howard Hawks, Robert Siodmak, Robert Aldrich, et al.), is a disillusioned, dark-shadowed urban poetry of losers, chippies, meatball thugs. But so much has been accomplished in the noir tradition, you can't do it straight anymore. So Tarantino works in banal daylight, on the L.A. streets, and we never do find out why the hit men kill the punks or what's in the stolen briefcase. And what had seemed incidental—the conversation about tending the boss's wife—turns out to be the essence of the first story.

Travolta is himself given the job of entertaining her for the evening. Witchy in dark hair, bangs, and matching ruby lips and nails, Uma Thurman's predatory moll has the lacquered beauty of those only-in-the-movies women (Veronica Lake, Jane Greer, Gene Tierney, et al.) from the 1940s. She takes Travolta to a glowing retro-1950s restaurant that features tables placed inside long-finned cars and a headwaiter imitating Ed Sullivan—the period references dance around deliriously. Afraid of his boss (if he sleeps with the wife, he'll die), Travolta walks on eggshells until the instant that Uma snorts heroin by mistake and the scene turns toward black comedy with moments so appalling you can't take your eyes off the screen even as you are close to nausea.

Most of the behavior on-screen is outrageous, yet each character feels justified in what he does and engages in long tirades of rational discourse when anyone disagrees. Samuel L. Jackson's blistering rant draws on the traditions of black street preachers and con artists; the rhetoric of insult and indignant, high-voiced hyperbole propels the language beyond Scorsese's tough-guy repetitions into a new movie poetry—Jackson dominates the screen. The movie is not so much a set of stories as a way of life and a habit of consciousness. Tarantino may be saying that Scorsese's kind of sincerity is no longer possible: These people know they are playing a role. Gangsters imitate movies and movies imitate gangsters in an endless chain. That situation could produce a stale, literary "postmodernist" cinema, but *Pulp Fiction* stays wild. The genre situations are invaded by weirdness, mess, coincidence. People talk much longer than you expect. The second story begins with a stoic Hemingwayesque loser—a boxer, played by Bruce Willis, who has been paid by the crime boss to take a dive, and who refuses to go down. Holed up in a motel room with his kittenish French girlfriend (Maria de Medeiros, who could be Maria in the sleeping bag from *For Whom the Bell Tolls*), Willis realizes he has to return home to retrieve a family heirloom, a watch his father once stored up his ass in a Vietnamese prison camp. A sacred treasure! What follows, as Willis runs into the angry crime boss, and they both wind up as prisoners in an S&M dungeon, is so startlingly funny—so far out yet logical—that Tarantino seems to be goosing the entire solemn history of action cinema. And the last sequence, in which the two hit men, with a dead body on their hands, require the services of a gentleman hood, the Wolf (Harvey Keitel), also seems a kind of preposterous valedictory. The dead bodies must be disposed of. Farewell to pulp fiction! As we return to the diner, and the two rabbity amateurs from the opening scene, the executioner played by Samuel L. Jackson movingly resigns from crime.

Tarantino has himself expressed his desire to make other kinds of movies. In the roundelay of violence and comedy that is *Pulp Fiction,* he has hilariously summed up an immense genre and gloriously achieved his exit from it. Life beckons from beyond the video store.

New York, *October 3, 1994*

KILL BILL: VOL. 1

In Quentin Tarantino's *Kill Bill: Vol. 1,* the trunk of a body, its head severed, spurts blood like a fountain, and other bodies twitch and gush at the shoulder after their arms have been lopped off. We know that the violence isn't "real," that Tarantino is playing with the conventions of Japanese samurai movies; we understand that the spraying blood, which looks like cranberry juice, is deliberately absurd. We get the joke of exaggeration carried out on a scale so grand that it becomes both homage and parody, and we may even appreciate Tarantino's skill in keeping a fight going between a lone woman warrior (Uma Thurman) and numberless black-suited goons for minute after minute, with individual duels fought on the floor, on platforms, on railings, and in midair. The prolonged fight has the exciting madness of a binge. And yet, entering into the spirit of Tarantino's video store fantasy of martial arts, we may still have a little problem. It's this: A filmed image has a stubborn hold on reality. An image of a rose may be filtered, digitally repainted, or pixelated, yet it will still carry the real-world associations—the touch, the smell, the romance—that we have with roses. Tarantino wants us to give up such associations, which means giving up ourselves.

In *Kill Bill,* Uma Thurman kills a fellow female warrior in front of the woman's little girl, who stares but utters not a sound. Again, we know the scene is meant as play. The two women have already been fighting in the living room, knocking down furniture and throwing each other about like rag dolls. But where's the joke in this particular unreality? If Tarantino is cutting us off from the real world, why use a child to bring us so perilously back into it? And, if he's bringing us back into it, why not allow the child some expression of fear or grief? Tarantino wants the shock of a mother killed in front of her daughter without the audience undergoing any discomfort at all. *Kill Bill* is what's formally known as decadence and commonly known as crap. It will doubtless cause enormous excitement among the kind of pop archivists for whom the merest reference to a Run Run Shaw kung-fu picture from 1977 is deliciously naughty—a frisson de schlock that, for them, replaces any other vital response to a movie. As for the rest of the audience, some people may like the brutal playfulness, but I don't think anyone should feel aced out by what he doesn't enjoy in *Kill Bill*. Coming out of this dazzling, whirling movie, I felt nothing—not anger, not dismay, not amusement. Nothing.

The New Yorker, *October 13, 2003*

INGLOURIOUS BASTERDS

In Quentin Tarantino's *Inglourious Basterds*—an extravagant jest about the Second World War—Joseph Goebbels commissions a propaganda combat film and assembles the Nazi leaders in occupied Paris in 1944 for its premiere at a lovely Art Deco theater. As the big night approaches, groups of European movie people and Jewish American soldiers plot to use the occasion to eliminate the Nazi command and bring an end to the Third Reich. (Some plan to set fire to the theater, others to blow it up.) The anti-Nazi cinemaphiles include the female theater owner; her black lover and projectionist; a leading German actress who spies for the British; and, of all people, a critic—an English expert on German cinema who attempts to pass himself off as an SS officer. The Americans are themselves right out of the movies: The Inglourious Basterds, as they are known, are a kind of Jewish Dirty Dozen, led by a Gentile, Lieutenant Aldo Raine (Brad Pitt), a blunt, jaw-jutting tough guy from Tennessee (which is where Tarantino is from). In brief, Tarantino has gone past his usual practice of decorating his movies with homages to others. This time, he has pulled the film archive door shut behind him—there's hardly a flash of light indicating that the world exists outside the cinema except as the basis of a nutbrain fable.

Since 1941, the Basterds have been killing German soldiers in occupied France, sometimes by beating them with a baseball bat. Then they scalp them (the explanation: Raine has Native American blood). The lieutenant also carves swastikas into Nazi foreheads. Whether the Basterds are Tarantino's ideal of an all-American killing team or his parody of one is hard to know. Very little in *Basterds* is meant to be taken straight, but the movie isn't quite farce, either. It's lodged in an uneasy nowheresville between counterfactual pop wish fulfillment and trashy exploitation, between exuberant nonsense and cinema scholasticism. In the middle of this crazy narrative, Tarantino pauses to pay his respects, like an unctuous film professor, to the immortals of German cinema. The great G. W. Pabst! Emil Jannings! (They are brought to Paris for the premiere.) The cinema, it seems, is both innocent and heroic; it creates great art, and it will end the war. The fire is started by the burning of old nitrate-based movies behind the screen.

Inglourious Basterds is not boring, but it's ridiculous and appallingly insensitive—a Louisville Slugger applied to the head of anyone who has ever taken the Nazis, the war, or the Resistance seriously. Not that Tarantino intends any malice toward such earnest people. The Nazis, for him, are merely available movie tropes—articulate monsters with a talent for sadism. By making the Americans cruel, too, he escapes the customary division of good and evil along national lines, but he escapes any sense of moral accountability as well. In a Tarantino war, everyone commits atrocities. Like all the director's work after *Jackie Brown,* the movie is pure sensation. It's disconnected from feeling, and an eerie blankness—it's too shallow to be called nihilism—undermines even the best scenes. At the beginning, for example, in 1941, an SS patrol, led by Colonel Hans Landa (Christoph Waltz), questions a French farmer about a family of Jews who may be hiding on his property. The scene is methodically staged. Colonel Landa is polite, even flirtatious, and Tarantino increases the tension gradually, shooting and editing the confrontation with classical rigor. Landa promises the farmer—a man of great dignity—that he will protect his family if he turns over the Jews, which he finally does, though unwillingly.

They are hiding under the floorboards, and Landa's men shoot all of them, except for a young woman, Shosanna (Mélanie Laurent), who disappears into the countryside. (We meet her again later, as the owner of the Paris theater.) Does Landa keep his promise and allow the farmer's family to survive? The scene ends, and Tarantino doesn't say. His refusal to show us how events play out comes across as sheer negligence, or indifference.

Moral callousness has been part of Tarantino's style in the past. In *Pulp Fiction,* his merry roundelay set among Los Angeles lowlifes, the aggressive acts that the characters commit against one another are so abrupt and extreme that they become funny. The movie's outrageous panache gave the audience license to enjoy the violence as lawless entertainment. But in *Basterds,* Tarantino is mucking about with a tragic moment of history. Chaplin and Lubitsch played with Nazis, too, but they worked as farceurs, using comedy to warn of catastrophe; they didn't carve up Nazis using horror-film flourishes. Tarantino's hyper-violent narrative reveals merely that he still daydreams like a teenager. It should be said, however, that the scenes set in Paris, in which Tarantino imagines the formal but abrasive nature of social life among the Nazi elite, are all beautifully designed (by David and Sandy Wasco) and photographed (by Robert Richardson). The director has also given prominence to a good actor new to American audiences: the Austrian-born Christoph Waltz, who, as Landa, exudes the kind of insinuating menace characteristic of Nazis in old Warner Bros. movies. The role may be a cliché, but Waltz is brilliant in it; he takes an intellectual pleasure in devilry.

The film is skillfully made, but it's too silly to be enjoyed, even as a joke. Tarantino may think that he is doing Jews a favor by launching this revenge fantasy (in the burning theater, working-class Jewish boys get to pump Hitler and Göring full of lead), but somehow I doubt that the gesture will be appreciated. Tarantino has become an embarrassment: His virtuosity as a maker of images has been overwhelmed by his inanity as an *idiot de la cinémathèque. Inglourious Basterds* is 152 minutes long, but Tarantino's fans will wait for the director's cut, which no doubt shows Shirley Temple arriving at Treblinka with the Glenn Miller band and performing a special rendition of "Baby Take a Bow," from the immortal 1934 movie of the same name, before she fetchingly leads the SS guards to the gas chamber.

The New Yorker, *August 24, 2009*

DAVID FINCHER AND
THE SOCIAL NETWORK

The Social Network, directed by David Fincher and written by Aaron Sorkin, rushes through a coruscating series of exhilarations and desolations, triumphs and betrayals, and ends with what feels like darkness closing in on an isolated soul. This brilliantly entertaining and emotionally wrenching movie is built around a melancholy paradox: In 2003, Mark Zuckerberg (Jesse Eisenberg), a nineteen-year-old Harvard sophomore, invents Facebook and eventually creates a 500-million-strong network of "friends," but Zuckerberg is so egotistical, work-obsessed, and withdrawn that he can't stay close to anyone; he blows off his only real pal, Eduardo Saverin (Andrew Garfield), a fellow Jewish student at Harvard, who helps him launch the site. Yet the movie is not some conventionally priggish tale of youthful innocence corrupted by riches; nor is it merely a sarcastic arrow shot into the heart of a poor little rich boy. Both themes are there, but the dramatic development of the material pushes beyond simplicities, and the portrait of Zuckerberg is many-sided and ambiguous; no two viewers will see him in quite the same way. A debate about the movie's accuracy has already begun: Doesn't the actual Zuckerberg have a girlfriend? Is it fair to portray him as arrogant and isolated? And so on. But Fincher and Sorkin, selecting from known facts and then freely interpreting them, have created an irresistibly entertaining work of art that's infinitely suggestive of the way personal relations are evolving—or devolving—in the Internet Age. Spiritual accuracy, not literal accuracy, is what matters, and that kind of accuracy can be created only by artists. The Zuckerberg of the movie is the Zuckerberg who matters to us because he's become part of us.

In this extraordinary cinematic collaboration, the portrait of Zuckerberg, I would guess, was produced by a happy tension, even an opposition, between the two men—a tug-of-war between Fincher's temperamental attraction to an outsider who overturns the social order and Sorkin's humanist distaste for electronic friend-making and a world of virtual emotions. The result is a movie that is absolutely emblematic of its time and place. *The Social Network* is shrewdly perceptive about such things as class, manners, and business ethics; it understands, with rueful regret, the emptying out of self that accompanies a genius's absorption in his work. Ardent and hard-charging, the movie has the excitement of a very recent revolution, the surge and sweep and pressured exhilaration (and sometimes nausea) of big money moving fast, and chewing people up in its wake. It's the very opposite of priggish: It knows that nothing is more exciting—and more destructive—than American enterprise in its lean and hungry early phases. Paul Thomas Anderson's *There Will Be Blood* had that kind of excitement, too—the wonder mixed with more than a little disgust.

We know from *The West Wing* that Sorkin can write the smartest and swiftest dialogue since Ben Hecht and Preston Sturges pulled their last sheets of paper out of a typewriter. Sorkin takes out the explanatory filler and overexplicitness that other screenwriters leave in. His adrenaline-pumped men and women anticipate one another's best shots; they fill out or overturn one another's fragments and questions, answering what's implied rather than simply what's said. They're racing ahead—ahead of *us,* too. Sorkin's method is both exciting and flattering; you feel yourself one of the elect of smart people when you listen to him: "Punch me in the face," Larry Summers, the president of Harvard, says to his secretary at one point in the movie. That punch is directed at us, too, and we take it, and enjoy it. Sorkin's script for *The Social Network* is a whizzing miracle—incisive and witty from moment to moment but expansive overall as a picture of college social life, hipster business enterprise, friendship, and rivalry. But Sorkin's scintillating skills in *The Social Network* are familiar. The unexpected element is David Fincher's work. The director of *Fight Club, Zodiac,* and *The Curious Case of Benjamin Button* is a master of sullen menace, convulsive action, uncanny and magical goings-on. Yet he treats Sorkin's real-world situations with extreme delicacy and precision. Fincher has always been obsessed with outsiders and rebels, but now, in midcareer, he has transferred that obsession into a subtler, more telling form, with both comic and tragic implications. David Fincher, it appears, has undergone his own revolution.

The Social Network draws on a 2009 book, *The Accidental Billionaires,* by Ben Mezrich, which appears to have been thrown together in order to be turned into a movie. Mezrich went to Harvard himself, and in both the book and the movie the Harvard self-love is laid on a little thick. The eager suburban college girls trucked in for parties, the rabbity competitiveness and status seeking among the men, the unspeakable excitement of being "punched" for one of the all-male "final clubs" (off-campus social sites for the chosen elite)—to outsiders, all this frenzied self-importance seems slightly mad. Yet the filmmakers don't satirize Harvard, and you can see why: They needed to re-create the pressures, the stratified social situations that led to Zuckerberg's revolt. Watching Zuckerberg and his friends toss beer bottle caps and ideas at one another in the dorm, we're meant to think that they really are the brightest (and perhaps the most obnoxious) boys in the country. And the brightest of them all is also damaged in some way. In the brilliant opening scene, Zuckerberg tells his lovely and intelligent girlfriend, Erica (Rooney Mara), that he could introduce her, a mere Boston University student, to important people if he gets into one of the clubs. He's prickly, overprecise, condescending; he keeps wrong-footing her and then scolding her for not keeping up. Yet, even as he acts like a jerk, you feel for him, because at some level he wants Erica, and the harder he tries to impress her the faster he drives her away. Sorkin created an emotionally stunted, closed-off young man, and Fincher pulled something touching out of Jesse Eisenberg. Slender, with curly light brown hair and dark blue eyes, Eisenberg pauses, stares, cocks his head, as if listening to some inner impulse far shrewder than the idiot standing before him, then rushes ahead, talking in bristling clumps, like a computer spilling bytes. The self-assurance he gives Zuckerberg is audacious and funny. It's also breathtakingly hostile. Yet, after many of Zuckerberg's haughtiest riffs, a tiny impulse of regret quivers across Eisenberg's lips. This is not a dead guy, emotionally. Something else is going on in him beyond mere insensitivity.

As Zuckerberg and his friends lay siege to computers in marathon doom room sessions—the pace is giddy, Beck's-enhanced—they turn women into objects, even prey. In the end, Facebook the invention becomes gender neutral, but the movie is sparked by a gleeful comic irony: A worldwide social revolution, capable of rattling authoritarian governments, began with nothing more urgent than the desire of two middle-class Jewish boys to be considered cool at college and meet girls without having to endure the humiliation of campus mixers. Fincher and Sorkin must have known how odd this geek-testosterone world is. They bring Erica back for a key scene, and then again at the very end. She's the three-dimensional person who's missing from the male code-writing orgies.

From the first scene to the last, *The Social Network* hints at a psychological shift produced by the Information Age, an altering of the way we perceive and address one another—a new impersonality. Zuckerberg may be the exemplar, but the shift affects almost everyone else as well. After all, Facebook, like Zuckerberg, is a paradox—a website that celebrates intimacy while offering the relief of distance; a site that substitutes bodiless sharing and the thrills of self-created celebrityhood for close encounters of the first kind. A hundred seventy years ago, Karl Marx, trying to grab hold of modernity as it was forming around him, suggested that, in the capitalist age, as goods fill up the spaces between people, we begin to treat one another as commodities. *The Social Network* suggests that we now treat one another as packets of information. Mark Zuckerberg, as interpreted by this film, comes off as a binary personality. As far as he's concerned, either you're for him or you're against him. Either you have information that he can use or you don't. Apart from that, he's not interested; he certainly doesn't register that you may have the same needs that he has.

At Harvard, Zuckerberg hacks into the university's computer system, a stunt that gets him into trouble with the administration but also brings him to the attention of the seniors Tyler and Cameron Winklevoss, who are identical twins and as close to aristocrats as you can get in America. In a weird touch, balanced between derision and awe, both brothers are played by the handsome Armie Hammer, digitally doubled. Devoted to physical cultivation, civility, and fair play, the twins row at dawn on the Charles River; they're headed for the Olympics. Yet the Winklevosses—or Winklevi, as Zuckerberg calls them—want to get into the social media business. Zuckerberg strings them along while he and Saverin develop the prototype of Facebook; that's the root of his eventual legal troubles. The movie is framed by the two civil suits brought against Zuckerberg a few years later—one by the Winklevosses, who claim that he stole an idea that they had developed with their partner, Divya Narendra (Max Minghella), the other by Saverin, whose shares in the company Zuckerberg intentionally devalued, in effect acing him out of the spoils.

The movie is a tightly fitted mosaic of agitated fragments. As the lawyers and the disputants throw verbal darts at one another across a conference room table, the filmmakers repeatedly cut, sometimes in mid-sentence, first back to Harvard and then to Palo Alto, where Zuckerberg lands in the summer of 2004, enticed by the siren song of Sean Parker (Justin Timberlake), the cofounder of Napster. When Zuckerberg first gets to Silicon Valley, he's as unworldly as a cloistered monk. Surrounded by pizza boxes and beer cans, and dressed in gray sweats, flip-flops, and a hoodie, he even looks like a monk. But Sean Parker, a hustler of genius, says to him, "A million dollars isn't cool. You know what's cool? A billion dollars." And though the hoodie remains, everything else changes. Parker, who foresees the universal success of Facebook, comes off as intelligent but reckless and dissolute—a candy man who brings the goods (venture capital, mainly, but drugs, too). Justin Timberlake, with his feline, insinuating charm, his physical dynamism, has a wicked visionary gleam in his eye. He embodies "scale"; he torques the movie even higher, and the colors in Jeff Cronenweth's cinematography change from Harvard crimson to the electric pink of a San Francisco nightclub.

The tempo is generally swift. Yet no matter how quickly the film moves, Fincher, working with the editors Kirk Baxter and Angus Wall, pauses within the fast tempo and, like a great opera conductor, lets the emotional power of the moment expand. The emotion is produced not so much by emphasis as by extreme precision—tiny shifts of inflection (a hesitation, a glance, a lowered voice); even the actors playing the lawyers add their bit of nuance to what might have been routine scenes of questioning and badgering. In the end, to an amazing degree, Fincher makes us care about the split between two college buddies, Zuckerberg and Saverin, tender friends who understood each other about as well as highly competitive young men ever do. Poor Eduardo! He's a decent guy but unimaginative and perhaps a little timid. He's our surrogate in this fast company, a fellow just trying to hang on who can't quite take in the scale of the invention that he and Zuckerberg have unleashed. As Saverin, Andrew Garfield, hardly raising his voice, has the emotional fluency—the fear, the indignation, and the hurt feelings—that Eisenberg has to suppress. The big money at stake forces both boys to grow up faster than they want to. In the legal hearing, a college prank that was once a joke between them—something about a tortured chicken—is recalled and used as ammunition, and the moment is almost tragic; it rips what is left of their careless youth to shreds. *The Social Network* is a linear accelerator that breathes, and Fincher is the one who created the breathing room.

Fincher has been a bit of an outsider himself, working at the edge and celebrating inspired screwups, marginal eccentrics, and monsters. Born in Denver in 1962, he grew up in Oregon and Northern California, skipped college, and, at the age of seventeen, went to work as a camera operator for the San Francisco independent filmmaker John Korty, the director of *The Autobiography of Miss Jane Pittman* and other gentle movies. A few years later, Fincher moved to George Lucas's Industrial Light & Magic, where he worked on the special effects for *Return of the Jedi* (1983) and *Indiana Jones and the Temple of Doom* (1984). By his late twenties, Fincher had found his own cinematic style in two forms: a series of razory, provocative, and beautiful music videos—for singers like George Michael and, most notably, Madonna—and some commercials that added exciting and disturbing images to our collective unconscious. There was the increasingly fast speed demons (a dog, a runner, a horse, a bullet train) racing across a sunbaked desert, made for Nike; a fetus slowly and thoughtfully taking a drag on a cigarette, for the American Cancer Society.

Fincher was never an outsider in the way that, say, an independent filmmaker like Jim Jarmusch is. But he may be one of the few directors who can flourish as an idiosyncratic artist amid the quarterly-return mentality of the conglomerate-controlled studios. There's no indication from his work that he has read much, or that he has lived much outside the movie world, yet he's not, thank God, another director obsessed with the movie past, like the pop-scholastic Quentin Tarantino, whose virtuosity with camera, mood, and tone Fincher more than equals. Fincher has his own obsessions. You can see many of them in the 1993 video for Madonna's "Bad Girl," which is a premature summation of Fincher's work in miniature. The police enter and examine a corpse (Madonna's)—a visual motif that he returned to in the grisly *Se7en* (1995), in which cops repeatedly walk in on deliquescing or bloody corpses. Madonna, it seems, has been murdered by a serial killer—and both *Se7en* and *Zodiac* (2007) are about serial killers. Outside Madonna's apartment, Christopher Walken, as some sort of angel of death, looks at his watch, which is running backward. That backward-running timepiece image became the key visual and metaphysical idea in *The Curious Case of Benjamin Button,* fifteen years later.

Fincher became a demon on the set, controlling everything, demanding, in *The Social Network,* seventy or eighty takes of a single shot. But, like any director working in the mainstream, he first had to fight to impose himself. He was only twenty-eight when he started on his first feature, *Alien³* (1992), and he got pushed around by the studio, Fox, which recut the movie. Still, there's a peculiar look to this noir sci-fi horror movie, with the camera often positioned beneath the actors and tilting up at black or mucky ceilings. It's a look that could have been produced only by a man ornery enough to attempt to have his own way with a prized studio franchise. In *Se7en,* the first real Fincher film, there's a prolonged philosophical dialogue between a pessimistic, isolated older cop (Morgan Freeman) and an idealistic, life-loving younger one (Brad Pitt). But then, at the end, a surprise: The killer, a religious fundamentalist nut calling himself John Doe, shows up in the hyper-articulate person of Kevin Spacey, and he's so cogent and comprehensive in his disgust for the world and for most of the people in it that you wondered if he didn't, in some way, represent a part of Fincher's temperament, too. Sympathy for the devil has always been a productive mood for an artist, and particularly for Fincher; he could probably make a thrilling version of Milton's *Paradise Lost,* with Satan reigning heroically in Hell.

Spacey's killer boasts of his ability as a murderer to overturn everyone's complacency, to disrupt the bourgeois order, and a version of that disruption is enacted upon the body and the spirit of Michael Douglas's wealthy and pleasureless banker, Nicholas Van Orton, in Fincher's *The Game* (1997). Terrible things happen to Van Orton, and it turns out that they are all part of an elaborate prank, a kind of benevolent shock therapy administered by his kid brother (Sean Penn) in order to jolt him out of middle-aged rigor mortis. Yet what one remembers from the film isn't the reassuring hugs at the end but the way the world falls apart for Van Orton—his pen leaks, staining his shirt; his briefcase won't open when he wants to close a big deal; a taxi races down a hill and tosses him into San Francisco Bay. The banker is toyed with—terrorized, really. Fincher's mischief was taking on a malevolent edge.

Genuine terrorism shows up in *Fight Club* (1999), which begins with another rant against bourgeois order and conformity. Hoping to escape mediocrity and boredom, a depressed corporate worker (Edward Norton)—an American patsy, a *consumer*—joins a sub-fascist group of disaffected men, a band of bloody brothers who happily maul each other in a basement club. The group grows larger and more organized, finally planting bombs. The movie has a wacko happy ending in which the bombs go off bringing down office towers. (It's a pre-9/11 movie.) Towers remain standing in *The Social Network,* but barriers fall; the barbarians not only enter by the gates but destroy them. Every Facebook user, Zuckerberg tells Saverin, becomes the president of the club, and the reign of the Winklevi and their kind is over. At last, Fincher has made a movie about a revolution that succeeded.

Despite the half craziness of the themes, the early Fincher movies have a visual distinction that makes them galvanic, irresistible. As critic Amy Taubin wrote, "No one comes close to Fincher's control of movement in a frame and across a cut," and I agree with that. Even Fincher's patented junk and mess, first seen in *Alien³* and then in the rubbishy, derelict rooms in *Se7en* and *Fight Club,* has a perversely attractive appeal, a glowing awfulness, as if it were lit from within. He doesn't hide the disintegrating walls, the sordid beds; we are meant to see the ugly poetry in them. Whatever locations he uses, Fincher brings out their special character. At the beginning of *The Social Network,* Zuckerberg runs across the campus to his room at night, and Harvard, its many enclaves lit with intellectual industry, looks glamorous, like an enlivened imaginary city. The scenes of the Winklevosses in their boat, crisply cutting through the water, are ineffably beautiful; the twins are at ease in their bodies and in nature, while the Zuckerberg gang slouch over their computers in the kind of trashed rooms that Fincher's anarchists and killers live in. The revolution brews amid garbage.

In the early movies, and in *Panic Room* (2002), a superlatively well-made but meaningless B movie, Fincher worked in "closed," overdetermined forms, with plot arcs as rigid as steel. Formally, the outlier in Fincher's work is *Zodiac,* based on the investigation of an actual serial killer in Northern California. Jake Gyllenhaal's Robert Graysmith, who pursues the murderer for years, is another of Fincher's inspired outsiders, an obsessive who so thoroughly gives himself over to his task that he almost destroys his own life. Graysmith comes very close to cracking the case, but, in the end, proof falls maddeningly out of his grasp. *Zodiac* feels open-ended. It lasts more than two and a half hours, but it might have gone on for hours more; it accumulates a series of suspicions rather than working toward a simple resolution. The truth, Fincher seems to be saying, is best approached with data, impressions, and interpretations; there's no final way of knowing anything. The double deposition scenes in *The Social Network* would also seem to be a way of attaining proof, but, again, truth slips away. Fincher and Sorkin have turned a philosophical position about uncertainty into a dramatic strategy. We see the events of 2003 and 2004 from different sides—Zuckerberg's, Saverin's, the Winklevosses'— and all the self-serving versions have a degree of validity.

The movie's evenhandedness is a masterstroke; it forces us to make our own judgments. For instance, Tyler and Cameron Winklevoss, despite their hilarious double perfection, are never caricatured as muscle-bound jocks. They're highly intelligent; they understand the idea of a social dating site. What they lack is Zuckerberg and Parker's intuitive apprehension of it as a new form of virtual social life. Fincher and Sorkin treat the brothers as traditionalists, men of honor tied to a formal notion of ethics and intellectual property, and therefore not ruthless enough for the Internet Age. They go to see Larry Summers (Douglas Urbanski), then the president of Harvard, to complain about Zuckerberg, and one can feel, in this seemingly unimportant scene, history falling into place, a shift from one kind of capitalism to another. Fincher and Sorkin wickedly imply that Summers is Zuckerberg thirty years older and many pounds heavier. He has the same kind of brightest-guy-in-the-room arrogance, and little sympathy for entitled young men talking about ethics when they've been left behind by a faster innovator.

Zuckerberg's tragedy, of course, is that he leaves behind his friends as well as his intellectual inferiors. It may not be fair to Zuckerberg, but Sorkin and Fincher have set him up as a symbolic man of the age—as our supremely functional prince of dysfunction. Charles Foster Kane was convivial and outgoing; Zuckerberg engages only the world he is creating. But those viewers who think of him as nothing more than a vindictive little shit will be responding to only one part of him. He's a revolutionary because he broods on his personal grievances and, as insensitive as he is, reaches the aggrieved element in everyone, the human desire for response. Facebook, whatever its banalities, meets this universal need; the outsider in the dorm room, in the office bank of computers, never need feel quite alone. Zuckerberg is meant to be a hero—certainly he's Fincher's hero, an artist working in code who sticks to his vision with infinite success but is helpless to prevent himself from suffering the most wounding personal loss.

The New Yorker, *October 4, 2010; revised 2011*

PART SIX / TWO CRITICS

INTRODUCTION

I first read *Agee on Film,* a thick selection of James Agee's reviews from both *The Nation* and *Time,* in the late 1950s or early 1960s when I was a teenager. I remember being stunned by the combination of high-flown moralized eloquence—the film critic as guardian—and the irrepressible outbursts of humor, which, often enough, brought the lofty sentences to the ground in an abrupt spill of blasphemy. I also remember being amazed by Agee's mastery of rhythm through the many clauses of his most complicated thoughts. Later, after reading Walt Whitman, Henry James, and John Updike, I could "situate" Agee's expansiveness in light of what came before and what followed. At the time, I had no idea you could *do* those things in prose, much less in film reviewing. Pauline Kael, as my long piece on her suggests (I have combined two separate articles), amazed and preoccupied me (and many others) for a long time—an obsession which I expunged by writing about her. Looking back, I'm very happy that she wrote as well as she did for so many years—that was the most important thing she did for the young critics who admired her and became part of her circle. I'm equally glad that she took me up in my mid-twenties when I was a nobody and that, for a while, we were friends. She may not have intended to do me a favor when she threw me out, but it was a favor nonetheless, since I might not have grown up for years if I had remained in that group. It's now a commonplace to say that she wrote criticism with a candid acknowledgment of the sensuous pleasures of movies that, in the past, educated people were unwilling to make. This is true. But now that her work has been revived (in a Library of America volume expertly edited by Sanford Schwartz), I would hope that readers will see how solid and shrewd she was on so many subjects, how responsible she felt for the actual content and effect of movies on the audience (if anything, responsible to a fault). Both Agee and Kael believed that the nation's soul was on trial in its movies. It's up to us, their descendants, to bring to our work the same measure of alarm, scorn, and heated partisanship.

JAMES AGEE

In 1947, James Agee, then in the seventh year of his career as a film critic, began a review as follows: "The elementary beginning of true reason, that is, of reason which involves not merely the forebrain but the entire being, resides, I should think, in the ability to recognize oneself, and others, primarily as human beings, and to recognize the ultimate absoluteness of responsibility of each human being. . . . I am none too sure of my vocabulary, but would suppose this can be called the humanistic attitude." The opening sentence has a grave but forward-moving rhythm—a sense of balance and momentum—that could only be Agee's. The sentiment, of course, is astonishingly high-minded. Can this really be the beginning of a movie review? Agee was writing of *Shoeshine,* Vittorio De Sica's Italian Neorealist classic. After saying more about *Shoeshine,* and defining further what he means by "a humanistic attitude," and noting its absence from contemporary movies, Agee goes on: "I know that *Shoeshine,* because it furnishes really abundant evidence of the vitality of this attitude, seems to stand almost alone in the world, and to be as restoring and jubilant a piece of news as if one had learned that a great hero whom one had thought to be murdered or exiled or corrupted still lives in all his valor."

Humanism as hero—as Achilles restored to battle after languishing in his tent? The review was published only two years after the slaughter of the Second World War had ended, a bloodletting that nevertheless left one of the totalitarian dictatorships still in power. In that grim period, Agee thought it necessary to point out that, putting it as mildly as possible, respect for individual human beings had fallen into abeyance. But now consider, even in the occasional absence of war, how much further that notion has been cast into neglect in the last sixty years, when humanism has suffered postmodernist theory and the everyday ravages of media irony. In America (though not in the recently democratic Eastern Europe) humanism has been discredited as an ideal. It has been called a sham—a tool of the ruling class, an intellectual fraud. Indeed, the "self" is a mere construct, the product of ethnic identity, class, power, the habits of language. The Marxist contempt for individuals may have vanished, but in the capitalist countries contempt has taken different forms: At the popular levels (magazines, the Internet, reality TV), it has turned into a nervous, automatic, reflexive derision, and by the commercial exploitation and self-exploitation of privacy as a commodity; and at the higher, more responsible levels, by a timid refusal to notice the individual character of people or groups for fear of insulting them. Humanism among the well-meaning has been replaced by a respectfulness bordering on squeamishness—a retreat into "rights," or formal respect, all quite necessary in the legal sense, but accompanied by actual indifference or fear.

And yet here is Agee in 1947 speaking of humanism as necessarily heroic. Certainly Agee didn't find much of what he was looking for. In the 1940s, the attitude of radical humanism was something Agee recognized only in the Italian Neorealist films, in Chaplin's *Monsieur Verdoux,* in certain documentaries, in revivals of Jean Vigo's movies, and in a few Hollywood productions. One can't help thinking, however, that Agee was proposing it as an ideal not just for filmmakers but for himself. The attitude, as he practiced it, was heroic precisely because the scrupulous fairness and respect he brought to reviewing movies did not exclude the most furious anger, a savage gaiety, a loathing of banality and self-delusion, and a remarkably complex attitude toward the vexing difficulties of representing reality. How much mealy-mouthed junk has to be scraped away in order to get to true reverence—for human beings or for anything else! Here is Agee's review (from *The Nation*), in its entirety, of a 1945 war movie:

> In *God Is My Co-Pilot,* the Flying Tiger hero, Dennis Morgan, tells a priest, Alan Hale, that he has killed a hundred men that day; he obviously feels deeply troubled by the fact, and is asking for spiritual advice. Since the priest does not answer him in any way about that but pretends to by commenting comfortably on a quite different and much easier perplexity—*every* death makes a difference to

God—it is regrettable, not to say nauseating, that they bothered to bring up the problem at all. Aside from these religious conversations, any one of which would serve to unite atheists and religious men in intense distaste for the lodgers in the abyss which separates them, there is a good deal of air combat on process screens, obstructed by the customary close-ups of pilots smiling grimly as they give or take death in a studio, for considerably more than soldiers' pay, a yard above the ground. The picture is not as bad, I must admit, as I'm making it sound; but it is not good enough to make me feel particularly sorry about that. God is my best pal and severest critic, and when He asked me for this touching March afternoon off, I didn't have it in my heart to refuse him.

In a little over two hundred words, the review expresses a disgust for false piety and a demand for emotional truth, a demand so stringent that it leads, momentarily, to the collapse of the cinematic illusion altogether. But all of this half-serious alarm is followed by a perfectly phrased and timed joke that both harpoons the movie's chumminess with the deity and restores the critic, in a nice soft landing, to his role as amused professional.

For Agee, the heroism of the writer's role consisted in harnessing an aggressive critical faculty, very modern in its temper, to an earnest, almost religious desire for celebration. He was a moralist, and one of the most interesting of the century: His affirmations survive a thousand distastes; his force outshines the innumerable qualifications that he added to his opinions. Agee's favorite word was *but*. He was always turning his judgments around, examining the other side, fairly patiently, tenderly, but without indecisiveness or timidity. For all his insistence on respect, Agee would have loathed the false respect of political correctness. He loathed it in its earlier guises in the 1940s: in the studio expert genteelism choking the life out of movies; in the dull softening of what had been tart and funny in the 1930s; in the lying Stalinist pieties of such pro-Soviet movies as *North Star* and *Mission to Moscow*; in the many films about combat that refused to face the elementary physical realities of pain, suffering, and death. His writing itself was an example of merry, high-principled, relentlessly muscular humanist aestheticism.

/ / /

Agee arrived at movie criticism in a way that might now seem odd. In July of 1936, a writer of richly resonant prose for *Fortune* and an avid Greenwich Village partygoer, drinker, lover, and talker, Agee found himself in the house of a taciturn family of Alabama farmers. Henry Luce's business magazine was then in its early, socially concerned phase, and Agee, along with the photographer Walker Evans, had been sent to the South to investigate the situation of impoverished cotton farmers. The report eventually became not a magazine article but a daunting four-hundred-page prose epic, *Let Us Now Praise Famous Men,* with Evans's extraordinary photographs preceding the text. (It took five years for the book to come out.) For Agee, the entire project was fraught with doubt, guilt, and miseries, relieved by brief moments of exaltation. At the beginning, he had denigrated the project as a fraud and a betrayal. In the book's first pages, a furious self-inquiry builds up. Agee was not wealthy, but he was privileged, an emissary from a powerful organization who had been authorized to "pry intimately into the lives of an undefended and appallingly damaged group of human beings." For what purpose—for money? For glory? In the name of "honest journalism"? After all, he wasn't going to bring the tenant farmers any kind of relief. A literary man in love with Joyce, Faulkner, and Céline, he had no intention of writing the kind of responsible report, with statistics and graphs, that might have spurred legislative action. Nor was he a Marxist, hoping to inflame protest meetings and rallies. The moral quandary of liberal journalism has never been stated with greater clarity.

Agee and Evans settled on three families, whom Agee called the Gudgers, the Rickettses, and the Woodses, and worked and stayed with them for a few weeks. Owning virtually nothing themselves—at best, a couple of mules and a few farming implements—the families were required to give their landlords half of their crops and a quarter or more of the earnings from their own half. They lived, literally, on quarters, and without electricity or running water. Having worked since they were children, they were hardened, shrewd, unlettered, inarticulate. For Agee, however, the point was not that these families suffered from atrocious social conditions. The point was that they existed. In an age concerned largely with the "masses," Agee was impressed by the notion that other human beings idiosyncratically and indelibly are what they are, in every ornery fiber. Flesh, bone, desire, consciousness—in almost every way, the farmers were different from him, obdurate in their singleness and as capable of pleasure and misery as he. A young couple sitting on a porch and staring at Agee had in their eyes "so quiet and ultimate a quality of hatred, and contempt, and anger, toward every creature in existence beyond themselves, and toward the damages they sustained, as shone scarcely short of a state of beatitude." Agee, born an Episcopalian, and religious as a child, was no longer an orthodox believer. But he had a consciousness of the sacred in people and in ordinary objects that believers associate with God's immanence. He loved, and took literally, Blake's proclamation "Everything that lives is holy."

It's an idea that, as a practical matter, most of us would find impossible to sustain, even absurd. And it imposed devastating, almost comically burdensome responsibilities on this ambitious young man (he was twenty-six at the time). Agee wanted to make a connection with the families, and to be liked by them in return, but he didn't want to swamp the farmers with sympathy—their pride wouldn't endure it. Try as he might, he could not resolve the disparity between the sullenness of his subjects and his own ravenous and unending sensibility. All that he could do was record. In the room where the Gudgers slept, there was:

> George's red body, already a little squat with the burden of thirty years, knotted like oakwood, in its clean white cotton summer union suit that it sleeps in; and his wife's beside him, Annie Mae's, slender, and sharpened through with bone that ten years past must have had such beauty, and is now veined at the breast, and the skin of the breast translucent, delicately shriveled, and blue; and the tough little body of Junior, hardskinned and gritty, the feet crusted with sores; and the milky and strengthless littler body of Burt whose veins are so bright in his temples.

Of the Gudger house itself, he noted that, in daylight, "each texture in the wood, like those of bone, is distinct in the eye as a razor: each nail-head is distinct: each seam and split; and each slight warping; each random knot and knothole." Then, burrowing under the house, he finds, among many other things, "the white tin eyelet of a summer shoe; and thinly scattered, the desiccated and the still soft excrement of hens." Agee's way of escaping from his compositional problem—escaping from sophistication and condescension, and from what we would call "attitude"—was to immerse himself in the materiality of the sharecropper's life in Alabama. The spoons, the stoves, the shoes, the beds, "a cracked roseflowered china shaving mug"—the things and stuffs and bodies and faces—this is the substance of *Let Us Now Praise Famous Men,* a magnificent expansive Whitmanesque text, as grained and serried as any work of American prose.

Famous Men was a commercial failure when it came out, and, even now, though perennially in print in one edition or another, the book remains essentially unread. It is a difficult, maddening, eccentric, very great work. One unequivocal success, however, can be extracted from it. The act of writing it honed Agee's ethical curiosity, tutored his relentlessness and gentleness, schooled his eye and prose in the immersive details that he would find in movies. Here he is doing physical description in much the same microscopically fearless manner, though with greater happiness— he is describing one of the great silent comics.

> [Harry Langdon] had big moon cheeks, with dimples, and a Napoleonic forelock of mousy hair; the round, docile head seemed large in relation to the cream-puff body. Twitchings of his face were signals of tiny discomforts too slowly registered by a tiny brain; quick, squirty little smiles showed his almost prehuman pleasures, his incurably premature trustfulness. He was a virtuoso of hesitations and of delicately indecisive motions, and he was particularly fine in a high wind, rounding a corner with a kind of skittering toddle, both hands nursing his hatbrim.

A man like Langdon—or Buster Keaton or Harold Lloyd—exhibited the absolute dedication to an idiosyncratic identity that he had seen in Alabama. But such expressions of unfettered being were rare, and the absence was heartbreaking. He had not the slightest doubt that movies represented "the grandest prospect for a major popular art since Shakespeare's time," and he insisted that the special strength of that art was photography, which, combined with sound, was capable of capturing "the paralyzing electric energy of the present tense." For the camera, "scrupulously handled . . . can do what nothing else in the world can do: can record unaltered reality; and it can be made to perceive, record, and communicate, in full unaltered power, the peculiar kinds of poetic vitality which blaze in every real thing and which are in great degree, inevitably and properly, lost to every other kind of artist except the camera artist." He was not naive: It wasn't "realism" as an aesthetic mode that he desired so much as a respect for reality. He liked stories, he liked the play of fancy, but fiction needed the charge of actuality. He was in revolt against the over-composed studio effort—the stultifying set-bound movie, the luxe period re-creations with their "wax-fruit dialogue [and] munificence of costume and social degree" which could not conceal the essence of tales told "without perception, honor, or irony from the center of a soul like a powder-parlor." He hated the too gentle evocations of small-town life shot on studio backlots; the dead literary adaptations (Wilkie Collins's *The Woman in White* was "given the studious, stolid treatment ordinarily reserved for the ritual assassination of a Great Classic").

When Agee began writing about movies (for *Time,* in 1941, and, concurrently, for *The Nation,* the year after), the issues of authenticity and the observer's moral relation to the subject—everything that he had wrestled with earlier—appeared with greater urgency than ever. After all, the war was on. How could you sit there, safe in the dark, watching it? Agee was hardly a prig, alarmed by pleasure. But he saw the war as the test of a pleasure-loving country's ability to deal with brutality, death, and dislocation. Hollywood had a serious role to play: It could bring American audiences within hailing distance of the hell that America's soldiers and people in other countries went through on a daily basis. It nearly drove Agee mad (guilt, perhaps, was part of his anguish) that the movies were screwing up their obvious task. There were the routine combat movies, some of them (like *Bataan*) hearty, patriotic, naive, and vigorous; and some, like *God Is My Co-Pilot,* embarrassing. At the more earnest levels of effort, there were the well-meaning resistance dramas, set in conquered Europe, but filled not with actual-seeming people but "with a pack of posturing Donlevys and Laughtons and Traverses spouting inhuman lines like 'You cannot keel de speerit off a free pipples.'" In Cecil B. DeMille's *The Story of Dr. Wassell*, a film about a compassionate doctor who remained with his patients during the evacuation of Java, the casting of Gary Cooper was a disaster. "One measure of the truth and goodness of the film is the difference between the elderly, simple face of the doctor and the simple yet far from simple face of the high-priced male beauty who enacts him. I like Gary Cooper; but God himself, assisted by all Nine Muses, could not have made an appropriate film of *Dr. Wassell* once that piece of casting was settled on." At the same time, Agee hated the violent fictionalized propaganda films coming out of Soviet Russia, which were filled with German atrocities committed against innocent villagers, and which, in their dubious appeals to revenge, threatened to degrade the audience more than the most softened representation.

More mortifications: When Hollywood tried to make leftish films devoted to people comparable to those Alabama tenant farmers, the results made Agee squirm. In the adaptation of John Steinbeck's *The Pearl*, for instance, "these simple folk speak a kind of pseudo-Biblical Choctaw, by Steinbeck; [and] most of the posing and camera work is earnestly luscious salon idealization. An extremely sincere and high-minded effort and, in my opinion, perfectly lousy as 'art.' . . . The very salt of the earth is reverently changed into so much stale saccharin." The dialogue between authenticity and responsibility never ends in Agee's work; the conflicts were never quite resolved. He wanted rawness, roughness, surfaces just as aged, gnarled, and worked as the wood of a tenant farmer's house; he also wanted delicacy and tact. The combination is what he meant by humanism.

When Agee got excited, it was over the poetry of the unforced image—something natural, spontaneous-seeming, "virile." In his beautiful review of William Wellman's *The Story of G.l. Joe* (1945)—a fictional war film he could love, at last!—Agee praised the movie's "taciturnity," which he compared to "a particularly strong and modest kind of prose," which yields a "long and gently rising arch of increasing purity and intensity." There is, for example, "the sudden close-up . . . of a soldier's loaded back, coldly intricate with the life-and-death implements of his trade, as he marches away from his dead captain," an image that Agee insisted was "as complete, moving, and enduring as the finest lines of poetry I know." And Agee found comparable virtues in John Huston's *The Treasure of the Sierra Madre* (1948). "There is not a shot-for-shot's sake in the picture, or one too prepared-looking, or dwelt on too long," but, rather, "a wonderful flow of fresh air, light, vigor, and liberty through every shot, and a fine athlete's litheness and absolute control and flexibility in every succession and series of shots." Agee wrote a memorably admiring profile of Huston as a leathery, reckless, canny, woman-devouring adventurer who has fallen into the Hollywood machine without being diced by it. Later, they worked together. For him, Huston was a tough-souled humanist-artist; Huston thought Agee a poet in everything he did.

Agee's work is pre-television criticism; he was not inundated by images, as we are, and he could be plausibly dismayed that film had devolved from art form to something that was only occasionally more than commercial entertainment or salesmanship. As an anonymous movie critic at *Time* (articles in the magazine were then unsigned), Agee did a terrific job summarizing plots and themes, grade-sheeting performances, highlighting directorial touches. He had an easy way with actors and actresses, and wrote sprightly, fact-filled profiles of Ingrid Bergman and Gregory Peck. He worked with enormous skill, displaying flashes of mischief and eloquence that propelled the columns out of the ordinary.

But those of us who know Agee's criticism almost by heart dwell on the *Nation* pieces. Having accomplished the basics in *Time,* Agee would offer just a line or two of plot or setting, and then take off, using his space to evoke the movie morally, aesthetically, physically. When he bothered to write them, the physical descriptions were stunning. In *Meet Me in St. Louis,* a mother and four daughters, "all in festal, cake-frosting white, stroll across their lawn in spring sunlight, so properly photographed that the dresses all but become halations." In a morose or philosophical mood, he would describe a movie as a revelation of the American soul, as a set of delusions or myths, as an innocent window on the country's not so innocent unconscious. Bad movies sometimes had their own kind of accuracy, a nagging, enraging faithfulness to the domestic life (say) of American

families, of community functions almost smothering in their acceptance
of mediocrity. The hard-drinking Village bohemian who saw authenticity
in the tenant farmer's houses and hands, recognized authenticity, too, in
the scrubbed new suburban houses of the 1940s, but hated what it said of
softness and philistinism.

Two historical forces merged in Agee's impatient aesthetics: the enthusiasm for "film as art" that animated, in the 1920s, so many little magazines, bristling manifestos, and avant-garde experiments; and the left-wing
and government agency excitement about film as a shaper of behavior and
consciousness that emerged in the 1930s. Writing in the 1940s, Agee was
still in touch with the heroic age of the cinema. In his six years on the job,
he found heroism in the moral daring of Chaplin's *Monsieur Verdoux,* in
Carl Dreyer's gravity, in Preston Sturges's high-velocity cannonball satire
of American types and small towns, in Laurence Olivier's soaring rhetoric
and flights of arrows in *Henry V.* But he saved some of his most detailed
concern and praise for such humble realist forms as newsreels and war
documentaries (*With the Marines at Tarawa,* John Huston's *Battle of San
Pietro,* and so on). In the hands of totalitarian propagandists in Germany
and the Soviet Union, documentary had become something poisonous; in
the more benign American and British forms, it held out the promise of
art. No one has ever taken more seriously the meat-and-potatoes issues of
documentary shot selection and editing, or heralded with greater fervor
the anonymous artisans of the wartime newsreels. He believed that the
mere photographic record of something, when skillfully shot, selected,
and arranged, could be tantamount to the greatest art.

Agee's moral disapproval of artificiality lent his writing satirical fervor,
but it also led him into his single major error—his inability to respond to
the dramatic strengths of the highly charged, deliciously fabulous or melancholy noir style. He wasn't much interested in films like *The Big Sleep,*
whose chiaroscuro lighting and night-world dirty-mindedness struck him
as little more than charmingly sinister. *The Big Sleep,* he said, was

> a violent, smoky cocktail shaken together from most of the print-
> able misdemeanors and some that aren't—one of those Raymond
> Chandler Specials which puts you, along with the cast, into a state

of semi-amnesia through which tough action and reaction drum with something of the nonsensical solace of hard rain on a tin roof.

"Nonsensical solace of hard rain on a tin roof" is wonderful. But Agee didn't see what we see—an incomparably witty insolence running through the farrago of murders, coincidences, intimations of debauchery, and extortion; a knightly virtue driving Humphrey Bogart's furious passage from one end of Los Angeles to another in down-at-the-heels jalopies; an investment in style, in cool, in pre-hipster hipness that did not exclude a lonely ethos and as serious a moral code as the 1940s would produce.

Despite such lapses, Agee, in his *Nation* pieces, invented the moral rhetoric of film reviewing. He had unlimited respect for the artistic capacity of the medium, but Hollywood in the 1940s was an industry in which a few "dangerous" individuals with "murderous creative passion" struggled against mediocrity and routine, and often lost. Agee created the myth that almost every critic since his day has drawn on—that the audience, collectively, was pure, and that Hollywood, except for a few people, was timid or corrupt. His use of words like "honor," "purity," and "courage" has left some critics cold (even as these critics were inventing equivalents of their own). His rival, Manny Farber, who wrote for *The New Republic* when Agee was at *The Nation*, later complained that Agee, "borrowing words from God, decided whether the latest Hollywood sexpot, in 'Blanche of the Evergreens,' was truthful, human, selfless, decent, noble, pure, honorable, really good, or simply deceitful, a cheat, unclean, and without love or dignity," and Pauline Kael, while acknowledging Agee's powers as a critic, complained of his "excessive virtue," which, she said, "may have been his worst critical vice." But Agee's "virtue" was shot through with dissidence, foul temper, and comedy. (He ended a grimly knowing review of Billy Wilder's alcoholism drama, *The Lost Weekend*, with the following words: "I undershtand that liquor interesh: innerish: intereshtsh are rather worried about thish film. Thash tough.") Farber and Kael missed something in Agee that was foreign to their own temperaments—the intricate and unending play of piety and blasphemy, the twin needs of an essentially religious man to revere and to let loose. One can only blink in wonder at the profanity that Agee got away with, artfully, as in his review of the excruciating *Carnegie Hall,* in which, he noted, the conductor Leopold Stokowski, "shot from the floor . . . seems to be undergoing for the public benefit an experience, while conducting a portion of Tchaikovsky's Fifth Symphony, which men of coarser clay wish exclusively on women, or perhaps on albums of prefabricated trade-union songs."

When he wasn't excited by the possibilities of film as art or as ethical passion, Agee exercised what can only be called the gallantry of reviewing, which is to bring the maximum of response to the most minimal of occasions. He worked with his characteristic "yes, but" or "no, but" fairness on movie after movie. His disparagement of so much that he saw may have been produced by disappointed idealism, but he never fell into sourness. On the contrary, disappointment fueled Agee's resourcefulness and gaiety. He was great at lightning-fast evocation of a bad movie—the tone, mood, style captured in a few sentences (among his predecessors, only Graham Greene, in his part-time tenure as movie critic in the late 1930s, was able to do this). The first twenty minutes for instance of Twentieth Century-Fox's 1944 adaptation of *Jane Eyre* are

> a lush, beetle-browed, unusually compelling piece of high romantic screen rhetoric. I suspect that Orson Welles [who played Rochester] had a hand in this stretch—for good and for bad; it has a good deal of his black-chenille-and-rhinestones manner. After that, all you get is a careful and tame production, a sadly vanilla-flavored Joan Fontaine, and Welles treating himself to road-operatic sculpturing of body, cloak, and diction, his eyes glinting in the Rembrandt gloom, at every chance, like side-orders of jelly.

That single phrase about Welles's eyes is worth more, as a spurt of energy, than ten academic essays about "the male gaze" and how it controlled the spectator's response to movies in the classic Hollywood period. Such a phrase is unprecedented and inimitable; no amount of theory can produce it. In *Tender Comrade,* the courtship and marriage of Ginger Rogers and her husband have "the curious accuracy of those advertising dialogues in which Mr. and Mrs. Patchogue eliminate their erotic blockages by wrangling their way through to a good laxative." About the musical *Good News,* Agee wrote that "Joan McCracken makes me think of a libidinous peanut; Mel Tormé reminds me of something in a jar but is, unfortunately, less quiet."

At the end of his time as reviewer, Agee was getting exasperated. He did not feel betrayal so much as exhaustion. *Hazard* was perhaps "an hour too much of the kind of edgy, intelligent worthlessness which Paramount turns out in its sleep." Studio complacency was beginning to close in on him; his later work moves toward the extremes of long appreciations and very short dismissal. In response to the title *You Were Made for Me,* he wrote only, "That's what you think." Unfortunately for him, he stopped writing years before a new heroic age—in the late 1950s in Europe, the 1970s in America—could get under way. The films of Truffaut, Godard, Buñuel, and Martin Scorsese and Robert Altman, I suspect, would have amazed him; the documentaries of Frederick Wiseman would have fulfilled his desire for a level-gazing, textured, unflinching critical realism.

In 1948, he quit regular reviewing (though he made a few return appearances—the silent comedy piece and a review of *Sunset Boulevard*). He had always wanted to write movies, and finally he did, working on *The African Queen* and *The Night of the Hunter.* These two films have their poetic glories, but none that were not anticipated by Agee in his regretful and exultant years as a movie critic.

Material in this essay was drawn from the Introduction to Agee on Film: Criticism and Comment on the Movies *(Modern Library, 2000)*
and The New Yorker, *January 9, 2006*

PAULINE KAEL / A GREAT CRITIC
AND HER CIRCLE

I became a follower of the *New Yorker* movie critic Pauline Kael, or a "Paulette," as her acolytes were later derisively known, in the spring of 1969, when I answered a summons and showed up at her apartment at 93rd Street and Central Park West. At the time, I knew her only slightly. I had been introduced to her two years earlier by Paul Warshow, the son of the critic Robert Warshow, and we had later met a few times and laughed a lot—in person, she was always funny. In 1969, I was a graduate student hiding on a shadowless California campus and putting off my life as much as I could. I was trying, I suppose, to find a way of easing into writing. Earlier that spring, I had written a letter to *The New York Review of Books* teasing the surly shenanigans of the avant-garde troupe the Living Theatre. The letter wasn't much—a mere gloss on a piece that critic Robert Brustein had already published in the *Review*—and it was never printed, but Pauline, noticing my odd, crablike gestures toward criticism, demanded to see it.

"Give!" she said as I entered her apartment. She snatched the pages from my hands, and without looking them over began to read to her guests, a documentary filmmaker and a publishing executive. Pauline read the letter the way that she read her own work on the radio—slowly, with a schoolteacher's weighted emphasis that brought out the structure of the sentences. As she read in her radio voice, my heart pounded violently, my ears turned red. I knew that hiding was no longer possible—the public reading was some kind of laying on of hands.

Not a singular honor, of course. Pauline had taken up many young people before me, and would famously take up a great many more later on. Young readers who dropped her a combative note about something she had written, or who sent her some pieces they had written themselves, even in a tiny small-town paper, might get called up and invited over or asked to send more writing. Pauline, who lived with her twenty-year-old daughter, Gina James, liked having company at night when she wasn't working. The Central Park West apartment, an odd, inviting place, had become a kind of minimalist writing-and-talking theater. A previous tenant had knocked down a couple of walls, leaving an irregular open area facing the park. Pauline worked on a slanted architect's table, which dominated one side of the room; her narrow bed, lying open on all sides, was behind it, only a few feet away. In the center of the room, there was a circular oak table illuminated by a hanging Tiffany lamp. At night, the lamp created a pool of light which threw the surrounding area into darkness, and Pauline, facing the windows and the park, her legs gathered under her, would sit at the table and sip a glass of watered white wine. Laughing steadily as a way of keeping the ball in play, she argued with the guests, leaping up now and then to provide food or drink or to kiss one of the barkless, hairless dogs—basenjis—that lived with her and Gina. She praised, ardently and in detail, and she blamed. Mainly she blamed, scalding the reputation of virtually every writer in town.

She had recently completed her second year of work at *The New Yorker* (in those days, she and Penelope Gilliatt alternated in six-month periods), writing sentences that leaped off the page with a brazen force unknown among the magazine's critics at the time. The sainted Ingmar Bergman, she wrote, had become "a tiresome deep thinker of second-rate thoughts . . . the Billy Graham of the post-analytic set." About *Charly*, the Cliff Robertson–Claire Bloom weeper, she wrote, "And now there's *Charly*, with that primitive, garbagey appeal that seems to reach through sophistication and education right to the primordial jerk. College students study Ionesco and Beckett and Artaud and then respond to—*Charly*. A surprising number of people seem to be educated beyond their own tastes." In her first two years at the magazine, she wanted to pep up the readers' ideas of what art could be, and, quickly, she set out her notions of the hybrid nature of the movie medium, celebrated D. W. Griffith's *Intolerance* and the career of Luis Buñuel, dismissed English directors as inept, and made the case for a gimmicky pop American movie, *The Planet of the Apes*.

As a writer, she had the natural beat of a good musician, alternating the tension and weight of a long sentence with the brutal quick jab of a short one. Her prose was so urgent and heated that a complexly argued piece seemed to burst forth in a single unbroken stream of words that combined sternly proper syntax with free-ranging, rowdy habits of phrasing. She was a master of informal rhetoric—the bullying mock question, the interjected taunt—and a great liberator of critical language, establishing the right, by means of charged rhythm and color, to speak one's mind on the page as one might talk to one's friends over a drink. She used slang, contractions, hype, insult, syncopated compound adjectives—anything for greater speed. The point was not to write like a lowbrow; the point was to write as an intellectual without closing the top button of your prose and thereby choking a strong, easy breath. Her *New Yorker* column was the most exciting regular writing about movies to have appeared in English since James Agee gave up his job at *The Nation* in 1948. Two years before Pauline arrived at the magazine, the paperback version of her first collection of pieces, *I Lost It at the Movies,* had sold more than 150,000 copies, an almost unimaginable number for a book of criticism. At fifty, after knocking around for years and falling in and out of many jobs, including many reviewing jobs, she had suddenly become successful and famous, and she was cocky, overbearing, and friendly all at once.

Pauline Kael was short (five feet), and she wore (typically) a flowered print shirt, slacks, and sneakers. Except for her eyes, which were a beautiful blue and eagerly darted this way and that, she was an ordinary-looking woman who spoke in a breathy, liltingly feminine voice (it was teacherly only when she read aloud). In that soft voice, however, she tore through conversations like a projectile. The first time I met her, in 1967, she couldn't believe that Paul Warshow and I had enjoyed *The Graduate* or that we had identified with Dustin Hoffman's Benjamin, a silent naïf adrift in a world of rancid grown-ups. She sighed, giggled, and then said, "Do you think that grown-ups are all predatory and corrupt?" Her voice reached into upper registers, suggesting that all of rationality lay on her side, none on ours. Well, no, we didn't think that. More sighs and musically insinuating questions: "How could you identify with someone who doesn't have an idea in his head?" Well, we shared some of his feelings.

"But he's a *blank*. Aren't you projecting your own feelings onto him?" She asked questions, she poked you to see what you were made of, and then she knew: Some people had it, and some didn't. Among moviegoers, there were taxi drivers who knew what a good movie was, and there were famous intellectuals, including a few movie critics, who did not.

I must have said something that impressed her as sensible, or I wouldn't have been invited back. In all the years since then, I have never met any man or woman so quick to understand what someone else was up to, so eager to honor ambition in the arts or in writing. Not all her friends were young, but she had a special way with the young, rousing the intellectual appetite and worldly ambition in, say, a surly twenty-five-year-old stuck in a pointless job or a graduate student drifting toward a half-dreaded academic career. In those days, she was nearly magical in her powers, a good witch with a wicked tongue. If you said something unfortunate, expressing a reservation about, say, Aretha Franklin or Gilbert & Sullivan or Claudette Colbert or a liking for Anaïs Nin, Frank Capra, John Wayne, or Clint Eastwood, she would gasp and offer a summary judgment on your taste, sometimes addressed to another person in the room ("Gee, he's really a very conservative boy, isn't he?"), but offered (usually) with such humor and cajoling affection that those who didn't turn away in a rage were convinced that she was rough on them for their own good. At least, that was the promise.

Pauline Kael was motherly but brilliant, erudite but entirely informal, morally alert but as bawdy as a San Francisco madam. She responded to everything she saw and felt—registering a soft breeze coming off the water or a curious-looking dog in the park, along with movies and books and people—and her responses were immediate, fearless, paralyzingly funny, and rarely altered or withdrawn. She never pretended that she was objective or above the fray, and she refused to place her opinions on the table as just another view. She insisted that she was right, right about everything, and you would be right, too, someday, if you worked like hell and stayed loose. To anyone in flight from the academy, she offered a shackle-breaking song of liberation: You didn't need the citations, the habits of obeisance, the props of authority; you had to experience an art form directly, stand on your own ground, and express yourself forcefully as an ordinary person. What she said and wrote came out of her reading and viewing and also from her experience of life; and so, for many of us, her tossed-out judgments on movies or books, and particularly her personal remarks aimed at us, kindly or razor-edged, were accepted as a pure expression of spirit—an authentic, spontaneous creation. People sought her praise so energetically because there was little chance she would ever give it out of politeness. And that praise, when it arrived, was enthralling. Literally so—some people got so addicted to it they belonged to her forever. Whatever they did in their lives, or didn't do, they felt that their existence was at least partly justified by Pauline's love.

To be included within that pool of light around her table and to be privileged to exchange opinions and to hear the work of well-known people analyzed (i.e., put down) was an electrifying experience for a young man or woman struggling with self-doubt. She read our own writing with violent attention, implying that she cared more about what we wrote than we did ourselves, an outrageous presumption that nevertheless kicked many a stalled young writer into gear. "It's shit, honey," she said to me about one piece still in the works, "and if you don't make it better I'll stick pins in you." She was highly encouraging, sometimes impassioned on my behalf, and full of shrewd career advice. At the end of the summer, while I was still a graduate student, she recommended me for a movie reviewing job at *The Atlantic Monthly*.

Those who started out in film criticism in the late 1960s and early 1970s— everyone, not just Pauline Kael's friends—slowly realized that they had stumbled into a happy moment. After years of the Vietnam War, the culture had attained a degree of bitter self-knowledge, a mood more productive of serious popular work than the shocked rage and frenzy and with-it giddiness of the 1960s, which yielded movies too often shrill, jumpy, consciously zeitgeisty—Richard Lester having a fit, *Easy Rider* careering out of control. Things were settling down aesthetically; a highly developed visual style, and such narrative elements as ambiguity, unresolved feelings, even unhappy endings were suddenly possible. Art was possible—the audience, sometimes in sizable numbers, was up for it. Young directors like Robert Altman, Martin Scorsese, Francis Coppola, Brian De

Palma, Woody Allen, Steven Spielberg, Hal Ashby, and the documentary filmmaker Frederick Wiseman, taking advantage of that mood, were just beginning to work, and critics led the charge for them and for the ongoing work of Bergman, Buñuel, Godard, Truffaut, Fellini, Bertolucci, Antonioni, Polanski, Kurosawa, Mizoguchi, and many other great directors from abroad. We were just a bunch of journalists, not political revolutionaries or the founders of a new science or philosophy, but, still, there was a spirit of insurgency in the air, and we were part of it. Like the boldest of the rock critics, Pauline was sure that American mass culture at its best was plugged into the country's most vital instincts—anti-authoritarian, even subversive, individualistic but yearning for community. "Good movies," she wrote wistfully in 1968, "make you care, make you believe in possibilities again. If someone in the Hollywood-entertainment world has managed to break through with something that speaks to you, then it isn't *all* corruption. . . . Sitting there alone . . . you know there must be others perhaps in this very theater in this city, surely in other theaters in other cities, now, in the past or future, who react as you do."

The people she had gathered around her made up one such community of moviegoers. Hoping to extend that community outward, she promoted an explosive American popular art in which violence and eros would join together, an art freed of the austere reticence and formal rigors that she thought often squeezed the life out of European high culture. In that period and just after, many of the young critics worked under the aegis of Pauline's canonical anti-canonical statement from 1964:

There is more energy, more originality, more excitement, more *art* in American kitsch like *Gunga Din, Easy Living,* the Astaire and Rogers pictures like *Swingtime* and *Top Hat,* in *Strangers on a Train, His Girl Friday, The Crimson Pirate, Citizen Kane, The Lady Eve, To Have and Have Not, The African Queen, Singin' in the Rain, Sweet Smell of Success,* or more recently, *The Hustler, Lolita, The Manchurian Candidate, Hud, Charade,* than in the presumed "High Culture" of *Hiroshima Mon Amour, Last Year at Marienbad, La Notte, The Eclipse,* and the Torre Nilsson pictures.

In 1970, as that specifically American energy—raw, playful, yet serious—
was breaking out in such movies as *M*A*S*H* and Frederick Wiseman's
Hospital, I left school after getting the *Monthly* job and returned home to
New York, where I spent a fair number of evenings at Pauline's apartment
gabbing until two or three in the morning. "That's enough for you," she
would say with a laugh, when we were both too tired to speak. Sometimes
I needed another hour or two to calm myself down before I could fall
asleep. She had made me a writer, or at least a job holder—and, it turned
out, a member of an increasingly notorious group of disciples. Around
town a look of misery and fatigue (what, *another* one?) passed over the
faces of established critics when I ran into them.

Pauline Kael had many friendships, and other people will have different
stories to tell. What I know of her is largely confined to my own observation and experience, much of it dating back thirty years or more. In my
hearing, she never revealed much of her earlier life (which she regarded as
a failure), except for the things that everyone knew—that she had grown
up on a chicken farm and then on a ranch in Sonoma County, California; that she had gone to Berkeley in the late 1930s as a philosophy major
but had run out of cash and had not graduated; that she had been married and divorced a couple of times; that she had worked as a seamstress, a
nanny, an advertising copy writer and other such jobs while struggling to
find a steady reviewing berth. When I asked her about her early writing,
she mentioned plays and philosophical essays and sighed, "Oh, you know,
honey, it was dead, it was shit." In the 1950s and 1960s, she ran twin film revival houses in Berkeley on Telegraph Avenue—"they made money, *pots* of
money"—and did critical broadcasts on KPFA, the renegade radio station.

In the pieces written at that time, and in her later appearance in
New York, Pauline presented herself as the Western country girl, direct,
plainspoken, a natural democrat amused by East Coast "cultural snobbery." She was not impressed by fancy art talk and big reputations and
by what she took to be the pomp of degrees and job titles. Some of this
self-mythicizing was just bluster. Pauline was an intellectual; she learned
a lot more from *Partisan Review* than from the chicken farm. People who
deplored the colloquial brashness of her prose failed to notice the steel

frames that held the bursting rhetoric together. In her own free-slinging way, she was as highly syntactical as Henry James, one of her heroes. She was an intellectual, however, in a raucous style perhaps not seen since the bohemian rebels of the 1920s.

Her early years as a success in New York, in the late 1960s and early 1970s, caused a sensation. Goethe is supposed to have said that when we are faced with the great superiority of another person we have no means of safety but love. Love? When Pauline Kael arrived in New York, many of the entrenched critics in town responded with loathing. It's quite true, however, that she frequently brought this on, or enhanced it, herself, by shooting an arrow into the heart of another writer's vanity. She was insistent, rude, always funny, often perverse, even perversely commonsensical. She enjoyed shocking the most important people in the room. From her point of view, she was merely setting them straight for their own good. In response, they piled up anecdotes against her, waiting for her to go up in a puff of smoke. Their frustration was palpable, but what could they do? If they took her on, they got knocked off their feet, more often than not, by a lightning comeback. "John, you're too old still to be writing like a punk," she informed the elaborately educated Europhile slasher John Simon at a meeting of the National Society of Film Critics. Some of the men walked away murmuring "ball breaker."

This charge, which I heard many times and in many versions, completely missed the point. Pauline was just as tough on women as on men, and, so far from hating macho, she had a deeply romantic appreciation of such leathery, hard-drinking types as John Huston, Sam Peckinpah, and Robert Altman. She loved the swagger and panache of critics like the Australians Clive James and Robert Hughes and the young American James Wolcott. No, the problem with the American movie critics was they weren't ballsy *enough,* or at least not in the right style. One of them described her in print as "a wet hen," and for years she congratulated herself for not calling him "a dry rooster" in response. Apart from her self-censorship on this one occasion, she believed in assertion, not in reticence or modesty, though she couldn't stop herself from correcting almost every assertion she heard. And every self-evaluation. The compulsion to tell people off ran wild at times. She had the peculiar notion

that everyone should possess exactly the right opinion of his own achievements. If you were mistakenly cast down, she would raise you up; if you
had a swelled head, she would shrink your cap size. Since virtually no one
has exactly the right opinion of his own worth, she became a sort of self-
appointed vicar of Criticism, restlessly extirpating the sin of inappropriate
self-evaluation. She wanted to straighten out the world.

When she was young, Pauline had hung around with poets and artists
in New York and San Francisco, but she had no mentor herself—she was
self-created—and she never used the word, which she rejected in interviews as corny and false. Perhaps it's obvious why she considered the subject hard to talk about: Over the years, she consciously attempted to shape
the careers and the morale of dozens, maybe hundreds, of young men
and women, and she accepted their love as her due. She was a den mother
who probably could never have accumulated so extensive a brood if she
weren't female and welcoming—her maternal tones softened barbs that
would have been warlike or humiliating if received from a man. Yet in
her tough-kindly way, she was more interested in power than any man or
woman I've ever met.

Apart from bestowing recognition and entertainment and straightening us out, what did she do for the young group that gathered around
her? The most important thing was the sizzling example of her own practice. Pauline kept a notepad at her bedside and scribbled in the middle
of the night. At dinner, among friends, she would suddenly dive into her
bag and retrieve the pad, attacking it with a mysteriously sharpened little
pencil, writing things down while laughing at the conversation going on
around her. The first drafts of her reviews were composed very rapidly.
Fearing that she would end up a secretary, she never learned to type, so
Gina would run the review through the typewriter while Pauline took a
break, drinking a little watered wine, or talking to a friend on the telephone. Then, staring at the piece in horror and exclaiming at her own
ineptitude, she would tear it apart, scissoring and recombining the paragraphs, writing in new observations and jokes in the margins or above the
lines, at which point the piece would be typed again. The process continued without interruption at the office, where, like Proust after an injec-

tion of caffeine, she would assault the galleys, rearranging and rewriting, adding and subtracting still more jokes—on and on, until the pages were reluctantly yielded to the press.

From week to week, she resisted fashion and studio-bought publicity and celebrated, when she could, the creative life in unheralded movies made by fresh talent; she looked below the surface of a movie without ever giving up on that surface, which is where the action was—the transfigured flesh, the hurtling movement, the sensuous and erotic power that drew people to the medium in the first place. She dealt firmly with studios and even with directors (Altman, Huston, Woody Allen, Warren Beatty), those overwhelmingly seductive creatures whom she occasionally befriended and, sooner or later, amid cries of betrayal from them, panned. Her young friends were dazzled, for here was the real thing, a genuinely independent person existing as an American writer, and with singular force. She was indifferent to clothes, casual about such worldly goods as furniture—the apartment, and, later, her house in Great Barrington, Massachusetts, was outfitted with "sticks," as she called the Bay Area–bohemian couches and Tiffany glass that she threw together with considerable taste. However much she loved power, she didn't give a damn about the outward trappings of it. In public, she did not carry herself like a woman aware of her position in the world; her tongue was her only weapon. One of the minor highs of hanging out with her was to see publicists, directors, and other critics quail before so unprepossessing-looking a person.

Fearless herself, Pauline created courage in others. But she also created conformity in some of the same people, and that paradox produced not only trouble between us but also the public talk of "Paulettes." Pauline liked people with spirit, but she liked to win, too. You couldn't agree with her too quickly, or you lost her respect, but, in the end, you did have to agree; in my experience, she could not remain friends for long with anyone who consistently fought her. She cajoled and honeyed the people drawn to her, but, if we held to our opinions, she tried to pull the rug out from under us. The generic form of her rug pulling was "Oh, honey, you've never been fucked by a bear." That is, we had never been down and out, living in a cold-water flat, selling goods over the phone; we had never taken care of someone else's children or done any of the body-numbing chores she had performed when she was young. This was certainly true. We were mainly upper-middle-class boys falling out of university into journalism. But no matter how protected, anyone who loved movies, I thought, had the right to an opinion.

I was not submissive by nature, and neither were any of the others, but we acquiesced in the bullying, in my case with increasing discomfort. Her need to dominate may also have accounted for her social habits: After all, she spent a lot of time hanging out with *us,* not with the literary and journalistic celebrities who were her peers. In the group of young admirers there were no equals or rivals, as there would have been at a Manhattan literary watering hole like Elaine's. The group became a cult that never admitted its existence, a circle that never discussed its exclusions, a set of friends that never acknowledged how much enmity lay around it, not even after articles had been written fingering us as guilty parties, complete, in some publications, with mug shots.

It was not just Pauline's rhetorical powers and her insatiable need to win arguments that made sustained disagreement with her so difficult. There was something in the nature of movies as well—a peculiar aesthetic indeterminacy which she understood and celebrated and also used opportunistically to quell other people. As far as Pauline was concerned, there was no curriculum or method that one had to master in order to write criticism, though she certainly had a personal canon—all the movies mentioned in the passage quoted earlier from *I Lost It at the Movies* and also screwball comedies in general; the films of D. W. Griffith, Abel Gance, Jean Renoir, Preston Sturges, Luis Buñuel, Vittorio De Sica, Carol Reed, Louis Malle, and Robert Altman; the early work of François Truffaut, Jean-Luc Godard, Marco Bellocchio, and Bernardo Bertolucci, and then the young American directors of the 1970s; the screenplays of Samson Raphaelson, Jules Furthman, Ben Hecht, Herman Mankiewicz, and Robert Towne; the acting of Cary Grant, Laurence Olivier, Bette Davis, Katharine Hepburn, and Marlon Brando. She admired such schoolroom classics as the early films of René Clair, Sergei Eisenstein, and Carl Dreyer, but she was sure that there was no academic tradition in film that could not be overturned in an instant. The old distinction between high and low, for instance, didn't much matter to her, for in movies, she was sure, art might not look like art, or at least what people had been taught to respect as art—something formally composed, balanced, elegant. Movie art might be rough and raw, even messy. She preferred vitality to refinement; the irregular and jagged to the well proportioned; the aggressive, lunging uproar of American pop to the contained austerity of certain kinds of European art. The young Europeans she loved—the lusciously sensual Bertolucci of *The Conformist* and the word-happy and graphically dazzling Godard—were prized for their audacity. "An intellectual who is not afraid of sensation," critic Robert Brustein called her.

For her, film aesthetics was eternally in a state of becoming—it had to be that way, for the movies, as she never tired of saying, were the mongrelized bastard child of the arts, a compound of theater, photography, the novel, carnival, pornography, journalism, and exploration, and any pure-cinema definition or even descriptive grammar (montage or deep focus or, later, "the male gaze") omitted too many of the miscellaneous and even anomalous pleasures that were part of the fun as well as the art of movies. She loved praising small parts of bad movies—a muttered aside, a single graceful number in an overweight musical. Apart from the great movies, which were all of a piece, subversion (a term of praise), she thought, came in small acts of protest by talented people trapped in a machine. In writing about movies, you had to know film history and to have seen a lot, but, finally, no method or aesthetic was sufficient, and knowledge of the other arts—literature, painting, opera, dance—was not only necessary, it was what separated the true critics from the screening room pedants with their airless theories and overwrought praise for auteurist "masterpieces," a form of praise, she thought, that often congratulated a director for doing the same thing, with tiny variations, over and over (in effect, the critic was valuing his own connoisseurship, not the movie).

Pauline wanted sensation in the movies, not the banality of serious, explicitly stated "themes," and she believed that sensation, at its most intricate and demanding, could force audiences into complexities of response unknown in the other arts. Sensation would inevitably arouse the brain of the canniest moviegoers, for the senses and the intellect were combined, not opposed. No critic I'm aware of has longed so ardently for faces, bodies, landscape, decor, clothes, sex, and violence (austerity was truly her enemy), while demanding, at the same time, that a movie hang together morally. At her most rapturously exultant, as in her review of Scorsese's 1978 *Taxi Driver,* she approached the ecstasy of synesthesia, a merging of the senses so powerful in its effect that extinction might be the only release from it:

> Scorsese's New York is the big city of the thrillers he feasted his imagination on—but at a later stage of decay. This New York is a voluptuous enemy. The street vapors become ghostly; Sport the pimp romancing the baby whore leads her in a hypnotic dance; the porno theaters are like mortuaries; the congested traffic is macabre. And this Hell is always in movement.

At the same time, she insists the movie's alienated landscape was a protest against "urban indifference." This constant tangling and untangling of the sensual and the ethical kept her judgments fresh, startling, seemingly contradictory. For it was never mere sensation that she wanted; violence had to mean something expressively, as it did in *Bonnie and Clyde* and *The Wild Bunch,* or she was repelled—a distinction easy enough to understand but willfully ignored by such attackers as Renata Adler (herself a failed movie critic) in a notoriously wrongheaded piece in *The New York Review of Books* from 1980. People who seized on one or two of Pauline's pieces and then built generalizations about her taste invariably got her wrong; they missed the largeness and variety of her thinking. Often surprisingly earnest and responsible and, if anything, concerned to a fault—as if she were the only one to whom a movie really mattered—she fretted over popular successes that she thought worthless (*Dirty Harry*) and good movies that failed (*Band of Outsiders*); she grieved over audiences too priggish to respond to the sensuality of screen violence and those too savage to reject primitive kicks. The world, particularly Hollywood, needed to listen to reason, her reason. She never tired of her arguments, never fell into the usual vices of pop-culture criticism—disgust, fatigue, or self-canceling irony. Sometimes the good talk seemed to go on forever, stretching into dubiously omniscient evaluation of the psychology and soul of the movie's creators. She anticipated readers' objections and flummoxed enemies yet to appear on the horizon. She wanted to do everything—not only show us the movie but bring us the candy, sweep up the theater, and walk us to our car after the show.

For her young disciples, the ability to exercise along with her a multidimensional responsiveness meant that we were Good—we even possessed an element of the uncanny in our lives. But would we keep it? At its happiest, the group embrace of a great new movie by Altman or De Palma was an exalted communion of believers bringing the news to a semi-indifferent outside world. "You're *with* this?" Pauline would ask at screenings with a squeeze of the hand. But the experience of being squeezed wasn't always pleasant.

Since critical standards were, by their very nature, unstable, the anxious fear of being wrong, or of missing the subtle and seemingly contradictory ways of being right, was rather intense. There was, it turned out, a correct answer for every critical question, but there was no way of being sure of judgment from within. There was, however, the certainty of *her* judgment. None of us ever spoke of the fear of being wrong in such abject terms, or spoke of it at all, but the fear was there nonetheless. In the end, the feeling of election, and the fear of losing it, caused many of us to conform internally to what we thought she approved of. In the conversation of publicists and other reviewers, one heard paranoid fantasies of nighttime telephone calls to young critics, telling them what to say—a central authority producing pack behavior. But there were no such calls; they weren't necessary; pack behavior resulted from the way Pauline had shaped our aesthetics, enhanced by what I've described as internal conformity. The way you remained among the elect was to write in your head for the person who conveyed grace. The only other choice was to turn away altogether, and some smart young critics—Frank Rich, for instance—did exactly that early in their careers. They elected themselves, and they were right to do so.

The desire to please Pauline certainly colored my own work. As a beginner, I had no rhythm of my own, or none that I could use to review movies (Lionel Trilling's exquisite hesitations would have fallen like houndstooth tweed across the jagged surfaces of *M*A*S*H*). Now and then, I imitated Pauline's rhythms. I exploited the taunting rhetorical question; the piled-up syncopated adjectives (*Love Story*, she wrote, is "a generation-gap variant of a neo-Victorian heart-wringer . . . written in a snappy, tear-jerking, hard-soft style"). Then there was the thumping-finger-in-the-chest use of "you." You feel this, you feel that; you hate, you love. She was trying, as she explained, to get at common responses, but the effect was alternately to flatter and terrorize the reader into agreement. My imitations were not conscious; I was reaching for the security of an authoritative voice. Looking back, I can say that as a young man I may not have had enough of a writing self to violate—that is, I had yet to develop the sense of shame which would have checked the practice of imitation. As late as 1980, I was capable of writing, about De Palma's *Dressed to Kill,* "You can see that he's using film techniques and tricks to get at unconscious fears and to extend the lyrical possibilities of violence, and you admire his sadistic virtuosity even as he's manipulating you unconscionably." I'll stand by the description of what De Palma was doing. What makes me wince now is that "you" were unlikely to "see" anything so damnably specific. The second-person hectoring is an attempt to hog-tie a very elusive emotion.

Though Pauline never said as much, word drifted back to me, two years or so after I started at *The Atlantic,* that she considered me an imitator. She let me know, now and then, that she wasn't crazy about what I was writing, and she grew distant. Then the axe fell. In late 1972 or early 1973, I can't remember which, she called one afternoon with grim news: I had no talent for this trade. "You're too restless to be a writer," she said. And then she called again a few hours later: "I've thought about this seriously, honey. You should do something else with your energy." She suggested film producing.

In between the first and second call, I felt a little weak and lay down on my bed. What to do now? There was a heaviness in my chest and a slight roaring in my ears, as if a wave had knocked me over and the waters were still swirling around my head. After a while, protest surged to the surface. By what *right*? By what right did anyone have to speak this way? She pronounced her sentence on me as if she alone had the responsibility and the courage to rescue me from a disastrous misunderstanding of my own nature. But there was a market for writing, wasn't there?—a *market* which offered its own palpable discouragement to the untalented. If she were right, the collective judgment of many people would let me know it. "No," I said into the telephone when she called a second time to reinforce the message. "I think you're wrong." But I said it weakly, in a tiny voice, and, between the calls, I had thought, Maybe she'll change her mind.

I did not become a producer. I continued as a film critic and cultural journalist. I had made a false start, so I restarted myself in 1976 and gained traction in a good weekly paper, *The Boston Phoenix,* and I began—slowly, much too slowly—to shake out the borrowed rhythms, line by line. During those years and in the years after, restraining my desire to reach for the telephone, I spoke rarely to Pauline, who was wary and distant in general and blew hot and cold on the subject of my writing. I longed to get away from the subject altogether, but she wanted only a power relationship with me, narrowing the channel of our conversations to the issue of her judgment of my work. When I inquired after her well-being, she answered in off-putting generalities; in person, the old friendliness would return now and then, but she could also be distant, and sometimes insulting. The implications of her manner were clear enough: I had been told, hadn't I? How odd that I persisted in this *bêtise* of continuing to write. It was a social error, to be regarded with embarrassment. Some of her friends, who were often my friends as well, dropped away. When I ran into them, they stared at me, an apparent impostor, with a slightly haughty disdain.

For years I thought about her, with fierce indignation alternating with long sighs of regret. Yet even as I tried to regain her approval and friendship, I knew all along I was better off without it. What I wanted, after all, was not to be Pauline but to be myself. After she dismissed me, I never squared my shoulders and announced my defiance, facing boldly into the sunrise of independence. Like most people, I'm incapable of such dramatic resolutions; instead, I put one foot after another, preserving myself from nullity by refusing her assessment. And, having been tossed out of Eden, I no longer suppressed what I had often suppressed in the past, my sense that there was something clammy and half dishonest on both sides of these master-disciple relationships. Critics, obviously, should be independent. To demand validation from an older, more powerful person was a weakness that should be overcome. That was true for all of us. On Pauline's side: She was a late success, and at times much resented in the world; she felt embattled, and she surrounded herself with followers as part of her protective armor. Situated at the center of a circle, she wanted to see the people facing her and to look out, but she did not want to *be* seen, and certainly not to be seen *through*. Everyone else, she insisted, had motives; they operated out of unconscious drives, or they were corrupted by money or love of power. Only *she* was disinterested, working feverishly at the job of uttering the Truth. Before speaking in such capital-letter words, she would have committed seppuku in the Algonquin lobby, but that was what she meant, and she did not accept (at least, not in my hearing) even an occasional suggestion from friends that she liked pushing people around or had written falsely about anything.

When the dreadful and quickly forgotten movie version of *Fiddler on the Roof* came out in 1971 (I remember exactly one good shot—a row of black-suited young rabbis dancing with black bottles on their heads), she wrote a long, nonsensical rave in which the clumsy picture was made a powerful source of the Broadway musical itself: "Though the techniques and simplifications are those of musical comedy, when they are put to work on a large emotional theme that is consonant with the very nature of musical comedy—is, in fact, at its heart—the effect on the large screen is that of a musical epic," etc. Calling her up, I used Yiddish to tell her that the piece was overblown. She cursed and slammed down the phone.

By staying on the offensive and keeping other people off balance, she could not be seen. In 1970, after a screening at the old New Yorker Theater, on upper Broadway, Pauline and I had lunch with the director Nicholas Ray in a Chinese restaurant across the street. In the 1960s, the auteurist critics in France and America had taken up the director of *They Live by Night, In a Lonely Place, Johnny Guitar, Rebel Without a Cause,* and other films. In these celebrations, Ray was the haunted poet of the cinema; later in the 1970s, the young German director Wim Wenders would put Ray in a couple of his movies, drawing on his glamorous mystique. A former actor, Ray was tall and gaunt, with a pile of white hair, a dark patch over one eye, and a guttural voice. For his students at a local university he acted the fallen genius with superb displays of disintegrating romantic splendor.

Though only in his late fifties, Ray was not in good health and was clearly finished as a Hollywood director, and yet Pauline, vexed by his recent critical deification, went through his films one by one—this movie twenty years earlier had a few good shots, another one had been overpraised, a third was terrible, and so on, and Ray, his face cast down into his shrimp and rice, was mostly silent. What digs at me now is that I said nothing in the restaurant in 1970. I knew perfectly well that the act of telling off Nick Ray was cruelly unnecessary, though Pauline, doing her missionary work of straightening everyone out, had the bit between her teeth and probably couldn't have been stopped.

When the rebellion finally came, I was unaware of it at first. Pauline's protest against classy surfaces and formalism was enormously influential on an entire generation of critics—not just Paulettes—who have celebrated every vestige of energy in American pop for the last forty years. By the 1980s, however, the notion that pop could be subversive was beginning to look a little tattered and even delusional. The conglomerates were tightening their grip on the studios, and the period of lawless creativity which had produced such masterpieces as the *Godfather* movies and *Taxi Driver* and *Chinatown* was clearly over. It's not clear now whether Pauline's writing helped produce the shift to pop or whether the change, driven by the marketplace, would have happened exactly as it did even if she had never written. Certainly, she had prepared the way critically, and the irony of her later years was that she was still looking for subversion when she should have known better than anyone that there was none to be found.

In the end, she was reduced to looking for it in more and more trivial movies. Her old revolt against highbrow orthodoxy had turned into a new pop orthodoxy of her own. Her terms of praise included "crazy," "jazzy," "scruffy," "zizzy," "nutty," or some other jumpy y-word. She was too hard on quiet, non-y directors like Eric Rohmer, too dismissive of the entertaining deadpan malice in Peter Greenaway's one good movie, the teasing formalist exercise *The Draughtsman's Contract*. She virtually lost interest in movies from abroad, ignoring the nasty but provocative Rainer Werner Fassbinder, attacking Wim Wenders's and Werner Herzog's rarefied movies as threats to her all-American vitality. Of Herzog: "His goodness saps our strength." Of Wenders's *Wings of Desire:* "It's enough to make moviegoers feel impotent." It's as if her vital juices were being drained by too serious art.

By the late 1980s, the kind of deep-dish European "art films" she had ridiculed in the 1960s (*Last Year at Marienbad, Persona,* and so on) had virtually disappeared, the schoolroom she hated so much was rapidly losing its authority, and the new ritual in this country was not respect for high culture but contempt for it. In the universities, ambitious younger faculty and graduate students were beginning to mount the canting ideological attack on "dead white males." It was the years of the curriculum wars. If the Western classics enraged so many people, I thought, maybe there was something subversive about *them,* and I wound up writing a long celebratory book about the experience of rereading at the age of forty-eight the core curriculum courses in Western classics at Columbia. Until the book was done, however, I never realized that by trying to get away for a while from pop—which had become omnivorous, threatening to swallow the entire culture—I was also trying to throw off a personal influence that no longer fit.

Well, let it go, let it go at last. If growing up is partly a matter of building strengths out of the bitterness of disappointment, I can't blame Pauline for not giving me the praise that I wanted. She was an astonishing woman who enhanced my life, and many other people's lives. There was much that was free-flowing and generous in her nature. She laid out food, drink, and incomparable talk, and took genuine pleasure in the friendships that formed around her. She discovered and brokered talent as if she were running a small movie studio, promoting alliances, reviewing boyfriends, girlfriends, and wives, blessing children, and she never stopped responding freely, spontaneously, to everything that passed in front of her. In 1970, I sat with her in the rear of a theater showing the stately and prissy costume epic *Cromwell.* Richard Harris, dressed in barrel bloomers as Cromwell, stamped his foot in impatience, and Pauline, without waiting an instant, loudly said "Oh, *drat!*" convulsing the back third of the house. A few weeks later she demanded I take her to a porno movie on the then lewdly outfitted Seventh Avenue. It was the time of *Deep Throat,* and she wanted to see what the porn craze was about. She was the only woman in the theater. On-screen, one of the studs melted for an instant and Pauline let out a loud, disappointed "Awww . . ." Men in black raincoats sitting nearby rustled in their seats. A few minutes later, two bottoms, through some athletic variation on the missionary position, were juxtaposed one on top of another, and Pauline said, "That's sort of sweet." The raincoats turned and glared angrily in our direction; some of them stalked out. Pauline redeemed a silent, furtive experience by bringing it into the realm of regular moviegoing—by turning it into fun. She later made a powerful metaphor in print out of the one live performer at the theater—an African American girl doing a strip while staring at the audience (including the two of us) in contempt.

In retrospect, I see nothing so terrible about a group of critics speaking as a single voice at a breakout time in the arts. During the 1920s, and afterward, Carl Van Vechten and the philosopher-critic Alain Locke and a group of young disciples promoted what became known as the Harlem Renaissance. In the late 1940s and early 1950s, the thuggish but brilliant Clement Greenberg gathered a cadre of critics around him and helped the Abstract Expressionist painters find their audience and their buyers. Art movements attract ardent critical supporters who want desperately to be part of history. In the 1970s, Pauline and her group were not the only ones pushing Scorsese, Coppola, Altman, Spielberg, and others, but we did it early, we did it hard, and we helped a group of directors make their way. The problem was not so much the united critical push as the habit of internal conformity to a mentor, so harmful to spirit and morale.

In movie criticism, Pauline is unlikely to have a successor. It is not a matter simply of talent. There's plenty of critical talent around, in part because of her example. But the movie culture has changed, and movie criticism with it. Movies have become a major business story, but, for long stretches of the year, a minor artistic story, and without heroic movies we are not likely to have heroic movie critics. In the 1970s, when an American movie was bad, people got mad about it—they felt outraged, even betrayed, because the possibility of art, or at least superior entertainment, was real. If a movie was bad, Pauline said so straightforwardly, with scornful wit. But rage is no longer possible on a sustained basis when art has been systematically eliminated. Who wants to whip himself into a froth every day or every week? What's at stake? In response to the new situation, critics have reduced their expectations and lowered their voices. Yet critics as a tribe may be more necessary than ever. It is a period in which a good part of the press—and even many of the bloggers—has been absorbed into the marketing effort for movies, and regard anything that isn't pop as "elitism," thereby identifying with corporate interests in the guise of populist fervor (a trick Pauline would have despised). At such a time, a few honest reviewers keeping score may be the only force standing between the movie companies and the public. Could the situation become more healthy? If American culture, under pressure of war and disgust for lying corporate and political leaders, should reach a crisis once again; if alternate funding sources produce a healthy independent cinema; if an up-from-the-bottom micro-budget revolution should spring forth, then movies could leap back onto center stage artistically, and the critics could claim their small but necessary piece of the action. Pauline Kael's influence—her notion that popular art could be cleansing, even subversive—may lie more in the future than in the past.

She retired in 1991, and in the years before her death in 2001 I saw her only once—at her eightieth birthday party, in 1999, at her house in Great Barrington, Massachusetts, a large, happy gathering of family, friends, disciples, and ex-disciples. She had been ill a long time, and she was then tiny and frail, a grandmother more than a mother. I wanted to speak to her, I tried twice, but even though she had invited me to the party she was silent when I came around, just as she had been silent on the telephone in recent years. "In both abundance and quality," I wrote in her obituary, published two years later in *The New Yorker,* her work "was a performance very likely without equal in the history of American journalism." Those felt like the right words, and it felt good to write them. And I laughed out loud when, the day after I finished the piece, late at night, as I was falling asleep, a small voice deep inside me said, "I wonder if Pauline liked that obit I wrote about her?"

Drawn from The New Yorker, *September 17, 2001,*
and October 20, 2003

PART SEVEN

AN OPENING TO THE FUTURE?

INTRODUCTION

What follows are three intimations of a possible better future. The filmmakers who have fallen under the rubric "mumblecore" hate the term, but my pragmatic view is that journalistic shorthand which helps bring attention to micro-budget filmmaking isn't completely useless. The mumblecore movies, which can be shot for a few thousand dollars, and are usually set in someone's apartment or in a few streets and a motel room, haven't gone very far in theaters. Small and quiet, they may be truly a home video genre, at least for the moment. What do they need to do to bust out? They need to work with much bolder scripts, a larger dose of happiness and misery, a lyrical flame burning bright. Writing out conflicts between characters doesn't necessarily diminish them.

It's possible that the most complex patterns and overtones can be accomplished only with careful planting and tending; improvisation, which the micro-budget filmmakers often use, is a tool, not an end; a means, not a goal. The micro-budget directors need to trust writers more and liberate the camera. But the sky's the limit: What follows here should be considered an early report on a burgeoning movement. Terrence Malick, intermittent and pretentious as his work is, nevertheless has to be considered a major artist. In my piece on *The Tree of Life,* which I expanded from a *New Yorker* blog entry, I contented myself with trying to understand as much of that prodigious, unbearable movie as I could. Placing the work in Malick's career will have to wait for another time. Right now, I'm still enjoying my shock at what Malick has done to reinvent storytelling and redeem a degraded language. So much of digital fantasy, for instance, bores me silly, but Rupert Wyatt, in the engaging *Rise of the Planet of the Apes,* expanded the conventional digital language to do something heartfelt and surprisingly complex. No flying masses, no instant transformations, no superheroes, just a bunch of apes pushed a little past conventional apish behavior—an expansion, using digital, of something physically inherent into a provocation.

What will it take to renew movies? It's not as if there's an absence of *talent* in America. One obvious development: A revolution from below combined with online distribution of inexpensive movies—an efflorescence of low-budget productions that can be sorted out, as I suggested at the end of the introduction to this collection, by a new kind of film magazine, on the Internet, which combined erudition and combative postition-taking. The studios, in their wisdom, could renew their specialty divisions, an action which would stop making it so hard for people like Benett Miller and Paul Thomas Anderson to make their movies. Those divisions were doing quite nicely a decade ago before the budgets got too large and the parent companies either too ruthless or too jealous to let the divisions continue to flourish. The studios could also lure grown-up audiences back to the movies—and not with action films starring elderly, thick-chested gentlemen like Sylvester Stallone and Arnold Schwarzenegger, but with contemporary dramatic material with guts. If you are the head of Disney or Warner Bros., do you really want to go to your maker saying, "I green-lit a comic-book franchise?" Wouldn't you also like to say, "And also an amazing little picture that won four Oscars in 2013"? Or even: "I brought smart audiences back to the theaters, and movies became a national culture that everyone talked about again." Sure you'd like to say that.

MUMBLECORE

You're about twenty-five years old, and you're no more than, shall we say, intermittently employed, so you spend a great deal of time talking with friends about trivial things or about love affairs that ended or never quite happened; and sometimes, if you're lucky, you fall into bed, or almost fall into bed and just enjoy the flirtation, with someone in the group. This chatty sitting around, with sex occasionally added, is not the sole subject of "mumblecore," a recent genre of micro-budget independent movies, but it's a dominant one. Mumblecore movies are made by buddies, casual and serious lovers, and networks of friends, and they're about college-educated men and women who aren't driven by ideas or by passions or even by a desire to make their way in the world. Neither rebels nor bohemians, they remain stuck in a limbo of semi-genteel, moderately hip poverty, though some of the films end with a lurch into the working world. The actors (almost always nonprofessionals) rarely say what they mean; a lot of the time, they don't know what they mean. The movies tell stories, but they're also a kind of lyrical documentary of American stasis and inarticulateness. The first mumblecore film, by general agreement, was Andrew Bujalski's 2002 *Funny Ha Ha*, a sweet-natured account of a young woman's post-college blues. But the style wasn't named until 2005, when the sound mixer Eric Masunaga, having a drink at a bar during the South by Southwest Film Festival (SXSW), in Austin, used the term to describe an independent film he had worked on. The sobriquet stuck, even though the filmmakers dislike it. In the films I've seen, however, the sound is quite clear. It's the emotions that mumble.

Apart from the yearly festival in Austin, where many of the movies are first shown, the movement has never developed a geographical center. The directors live in Chicago, Boston, Portland, Brooklyn. What makes them part of a movement is the technology they use and the paucity of their funds, which, together, help create a subject matter and an aesthetic. A typical low-budget independent film with professional actors and a good cinematographer may cost upward of $2 or $3 million. The budget for a mumblecore movie may be as low as fifteen hundred dollars. The films are usually shot with a digital camera, in somebody's apartment, and run about eighty minutes. The filmmaking ensemble gathers around a writer-director-editor figure; they act in the movie, add ideas or lines of dialogue, write music, play or sing on-screen. Few people get paid much, if they get paid at all. Youth is the subject of mumblecore and also the condition of its existence. But these sociable movies exist at a lower level of intensity than comparable youth-loving movies of the past. The young people in the quickly made Godard movies of the 1960s dreamed of becoming gangsters, thieves, revolutionaries—characters, so to speak, in a movie. The studs and the female "superstars" of the Warhol films played at Hollywood glamour while enacting the ceremonies of decadence and self-destruction. Mumblecore disdains flamboyance; its reigning mood is diffidence.

The critic Amy Taubin, in *Film Comment,* once referred to the director Andrew Bujalski—now thirty-one, and perhaps the most fluent and talented of the group—as "a poet of demurral, hesitation, and noncommitment." In Bujalski's engaging *Mutual Appreciation* (2005), there's a potentially dangerous conversation on the edge of a bed between a young musician, Alan (Justin Rice), and Ellie (Rachel Clift), the girlfriend of Alan's longtime best friend. Ellie hints that she's attracted to Alan, a sweet, rather hapless guy with an enchanting smile, then retracts what she started to say, and apologizes. Alan reassures her that it's cool, it's all right, no problem. So she tries, haltingly, to say it again. Starting and stopping, she's like a puppy shyly nosing a toy into a room and looking up to see who's watching. The scene is a comic duet for two affably passive-aggressive people, each of whom wants the other to take responsibility for anything that might happen. In conventional terms, nothing does happen. For Bujalski, however, the passing desire, the impulse not acted on, is a major dramatic event, and a good part of the rest of the movie is devoted to discussing this ineffable conversation. The edge-of-the-bed scene is partly improvised, which gives the hesitations and silences a tone of exquisite embarrassment. The moment plays like a scene from one of John Cassavetes's semi-improvised movies (*Husbands* et al.), but without the high-pressure acting.

Some critics have deplored mumblecore movies as smug portraits of a new generation of privileged white slackers. But a critic, I think, should grant a filmmaker his subject. When the material is emotionally raw, and the nonprofessional actors show some strength, mumblecore delivers insights that Hollywood can't come close to. Aaron Katz's *Dance Party, USA* (2006) has a sequence that may be the most moving and effective in the modest mumblecore canon: A good-looking seventeen-year-old boy (Cole Pensinger), who is rapidly becoming a lout, confesses to an aimless young woman who interests him that he once raped a drunken fourteen-year-old girl. The confession moves forward, but with innumerable pauses. The boy enjoys boasting of his ruthlessness, yet he also feels ashamed; the woman's silence goads him, finally, into completing the confession, which for him becomes an act of purgation. The movie tracks his gradual passage from smarmy adolescence to something like decency.

The characters in mumblecore may lack ambition, but the directors are clear enough in their desire to make full-length movies. Bujalski, the director in the group whose work most resembles European art films (he even shoots on film), has made three features since 2002; the earnest and lyrical Aaron Katz has made five films of one sort or another in the past four years; and Joe Swanberg, the most sexually explicit of the directors, who sometimes appears in mumblecore movies sporting a tuft of devilish red beard, has made six features and three shorts in five years. This kind of busy-beaver, spontaneous activity is, of course, a de facto rebuke to Hollywood's elephantine methods and inane formulas—the snippy-snappy Kate Hudson comedies, the digital action films that whirl into nowhere. Is there a revolution brewing, a rattling of the gates? One might like to fantasize about mumblecore and other independent directors taking over the studios and junking all the dumb projects, but no such thing will happen. Theatrical attendance for commercial movies is on the rise; the executives are not about to abandon their movies or their methods. At the same time, the theatrical distribution of small movies has become commercially hazardous—the land of high ideals and broken hearts—and many young filmmakers are looking to shake up distribution patterns. Some of them hawk their movies themselves, selling DVDs on the Internet. (You can buy Bujalski, Swanberg, and Katz movies that way.) But a larger audience can probably be built in the future through video on demand or by direct Internet download. For instance, *Alexander the Last,* the most recent picture written and directed by the prolific Swanberg, will be shown at the SXSW festival in Austin, on March 14, and made available the same day as a video on demand.

It turns out that Swanberg, now twenty-seven, is changing his game. In his earlier movies, there was usually a project of sorts going on amid the sexual encounters—a set of taped interviews with people whose love affairs had gone bad in *Kissing on the Mouth* (2005); an audio montage of people making funny noises which a musician assembles into a rhythmically charged composition in *LOL* (2006). In *Alexander the Last,* the project is a local theater production. A married actress (Jess Weixler) attracted to a good-looking actor she's working with contemplates an affair with him, only to discover that her sister, with whom she's very close, is already sleeping with him. The story, in its formal symmetries, suggests one of Eric Rohmer's narratives of advance and retreat in "Six Moral Tales." In the past, people in Swanberg's movies slept with one another without much consequence—the plots were not fully worked out, and many implications, not to mention relationships, were left hanging. The slapdash style of storytelling was part of Swanberg's cool contempt for mainstream filmmaking. But in *Alexander the Last* he's advancing toward a firmer structure and more emotionally explicit scenes. He has a producer this time, and sets, or at least a theater, and he uses trained actors, who work up an emotion much more clearly than the earlier casts of amateurs did, though without the surprises. In brief, Swanberg is giving up some of the methods of mumblecore.

It remains to be seen, in fact, whether mumblecore's ethos can survive in a period of violent economic downturn. Those penny-budget movies were made in a time of prosperity. Now that the parental check or the roommate's job may be drying up, the movies could dry up, too, or turn from dithering to rage. Of course, fresh young directors, willing to work cheaply, will emerge. But will they mumble if their bellies are beginning to growl? The new distribution channels may be the key to keeping this low-key but cheering movement alive.

The New Yorker, *March 3, 2009*

TERRENCE MALICK'S
INSUFFERABLE MASTERPIECE

Interminable, madly repetitive, vague, grandiose; an art-history *Summa Theologica* crossed with a summer camp documentary on the wonders of the universe; sexless yet sexist, embracing of everything in the world but humor (and is wit not as essential to our existence as air?)—Terrence Malick's *The Tree of Life* is insufferable. It is also, astoundingly, one of the great lyric achievements of the screen in recent years and a considerable enlargement of the rhetoric of cinema—a change in technique which is also a change in consciousness. An insufferable masterpiece, then; a film to be endured in a state of enraged awe. Its central idea can be paraphrased only in the grossest terms, which make it sound irredeemably banal. All of life—the creation of the universe, birth, childhood, marriage, death, the teeming oceans, the stars, the hereafter—can be dramatized through the fragmented history of a single family living in small-town Texas in the 1950s and 1960s. We see this family in the everyday phases of its existence and also in moments of crisis and mourning. Yet, except for its concluding scene, which has become notorious, *The Tree of Life* isn't banal. Years from now, the movie will be remembered as a freshening, even a reinvention, of film language. "If the doors of perception were cleansed, everything would appear as it is—infinite," said Blake. That was a notion much loved in the acid-soaked 1960s. It's a relief and an amazement to see the same sentiment embodied in a work of art.

The beginning is hardly promising: a quotation from Job, whispered prayers to God, undulating gaseous colors, indefinite in shape, indeterminate in meaning. Where are we—in a sepulcher? In a museum for 1960s experimental movies? No, we see some children, and a young woman utters words about grace. "No one who lives the way of grace comes to a bad end," she says, which is a statement of Christian faith, and particularly of Catholic faith, that others may quarrel with or find inadequate. A telegram is delivered: One of three sons, at the age of nineteen, is dead (presumably in war, though no cause for the death is given). Some scenes of grief follow—a father (Brad Pitt), a mother (Jessica Chastain), clinging to each other on the front lawn on their house, which is where much of the movie will take place. These scenes are intercut with silent shots of another of the sons (Sean Penn), years later, working in an urban office tower in Houston under a glass cathedral ceiling, and still inconsolably obsessed with his dead brother. There are more whispered questions, a vague reaching toward God. By degrees, the movie changes into a lengthy evocation of natural phenomena, all suggestive of violent creation—churning water, perturbable gases, bits of the galaxy spun into spectral dust, the sun seen close as a seething, roaring landscape of flame. It is creation not as a single Big Bang but as a pouring, tearing, burning and incessant convulsion. We get the point: Creation has always gone on; it never ceases. Destruction never ceases, either; both are happening all around the Texas family.

What is there to say about this footage except that it's extraordinarily beautiful? Half the time, I'm not sure what, exactly, we are looking at. Are these natural happenings, captured with high-powered telescopic lenses? Gleanings from the Hubble? The swirling nebulae or exploding novae, or whatever they are, could be NASA footage or the digital work of twelve sexually undernourished nerds sitting in a windowless room. Probably they're a little of each. And I think Malick might respond that it doesn't matter. The exploding novae are what we *should* see if we could—if we had the right vantage point, or if we had enough curiosity and bravery to face the elemental facts of the universe. This use of the telescopic sublime is overwhelming, but, in the midst of awe, a belligerent impression begins to form: A movie that is about everything can't be about anything in particular.

That impression, however, turns out to be false. Malick returns to the family and begins his story over again, and now it takes hold. The father had wanted to be a great musician, a great inventor. He wound up an engineer at an industrial plant, which goes bust. He feels himself a failure— "nothing"—and he takes out his frustrations on his sons, particularly on his oldest boy, Jack (Hunter McCracken), a tough little kid (he will grow up to be Sean Penn) who is sure his father wants to kill him. The father is loving but dictatorial, almost abusive. He demands love but gives it only when his boys agree to live as extensions of himself; they may not speak at dinner unless he allows them to say what he wants them to say. As this troubled man—a failed god, who wants to be called "Father," never "Dad"—Brad Pitt has given his first great performance. In his work as the husband in *Babel,* there were hints of fire and a fallible rage. But who knew he had this kind of anguish in him? His back is straight and stiff, part of a long plane extending through his neck and head; his jaw juts out; his eyes, so often dead in the past, are full of hurt. A willful, foolish, good man. His anger is self-wounding and tragic.

It is this central part of the movie—the family drama—that strikes me as revolutionary. Malick has done away with the sequence as normally understood. Apart from two brief episodes at the dinner table—in both of them the father loses his temper and tries to squash his boys—the rest is fragments, with minimal dialogue, and shot by a camera that never, as far as I can see, stays fixed on a tripod. The great Emmanuel Lubezki did the cinematography, and the camera floats, evenly, smoothly, gently, moving behind the actors, around them, underneath them. It communes with them, cutting them off at mid-body, sometimes in mid-forehead. Our intimacy with the characters is startling, privileged, almost painful—an intimacy that extends to the little boys and their friends as they run lawlessly through the back alley of the town, smashing things and tormenting toads; or as they put each other through rituals of daring and forgiveness. We have never seen childhood re-created this candidly in the cinema. A comparison to Mark Twain feels necessary and right.

The shots in all these family sequences are not quite continuous—that is, they don't match up in the manner of classical shooting and editing, in which a given body movement is carried over from one shot to the next. In itself, that is hardly a surprise: Highly fragmented editing has become commonplace in recent years, and much of it is jarring and larcenous— say, the whirling movement in bad action movies, in which the mere impression of violence substitutes for the coherent staging and editing in an integrated space. But if the shots in *Tree of Life,* strictly speaking, don't match, the moods match, and you can certainly see everything you want to see. The conflict between the father and Jack coheres into physically detailed, dramatically overwhelming sequences. The slight gaps in visual continuity are like pauses for a breath in fervent speech. Or, more to the point, like metaphysical questions: How is it that we are in this place, at this time? This lawn, this house, these trees—are they not connected to all eternity? The floating camera in *Tree of Life* lifts us just slightly out of the here and now and achieves what I assume Malick wants—a sense that these spasms of conflict and love, out there on the lawn of an ordinary Texas house, are as momentous as the seething gases and exploding novae. A father who has been fighting with his son confesses his love for him and grasps the boy in a tight embrace, both of them too moved to say much of anything. It is commonplace; it is everything. "Holy, holy, holy!" Allen Ginsberg exclaimed, echoing Blake. And in that holy is included fields, seas, the saurian past, the light-filled office in Houston, which, I believe, is another example of the Malick sublime and not, as some critics have said, a soulless view of an antihuman present.

If Malick has reinvented the sequence, he has also reinvented the frame, with equally satisfying results. Among other things, *The Tree of Life* is Malick's memory of growing up in Texas, and, as Richard Brody put it in his *New Yorker* blog, "Memories have no frame; they slide out of a pictorial boundary to remain infinite at the edges, bending around to include oneself—and maybe even several versions of oneself, present and past, as seen from without and from within." That moving camera is the eye of consciousness. How great a license Malick has given himself! And how superb his control even as he violates the standard rules of craft! If you want to get a sense of Malick's boldness, think of Woody Allen's *Midnight in Paris*. There you have a perfectly elegant classical frame—the characters firmly and stably planted in space and in clear relation to walls and streets. As Owen Wilson waits for his midnight carriage to take him back to the 1920s, Woody sends a shimmer of light across the top of his head to set him off from the building behind him. Classical, and pretty similar to what Michael Curtiz did with Bogart in *Casablanca* seventy years ago.

Photographing the ineffable seems like a contradiction: Of all the arts, the cinema depends most on the effable—on matter that reflects light, impressing itself on celluloid treated with silver nitrate or, increasingly, on bit-mapped receptors. But Malick has done it; he has captured spirit. How hard that is! The sense that no act is meaningless, the certainty that we are not alone, isolated, or lost is shared by mystics, believers, and sentimentalists. But Malick makes the certainty palpable. And the use of sublime passages of music seals the palpability—especially the concluding pages of the Berlioz *Requiem,* whose circling string motifs and quietly thudding drums suggest the utmost consolations of belief, especially in times of tragedy and death. For long stretches, the moods are sustained, eloquent, encompassing. As visual art, the movie's celebratory religious view of existence comes within hailing distance of the great religious painters of the Renaissance.

But some of us will hold back from the movie emotionally, and even morally. *The Tree of Life* wants to be a universalizing view but, actually, it's a highly particularist view, and one bounded by doctrine and history. "Grace accepts being forgotten, slighted, accepts injuries," the wife says. But it is *she,* not just anyone, who is forgotten, slighted, and injured, and not just by her husband, who hardly addresses a word to her in a 138-minute movie; she is slighted by Malick, too. The mother, in flowing dresses, playing, teasing, reading, chasing around the house and yard, glides through wordless scenes with the boys. Jessica Chastain is pale, with reddish hair and blue eyes; she has some of Liv Ullmann's luminous quality and a strong, pliant body. A bending, twisting, undulating female figure, she is the consoling Eternal Feminine, Christianized as "grace," and, at one point, she floats horizontally, near a tree in the yard. Malick photographs her the same way he photographs some of the translucent underwater creatures that float toward us—the jellyfish for instance. In Malick's vision, temperament, ambition, and failure are male, sacrifice and love are female; ego is male, charity is female. The wife is passive, awaiting God's rescue; she is the latest embodiment of the Virgin Mary; she is not a sexual being. Yes, most of the movie is set in the 1950s, but even in the 1950s wives talked back to their husbands and expressed lust and tried to run households. The movie is a Catholic and patriarchal vision, presenting itself as universal. For Catholic believers, of course, it *is* universal, but those of us with different beliefs or no religious convictions can't help seeing history, culture, and sexual politics flowing around Malick's embrace of life.

The Tree of Life raises an ornery question: Could a worldly movie with humor, sex, work, society—everything that Malick ignores—also capture spirit? Could a secular temperament capture it? A temperament acting outside of religious doctrine? I wonder, in fact, if Malick has embraced enough of life to pronounce it good. Hasn't he narrowed life down only to those elements that can be etherealized? Play is at the center of his notion of being, but *only* play, which leaves out an awful lot. I admire *The Tree of Life* enormously, but I think I would be less than candid if I didn't say how far away from it I feel emotionally. It's a very solemn piece of work, and it ends with a pathetic sequence of the hereafter, in which all the characters wander around on the beach and embrace one another like stoned party-goers at dawn. Just before the end, speaking to God, the mother raises her arms and says, "I give him to you. I give you my son." As an apotheosis of belief, that moment is fully earned by the rest of the movie. But let me say categorically that no woman I've loved, or even merely known, could raise her arms and yield up her son to any god whatsoever.

Published as a New Yorker *blog, June 23, 2011; revised 2011*

RISE OF THE PLANET OF THE APES

Among the trillions of binary digits skittering across screens this summer, a vibrant minority have been gathered into a shrewd, coherent, and fully felt movie. I'm speaking of the expertly crafted *Rise of the Planet of the Apes,* by far the best spectacle movie of the season, and one of the few films to use digital technology for nuanced dramatic effect. *Planet,* of course, draws on the old species-reversal conceit worked out by Pierre Boulle in his 1963 novel, *La Planète des Singes,* a book that launched a cluster of movies and television shows, most notably Franklin J. Schaffner's *Planet of the Apes* (1968). In that mock epic, the manacled, nearly naked Charlton Heston is rated an interesting specimen by a variety of simian overlords. The new movie draws not only on Boulle's outrageous idea but on some of the most enduringly suggestive fables we know. It begins as a benevolent version of the Frankenstein story. Will (James Franco, trying harder than usual), a young genetic engineer working for a San Francisco biotech company, creates a serum that reverses brain damage. (He wants to treat his father, Charles—played movingly by John Lithgow—who has Alzheimer's.) The company tests the serum on apes, one of which goes mad and has to be destroyed. But Will takes home the ape's baby, Caesar, who has inherited his mom's supercharged gray matter, and he and Charles raise him as a pet. Caesar swings through the house, leaping up and down stairs and throwing himself in and out of the attic, but he sits quietly at the dinner table, too. He listens, he grunts, he eats, he makes signs. He's a darling little ape, but there's a joke buried in our wonderment: We all anthropomorphize our pets, finding spirit, even conscience, in beautiful collies, in cool, blue-eyed Siamese cats, in potbellied pigs. Out of affection, we see what we want to see of ourselves. But Caesar really *is* like us, in many ways.

He plays and chatters like a chimp, but, like a child, he needs protection and reassurance, and then—a fellow primate to the rescue—he rushes to the defense of Charles, his ailing "grandfather," when he's attacked by a neighbor. An empathic ape! The screenwriters, Rick Jaffa and Amanda Silver, and the director, Rupert Wyatt, create many small gestures, glances, and pauses that anchor the improbable turns of the story. At one point, Charles, confused, holds a fork by the wrong end, and Caesar slowly, gently takes it out of his hand and turns it around. The scene is ineffably, absurdly touching, the sweetest expression of family love seen in recent films. Pierre Boulle's novel was sardonic, even maliciously satirical—science fiction with a tickle. But *Rise of the Planet of the Apes* discovers a new emotion: what you'd have to call interspecies pathos.

Andy Serkis, who was the emaciated, depraved, ground-hugging Gollum in the *Lord of the Rings* trilogy, plays Caesar—that is, he lends his body and face, covered with reflective markers, to image makers who then, employing the techniques of motion capture, create a digitized simulacrum of an ape, but an ape that has unrivaled flexibility and expressiveness. The filmmakers have pulled off a stunning paradox: Caesar is much more human than an entirely digitized creation, and much more apish than an actual ape—faster, stronger, more exuberant in his knuckle-dragging, chin-thrusting, lunging glory. Caesar becomes an adolescent; hormones kick in, and he turns violent, doing bongo numbers on his enemies with his fists. At last, digital fantasy means something: We are not watching a dull-brained superhero banging off walls like a fly in a bottle; we are watching an animal with suddenly enhanced powers who still behaves recognizably like an animal. But a juiced-up ape can become something more than fun for us—he can shock us with his power, even inspire terror. There's a premonition early in the film: When a leashed German shepherd barks at Caesar, he roars back at the dog, and then, climbing into Will's car, surly and sad, he signs with his hands that he feels like a pet—it's a complaint, a question, and a challenge.

A second fable moves into place. The violent Caesar gets sent to an ape compound, where he's forced through steel mazes, prodded, and stungunned. The imprisonment is unbearable: He experiences the humiliation that a mere dumb animal would never feel. Gorillas, orangutans, and other chimps live with him in the compound, and Caesar quickly becomes a leader of apes. For a while, the movie turns into the latest version of *Escape from Alcatraz*, reaching its climax in a single syllable, a roaring "No!"—Caesar's first word, a refusal that caused the audience when I saw the movie to go ape. Caesar spreads the serum to the other animals, and what starts as a prison revolt quickly becomes a species revolt. The changes in the apes' intelligence are so vivid that we experience the alterations as a stirring birth—the origins of revolutionary consciousness—even though it is we humans, in the end, who will get overthrown. In a truly creepy moment, Caesar goes back to the house in which he was raised and stares silently at Will and his girlfriend (Freida Pinto) in bed together. The scene marks a sexy return to Boulle's idea: For apes, human behavior becomes an object of avid curiosity and study. And we wonder, Who's the prime primate, at the top of the species hierarchy? The position is suddenly up for grabs.

Digitized acting (if that's the right phrase) should be as warmly recognized as any other kind of acting. When Will arrives at the pen, intending to take Caesar home, the ape sees the leash in Will's hands and sorrowfully but firmly closes the door of the cell—staying behind with his own kind forever. To register the moment, Serkis lengthens his jaw in sullen resolve, turns his back, and gives Caesar a regretful shudder—the scene is almost tragic. Throughout the movie, the filmmakers capture tiny changes in mood and physical appearance, and the grand effects are startling. Finally, the apes break free, running all over San Francisco, busting into the biotech company's corporate headquarters and liberating the remaining apes in Will's lab. For once, the riot of movement is exhilarating rather than just extravagant. I've seen dozens of digital creatures and endless cars smashing through windows, but when the freed apes, like water bursting through a dam, pour through the building's glass walls at different levels, the image is a pop epiphany of freedom. *Rise of the Planet of the Apes* is spectacle with a kick: The transcendence of the normal in creatures so like ourselves is both an entertainment and a needling rebuke to human vanity.

Digital is here to stay, but this terrific movie tells us that it's time to move on from the current clichés. The superheroes and the thundering plastic toys need to be tossed into the back of the closet, where they be-long. If invention, wild and free, yet tied to emotion and philosophical speculation, is given a chance, digital filmmaking could have a more brilliant future than any we can now imagine.

The New Yorker, *September 5, 2011*

ACKNOWLEDGMENTS

Most of these pieces first appeared in *The New Yorker,* where I've enjoyed intense conversations about movies with the magazine's writers and editors encountered here and there, in the corridors, in the Condé Nast cafeteria, in the elevators, on the street outside the building. Virginia Cannon, who edited most of the pieces, likes the arrow to fly straight to the target. I'm grateful for her enormous skill and patience. And I would like to acknowledge as well the interest and passion of Susan Rieger, friend and wife, who likes stories so much that she demands to hear about movies as soon as I've seen them, and then asks the questions that drive me to see what is right or wrong in the movies and in my own feelings about them; and also the work of Kathy Robbins, ace literary agent, and Alice Mayhew, friend and longtime editor at Simon & Schuster, both of whom helped me to shape this writing into a book.

INDEX

ABOUT THE AUTHOR

David Denby has been film critic and staff writer at *The New Yorker* since 1998; prior to that he was film critic of *New York* magazine and *The Boston Phoenix*. His reviews and essays have also appeared in *The New Republic*, *The Atlantic*, and *The New York Review of Books*. He is the author of *Great Books*, a nominee for the National Book Circle Award; *American Sucker*; and *Snark*. He lives in New York City.